PRETTY GOOD AT WALKING

A FAMILY JOURNEY

VINCE STRAWBRIDGE

Pretty Good at Walking, a family journey

Sponsored by Clerestory, Inc. *Clerestory is a 501(c)(3) that implements economic development initiatives for the benefit of the poor and at-risk; we also exist to help powerful stories get told. Our federal tax ID number under section 501(c)(3) of the Internal Revenue Code is 27-4967363.*

For information about special discounts and bulk purchasing, contact:
Small Stories Studio at info@smallstoriesstudio.com, or call 205-757-7825

Library of Congress Cataloging-in-Publication Data
ISBN 979-8-218-37709-0
Printed in the United States of America.

Visit Small Stories online at smallstoriesstudio.com

Partial proceeds from the sale of this book have been directed to the Pacific Crest Trail Association in gratitude for their continued efforts to maintain this remarkable footpath from Canada to Mexico.

For my future grandchildren, live an adventure.

"This isn't the *worst* idea you've ever had."
—**Uncle Bill**

When the tires dropped from the lip of the pavement, I turned toward the back. I slapped my son's leg just above the knee and squeezed. "Alright, buddy, here we go!"

Henry pushed my hand away and rubbed his pant leg. "Why can't we just start at the start?"

I wagged my finger.

Behind us, the van kicked up a thin wisp of dust from the gravel road, a recent spring rain having damped it into submission. Beside us, power lines dipped their way back out toward the highway. I waited for Henry to look me in the eye. "What did I say about asking me that question?"

"But Dad?" His eyes welled.

"What'd I say?"

"You said not to ask you again." He pressed his forehead to the glass. "Stupid."

We rattled over a bridge and turned left to follow a creek up the valley past the few wooden buildings of Mazama Village. Each wide front porch leaned across a narrow front lawn. Giant trees rose before us on either side of the road. I looked up to follow the trunks to their tops where, between them, they left only a sliver of bright sky.

John Smith stretched high in the driver's seat. "Hey, Vince, can I get a peek past you at that rear view?"

I leaned back. "There's no easy way across these mountains in winter, is there?"

"Highway 20 just opened on May twenty-fifth. You'd have to go all the way down to I-90 to find anything open year-round."

I twisted in my seat to look back. My wife met my glance with wide eyes. "This is crazy," she mouthed. I reached out my hand. She folded it into her own hands and squeezed.

My three daughters sat in the row furthest back. Aiden, my oldest, was sandwiched between June and Georgie. When John slowed at a bend to pick his way over a tricky washout, the front tire dropped into the rut. We all wobbled, but Georgie's head bounced off the glass.

"Oof," I said. "Are you okay, kid?" I held up my four fingers and kissed them, then blew her the kiss.

She made a motion as if to catch it and pressed her hand to her head. "Ouch."

"She's fine, Dad," Aiden said, embracing her. "Aren't you, Georgie?"

When we rounded a bend, the road leveled. Up ahead, a distant saddle was shrouded in clouds. I shifted in my seat. "I haven't seen a power line in a while. I guess no one lives this far up here."

"You wouldn't want to live up here," John said. "Not year-round anyway."

"This was a heavy snow year for Washington, wasn't it?"

"It was a big winter, but you should be fine," he said. "We had a warm spell early this spring, so it's been clear for a week up here at the pass."

"I'm glad to hear you say that. That guy from the forum would not agree. He'd say to wait a minimum of two weeks."

"Which guy are you talking about?"

"The one that told us we shouldn't attempt the trail southbound."

John turned toward me with a half-smile. "No, he wouldn't." He paused. "But keep in mind, he is selling courses in winter preparedness."

My brother interjected from the third row. "Is that how you guys know each other?" He passed his miniature poodle from his lap to his son's and moved forward to sit beside my wife. "You met on an online forum?"

"There are so many voices in this van," John said. "Would you mind announcing yourself and trying that one more time?"

"Sorry about that, John. This is Stephen, Vince's brother."

"Stephen," I said, "John reached out to me right after that guy said all that stuff. It was a good thing too. He was making me nervous." I turned to John. "You told me not to let him get to me."

"Something like that." He tilted his head.

I turned to Stephen. "Since then, John and I have messaged nearly every day."

"That's incredible," Stephen laughed. "What's the big deal about going southbound?"

"It's a much tighter weather window," John said. "You have to hike north from here to Canada for thirty miles, then turn south and walk all the way to a little town just on the other side of the Sierra Nevada Mountains. And, if you don't make it before winter, you don't make it." He worked his way through a rut in the road with care, then added, "Technically, Kennedy Meadows South is still a part of the Sierra Nevada range. You aren't officially clear of them until you make it to Tehachapi."

"Kennedy Meadows South is …" I paused and looked toward John. "What is it? 1900 miles?"

"That's about right." John smiled. "But there's a lot of great stuff to see in between."

"I can't believe how far you've driven for these ruffians today," Stephen said. "Six hours one way. Not to mention coming up to Rainy Pass to pick me and Silas up from our car."

"Don't forget about Maple," his son, Silas, said and lifted their miniature poodle by the loop of her harness.

The growl of the gravel subdued our conversation. We snaked above the trees to round a tight turn cut into a sheer cliff face. Below us, the wide valley and Highway 20 stretched far away.

"Woah, guys." Stephen tapped the glass with his finger. "We're getting up there."

When the noise of the gravel subsided, John told us about a recent trip to Olympic National Forest with his Boy Scout troop. It had rained on them every day.

"Was it cold?" I said.

He nodded.

"I can't imagine." I crossed my arms over my chest. "How'd you keep your gear dry?"

"Not everyone did," he said. "Of course, you know, if you get wet, you flip your rain shell to the inside of your puffy jacket. You'll keep some insulation value of the wet down, and at the same time stay mostly dry."

"Of course." I leaned back toward Monica. "Is a shell the same thing as a rain jacket?" I touched my lips to her ear. "If he knew how little we knew, there is no way he'd let us out of this van with our kids."

She said, "Are you nervous?"

"It's a long way to Mexico."

"Yeah," she said. "Me too."

—31.1.2

Henry leaned hard on the handle and slid the side door open with a thunk into heavy rubber stoppers. The cold air rushed in. We all gasped. Having hopped to the ground, he turned to yank his backpack from under Monica's feet and huffed.

"Be patient, Henry," she said.

We poured from the van like the uncorked content of a bottle and shifted on nervous feet. To the right up a short bank behind a small ranger cabin stood an outhouse. I bounded up to inspect it. The wooden locking mechanism dangled from one end, useless. I kicked a rock from the corner and swung wide the door. Above the toilet seat, fifteen crowded stuff sacks dangled from the rafters. One opaque bag contained dog food.

"I guess Stephen isn't the only one bringing a dog."

I replaced the door and the rock and half slid down the slope, where, overplaying the effect of momentum, I crashed into Henry. "Oh buddy, I didn't see you there," I said, and wrapped him up in my arms.

"Were you trying to knock me over, Dad?"

I stepped back, leaving one finger to linger on his elbow. "Are you okay?"

"I don't understand why we don't just start at the start."

"This is the start." I pointed to the ground, then placed a hand on his shoulder. "If I tell you once more, will you promise not to ask me again?"

He nodded.

"I'm going to say this very slowly for you, okay?"

He shrugged.

"This is the closest we can get to the border by car. They used to let southbound Pacific Crest Trail thru-hikers start eight miles north of the Canadian border. But they don't let us cross the border from that direction anymore. So, now, we have to start here and walk north. When we get to the border, we turn back." I patted his shoulder. "Nod if you understand."

He lifted an arm as though it were leaden and pointed south. "We could just go that way instead of wasting thirty-three miles."

"By the time we make it to Mexico, this extra thirty-three miles won't make any difference." I bent low to catch his gaze. "It's going to be okay," and I pulled him toward me. I held him there for a long time.

Henry mumbled something and pointed toward the van.

Out of the corner of my eye, I saw Monica tumble over her backpack and catch herself with her hands.

"Mom fell." He wiped his eyes.

I let go of Henry and jogged toward her. She rolled herself into a seated position and groaned. She brushed off her hands and shook her head. "I'm such a klutz." She looked past me and said, "Wasn't it sunny at the bottom of the hill? "

Behind her, John stood beside a slight man with red hair. "Yes, they're a family," he said.

"A family?" He leaned forward and looked toward Monica and me. "Man, that's cool."

John pointed to Stephen and Silas. "These two are only hiking as far as Rainy Pass, but these six are going the whole way."

"Attempting," I interrupted, and turned back toward Monica. "At this point it feels safer to call it an attempt."

She lifted her arms toward the darkened sky, spread her fingers wide, and said, "Is it raining?"

Georgie jogged a few strides from the van. "Look on the top of your feet, Mom," she said. "I think it's snow." Small, white flakes fluttered onto her shoes and held there for a moment, then disappeared. Georgie looked at us with wide eyes. "I've never seen snow actually coming down from the sky before."

I raised my hand, half turning, and snapped my fingers. "Listen up everybody! Get your stuff inside your trash compactor bags, so nothing gets wet. And separate out the food you don't need. I'll hang that in the outhouse for when we come back through."

June clapped her hands to her side. "Dad, why am I always the last one?"

"What's wrong, Bug?"

"None of my stuff is inside my trash compactor bag. Can you help?"

"No problem, kid. We are going to be fine. We don't have to be in a rush."

"But they are all going to leave me and go up there to the fire."

Beyond the small rise to the left I heard laughter and a faint bass line from a song. Further down, along the bank, I could see the top few inches of a brown VW van.

Below June's sleeping quilt I felt something solid. I pulled the quilt out and reached back inside.

"What is this?" I held up three paperback books and fanned them in front of her face.

"I'm reading them."

"I thought you brought your Kindle."

"Yeah, but these ones aren't on our account."

"Pick one to carry, I'm sending the other two home with John."

After I clipped her bag closed, she carried it to the side of the hill. I crawled into the side door of the van and laid the books on the console. It was as cold in the van now as outside. Bending to check the floor for any forgotten thing, I slid my hand inside the cracks of the seats to find them still warm.

We had left nothing there either. I sat down for a moment, watching Monica and Stephen talking. Their laughter sounded far away. Behind them, at the top of the rise, a weathered sign read, "Pasayten Wilderness." I sat and watched my breath for a while, until Aiden approached me. I slid forward and stood on the running board with my toes hanging over the edge. "Oh well," I said and hopped to the ground.

"I can't believe we're actually here, Dad."

"Here goes nothing, eh kid?"

Aiden reached toward me for a hug. "I'm going to go up to the fire with the others." I watched her hop up the steps to disappear over the rise, then looked over each of our backpacks piled about, all of them brightly colored and clean. "I don't guess they'll look that way for long, eh, John?"

"They sure won't."

I nodded toward his van. "I left a couple of June's books in there, if you don't mind tossing them out for us. I think I got everything else." We stood in silence for a while until I toe tapped my backpack. "I guess this is everything I need."

John smiled, and after a few minutes more, he took a step toward his van. "Thank you."

"It's my pleasure. I'm proud to be a part of this."

"We'll see how it goes."

"They're all about it." He patted my back and released me. "Vince, I mean it when I say it is an honor to be a part of this … And try not to let yourself worry about what you don't know yet. It will seem overwhelming at first, but the trail is a good teacher, the best of teachers."

Monica and I watched the back of the van until its brake lights shone red as it rounded the bend.

I heard June's voice from a distance. "Dad, come up here to the fire." She invited me to the top of the rise with a wave of her hand.

I lifted a finger. "Give us a minute, kid." Monica and I stood facing the empty road. "He wouldn't take any gas money."

"I don't even understand why he would do this," she said. "I would never have done something like this for a stranger, would you?"

"Not before now."

We found June kneeling in front of the fire. "Look, Dad!" She reached her gloved hands over the flame. "I'm drying my gloves from the snow." Opposite June, a hiker sat with arms crossed and two feet propped on one of the rocks in the fire ring. I said, "Have you been there and back?"

She half nodded.

"How was it?"

She shrugged.

"How was the snow?"

"Twenty-five percent coverage, but it's melting fast."

"Well, June? I guess that's our cue." I tapped her on the head. "Alright, everybody, I guess it's that time."

We funneled down the steps to the parking lot, stepped over the tire tracks in the dirt, and stood for a last picture by the Pasayten Wilderness sign. I broke away to hang our extra food in the outhouse while the others took their first steps up the trail without ceremony. Monica, alone, waited for me beside the sign. She stretched her arm toward it and traced her fingers across the weathered wood, into the depression of the carved-out letters. She turned to me and whispered, "Canadian Border thirty-three miles. Do you think we should pray?"

"Without ceasing," I said.

After she set off, I stood for a while. I stared down at the trail and dragged decomposed granite under my foot. To the south, the trail cut a meandering line through the green. "All the way to Mexico," I said aloud, and tapped the sign with my trekking pole. "See you again, in a few days."

In a few minutes, I caught up to her. A few minutes more, and we caught sight of the others. I called, "Hey guys! Let's gather up. We need to pray."

After our first two hours of walking, we regrouped under the trees. Georgie stepped toward me. "Dad, we have already had snow, sleet, and rain, and it's only the first day."

"What do you think?" I said.

"I think it's really fun, Dad," she said. "And we've walked almost four miles already."

—18

Rain fell on us in varying portions the following morning. We traversed steep escarpments blanketed beneath intermittent fields of snow. Dotted lines traced across them, the footsteps of hikers ahead of us. We secured our steps in the deep foot holes. By the late afternoon, puddles formed in the bottoms of the holes. We lifted heavy wet feet from one to the next. On level stretches, Georgie opted out of the holes and skated on top of the snow. She slipped often, and we fell behind the others.

After yet another hard fall, she cried, "My feet hurt. Can we take a break?"

I watched the others disappear around the bend as I sat down beside her. The snow was cold through my shorts. I reached a hand down to touch them to ensure they weren't wet, but they were damp. Everything was damp. "How long do you think, kid?"

Georgie glared at me.

I held up my hands as if to surrender, and then gave her a hug. For as long as I could be patient, I wore grooves in the snow with my heels. Five minutes later, I stood and extended a hand. " Georgie, I'm sorry. You are just going to have to walk and cry."

She lifted her eyes, then both hands and sighed. I pulled her to her feet. Her foot slipped hard against mine. She collapsed again to the snow, rolled onto her stomach, and pulled her hood over her head.

"Dad, you promised it would only rain five days on the PCT."

"So?"

"It's already rained two days, and this is only the second day."

"That's what everyone told me." I sat down beside her. "Let me help you sit up, Georgie." I pulled her to a seated position. "Scooch over a bit." She pressed her palms to her eyes and bowed her head. After a while, the rain stopped. I looked out, as if for the first time, into the deep greens of the valley below us, and into the haze where distant lines of mountains faded away.

I pulled back her hood and placed my hand on her curly, red hair. I said, "God made a beautiful world, didn't he?"

She did not look up.

"Well, at least it's not sleeting anymore," I said.

We walked on. Far below us, beyond several long switchbacks, some of the others appeared. They stopped as a group before a dense stand of trees. Scanning uphill, Monica spotted us and waved. Beside her, Stephen stretched his arms wide toward the valley and called, "Isn't God amazing? You guys, this is amazing!" They all disappeared into the trees followed by Maple, the dog.

"Dad, we're never going to catch up."

We stepped out of the snow onto a hard-packed dirt path. Our feet struck a slow and hypnotic cadence. I looked at my phone—three miles to the next tentsite. "Just an hour and a half," I said.

"Yeah, right. Just? What time is it?" She dropped her head and began to cry.

"I guess it's cry-thirty."

"That's not funny."

"It's only been ten minutes since we started walking again. Does your foot still hurt?"

She nodded and touched her foot on the instep.

"Okay, let's take a look." I took off my pack and dropped it on the ground. "Here, sit on that." She pulled herself onto my pack, and I prodded for tender spots 'til she winced. "I think the best thing for this is going to be a good night's sleep, but let's work on it tonight before you get in your sleeping quilt. Will you promise to remind me?"

She said, "Dad, do you think they will stop at that tentsite?"

"I don't know where they will stop. We forgot to make a plan."

"I hope they stop."

After a while walking she asked for the time, but this time when I told her, "Cry-thirty," she laughed through her tears. We re-entered the snow patches on the next long climb. She no longer skated the tops but lifted heavy feet from each hole and stretched with a longer than normal stride to the next. "Georgie, I wish I could carry you."

"It's okay, Dad. I just have to get all the crying out of me, then I'll be fine."

We saw the others where they waited at the top of the climb. They seemed to be taking turns walking to the edge to look down.

When we joined them, at last, on the high flat, Aiden said, "Dad, look behind you. Did you guys see that rainbow?"

Below and behind us it spread above the wide valley. "I didn't even notice that," Georgie said. "A full rainbow."

I stepped close to Monica. "I can't believe we get to do this," she said. "It's beautiful."

Georgie tapped my calf with her trekking pole. "Dad, how did we not notice the rainbow?"

"I see it, Georgie. It is an impressive rainbow." I turned to Monica. "Georgie's arches are hurting."

"Mine too," Monica said.

—6.3

On my back in the dark tent, I lie. What little light there is lands gently on the tent's single wall. It glows. When the wind flutters the fabric, it plays. I can't sleep. It's my third sleepless window in the night. On the first night, it had been the same. I had hoped it would be different tonight.

I reach a silent hand above my head to press blindly into the pile of gear. Each thematic bundle is identifiable. An electronics bag, a toiletries bag, the shovel kit, and a clothes bag. I move them from one side to the other, pressing into them, feeling each item they contain. This is my third time through everything, but I still can't find my phone. If I touch the tent wall I will activate the transfer of moisture from the outside to the inside, so I am careful. I am quiet.

It is quiet here. There are no bugs. In the stands of trees, the wind is only a whisper. At home, a chorus of cicadas or crickets would repulse the silence. Here, I want something to break it.

I don't want to wake Henry. I did not hear what he said to Georgie, but in her retelling, she tipped Monica's sympathies her way. Monica switched from our tent to theirs. A parenting loss. By separating them, we have rewarded Henry for irritating his sister. We will have to sort out a better response.

At home, if I wake in the night, I open my phone to find something inane to numb me to sleep. Often, an unworthy, but bingeable television show. The impulse igniting my search for the phone is a defense against a silence that offers space and time. Aloneness is amplified here.

Still, I would like to know what time it is.

I have no watch. It is costly to power up the phone just to power it down. My Anker two-port, three-panel solar charger is folded and velcroed around my two cylindrical 5,000-milliamp Anker battery pucks. I haven't used them yet, because my phone still has 24 percent of its original charge.

I tap a plastic bag beside me. Henry and I have the shovel kit tonight. It is two plastic bags to keep the two parts separated, one inside the other. One is for the toilet paper, and one for the shovel. We have yet to master the system of which bag is for which. The toilet paper is smudged with dirt. I hope it is dirt.

I touch the bundle of paper maps we have brought as a just-in-case. Monica's sister spent two days at the church office laminating each quarter page. I hope we never have to use them. The phone is easier to use for navigation.

I feel my phone at my feet. Yes, that was it, I had tossed it into the toe box of my quilt the last time I was awake. Someone told me that the battery drains faster in the cold. I muffle the sound of my phone's powering up. I open my YouTube, but I have nothing downloaded. There is no cell coverage here. It is the force of habit.

I launch another app on my phone. Guthooks utilizes the phone's GPS and marks us as the blue dot on a red line over an embedded map. Users add comments to waypoints as they go. We uploaded the latest in town. Beside the map is a tab for elevation. On the graph, we are the blue dot near the bottom of a long drop. Ahead is a gentle descent to the border, just six miles.

I scroll backward on the map and tap the waypoint where we'd stopped for lunch. We'd all piled under low-hanging pine branches to escape another light drizzle and boil water for lunch. A hiker had walked in wearing sandals. She'd sat down with us. Monica had asked about her sandals, and she'd said she wore them throughout her entire hike on the Appalachian Trail. Henry then asked if she also wore them in the snow. "I live in

Canada," she had said as she pulled out a plastic jar. "I've been cold soaking all morning, so this would be ready to eat." I'd never heard of cold soaking, so I said. "All you do is drop your food into water and let it soak?" she had said. "That way you don't have to worry about carrying a stove with you."

"How long does it take to be ready to eat?"

"A couple of hours, I guess. I set my lunch to the side in the morning when I break camp."

In five minutes she was gone again.

We'd been passing our titanium cups to Monica when the sun came out. It had been the first time the sun broke through, really broke through. We'd all raced into the meadow and stood, palms open. With her eyes closed, and her face turned toward the heavens, Georgie had said she'd never been so happy to see the sun in her life. "Don't get used to it, kid," I'd said. "There is a bank of clouds moving in."

I power down my phone. I close my eyes and see white circles. It is soothing to press my thumbs to my eyes. When I release them, the circles are brighter and clearer.

New sounds crack the silence: a distant cough, the ripple of a tent's fabric, the loud crinkle of a half turn on a loud groundpad.

My bladder is full. I needed to go the last time I woke, but I thought I could make it 'til morning. It couldn't have been much after midnight. To achieve the momentum to break the seal of my warm quilt will take motivation.

I close my eyes and sleep.

I wake again in the dark and listen into the silence. There is a buzzing, a low drone. It is constant. Inside my ear, attaching to each sound that enters. How long has it been since I have heard a pure sound, unfiltered, unflavored, unmixed with my own buzz?

There is a rhythm to this place I can't swing with. It's a steady pulsing, and

I'm out of time. I am abuzz with a nervous white noise, discordant, unsettled, half tempted to scream. I may scream, or I may laugh at myself. Out loud.

In the daytime everything's easier, offering up attainable markers. One hour 'til break. Two miles to water. Three hours to lunch. It's not that I find myself in swing with the rhythms of the day; it's just that I can endure the dissonance with a view to the next coming thing.

The steady beat of the walking is beginning to help, a little.

The night stretches on in a long line of time. Nearly endless.

Come quickly, morning. If it were 5:30, I would wake everyone and get them moving.

I power up my phone. 3:26 a.m.

Now I really can't hold it. I sit up and slide my arms into the sleeves of my 8 oz. down jacket.

I check on Henry, worried the noise of my groundpad will awaken him. He doesn't stir.

The air is cool, the dark sky pinpricked with bright stars. The moon's hollow light is enough, so I abandon my search for my flashlight. I push myself to my feet and test them against the cold grass. I feel only a low-level burning, so I remain shoeless. On my third step, mud squeezes up through my toes. There are eight tents in the meadow including our four. I see more tent tops away in the trees. I don't know how many have camped here at Hopkins Lake. Those that have returned from the border, and the ones that have yet to see it.

I step away from the tent to the path through the meadow. There is no risk that I will be seen, even in the open. I snap my waistband back into place and look toward the lake. It glitters with reflected skylight. I hear a faint lapping of water against large stones. I walk toward it.

The ripples glisten on the near side of the lake, but fade smooth, into blackness below a towering glacial bowl. A field of talus, now hidden in darkness, slopes upward from the lake into sheer granite faces below a sharp peak. The peak is the high point on the jagged line that differentiates dark land from dark sky.

I sit on the same stone where June had jumped earlier. We call her the Polar Bear. She had been dog paddling in a circle ten feet from shore long before I'd jumped in. When I had scrambled out, teeth chattering and breathless, she'd continued to paddle. "Where are you going, Dad?" she had said, and giggled.

I am glad she has that. Most things are harder for June than the others.

This is the good kind of alone. I look up into space and know I am small.

Time passes.

I rise to pick my way across rough rocks to the soft path that leads back to the tent.

From the dense forest, we stepped into a bright and unnatural clearing, like one cut for power lines. Across the thirty-foot span, the far line of trees stood brilliant in the full light of the sun. In the center, a monument marked the northernmost endpoint of the trail. Not far from it, stood a silver obelisk, not much more than waist high.

Three other hikers were already there, so we made introductions. Mad Max held court, enthroned on a wide log to our left. To his left, Paige sat cross-legged, inches beyond the shade line from the nearest row of trees. Behind her, Andrew leaned against a tree, chewing something.

"I started the trail northbound from Campo in April," Mad Max said, "but got off in Tehachapi for a family emergency. I live not too far from there. After that, I figured I'd just flip up to the top and walk home. Are you hiking the whole thing?"

"We're hoping to," I said and stepped apart to rest my hand on the point of the obelisk. In either direction, the clearing delineated the border between nations, north and south. To the west, visible for miles, the line traced away, until it reached the top of a rise. To the east, it disappeared within a few hundred feet, over a small hill. "I guess you've already got your trail legs then?"

"I guess I do," Mad Max said.

Henry sat up on his groundsheet. "Dad, do you care if I do it?"

"I don't have any problem with it."

As he walked past us toward the clearing, Paige looked toward Monica. "What's that about?"

"He lost his tooth." She nodded toward him. "For some reason, he wants to throw it into Canada."

Henry took a few more steps beyond me and threw his tooth into Canadian trees. He turned to me and spoke from the corner of his mouth, "Let them deal with it."

I stepped back into the United States. "Yeah," and, as if answering Mad Max's question again, I said, "we are hoping to go the whole way."

He nodded and turned to Andrew. "Pass that back to me when you've had a swig, would you?"

Andrew put his Clif Bar in his mouth to free his hand, bent to grab a small bottle of Fireball whiskey, and held it out.

"Thanks." Mad Max turned the bottle in his hands.

"Now that was a good idea," I said.

"I started carrying a bottle after a long-distance bike race." He unscrewed the top. "I can't recommend the race. It might be the hardest thing I've ever done. I couldn't hardly ride half the time. I was following these two women up the side of the hill, and I swear they rode straight up the damn thing. It wasn't even a trail. I had to take my bike apart and strap the parts to my pack with bungee cord and dental floss. I'm telling you it was all loose gravel and dirt. A scramble. I'd take one step and slide back two. I crawled on all fours. It was so hot it burned my hands. I had to wrap them all up in gauze. After two hours of climbing, I slipped and everything busted loose from my pack. My bike went everywhere." He paused and lifted the bottle toward his lips. "All down the hill in pieces."

"That sounds awful," Monica said.

"It was bad for me, but you should've seen the guy behind me, dodging that stuff." He touched the bottle to his lips again and tipped his head back. "I didn't win the race, in case you were wondering."

Paige asked me how we were liking the hike. "It's intimidating," I said, "but I think everyone is doing great." I nodded toward Monica. "Especially, my wife. She's in her element here."

"You mean she likes being outside?"

"It's that, a bit, but that part of it is more the thing she endures for the beauty. She'd have been an artist, if she hadn't been strapped with all these dratted kids."

"Oh, Monica," Paige said, "you are an artist?" She reached into the top pouch of her pack, lifted a small clay pot and stood up to walk it over. "I am too, I work in clay, but I do a lot of other things too."

Monica held out one hand for the pot and patted her Tyvek to invite Paige to sit down. "I'm not really an artist," she said. "I just paint now and again."

As if from nowhere, June referred to the overgrown brush as a washing machine, Andrew coughed. "This is nothing. Wait 'til you get to the Suiattle River. I hope you brought long pants." He unwrapped a Clif Bar. "Do you have gaiters?"

"Just the ankle ones."

"That's too bad, because that kind won't do any good." He reached down and tapped the top of his gaiter where it cinched just below his knee. "It straps tight below the boot so nothing can get in your shoe." He turned and lifted his boot to show us the strap, and touched the logo on the outside of his calf. "These are Gortex, so they are waterproof and breathable." He nodded toward me. "And, I guess you fell for the fad of hiking in trail-runners instead of boots."

"Careful there, Andrew," Mad Max said, nodding down toward his own pair of faded, black Altra Lone Peaks. "There is nothing wrong with trail-runners."

Paige returned to her place, picked up a Tuperware bin, and pulled two slices of bread from it. She reached into her food bag and searched with her hand.

"Oh, that's a good idea," Monica said. "We should eat here." She pulled out the cook pot and shook it.

Paige looked up again when she heard the rattle. "You boil water at lunch?"

"Yes." Monica screwed the tiny stove onto the isobutane canister. "We're eating our hot meals at lunch now, because we are so tired at night, we don't have the energy for it."

"That is a good idea. I may have to try that."

"Can we take pictures first?" Aiden pushed herself up from her groundsheet. "And get it out of the way."

"Would you mind, Paige?" Monica said.

Paige set her Tupperware to her side, brushed her hands together, and stood up. "I'd be happy to."

When Stephen and I also handed our phones to Paige, Mad Max hopped up to help her.

We crowded in front of the monument. Silas pushed past Henry to climb to the top of the assemblage of 8x8 posts. The words carved into them were weathered smooth, but still legible. Paige counted down, "Three, two, one, cheese."

"Shoot, I may as well take mine while I'm up," Mad Max said. "Would you mind?"

He knelt in front of the monument, and Maple ran to him. He swept his leg toward her. "Get this dog out of my picture! If there is a damn poodle in my shot, my friends are never going to believe this was a tough trail. Kids are one thing, but a miniature poodle?"

"Come here, Maple." Silas clapped his hands. "Come here, Mapes."

Mad Max didn't sit down again. He swung into his pack and said, "These miles won't walk themselves," and disappeared into the trees. After they made their goodbyes, Andrew and Paige followed soon behind him.

"Well, everybody," I stood up. "These miles won't walk themselves."

Monica tilted her head up toward me. "Give us a few minutes more. We've made great time this morning, and it's so nice here. I think lunch might be my favorite part of the day."

I sat down again.

"Hey, Daddo," June said. "How far does your map say from here?"

"2662.6 miles."

"Oh. That's easy." Aiden laughed. "We've already done one one-hundredth of it."

"We've done more than that," I said.

"Technically," June said, "we haven't done any of it yet, because this is the start."

0.0.2

"Go ahead, June," I said, "I'll catch up in a minute."

I turned back to the monument, wooden eight-by-eight posts, stacked in a jumble. All of them rotten and weathered.

At the sharp sound of a cracking stick, I startled and turned. "Oh, sorry about that." The hiker dropped his pack where the trail entered the clearing and walked toward me. His shirt was ragged and stained with holes worn on the top of each shoulder. It was stretched so tight at his waist that between each of the buttons the two sides of the shirt separated. "I didn't mean to scare you," he said as he pulled off his hat and wiped a hand over his bald head. He then covered his mouth and didn't move it away before he spoke. "There it is." He looked past me toward the monument. "There it is." He stepped beside me as if to admire it from a distance.

"You've been out here a long time," I said and pointed at his shirt.

He pinched it and pulled it away from his body. "This is last year's shirt. I only made it as far as Rainy Pass, too late in the season to finish. I've waited all year to get back out here. I wanted to finish the trail in last year's hiking shirt." He stepped back and struck a pose. "Clearly, I was in better shape last year."

I laughed. "I'm hoping the same thing will happen for me."

"Nah dude, you are skinny enough already." He nodded past me toward the monument. "They are replacing this thing soon, and I was nervous I wouldn't get here in time to touch the same one all of my tramily touched."

"Tramily?"

"My trail family." With his legs straight, he bent from the waist and placed his palms flat on the ground. When he stood up, he groaned and continued, "We all came together somewhere along the trail, mostly between Southern California and the Oregon line. I had to get off-trail a couple hundred miles into Washington for an injury, and they all pushed on without me."

We stood there in silence for a while.

"Excuse me." He breathed out a deep breath. "I've got to do this thing." He took a few halting steps toward the monument and stopped there, as if he could not decide what to do. After a while, he stretched out his left hand. But, without touching it, he dropped to his knees as if prostrate before an altar. And, as would be appropriate before an altar, he bowed with his face to the ground.

I felt caught between staying and going. To leave would be to make noise and break whatever trance held him. I looked away into the trees.

"Hey, buddy." He snapped his fingers. "Would you be kind enough to take my picture?"

As he climbed onto the monument, I said, "On our way in here to the border, I had thought being here in this place must feel much different for the northbounder."

"You have no idea. I can tell you. Wait till you reach the southern terminus. I assume you are a part of that family, right?" He smiled and touched the side of his temple as if remembering something. "You know what? I meant to tell you. One of your kids is waiting for you, just up around the bend."

I handed his camera back to him, and motioned with my head, "You coming back out to Hart's Pass?"

He pointed north. "My trail goes that way," he said. "Canada won't turn U.S. citizens away."

When I stepped from the clearing, I saw June through the trees. "I'm coming to you, Bug. You don't have to wait." When I reached her, I placed a hand on her shoulder and said, "You can see that this place would be iconic for them." We walked through a clearing in silence. When we stepped into the trees again, I said, "It does feel like we have earned our way to a start."

6.3

I turned off the trail and walked toward Hopkins Lake. "Monica, don't wait up. I need to grab some water." As I neared the lake, I reached back to pull my water bottle from the side pocket. It was full. "Well, these were unnecessary steps," I said aloud. I walked to the lake, anyhow, and found again the rock from which June had jumped. In the daytime, it seemed a more hospitable place.

Climbing up the trail from the lake level, my conversation with three passing hikers was filled with familiars. "Yes, we are all a family. Six of us are going the whole way. Yes, we've been to the border. Yes, she's eleven years old. We have seen the father hiking with his son. They are a good bit ahead of us. We saw them the day before yesterday. No, I think he's thirteen."

After I answered all their questions, they told me their story. One of the hikers was just out of high school, with a medical waiver his parents had signed. The two others had been friends in college, and dreamed up the idea in the dorm during the second semester of their sophomore year.

When we set off in our different directions, we did so with a "see you down the trail."

Within a few minutes, I caught June and slowed to keep pace behind her. A cheery, though disheveled, hiker passed us on the climb. She smiled and said hello but seemed in a hurry to make it to the top.

When we reached the top, I dropped my bag on the snow beside Henry. "Let June and I rest a minute, everybody. I tapped Henry's leg. "What do you think of this? Have you seen such a view?"

He rolled his eyes toward me and said, "I've seen better," then jumped up to join Silas further up the snowbank.

"Monica," I said. "Who was it that you were talking to when June and I were almost to the top? I think she passed us on the way up, but we didn't talk."

"Oh yeah, she's great, her name is Bear Hair. She's from Germany. When she passed, we were listening to Tolstoy on the speaker. She focused on Russian literature in university, so we talked for a while about that."

"She seemed like she was in a hurry when she passed us."

"Today is only her second day out here. She said she's going all the way to Harts Pass tonight."

"Wow, that's a long way." I moved over to sit beside her. "And Bear Hair? How did she come by that name?"

"Oh, Dad," Aiden said. "This is funny. You know all that Old Man's Beard we've been seeing that Silas and Uncle Stephen use to start fires. Apparently, she thought it was all from a bear that had rubbed its hair off onto the branches."

After a while, June joined Henry and Silas in the final phase of an intricate snowman project. It was of an impressive size. When they adjusted its hat, the snowman fell to the ground but stayed assembled. Even the eyes, nose, and arms retained their place. Undeterred, Silas found, in it, a Biblical scene. He crossed the arms of the slain giant so that it might rest in peace. He then fashioned a David from the dirty snow. He set his small creation, once erected, upon the vanquished foe. His placement of his David, however, was unfortunate.

I snapped my fingers. When Monica looked my way, I directed her attention to the snowman. "Wow, you did great, guys," I said, "but doesn't Goliath look overly happy, for a guy that lost a fight?"

14.6

"Are you the Parents?"

I smiled. "That all depends. I don't always like to admit it. How far back did you pass them?"

"No, they were great. They were singing when they passed me." The bearded hiker turned his head to look behind him down the trail. "It wasn't more than a tenth of a mile. I did see a father and son at the top of the next pass."

"Was there a little poodle with them, the father and son?"

He nodded.

"Making a snowman?"

He nodded again.

"That's my brother and his son. They are hiking with us as far as Rainy Pass."

"Then all four of the other kids are yours? How far are you going?"

"All the way."

"To Mexico?" He shook his head and smiled. "That is so cool." He bent to shoo a fly from the back of his calf. "What are their ages?"

"I guess I should have said that we are attempting to go the whole way, but the youngest, Georgie, she's eleven, the redhead, Henry, is thirteen, June, that's the dark-haired one," I held a hand up to the middle of my chest. "She is fourteen, and Aiden is sixteen."

"Where are you from?"

"Florida."

"Oh, yeah, what part?"

"Lakeland."

"No kidding? I lived in Lakeland one summer. I worked on a farm up in the Green Swamp."

"How cool. How did you like it?"

"Honestly, I hated it." He laughed. "How did you …" He paused. "I hope you don't mind me asking questions." He paused again. "It's just that I think what you are doing is great. My mom dragged me all over the world when I was a kid, and I don't think she could have done anything better." He placed his palm on his chest. "My name is Dahn."

"No trail name?" I tilted my head. "It seems like everyone else out here has a trail name."

"It's just Dahn." He smiled. "What about you?"

"I'm Vince."

"And I'm Monica." She leaned against me. "When did you start?"

"I'm doing it a little differently than most people. I started in Kennedy Meadows South, and I am flip flopping around trying to hit the different parts of the trail in the best weather windows."

"But you are hiking the whole thing?"

He nodded and looked me in the eye, but as if some other thought had surprised him, shook his head slightly. "They are going to see things … wonderful things ... this will be so good for them. How did you decide to do this?"

"It's all her fault." I looked at Monica. "She loves to walk, and for a few years she and a friend of ours have talked about thru-hiking the Appalachian Trail after the kids were gone. But last year we took the kids on a sixty-mile loop hike in the Smoky Mountains and they got stronger every day. I meant it almost as a joke when I suggested taking the kids along on her thru-hiking dream. I was shocked when she said yes."

"In my defense, I didn't think he was serious."

"That's not all of it," I said. "It's a confluence of several things, most of them tied to the housing market crash in some way."

Dahn tilted his head.

"I was a builder and got overextended on a bunch of projects when the money tightened up, and I went bust. I went into debt pretty badly, and bankruptcy wasn't an option."

"Why is that? If you don't mind me asking."

"Not at all. If I went bankrupt, I couldn't legally pay back any of my subcontractors, and I knew how important that money was to them. We got into backpacking then, because it was the only vacation we could afford. I figured that none of the people I owed money to would begrudge me a trip where I was sleeping on the ground."

"Vince, are you going to tell him your life story?" Monica placed her fingers on Dahn's forearm. "You wanted the long version, I guess."

"I prefer the long version, truly."

"Well, anyway." I looked at Monica. "We've recently paid everyone back, so this is also a sort of celebration."

"Yes," Monica said. "And to be clear, I didn't think there was any way we were going to pull this off."

"But you went through with it?" Dahn said.

"Well, I told him we couldn't do it if it would mess up Aiden's school track."

"She's in an IB school," I said.

"International Baccalaureate," Monica said.

"I'm aware of IB. I'm a teacher. Well, I was a teacher." He paused. "I was going to ask you about school."

"The youngest three are homeschooled," I said. "So that was no big deal to rearrange, but Monica was sure they wouldn't let Aiden drop out of IB for a year and come back."

Monica leaned into me. "I was sort of counting on it."

"I made an appointment with the principal and told her what we wanted to do, and she was all for it. She said, 'I wish I'd done something like this. Go and I'll work out the details.'"

"Her two sons are in their mid-twenties now," Monica said.

"She let Aiden drop out for the year, and she'll pick up where she left off when we are back."

"A true educator," Dahn said. "What about school out here, will you try to do anything on-trail?"

Monica looked at me and laughed. "We have different opinions about that, but we are probably going to have to work through the summer to catch up."

"What they'll gain here will be more than they ever would in a classroom."

Monica looked up at me. "We have different opinions about that too."

"This much time away from phones and screens alone will be worth it," Dahn said, stepping to the side of the trail.

"Now on that," Monica said, "I agree."

"It seems almost as though"—he pointed a finger toward Monica—"you were the more reluctant of the two. Is that true?"

"I'm always the more reluctant. He's the eternal optimist. I tend to see all that can go wrong, and there was so much with this that could go wrong. There is still so much with this that could go wrong." She laughed. "But, he was persistent, and to be honest, I love walking, especially out here. You just get to have everything be so simple, and so beautiful all the time." She reached her arm toward him. "And the birds."

"Oh, I love the birds."

"Which is the little yellow one?" Monica said. "We've been trying to figure that out."

"Is it the goldfinch?" He held his hands close together. "With the little stubby body?"

"I'd have said it looks more like a swallow."

He shook his head. "Maybe it is a swallow."

"You know what I think I like best?" she said. "I like waking up with the sun, and going to sleep as soon as it's dark. I think that's the rhythm we are made for. It feels so much less artificial to me. It makes me feel a little less crazy."

"You guys are so great. I could talk to you all day, but you'd probably better catch them. It was great to meet you. I hope to see you again."

Monica waved her hand and we stepped past him.

As if an afterthought, he said, "How did you talk the kids into this?"

"You go on, Monica," I said. "I'll catch up." I turned to Dahn. "Talk them into it?"

"How did you get them to agree to do this?"

"Agree to this?" I paused to shoo away a fly. "I don't mean to seem cavalier, but that's not how I parent. If something is good for them, I don't ask their permission."

"How did they feel about the idea when you announced it?"

"There was more than a little eye-rolling and quite a few tears. But they were excited, too. They love camping and being outside. Other than June, they are all athletic. I doubt the magnitude of five months and twenty-six-hundred miles has hit them yet." I paused. "I'm not sure it's hit me yet, for that matter."

29.9

June and I sat with our legs splayed across the trail. With her left hand, she slapped her leg and loosed a cloud of dust. With her opposite hand she pointed toward the dust cloud, looked at me, and giggled.

I tapped the sole of her shoe with my toe and nodded out across the downslope. The broad grassy field that spread out between us and the sharp forest line lower down was of deep green and dotted about with wildflowers, muted purples and pinks, bright yellows and whites. I pointed to a stand of trees in the meadow. "What kind of tree is that June?"

"Which one?"

"The one that looks kind of like an aspen. There are all those little islands of them down in the field."

"Maybe they're aspens."

"I like these places where the snow is all melted and the flowers are coming out." I pointed my finger to the tops of the trees that made up the treeline. "Look at that kid, you can just see the tops of those mountains. I wonder if those are all a part of the Cascades." I kicked the sole of her shoe again and said,

"It feels like we're finishing something. Doesn't it, kid?"

"Yeah, but it's only starting." She dug in her heel, pressed out and back, and worked a trough into the dirt. She turned her head toward me, dropped it to her backpack, and sighed. "I'm tired."

"It's still early in the morning."

"I don't mean like that. I just mean I'm tired."

"You want to go home?"

Two bold dirt lines on her face disappeared into the crease of her smile. "No, I like being out here."

"Look, Bug, here comes your mom."

"What are you guys talking about?" Monica pulled her hands from her pockets to warm them with her breath. "Can you hand me my trekking poles?"

I stood up and fished them from her side pocket.

"Look at what Henry is doing." June pointed with her trekking pole. "Are they just taking the road? You told them to stay on the trail. Why doesn't he ever do what you say?"

"Henry," I called. He heard me and half-turned. I pointed him down the embankment. He stepped toward it and took a first careful step over the edge.

Below us Stephen and Aiden emerged from behind one of the tree islands, picking their way on a diagonal back toward the trail through flowers and grass to their mid-thigh. They both had their hands up over their heads.

"Oh, that looks cold," Monica said. "How did they get that far off track? Will you wait with me?"

"For what?"

"I need to use some trees," she said.

"Or you could just wait 'til the trail takes us into some trees," I pointed. "We'll be walking through that forest again soon." I kicked the sole of June's shoe. "You'd better go. We may be here a while. Two more miles and we'll be back at Hart's Pass."

June remained seated as if she hadn't heard me. "Mom, there aren't any mountain lions waiting to attack you."

Monica dropped her pack beside us. "I know, but at the same time I don't know if you know what I mean." She pointed to a small grouping of trees one hundred yards downhill. "I think I'll go there." She pried the shovel kit from her back pouch and walked away.

I dropped my pack and sat down again beside June. We sat in silence until Monica was halfway to the trees. I called out, "I think mountain lions prefer the isolated trees."

She turned and stuck out her tongue.

"Why is she so obsessed with mountain lions, Dad?"

I shrugged. "You know she woke me up a few times in the middle of the night watching YouTube videos about mountain lions?"

"You told me."

"It was every night for a while, June."

Out of nowhere, a shock blond-haired hiker bounded toward us in bright, unsoiled shoes. "Are you guys a part of the family?"

"We are," I said.

"How's the snow out there? I talked to some of your other kids down the trail. They said it wasn't too bad."

"It's changed a lot in the last few days. You won't need your ice ax. I mean, there's some sketchy stuff, but there are steps kicked in. If you want, I can take your ice-ax down and leave it for you in the outhouse."

She thanked us and declined.

"Have a nice hike," we all said in turn.

31.1

With tired feet propped toward the fire, I reached down, pinched the bottom of my food bag, and shook the last of its contents onto the dirt. Henry bent and put his hand on my shoulder. He raised his food bag by its drawstring. "What do I do with this?"

"What do you mean?"

"The trash, what do I do with the trash?"

"There's a barrel inside the ranger hut. Go put it in there."

He slumped his shoulder, his food bag dangling to the ground.

"Wait, take mine too," I said as he turned away, "and don't drag that thing in the dirt."

I stretched for my trash bag and lost my balance but caught my fall with the heel of my hand. On my second attempt, I dragged it to me.

"Come back here, Henry." He stopped without turning, and I frisbeed my trash bag but landed it short. He moved back toward it with slow, backward steps.

I brushed my palms on my shorts and looked at them closely. Each line and crease of my hand was distinct, marked with a black line of dirt.

"Why can't you just make Aiden do it? I'm gonna miss out on the hiker box. People left all kinds of cool stuff they didn't want to carry anymore."

"What is so great in the hiker box?" I laughed. "You can't carry anything else with you."

"Well, there's tons of food."

"They haven't finished setting everything out, but if you just stand there, all the best stuff will be gone."

From the stack of wood behind me I grabbed a hand-sawn round of pine, three inches in diameter. I tossed it on the fire. Orange flecks of spark, bright against a backdrop of clouds, leapt high and vanished.

I heard knee-length gaiters over a pair of long pants swishing behind me. "Hey, Andrew, I haven't seen you since the border, grab a seat."

He held up a finger. After he swallowed a bite of his Clif Bar, he nodded toward the picnic table. "What's going on over there?"

I raised my arm and searched with my finger until I found him. "You see that guy over there? The redhead. He's called Broken Toe. He's been up here doing trail magic for at least a week. He's got several hiker boxes with food and gear that people have dropped." I turned back to the fire and pushed the larger log at the base to make room for the newest log to drop in at an angle.

"I could use some more calories," he said. "What do you know about him?"

"Not much, I talked to him a little bit when I first got here. He hiked the trail last year, until he … broke his toe," I spoke the words slowly. "But he says he may spend the whole season working his way up and down the trail feeding people."

I turned when I heard Monica walking up from the trees.

"Are you ready to check out the hiker box?" she said.

"Excuse me, Andrew." I leaned forward from the log to stand up.

"Oh, he's got the food out?" Andrew said. "I'm gonna check that out, too."

Aiden and Georgie moved between various bins and boxes Broken Toe had moved from the back of his VW van. He tossed most of the food from the bins onto the picnic table, leaving it just as it landed. He turned toward his van for another box.

"You need help with that?" I said.

"No, this is the last of them." He stopped to prop one leg on his bumper. He looked at me. "Nice to see another redhead out here." He nodded toward Georgie. "Where does her curly hair come from?"

"I always tell her, 'I love you, I don't care who your dad is.'"

He looked back and forth between us.

"I'm joking."

"I heard that, Dad." Georgie did not look up from the pile of food on the table. "He always says that. I don't know why he thinks it's so funny."

We stood aside and watched while the kids raked through the food on the picnic table. "This is great, man. It's nice to have a little variety. Our food is exactly the same all the way through Washington. We shipped everything before we left home to different resupply points down-trail."

"Mom, look at this." Aiden lifted a bag.

"Chili Mango." Monica smiled and reached out her hand.

"Oh, you gotta check this out." Broken Toe reached around Georgie. He stepped back with a beige brick wrapped in cellophane. I leaned in close. The beige was speckled with green and brown throughout. "You know what that is?"

"I have no idea."

"Pemmican. 3,500 calories. At least that's what the guy told me. And he made it himself. Of course, he also said he's been throwing up every day on-trail so far. I'm not sure he put the two things together."

"Did you try it?"

"Hell no." He tossed it back on the pile. "I have good food." He motioned me to follow him. "You feel like a burrito? I'll make you one."

"Are you serious? I'll be right there, I'll just pick through this stuff real quick." I stepped into a space beside Andrew.

He looked over his shoulder. "I'm just carb loading here." He picked up a Pop-Tart. "I hate the fruit flavors," he said. "I'd love one of those cinnamon ones."

Georgie pinched my elbow. I bent down to her, and she whispered, "I have an extra. Can I give it to him?"

"Sure, go grab it."

A few minutes later, Broken Toe poked his head through the window he'd cut in the side of his van and held up a plate.

"Excuse me, Georgie," I said.

Through my first mouthful of burrito, I said, "Emily and Ryan, did you see them?" I set down my burrito and touched my hand to my arm. "She's the one in the arm sleeves."

"No, I didn't see them."

"They said they were hitching out to Winthrop. Maybe they got a ride from here. How about the one who hikes in sandals, did you talk to her?"

"Yeah, Trouble was here. She came through here a couple days ago."

"We ate lunch with her on the way up to the border. I doubt we will be seeing her again."

"The trail is long, but only a few feet wide. Some of these people, you'll see them again and again, and some of them, you may run into them seven hundred miles down-trail. It's a funny trail in that way. I may flip down south and keep doing trail magic, so I may see you again. It's that, or head east to the Appalachian Trail. I haven't made up my mind." He set an empty plate on the counter and turned to make another burrito. "Did Trouble tell you her body doesn't regulate temperature well? She and I talked a long time about it. I wonder if it will end up a problem for her in the desert. Depends on when she gets there, I guess. In November it shouldn't be too hot."

Andrew appeared as if from nowhere. "Can I get one of those burritos?"

"Step right up," Broken Toe said.

I took another bite of the burrito and stepped out of the way for Andrew. He leaned through the window and began a rehashing of each previous conversation.

"Well, I'll leave you two to it," I said, and walked back toward the table.

When I was almost out of earshot, I overheard Andrew say, "I'm heading out soon. I gotta make sure they don't take all the spots."

We circled up around our communal pile of food we'd dumped from the bags I had stored in the outhouse, and began dividing it up.

"It's just thirty miles, right?" Stephen said.

"Hey, only two Snickers," June said. "Henry took five."

"Three of these are leftovers from last time."

"Why aren't you eating your Snickers?" Monica said.

"I hate Clif Bars, so I try to eat them out of the way first. I just can't 'cause they're so disgusting."

"June, he can have his two Snickers for this time," I said.

"Dad, what do we do about the food we got from the hiker box?" Georgie said.

"Trade it out. We can leave anything extra with Broken Toe. We will have more food in Uncle Stephen's car tomorrow night." I winked at Stephen. "Let's hope, anyway."

43.1.1

As long as we walked high on the western traverse, we stayed warm. When we curled over a cut to drop into the shadow of the mountain, we grew cold. We added a layer of clothing. As we dropped lower in elevation, the undergrowth overcrowded the trail as high as my chest. The trees above formed a dark tunnel, and the rain came. It dripped through to the brush. The leaves held the droplets. The droplets collected and grew colder. When we brushed by, they transferred to our clothes and soaked through to our skin.

Well into the day's cry-thirty, Georgie said, "This is the fourth day of rain."

"Hey, at least we're getting them out of the way, right?"

June said, "That's not funny, Dad!" And they both cried.

In an hour and a half it would be dark. We walked for a mile parallel to the creek through soaked-soft bottomland. "I think there are some tentsites on the far side of the creek," I said. If they were all taken, it would be 3.4 miles to the next one.

I didn't want to raise unfounded hope. "Girls, there might not be any spots here."

"What?" they both said.

"I know, June, but I want to prepare you, just in case."

June turned to me. "I can't walk any farther."

We crossed the swollen creek on a bridge. "Our first bridge," Georgie said.

Aiden jogged over from the group to greet us as we stepped off of the bridge. She pointed up to the top of the sharp shelf toward the cover of the dense trees. "Andrew and Paige are in the only two tent sites, but we're hoping there are a few more nearby."

At the top of the bank and pinched into a tight spot to the right was a tent with its door open. Paige was inside, dry, and reading a map. She looked up and waved. "Oh, you guys look miserable."

On a slant to the left, Andrew had squeezed his tent into a stand of young trees.

"I think he's asleep," Paige said.

"Did you see any other tentsites nearby?"

"I didn't see anything else. I'm so sorry. I hope you find something."

Monica looked at me. "Vince, what are we going to do?"

"Why don't Henry and I run ahead and see if we find anything?" Aiden said.

Monica nodded.

They dropped their packs and disappeared up the trail. Monica looked at me. Then to Georgie. Then June.

"I already warned them," I whispered. "If there's nothing here, there's no tentsites for a while. Nothing on the map anyway." I tipped my head forward and rainwater poured from my hood onto my feet.

"My shoes are soaked." Monica pressed down into her shoe, and the water sloshed out. "I can't wait to get out of these wet clothes."

A few minutes later, Aiden jogged downhill toward us, ahead of Henry. "We found enough places for three tents, but we can fit another one if we squeeze." She put on her pack and set off. We followed them thirty yards up the trail before they veered off onto an overgrown offshoot. We ducked around scrub trees hanging in from either side of the cut.

"This almost looks like an old forest road," I said. "Are you sure there are enough spots up here?"

"It ends right up here," Aiden said. "C'mon, Uncle Stephen, there's a great spot for you and Silas behind this big boulder. Somehow, it stayed dry."

As they moved out of hearing, I reached for Henry's sleeve. "Where do you see a third spot?"

"You're standing on it."

"This? This is as bad as Andrew's. I'm going to look around a little more."

I walked a faint path along a downslope for ten feet until it came to a thicket. I stepped closer to peer down over the berm where I slipped on a thin leaf layer, sliding with clumps of torn-loose, wet loam, eight feet to a flat at the bottom. I brushed myself off and looked up to find two large gravel pads, bordered about with milled lumber, with branches hanging low over the top of them.

"There used to be two tentsites here. Designated," I called. "It's grown over, but one of them can still work."

"Should we come down there?" June said.

"Yes, come on down."

Each set to our own shelters. Henry, again partnered with me for the night, staked down the far corner of our tent. On our third attempt, we laid it out right.

"It's going to be a long night, Henry."

"Why?"

"We'll be sliding all night."

"It's not that bad."

I was sinking the last of my stakes with my heel. Silas barreled down the path toward us, shielding his eyes to crash through some thin branches. At the uphill corner of our tent, he swerved a sharp left to run along the far side.

His leg caught two guy lines and sent two stakes flying over my head into the bushes below. My tent folded in on itself, like a deflating balloon. I clenched my fists. "Silas."

"Okay, Uncle Vince, I was just going to go to the bathroom."

I shook my head and turned away from him. I stood for a minute looking into the bushes below me. When I turned back, I said, "Bring me the shovel when you come back. I need to take a turn."

I watched him run up the hill.

In too short a time he came racing back into view. "I'm done, Uncle Vince." The shovel kit clinked at my feet.

At the same moment I touched it, I smelled it. "Silas, get back here!"

"What, Uncle Vince?" He stopped.

"Silas?"

"What is it?" He tilted his head.

"If you don't know, come take a whiff of this bag." I held it toward him, and he pulled back. "You know exactly what I am talking about. This is disgusting. Just go up there to your dad."

To find my way to uncontaminated paper, I had to discard half of the roll. Without resupply until we made it to Stehekin, we would have to ration.

I re-pitched the tent and walked toward the creek to wash my hands.

"Can I go help Uncle Stephen with the fire?" Henry said.

I squatted on my heels for a while by the creek, watching rain drip from the front of my hood. After a few minutes, it stopped raining. Aiden jogged down to invite me up to the fire. When I told her I would go up alone, she said, "No, I can wait, and we can go up together."

When we arrived, we found them in a close circle, huddled tight to the fire. "Let's make room for everyone," Stephen said. "Let them squeeze in." He offered to read aloud from his Bible, and afterward we all sang a song.

When we finished, he called for high fives all around. "What a day, everybody! Good job."

"Hey, Silas." Henry held up his hand. "Can I get a poop five?"

"Henry!" Monica said.

Silas burst into tears and ran into his dad's arms.

50.7

The glacial surrounds pulsed with life sound. The first high pitched squeak of the pika, I mistook for a mouse. Marmots screamed shouts of warning. An occasional "whoop whoop" of we-still-didn't-know-what. The "scree, scree" of a porous rock grinding under our feet would give way to "thud,

thud" on the hard packed trail, then a "sloosh" in the wet snow and mud.

We followed wide, slight downward traverses, with the trail winding forward and visible for miles, gliding together in a symphonic stride. I called it making hay. "June, let's make some hay while the sun shines." I updated her on our progress each climb, every fifteen minutes or so. "1.2 to go. You can do it." If she could get to within 0.8 miles of the top, she would believe she could make it.

Georgie would drop back on the climbs to ask me how much farther with uncanny consistency, 0.3 miles to go, on the dot.

On the steeper downs, in the pounding, our joints hurt, and our feet ached. I thought about my walking and sat deep in my stride to transfer the strain from my frame. We called it the "old man shuffle," and we made up a song.

Old man shuffle
Gonna get me down the hill.
Old man shuffle
Oh Lord, I know you will.

It was best when there wasn't too much of one thing for too long.

Silas, impatient to press, stabbed my heel three times with his trekking poles. Once, he drew blood. Henry, too, heel-walked. I counted for one hour with Henry behind me. He stepped on my heel fourteen times.

Silas didn't tell us about his blisters until a few layers of skin on the bottom of his foot nearly peeled off in a single sheet. He cried when we taped him down tight. He had no choice but to go on. "These miles won't walk themselves, Silas. You can do it. You have to."

Stephen and I discovered a pre-trip miscommunication, and the cost was high. He had said, "We will be with you for eight days."

I had divided by eight for the mileage, but we hadn't walked far that first day, and Stephen needed to drive away on the eighth day. Before we left home, I had promised the kids. "We will start with no more than fourteen miles a day." I had to move the goalposts.

In the mornings I didn't mind the ambition. It gave us a reason to get going early. But in the afternoon weary, when the crying began, I was angry. One of us could get injured, pushing that hard. "The stakes aren't as high for Stephen," I thought. "He'll be back home in a few days."

The afternoons were my cry-baby-thirty, every day.

Before the trip my Uncle Ted had said, "What are you saying to people who are telling you this is a stupid idea?" I told him that no one had said that to me. "Well, you aren't talking to the people I am talking to, then," he had said.

On most of those before-the-trip mornings, I didn't mind. At 7:30 a.m. I could defend the idea of a grand adventure. After lunch, talked-out and tired, I believed myself fully a fraud. I would call Stephen. "It's 2 p.m., and you know what that means."

"What an adventure! It will all have been worth it, you'll see," he would say.

"I'm not seeing it, not today."

"Hang in there, Vince. You won't regret it."

Why had I thought we could do this?

Georgie was nauseous. I walked with her all morning. We climbed to our new highest elevation and stopped to take pictures above another wide glacial surround. Cascades spouted from every cut and crevasse, crashing downward into a turquoise, teardrop shaped lake at its base. An outflow, discernible by the break in the trees, bent away to the west where it joined a long river valley that trailed away out of sight.

We switchbacked down an open hillside into dense valley forest with icy snow patches for a floor. Each mud patch between was its own kind of slippery, equally tricky. We followed scattered tracks through these bottoms in various directions, lost, until each scattered path rejoined.

"Georgie, are you sure you weren't feeling sick at the top? It might just have been the high elevation."

"No, Dad." She bent from the waist. "It started lower, down the other side of that climb."

I reached a soft hand to her head. "Kid, you can do this. We are going to make it. I am with you."

"I have that taste in my mouth, but I can't throw up. I know if I did, I'd feel better."

"I have always hated it when you were sick. Do you remember when I used to sit in the bathroom with you for hours? You would hunch over the toilet waiting for it to come up?"

"Dad, I don't want to think about that."

A hiker appeared out of nowhere and heard me. I turned toward her quickly. She reached a quick hand up to fidget with her necklace and walked to Georgie. "Oh, Sweetie, are you okay?" She turned her head to me. "I'm Sassafras. Georgie and I walked together for a little while yesterday. June was with us too. I had such a lovely time."

Georgie forced a half-nod.

Sassafras straightened and addressed me. "I know that look. How long has she not been feeling well?"

She stood with us there for a long time, rattling off a wealth of trail information. "Oh, Bear Hair, heavens, yes, she's such a darling, but she's long gone by now, running away from a crazy guy from what I heard." She left us with a cheery, "Sweet Georgie. I hope you feel better. You can do this. You are my inspiration."

Georgie bent over again. I groaned and looked at my phone.

"I think it's coming up, Dad," she said.

A second hiker surprised us. I hadn't seen him before I said to Georgie, "Come on, already. If you are going to throw up, throw up. We can't die here. You can cry while you walk, let's go." How much had he overheard?

We climbed a slope upward. The melting snow seemed to be a living organism on a downward slide. We sloshed up the switchbacks through the trees. Too many turns to count. "Dad, how much farther?"

"You won't believe this, but it's 0.3 on the dot."

When we topped Methow Pass, she lay down and felt better. I reached into my bag, pulled out every damp thing, and laid it all open to dry. I looped my tent over a line in the sun that Stephen had hung, and I looked back over toward Georgie, asleep.

When I sat down, Monica moved over to sit beside me. She said, "It looks like we are having a yard sale."

"We are the Clampetts gone camping." I put my hand on her back. "Even so, it is beautiful here." The tent fluttered in the gentle breeze and slipped on the line. I rose to adjust it and returned to Monica and sat down beside her again.

There is here, an unremarkable hum of another long lunch in the warm sun, another panoramic view of a valley below us, each one fading into the next. The slowness of the undistracted. Of watching our kids build a fire to melt snow. June with Aiden and laughing. Georgie, still sleeping.

"We will forget this, I think," I said.

"Forget what?"

"These unremarkable moments."

***

When Emily and Ryan, a couple we had crossed paths with several times, came over the rise, I felt compelled to apologize for our mess, and I did. They overlooked it. "Don't worry about it."

"I wonder how we got past you again. Didn't you pass us already this morning?" I said. "Where are you from, Ryan?" I looked at Monica. "Have I already asked him this?"

"I'm from England."

"Who is your team?" I said.

"Ipswich is my team, but for the Premier League, I'd have to say Liverpool."

"Up the Reds," I said and started to sing. He joined me for a few lines of "You'll Never Walk Alone."

Monica shook her head.

"Yours too?" Emily said.

"But you started the trail together," I said. "Emily, you aren't from England."

"No." Emily looked over at Ryan. "We are an odd couple. I'm from Arkansas."

"Oh," I said. "What's the story there? I don't imagine Ryan was wandering around the backwoods of Arkansas."

We talked a while longer before they moved out of earshot. Monica nodded toward them. They prepared for their lunch, as if rehearsed. They flapped open a Tyvek groundsheet and swiped it down flat, strung a line between two trekking poles, hung out a few items of clothing to dry, and began to stretch.

"We need to start doing that." Monica nodded toward them.

"Doing what?"

"The stretching part."

We sat in a large circle and passed out boiled water for meals. "Do you remember meeting them, Henry?" I said.

He shook his head.

"It was at that snow patch where I told you to wait for me? Remember that? They are the ones you walked with over that scary bit."

"I don't remember you telling me to wait. Besides, it wasn't that scary."

We lay back in the sun, and I closed my eyes. After a while Monica tapped my chest with her fingers. "Is it Cutthroat Pass next?"

"Why did you say it like that, Mom?" Georgie yawned and rolled onto her back.

"Good morning, sweetie," Monica said. "Did you have a nice nap?"

"Why did you say it like that, Mom? Is it scary?"

"Not as bad as Knife's Edge," I said. "Did you not hear Sassafras telling me about it?"

Georgie stretched her hands high in the air and yawned again. "I was a little preoccupied with trying to throw up."

56

"Hurry up, Georgie, someone is coming."

There were no trees on the wide slope, only snow and gray granite. The large boulder she chose was a last private place.

"I'm coming, I'm coming!" She stepped out with defiant hands on her hips. As she slid down the scree, she kicked loose a slide of small pebbles that peppered our feet. "You guys are being jerks!"

"Look, Georgie," Aiden said and pointed toward the two approaching hikers. "Emily caught us. See her arm sleeves?"

Monica stepped up from the trail. "We had better let them pass. This is going to take us a while."

"No wonder they call it Cutthroat," I said. The trail cut its traverse beneath spires of granite that rose like the sharp teeth of a giant from the snow to the sky where they blocked the afternoon sun.

"Look, Dad, there are people in the middle of those rocks down there too."

"Where, June?"

We did not recognize the hikers that picked their way through a small boulder island below us.

It didn't take long for Emily and Ryan to catch us. "Sorry again about the yard sale back there," Monica said. "We are a mess."

"Don't worry about it," Ryan said.

"You guys seem to have quite a routine down," I said. "Monica has threatened to institute a stretching regimen now."

"We are going to be slow through here," Monica said. "Why don't you go ahead of us?"

"Thank you." Emily waved her hand. "I'm sure we will catch you guys again after Winthrop."

Georgie took her time placing her first cautious step. At the connection of rock, the snow was slushy. She poked about with her pole, until she finally placed a foot and moved it around. She pulled it back again and said, "I'm scared."

I stood behind her. "You got this, Georgie. Don't sweat it." After ten minutes I said, "Georgie, this really is sketchy."

"Uh, Dad, will you do me a favor?"

"Sure."

"Don't tell me which are the sketchy parts 'til we are finished, okay?"

The sun-warmed rock melted any proximate snow and formed cavities. When we stepped too close, we sank to our thighs. I asked Georgie to stick close to me through the boulders, to place each of her steps where I stepped. I shortened my stride to match hers. Near the end of the boulder pile, she slipped. She cracked down on her tailbone.

I hugged her and sat beside her. The rock was cold to the touch in the shadow of the granite. I gathered her hands into mine and balled up our fists to blow into them.

When she stopped crying, she said, "It is the pain too, Dad, but some of it is the tired."

A voice behind us surprised me. "Excuse me, do you mind if I go ahead of you here?"

We slid apart. "Weren't you just leaving Hart's Pass for the border right when we had returned?" I said. "You must be walking big miles."

"Somewhere between thirty and forty."

"Oh my goodness!" Georgie said. "That's amazing."

"You are the one who's amazing. How old are you?"

"Eleven."

"You see what I mean?"

As soon as the hiker passed out of earshot, Georgie said, "Dad? Forty miles a day? What the heck?"

When we came to the giant wall of granite, I pointed toward the base where the snow peeled away from it. "Look, Georgie, it's like these things are giant granite teeth, and the giant has gingivitis." I kicked a few steps up to the lip. I looked down along the granite. The gap narrowed as it descended. I could see at least forty feet down. "Yikes."

"Daaad! I told you not to scare me." Georgie stopped and looked for the others. "They are so far ahead." She pointed. "Wait! What is that?" A roughed-up trough in the snow ran a perfect perpendicular down from the trail.

"Someone slipped out there. You see their trail. They didn't keep sliding all the way down, so that's the good news."

"Dad, I don't want to slip. Why didn't we bring ice axes?"

After we climbed the last steep bit and stepped out of the snowfield to safety, Georgie tugged at my shirt and pulled my ear close. "Which were the scary parts?"

I stood with her and pointed. She followed my finger to where large, jagged boulders jutted up below steep banks of snow.

She looked to me, then back across the snow. "I'm glad you didn't tell me before."

59

Stephen ran toward me when I rounded the bend. Across the creek, Aiden sat with her head between her knees. Both Henry and Silas leaned down toward her, each with a hand on her back, as if to comfort her.

"Vince. Oh, man! That was close. She could have been hurt, really badly. I messed up. I set up a log in the creek for her to walk across, but it wasn't secure, and it rolled when she was out on it. She came down hard right next to that sharp rock in the middle. I mean, if she had landed on it, she might have cracked her hip. I feel so terrible."

"Is she okay?"

"She says she is, but man, I'm shaking still. It's crazy how one little moment could change everything. I'm so sorry, man."

I put my hand on his shoulder and patted it a few times. "You okay, kiddo?" I called.

She looked up. "I'll be fine, Dad. I just need a minute." She put her hand on Stephen's shoulder. "It isn't your fault, Uncle Stephen. Don't worry about it."

61.1

"That doesn't hurt." He pointed at my bare feet. "Walking on that asphalt?"

I looked down. "I'm from Florida."

He laughed. "What does that have to do with anything?"

"We never wear shoes in Florida. We used to call ourselves the Medulla Alligator Feet in the neighborhood where I grew up."

"What are you doing out here?"

"We're on the PCT." I waved a hand toward the upper end of the parking lot. "My family is camped in the trees just past that sign." I pointed. "You see the rock wall there and the pine trees beyond it. There is a hitching rail there for horses. We set up our tents right there in the horse manure."

"You said it was the PCT?"

"Sorry. Pacific Crest Trail," I said. "Are you not from around here?"

"I'm from Oklahoma. I'm on a road trip, retracing my grandfather's steps." He pointed out toward the highway.

"He came right through here? How long ago?"

"The last letter we have from him indicated he would be coming right through this pass to cross the Cascades to return for the family."

"He came west for work?"

"Yes, to Seattle. My mother was very young, and her mother had fallen ill, so rather than send for them, he decided to come back for them himself. After that, there is no record, nothing." He stared into the trees for a while. "I look at these trees, and I wonder if he saw them. I wonder if he drank from a nearby creek. I wonder where it ended for him."

"Have you found any trace?"

"Nothing. Not yet." He shook his head. "I have no idea what I'll find, if anything at all. This whole thing is a reset of sorts for me. I'm in the middle of a divorce, so you know …"

"Ever thought about hiking a long trail?"

"That's what this is?" He moved a hand back and forth as if to trace a line in the asphalt.

"You are on it." I pointed. "That way is Canada, and that way is Mexico."

"No kidding?"

"It's true. We just completed the first sixty miles between here and the Canadian border."

"We?"

"My wife and four kids." I paused. "Well, my brother and his son came with us too, but they headed back toward Denver last night. That's why we camped here."

"They quit the trail?"

"No, he and his son always intended to get off-trail here. They were just helping us get started down the trail. I can't tell you how good it was to have them as a distraction for my kids. For me too for that matter. Plus, he's just one of those guys, you know. He's always kicking the encouragement up one level higher than you'd think it could go."

"Sounds like a good brother."

"Sorry to go on about it, but ya. I guess, I'm just feeling grateful this morning."

"How about your kids? How old are they?"

"My oldest is sixteen, and my youngest is eleven."

He whistled. "And how long is this trail?"

"2,650 miles if we manage to do the whole thing."

"That's incredible, and it runs all the way to Mexico?"

"All the way from Canada. If you start this direction, it runs through the Cascades down into Oregon along a volcanic spine, Mount Adams, Hood, Jefferson. Into Northern California it's more of the same thing along Mount Shasta, and through Mount Lassen. Then it goes through the Sierra Nevada. You know, the Yosemite type stuff, and then out through the desert of Southern California all the way to Mexico."

"How many people do this?"

"This direction, southbound, is less common. Only around six hundred people got permits this year to go this way. But around three thousand every year get permits to come north."

"How about families?"

"I don't think so." I laughed. "As far as I know, Georgie is the youngest person on-trail this year. There are a few lifelong sojourner types, but it's mostly people in stage-of-life changes." I held up my fingers to number them off: "Graduating from college, burned out in white collar work, retiring … That kind of thing. People trying to find themselves."

"Like me?"

"We all have a little of that in us, if we are honest, don't we?"

"Do you carry your food the whole way?"

"Four to six days' worth at a time. We have packages of resupply waiting for us in Stehekin, about twenty miles that way," I pointed. "We shipped from home for all of our Washington resupply."

"To volunteers along the way?"

"There are some hostels, but mostly to post offices, general delivery."

"What's going on with that?" He nodded toward the deflated groundpad draped over my left arm.

"My daughter's groundpad." I pointed toward the highway. "I found a puddle across the highway so I could find the hole and patch it. I am letting them sleep in as a reward for pushing so hard these last seven days."

"Sixty miles in seven days?"

"It's really ninety miles. You have to walk north thirty to get to the start, and then turn back."

"That sucks." He turned his eyes up. "It's that much extra walking?"

I laughed. "You'd get no argument from them on either count."

"I'm going to have to look into this some more." He paused. "I guess you all are about to head out?"

"What time is it?" I pulled out my phone and chuckled. "Eight-thirty. I told my youngest she was in charge of the start time this morning, so it may be noon before we get moving for all I know. That kid likes to sleep. You haven't seen any of them, have you?"

"I haven't seen anyone."

We stood in an awkward silence for a while.

"Best of luck in your travels," I said.

"You too." He turned toward his car.

I started off toward the end of the parking lot and then changed directions toward the privy. When I put my hand on the handle, I turned. He was opening the door to his car.

"See you down the trail," I called.

We waved one last time.

75.6

I open my eyes in the predawn dark with my head pressed against the side of the tent. My hair is dry to the touch, and when I drag my hand along the silnylon material above, it is also dry. For a while I try to sleep, but sleep will not come. Without waking Monica, I step from the tent.

The trees, towering Douglas firs, stand silent in the mist, as if expecting some coming thing. Their even disbursement in straight rows down the gentle hill betrays the careful hand of some logger or farmer that once counted out even steps, pressed seed into soil, and watched season roll into season. How high had the canopy stretched into the sky before he last stood among these trees? Before he retired to some valley town to spend his last days dreaming of this wood and these trees. It may well be his return they are expecting.

I ghost in and out of one of the rows on the way down the gentle slope. From out of the grass and the fog the shape of an old and rusted tractor emerges. Its skeletal contours are minimal and raw, each piston housing a rippling rib. I settle a hand on its rusted hood.

My dad had put me behind the wheel of a Massey Furgeson when I was eleven years old and left me to bush-hog an orange grove. My brother had been given the Kubota tractor. His was sleek and new, and easy to turn with its power steering. I had preferred my own tractor. One day, on Lee's tractor, I had been unable to find the brake on the way down toward the pond. I had decided it would be better to bail than to ride with it into the water. I jumped clear. I had watched with relief as it perched in perfect balance on the tree it toppled at the water's edge. My dad had only laughed and reminisced about a story of one of his father's mishaps. Then, he had added one of his own. "Pretty good shot," he'd said, "managing to park it right on that tree."

I am not the first to have rested my hand on this rusted bucket seat, pulled it down to test the springs. I doubt I am the first to have had these thoughts. My thoughts run backward this morning.

Stephen and Silas are gone. The morning after they left, Georgie hadn't stirred until 11:00. My brother's car had been our last bailout, our last sense of safety. It is as though, after he left, this thing became real. We are alone with only our feet to carry us forward to Mexico.

I turn back toward the tents, and to sleep. I don't sleep long. It is quiet here. One of the kids shifts on their groundpad. It has been eight days, and I still don't sleep through the night. I wonder if I ever will. I'm a heavy sleeper at home. Here, I wake every two hours.

It is only the birds and me now. We are not in a rush. Monica stirs. "Where are you going?"

"Sleep in. I'm going to take Henry fishing. We have three and a half hours before we have to meet the shuttle."

I duck into Henry's vestibule and unzip his tent. I tap him on the head. "Grab your pole, let's go."

"Why are you whispering?"

"I don't want to wake the girls. Let's go."

"It would take them an hour and a half to get ready anyway."

"Don't be a turd. Let's go."

"Do I need shoes?"

I pointed to my bare feet.

Henry pulled his pack from his tent and slid his Tenkara fishing rod from the side pouch and dropped it to the ground. He turned his pack around and slid his water bottle out before dropping his pack to the ground. We both heard the crack, and he looked up at me with his mouth shaped in an *O*.

"Oh my gosh, Henry. You broke your rod." I flipped his pack over to inspect. "Yep, you sure did." I looked at him and shook my head. "I guess we're going to have to share now. Maybe we can get one ordered to be delivered down trail." I rubbed his hair with my hand. "You know, the biggest bass I ever caught was on a rod that I had snapped in the screen door. I lost six inches off the tip. Did I ever tell you that story?"

"A few times, at least."

80.6.1

June gathered her flowy skirt in both hands, and her bare feet peeked out beneath it. She shifted her weight from one foot to the other. "This feels nice."

I looked behind me up the narrow lane that wound through the trees toward the bathhouse, then down to my own bare feet, and past them. The time-worn asphalt had given way to an aggregate of medium size. "When I first met your mom, she was wearing a skirt like that. Where did you get it?" I reached a hand to June's shoulder and guided her toward the shoulder of the road. A dusty, blue Prius came toward us around the bend at a crawl. Our nod toward the driver was met with a smile and a vigorous wave.

"They have extra clothes for the hikers up in the laundry room," she said as she hobbled back onto the pavement. She stopped and looked down toward her feet, lifted one foot in the air, and wobbled, but regained her balance. "This road feels warm too. It's like my feet are getting a massage."

I looked over my shoulder again to the bath house. "Wait here a second. I'll be right back."

I found Monica pulling clothes from the dryer.

"Do you want to come with us?"

"What are you doing?" I made a motion as if I were swimming. She placed a shirt on a stack of clothes on the top of the dryer.

"I have to finish the clothes." She patted a pair of socks on the top of the stack. "And I am going to take a shower when it's free."

"Shower?" I squinted my eyes and turned up my chin. "The lake is right there."

Before I stepped out the door again, she stopped me. "If you see Henry, tell him to bring me his dirty clothes. I don't think he gave me everything."

"Would you grab June's Kindle when you come?"

"Where is it?"

"It's charging around the outside of the building."

She nodded.

June was leaning back against the grassy bank on the high side of the road when I returned. When I leaned over her, she reached up with crossed arms, so I crossed my arms too, and we clasped hands. I pulled her to her feet.

"Hey, Daddo, I just thought of something. If you can't get here by car, how come there's cars here? I mean, they can't come over the mountains, because there are no roads there. Do you think they've all been here from before they dammed the lake?"

"Cars can come across the lake on the ferry just like the people."

"Except for the hikers." She stepped back onto the road. "We walk here." She took a few steps and stopped. "It must be a big ferry to be able to carry cars."

"It's a big lake."

Within one hundred steps, the road came to a T. The town bus crossed our path on its way toward the waterfront shops of Stehekin. We waited and watched it pull away. At the fork in the road, it veered downhill, toward the water.

"Dad, I wonder if anyone we know is on that bus." After descending the hill to swing a wide circle on the wharf, the bus pulled to a stop, and its passengers began to unload.

"It feels like a lazy kind of day," I said and placed a hand on her shoulder. "Where to now, kid?"

She looked left and then right, and then shrugged. We looked out across the wide turquoise lake to the far side. Sheer granite cliff faces split its surface.

"This kind of reminds me of Minas Tirith," she said.

"Don't you mean Lothlorian?"

"No, Lothlorian is the woods where Galadriel lives."

"Then what am I thinking of?"

"Rivendell is more like this. Remember, that's the place where they gather to decide the fate of the ring. There aren't any lakes in either that I remember, but there's just something elvish about this."

"You think the others would want to listen to *The Lord of the Rings*?"

"The whole trilogy? It's too long. We don't walk together enough to finish it."

I pointed toward a promontory that overlooked the water. June nodded, and we crossed the street. On the edge of the bluff, we leaned against a stone wall. To the right, a small jetty jutted out into the water. In its center, a few small trees shaded a well-manicured lawn that was bordered by a gravel walk. A few small benches lined the walk. Bobbing in the small bay between us, a large tree trunk, too large to call a log, barkless and branchless, floated around.

"Seems dangerous to have that thing in the lake." I pointed.

"I saw that, but look at the end of it. It's chained on both ends. You can see them go all the way to the bottom." She tapped her lips with her finger. "How deep do you think it is?"

"We could check." I made a swimming motion.

"Really?" She smiled.

"Want to get the others?"

"In a while," she said. "What's the rush?"

"Okay, but let's sit in the grass." We spent several minutes in silence. I lay back in the grass and shielded my eyes. June put her head on my chest. "Daddo, this is hard."

"Do you like it?"

"It's just that everyone is faster than me, so I feel like I'm always behind." She rolled to her side and re-situated her head on my chest. "I miss my goats." She laughed, as if at her own private joke.

"For some reason I was thinking about how Maggie jumps up on the roof of the goat shed and bites the oak tree branches and pulls them down so Boots can eat the leaves. She just looks so ridiculous up there on her hind legs."

80.6.2

June remained in the water long after the rest of us grew tired of playing king of the hill. We lay in a line on the log to dry in the warmth of the sun. "I wish your mom had come," I said. "She would love this."

"Yeah, she just had to have a shower," Aiden said.

Henry raised his hand to shield his eyes. "This is my shower."

"I don't know how you are still in that water, June," Georgie said. "It's freezing."

"It's not that bad." June laughed. "Not for me."

I rolled from the log, let out my breath, and descended, motionless, into the silence. For a moment, almost outside of time. I hovered above the bottom of Lake Chelan, listening, as though I might hear some long locked-away story. None came, and too soon the sound of a distant motor broke the silence. I swept my arms in a wide arc, gained the surface, and gasped. When I kicked myself onto the log again, I lay on my stomach with my head near one end and dropped my hand to rest underwater on the chain. I said, "Aiden, what superpower would you have if you could choose?"

"I don't know."

"I would invent magic shoes," June said.

Henry propped himself on his elbows. "That isn't a superpower."

"Okay, fine," she said. "I would be able to walk as fast as I wanted with the same amount of effort. Whenever I passed people on the trail, though, I would make sure to slow down and act like it was hard." She ducked under the water.

A rogue wave splashed cold water on my side, and I lurched into a seated position. I waited 'til June came up for air. She grabbed the log and dipped her hair one more time with her head tilted back. "Why would you slow down?" I said.

"If other hikers found out how easy it was for me, they might not give me credit for a thru-hike. I wouldn't want to make them jealous."

"Oh, pfft," Aiden said. "Why would you care about what they think, anyway?"

"You know what I'd do?" I lay down again. "I would be able to breathe underwater and in the air."

"I bet you could see some crazy stuff," Aiden said, "like old houses even."

Henry sat up and looked across the lake. "Dad, why would there be houses buried under a lake?"

"Because it wasn't always a lake. Do you remember Lake Fontana, in North Carolina? They flooded entire communities there. That one is dammed just like this."

"Could you dive down and see them?"

"I don't think Lake Fontana would be clear enough," Aiden said, "but you could see them here if they are down there."

She rested her chin on the side of the log and looked down. "It's crazy when you look into the lake this way. Look along your arm to the bottom. It's so clear. How deep do you think it is?"

I let my eyes follow the chain into the deep and then back to my fingers and moved them slowly.

The slippery fuzz coating the rocks on the lake bottom gave the blue water a hint of glacial green. I dropped my arms away from the chain. As the log bobbed up and down, my elbows submerged and returned to the air in a slow rhythm.

"Imagine you came here to homestead and built a house with your bare hands," I said, "saw your kids take their first steps in a meadow nearby, found all the best fishing holes, ran around these hills 'til you knew them like the back of your hand, saw bighorn sheep climb on those high cliffs there, even some of the cliffs that are now under water. This was your own piece of the world, and then one day you wake up to a knock on the door, and some guy from the government says, 'You've been eminent-domained.'"

Henry said, "Can they really do that?"

I muttered under my breath.

"What did you say?"

"Nothing," I said, "don't worry about it."

"The air is so dry out here." Aiden touched her hand to her arm. "Look, I'm already dry."

"The only bad part is," Georgie pointed toward the bank, "we have to get in the water again."

"It's not even that cold." June laughed.

I stood up from the log, bent over, and flapped my arms in preparation to dive. I said, "I do not feel the cold! I only feel its power!"

"Dad," Georgie said, "you always say that when you are scared to go in!"

"Come on, guys, let's race. On three, Henry. Count it down."

We reconvened on a warm concrete slab at the water's edge to re-dry. I looked up the hill. "This reminds me of drying out on the basketball court at home after swimming," Aiden said.

Monica was standing halfway up the hill near the intersection talking to Paige. I waved to get her attention.

June opened her eyes. "Why is Mom wearing a backpack?"

"She's got all the laundry in there," I said.

"Oh, Georgie. Guess who Henry and I saw earlier," Aiden said, and without pausing, continued. "We saw Mad Max. He was already leaving town with that bearded guy."

Henry laughed. "The bearded guy? That narrows it down."

"It's the one that said he spent some time living near us in Lakeland," Aiden said.

"His name is Dahn." I lay back and closed my eyes. "I could fall asleep here."

The tapping of Monica's toe on my shoulder woke me from my nap. "Did you tell Henry about his clothes?"

I shook my head.

"He's not going to have anything clean to wear. Are none of you going to take a shower?"

"This is our shower, Mom," Henry said.

"I don't know," Aiden said. "I might take one. Was there a long line?"

"You guys are disgusting." Monica slipped her thumbs under her shoulder straps and adjusted her pack.

"Look at that water," I nodded. "There's no shower on earth as clean as that lake."

Georgie and June followed Monica toward the campground. I tossed a pebble toward Aiden. "You want to go sit on the bench for a while?"

Henry stood up and brushed off the back of his legs. "I'm going up to the campground with them to take a nap. Did you already get the packages from the post office? I'm hungry."

"Eat your stomach lining," Aiden called after him.

"Hey, that's my line," I said and pointed her toward a nearby bench.

We sat down and looked out across the lake to the mountains that seemed to climb from it. Their dark and rippled reflection stretched across the water and gave way to a deep blue copy of the sky. "What do you think, Aido?"

"I can't believe we are here, but I do like the way the PCT is set up. I mean, if you count the thirty-one miles to the border, we've walked over one hundred miles already, but we haven't even passed the official one-hundred-mile mark yet, so it's like we've already done something big, but haven't quite done it yet. It makes you want to keep going. You know what I mean?"

We sat for a long time in silence. I rested my arm on the park bench behind her head and turned to look at her.

Near our house back in Lakeland, there is a twelve-acre phosphate pond, a strip-mined scar in the earth that is shaped like the number four. Our home is built on the peninsula that forms the top of the four. These days, they enforce reclamation, but our pond predates that demand. Even so, given time and the persistence of nature, neglected open pit mines heal themselves. Ours, like so many, is teaming with life. Many a mid-morning, after I finished my phone calls for work, I would wander out the door with my fishing pole in my hand. Aiden would trail along and talk, or not, and fish, or not.

One early morning, when Monica had gone for a walk with a friend, I walked out the door to fish. After I rounded a bend out of sight of our house, I had a feeling there was something behind me, so I turned around. It was Aiden. "What are you doing here?" I'd said. "Who is babysitting the other kids?"

"Dad, I'm seven. I'm not old enough to babysit," she'd said.

I kneeled in front of her and placed a hand on each shoulder. "Aido, look me right in the eye. You are as competent and capable a seven year old as I have ever known, and I know you can handle this."

She didn't question or challenge the wisdom of my directive. She didn't wonder if she was up for the task. Without her knowledge, I followed her back a few feet to a spot with a view of our front door. Not once did she turn around.

The fish were biting that day.

When I entered the house over an hour later, I found her standing on a stool in front of the kitchen island, wearing Monica's apron, and leaning, elbows deep, into a mixing bowl. There was a streak of flour running up the side of her face and into her hair where she'd been brushing it back. But that was not the only flour outside the mixing bowl. On the floor below the stool, June sat cross-legged, leaning forward to sweep more flour into the pile she was making. "June Bug," I'd said, and she'd giggled and shown me her hands.

The first thing I'd done was look at my watch. "Don't worry, kids, we have time to clean up this mess."

"I'm making scones, Dad. Don't you want some?" she'd said.

I moved my arm from the back of the park bench and brushed Aiden's hair behind her ear.

She turned to me. "What's up, Dad?"

"You've always been such a good helper," I said

She scrunched up her face as if she were confused.

"Guys," Henry ran up behind us, "you gotta come check out this hiker box. There is so much candy. I got five packs of Skittles. Mad Max was right."

"I thought you were going back to the campground." I patted the bench next to me. "Here, sit down with us."

"I changed my mind. I'm going back to see what else is in the box."

"First, tell me what has been your favorite part of the hike so far?"

"You mean my least worst part?" He smirked, but he tapped his lip with his finger. "That cinnamon roll from the Stehekin Bakery." Then he jogged away.

80.6.3

We stepped out of the bus in front of the Stehekin Bakery and found a place on the front lawn. I tapped Monica's leg. "Can you guys go grab some cinnamon rolls while I find a place to charge the phones?" I nodded toward the log building. "There has to be an outlet or two on that wraparound porch."

After we ate, we lay for a long time sprawled under a warm sun. Monica rolled her head toward me, her hand shielding her eyes. She nodded toward the bus. "I guess we ought to catch this one."

"I'll check with the driver," I said. After a stream of hikers disembarked, I leaned in and queried the driver.

He took off his hat and leaned his opposite ear toward me. He answered, "Plenty of room. I'll give this group about fifteen minutes to get what they need."

The bus was crowded as the driver edged the shuttle into the roadway from the bakery. A hiker chased the bus down and slapped the door. "Sorry, my good man, we couldn't pass up a chance to grab some more pastries," he said.

The driver smiled and waved him in.

"Would you be so kind as to wait for the remainder of the Royal Family?"

The driver nodded again.

The hiker stepped onto the first step with a big grin, doffed his hat, and bowed. "Thank you, one and all, for your patience." After the rest of his group boarded, he took a poll on the merits of the bakery. Whether by the benefit of location or true assessment, the consensus among the bus full of hikers was unanimous. It was the world's best bakery.

"Did you all start the trail together?" I said. "Or have you joined up along the way?"

"No, we have grouped up since the border."

"It's the Royal Family, you say?"

One of them chuckled under her breath, as if with disdain. "Yes, have you never heard of a trail family?" She turned away and held up a huckleberry pie. "I'm not sure what possessed me to buy the whole thing. Does anyone want any of it?"

Henry's eyes widened. Every last member of the Royal Family jumped up to help her, and Henry's head drooped.

At the trailhead we sat down to rearrange our packs and top up our water. When I clipped my pack closed, I groaned and sat up from the bench. "I guess we'd better get going. These miles won't walk themselves."

Monica and I crossed the parking lot together and stood at the trail sign to look up the steep path. "This is an awful way to start," Monica said. "June isn't going to like it."

"Me either," I said. I waved the others past me in order to wait for June. "Concentrate on your breathing, June. It's the first fifteen minutes that are the hardest."

Within ten minutes of the start, the Royal Family overtook us. I shouted up the hill, "Hey guys, move out of the way for a second."

The King stopped on a switchback above us. "Have you heard about the water crossing the day after tomorrow? It is supposed to be a pretty bad one, so try to get there in the morning before the snow heats up."

115.8

"Look at this, Dad." Henry stood with his trekking pole and tapped a pile of fresh sawdust.

"It looks like the maintenance crews are ahead of us now."

Aiden traced her finger on the number carved into the log. "What do you think this means?"

Henry stepped beside her.

"I think it's"—she tapped her finger to her lips—"I think it's how they keep track of how many logs they've cut."

"Come on, Aiden," I said, "think about it."

"What, Dad? The one back there said 14 and this one says 96."

"It's amazing to me how much different it is to walk on this trail now that we are walking where maintenance crews have already been through. They do such a good job of clearing the trail. It's like walking down Main Street now. Do you guys think you'd ever do that kind of thing?"

"I think it'd be fun," Aiden said. "I just think I'd be jealous of all the hikers passing by."

June rounded the corner and stopped and leaned over her trekking poles.

"June," Aiden said, "what do you think these numbers mean on the side of these logs?"

She didn't look up. "It's the year the maintenance person walked the trail. You didn't know that?"

"Well, it could mean that, sometimes, I guess. How far ahead is Mom, you guys? I need the shovel."

"She said she'd wait at the nesxt water stop," I said.

I walked out behind them through piles of clean-cut blown-down timber. Up the hill, a wide swath of trees toppled by an avalanche let the sun through. Some of the trees were fresh-cut, and some cut in previous seasons. Some were so thick that they were only notched with steps for us to climb up one side and down the other.

June traced her hand across a fresh-cut log. "I am glad they got here before us."

"Me too, kid." I thought of the next day's water crossing. "Do you care if I go by you and catch up to your mom?"

***

That night in the tent, I whispered to Monica, "What if we have to turn around at the water crossing in the morning?"

"You think it will be that bad?"

"I don't want to risk it if it is too sketchy, but what are we going to do, turn back and walk a day and a half out of here? When Sassafras passed me earlier today, she sounded nervous. She said they were going another two miles tonight to get closer to it, so they could cross early in the morning before it gets hot."

"You think it makes that much of a difference?"

"Afternoon snow melts faster, so the creeks rise. It's strange to think that there might be a barrier across the trail, so significant that we might have no choice but to turn back."

"You really think we might have to?"

"I wouldn't have thought so, but the way everyone is talking about it ... I don't know. I just keep envisioning these crazy scenarios where we get there to the edge of the creek, but it's not a creek, it's a gorge. There's some log across it that we have to shimmy across, and then I have this vision of Georgie getting halfway across and slipping and getting swept downstream. It's irrational, I know. I just can't shake it."

Monica laughed.

"What are you laughing about?"

"Now you know what it's like to be in my head all the time."

119

I was standing on the lip of the cutbank looking down when Monica grabbed my elbow. "What do you think?" she said.

"Listen."

She pulled her hat off of her head. "It's loud."

"It's roaring." I pointed toward a boulder in the middle of the creek. "That first part doesn't look that bad. I think if I stepped over to that rock, I can stand in the big eddy behind it, I could help everyone across the worst of the flow. It only looks about four feet of scary."

"It really doesn't look that bad."

"It's not not the crossing that's bad." With my trekking pole, I pointed downstream. "You just don't want to get swept." About ten feet below the crossing the stream dropped out of sight. Beyond it, a thin mist filled the air. It doesn't sound like a soft landing."

She put her hat back on and pulled it down tight, then tightened the strap up to her chin. "Waterfall?"

The wide gully cut by the creek was u-shaped. There were jagged boulders, exposed tree roots, and sharp lines where a recent flood had reshaped it.

"Wait for me down at the bottom," I said. "I want to talk to Georgie when she gets here."

I was first into the water. I inched my foot in and looked back. "Oh, that's cold," I said and took a long step into the eddy behind the big rock and shuffled my foot around until I found a solid fit for it. I found a good handhold for one hand the large rock in front of me and reached back with the other. "Come one at a time and I'll help you get past this part."

Georgie waited 'til last. I flung her over the heaviest part of the flow with ease. On the far side of the creek, we stood looking back. She said, "That wasn't bad at all, was it? What were we worried about?" She clipped her chest strap and looked up at the bank ahead of us. "I guess they aren't planning to wait for us."

"It was moving pretty fast," I said, "but it was narrow, so it wasn't too bad."

"Maybe we should see how bad something is for ourselves next time," she said, "instead of worrying about it before we get there."

We climbed the embankment and the trail leveled out. "Dad, why did we decide to come on this trip?"

"Why do you ask?"

"You told that guy yesterday it was because we finally got out of debt. I didn't know we were in debt."

"That's one of the reasons, kid. Did you want to hear about that?"

"Can you answer so I'll understand?"

"I can try. Do you remember that I was a supervisor for your grandpa? Well, at some point, I could tell things were slowing down in the building industry, and I could see there wouldn't be enough work for me and Mr. Morrison and Jared, so I just went out on my own under your great-grandpa's, my grandpa's, license. Everything was going great for about a year. But do you remember that neighborhood where I was building houses?"

"Highland City? Over by the church?"

"Yes, I thought I was so smart for building there. Highland City had a bunch of those run-down and abandoned mobile homes mixed in with the houses, so I would buy them and replace them with a house because then I didn't have to pay any impact fees."

"What is an impact fee?"

"It's a tax that the community charges for a new home in an area to offset the impact the new family will have on the infrastructure. Like schools and roads and such. Anyway, the other reason I built there was that Publix was putting in that new grocery store across the street, so I figured they had done all the demographic studies about growth in the area."

"What does that mean?"

"It means they thought more people would be moving into that neighborhood. They paid a lot of money to do studies to find that out, so I figured I would just cheat off of their test."

"Dad!"

"It didn't work. Well, I don't know if it would have worked or not. I thought I did everything right. I lined up buyers before I even started building, but because my buyers couldn't qualify for a construction loan, I had to line up credit borrowers."

"What is that?"

"It is a harder loan to get. It lets you borrow to build, rather than borrow on something that already exists."

"Why is it harder to get?"

"Because if you are the bank, you know that more can go wrong when you loan against something that doesn't exist yet. They prefer to loan against something that already exists. There for a while the bank had loosened the requirements for borrowers on regular loans, but about halfway through those six projects I was working on, the rules changed. After that, none of my buyers could qualify for the loans."

"So you had to pay for them."

"Some of them. Some of them were investments that friends had partnered on. I didn't want anyone to lose their money, so I took all the money I had and tried to finish everything up."

"Is that why we moved in with Grandmommy and Grandpa?"

"Yes, I gave up on our house payments first. By the time it was over, I owed a pile of money. We moved into their house, because I didn't want to go bankrupt."

"If you go bankrupt, you don't have to pay?"

"Yes, mostly, but I found out that if I went bankrupt, we wouldn't be allowed to pay anyone back, anything, and many of the people I owed money to were my friends."

"We've lived there a long time."

"It was a lot of money."

We walked for a while in silence.

"Dad?"

"Why did they change the rules?"

"Well, I blame the government more than I blame the banks, if you want to know the truth."

"What?"

"Yeah, it's like this. The banks know who is good to give money to and who isn't. They know how much money they need to get from someone to protect their investment. You know why?"

"No, why?"

"Because their paycheck depends on it. But in this case, they didn't follow
their own rules. You want to know why?"

"Why?"

"Because the government wanted more people to own houses. So they went
to the banks and said, 'You know those people you know better than to give
money to? You know that big down payment you know you need to ask for?
Yeah, don't worry about that anymore, just give it to them.'"

"Why would the banks do that?"

"Georgie," I looked back at her over my shoulder, "I think you may be the
only eleven- year-old in the world talking about this today."

She looked up at me. "It's kind of interesting. I never knew why we didn't
have money before."

"We had money, Georgie. We just had to give it to the people we owed it to,
so I guess it wasn't ours in the first place, was it? Anyway, what was I
saying?"

"Something about the banks."

"Oh yeah, It's like this. If you knew Henry was terrible with money, and he
asked for some money to spend on candy. But you knew he wouldn't ever
really pay you back. Would you give him money?"

"No."

"Well, what if Grandpa came along and said, 'Georgie, I know Henry might
not pay you back, but I want you to give him some money anyway. If he
doesn't pay you back, I will.' Would you give him the money then?"

"Yes, because Grandpa would pay me, right?"

"Well, that's basically what the government did. Except it would be like when Henry didn't pay you back, Grandpa blamed it on you for making a bad loan. You see, so it was around this time that I thought it would be a great time to go into business for myself."

"Good timing."

"Speaking of bad timing, I have to stop for the bathroom."

When I finished, I scooped up the shovel kit and walked quickly to catch Georgie. Thick undergrowth crowded the trail. I reached down to brush aside some branches with my hand and realized I had dropped my sun glove back where I'd stopped. I turned to retrace my steps.

With each step in the northbound direction, I felt Georgie getting further from me. The low river bottom below began to feel like an easy place for her to get lost. I imagined I saw something move in the bushes. Georgie was walking alone. "Forget the glove!" I said aloud. I turned and ran to catch up to her.

Around every corner when she didn't appear, I grew more certain I wouldn't see her again. I was out of breath when I caught her.

"What's wrong, Dad?"

"I got nervous about you walking alone and started imagining all sorts of crazy things." We walked in silence. After a while, I said, "I should probably say something else about the government. I don't think they set out to create a problem. I think they intended to encourage home ownership for people who wouldn't ever have a chance otherwise. Private property is extremely important."

"Is this private property?"

"What?"

"Is the trail on private property?"

"I don't know. I bet most of it isn't." We walked in silence for a while. "Georgie, when we catch them, I'm going to drop off and use the shovel again. Will you stay with them, so I don't have to worry about you?"

123

I turned onto the trail and felt my gaiter flap against the toe of my shoe. When I stood up from having reclipped it, I was startled by a man sitting just twenty feet from me on the trunk of a tree. He seemed not to have seen me, as if engrossed in an attempt to reach his feet. I coughed to announce my presence, and he turned.

"Taking a little break?" I said.

"Yeah, I can't seem to keep my shoes tied." He unzipped his heavy, green Arc'teryx rain jacket, flung it apart, and leaned forward over his knees. With what seemed to be some awkward shifting about, he pulled a handkerchief from his pocket and wiped his brow, then turned his head up to me and shook his head.

I stabbed one of my trekking poles into the ground just off the shoulder of the trail opposite him and bent to reattach my gaiter. "I'm having trouble getting my gaiters to stay clipped too. Do you mind if I sit down for a minute to try to tighten up this clip?"

He shook his head.

"How is your hike going so far?"

"Man, I've been throwing up since I started. You probably can't tell, but I've lost twenty pounds already."

"Are you holding anything down at all?"

"Yeah, it's only like every other day now. It's gotten better. Now my problem is my ankle. It's been killing me. I rolled it in the rocks yesterday, and I'm in constant pain." He pointed toward his plastic Nalgene bottle next to his pack. "Do you mind handing it to me? I'm dying of thirst."

"That sucks, man, not being able to eat." I scooped up his bottle and handed it to him. "What's your name?"

"Survivor Man."

"That's quite a name," I said. "How'd you get that name?"

"Before the trip I was trying to think of something that would be good, and I landed on that one."

"I didn't know you were allowed to make up your own trail name. Wait, are you the one that brought the homemade pemmican?"

He turned his head up toward me. "How did you know that?"

"I saw a block of it in Broken Toe's hiker box when we came through."

"Yeah, I made too much of it for the start. I wasn't really that hungry for the first several days. I've added other things to my diet now, so I may send the rest of it home when I get to my resupply boxes."

I laughed. "You are lucky no one tried to name you Pemmican. Have you been walking with anyone?"

"I walked for a few days with Bear Hair. When I hurt my ankle, I told her just to go on ahead without me."

I pushed myself to my feet and grabbed the grip of my trekking pole, twisted it in the dirt a few times, and stabbed it up and down. "Well, I think I'll get moving and catch up to my people."

He lifted his hand as if to stop me. "Do you mind retying my shoes for me before you take off?"

When I stood back to my feet, I waved goodbye and said, "If we run into Bear Hair, we'll tell her we saw you."

131.7

"Well?" I looked at June. "You want to?"

"Seriously?" She dropped her pack on the snow.

"If you will, I will."

June looked at Henry. "Are you coming too?"

Henry shook his head.

Mica Lake lay under a heavy blanket of ice and snow, save for the small opening below us. I made my way along the snowbank bordering the outflowing creek in order to find a good place to drop down. When I found it, Henry said, "Help me down too, but don't get any ideas. I'm not swimming in that."

I slipped off my shoes, placed my bare feet on the rocks, and waited for the others to join me. I looked at June. "If these rocks are this cold, think about that water."

"Hurry up, Dad." Aiden put her hand on my back. "Just go."

"Hold up, Aido," I said.

June reached for my elbow. "Dad, wait for me."

I found her hand and we steadied ourselves on the last rocks. "Do you want to jump in at the same time?"

Aiden backed away from the edge. "I'm going to let you guys go first." She wrapped herself in her arms and shivered. "That looks so cold."

June and I stood at the edge for a long time. June leaned forward again and again. Each time as if she would jump. "Sorry, Daddo. I'm scared."

"It's okay, kid."

I didn't want to be the first to go, neither did I want to refuse the challenge. Henry stepped up on a rock behind me and peered past.

"Are you coming too?"

"No way. I'm going over there." He picked his way over creek stones to the far side.

I was in the air over the water regretting my decision for what seemed like a long time. It was a familiar experience, that mid-air regret. It's a here-I-go, what-have-I done sort of feeling. I jumped from eighty-five feet above Linville Falls in North Carolina once. This feels familiar. You fall for a long time when the water is eighty-five feet down. This felt longer somehow.

When at last I broke through the surface of the water, it was as if I had fallen into a bed of a thousand hot needles. It was as if everything in me closed up shop. Slammed shut. Including my mind. Like a full body gasp. Like a full body panic. My dive carried me far from shore. At the end of my momentum, I curled upward and broke the surface. "Oh. Oh. Oh!" I gasped. And with frantic strokes, I raced to the shore.

"How was it?" June reached her hand down.

I shook my head. It wasn't until I was standing on the rock again in a wave of inexplicable warmth that I could speak. "It's not even that cold. You should try it."

"I know you're lying." Aiden stepped away. "I don't think I want to anymore."

"It's warm when you get out. It feels weird."

She reached an arm behind June's back and swept her forward. "You go first. You're the Polar Bear."

June held out her hand. "Come with me, Aido. I'm scared." And they jumped.

Atop the drift again we stood on our groundsheets and scraped our skin dry and inched into the rest of our clothes.

Aiden pointed. "Look at Henry."

As soon as she'd said it, we heard the splash. He looked up, bewildered from beyond the outflow where he'd slipped, as if to say, "Are you going to help?"

He was back on the shore in an instant and sloshing his way through the rocks.

"We should pack up and leave before he gets back here." Aiden said. "Huh, June?" She looked down at June's feet. "Slip that shoe on, June, and I'll help you get your traction devices on. I know they can be a pain in the booty."

Monica hoisted her pack, shook her head, and said, "I can't believe the three of you went in that water."

"Four!" Henry popped his head up from below the snowbank. "Four!"

"You slipped, Henry," June said. "That shouldn't count."

June and I were the last to start. She stopped above the lake for a last look back. "Daddo, I just thought of something. Maybe I shouldn't be called the Polar Bear anymore. I'm not as good at swimming in cold water out here."

148.6

I drop my pack into the dirt at the top of Red Pass and collapse into it. Georgie scooches over to rest her head on my shoulder, and we begin tossing small rocks at a large one.

Aiden and Henry stand up from where they sit a few yards away and walk to look back down the side we climbed.

"Ugh." Henry turns to us. "Why does she have to take so long?"

Aiden taps him on the elbow and points up the hill. "I bet the view is killer from up there." They race toward the steep slope and scramble, half running, half on hands and knees toward the summit of Portal Peak.

Monica, Georgie, and I stay where we are, lazy in the warm sun.

"Look at that view, Mom," Georgie says. "It's like an ocean of mountains. Rolling and rolling and wave after wave." She pointed. "What is that big one that's still covered in snow."

"That's Mount Rainier."

"All the other peaks look tiny around it."

"They aren't any tinier than this one. Rainier is just that big a mountain. It's where we are meeting the Browns."

"Oh really?"

It seems fitting that we get to see them out here, since they are the ones that got us into backpacking in the first place."

"How long will it take us to get to them?"

"If we had a car we'd be there in three hours. By foot, if we are going to make it in time for pizza, it will take thirteen days and two town stops, one hundred and eighty miles. We've already walked one hundred and forty, so we just have to do it again." I pinch my fingers, almost together. "Plus, a little."

"Are you counting the extra thirty-one miles to the border?"

"No."

"Then we walked one hundred seventy-one, so we really are halfway there, or we will be by tonight, anyway."

June appears over the saddle, as if from nowhere. "Don't even think about getting up. I need a rest." She collapses beside me, opposite Georgie, and lays her head on my chest.

In the hottest part of the following day, Henry punctuates our summit of Grizzly Peak with a complaint. "It's stupid to make us come up here when we could just go around that way. It should be called Pointless Peak."

"Henry," I say and point to the ground at my feet," We are here to walk this trail, and we will follow wherever it leads. Do you hear me?"

These days, first light comes early. We are walking as day breaks now. We target twelve miles before lunch.

At Stevens Pass, where the highway passes the ski resort, we split into two groups for a hitch down the hill into town. The cafe there is crowded with hikers. Columbus, Bluebear, The King, Shivers, and the rest of the Royal Family are gathered there. I order the Trainwreck, a jambalaya of everything you could think of for breakfast. Before I finish my first plate, I order another.

We catch another hitch to the Dinsmores', just out of town. Fifteen years earlier, Jerry Dinsmore had offered a stay to some hikers he had mistaken for homeless. He has taken hikers in ever since. He carries on now without his wife Andrea. Cancer took her from him last year. He speeds up and down the ramp on his all-terrain scooter, stokes the fire, and tosses hot dogs to everyone.

Sassafras and Beamer play the kids in Backpacker's Monopoly. Sassafras wins. We list off the people we've come to know and ask if they've seen them. "Bear Hair came through here yesterday, but she seemed in a hurry to get out of town again," Beamer says. "Other than that, I haven't seen any of the people you named, have you, Sassafras?"

Everyone warns us. "The mosquitoes are bad through this next section."

"We're from Florida. How bad can they be?"

Back on-trail, the mosquitoes emerge from under melting snow, solo and sluggish. "They don't even bite when they land." We laugh and shoo them away. But the next day they come swarming together. Repellent is useless. We pray for exposed ridgelines and high winds. Near stagnant ponds, the buzz becomes an enduring scrape on an endless chalkboard.

"Make it stop, Daddy," Georgie cries.

"I can't make it stop. The only way to make it stop is to walk, and to walk fast. Anything above two miles per hour seems to be the magic number."

"I can't, I can't. She dances in place, waving wild hands and says again, "I can't!" She throws her face toward the sky. "Make it stop."

But we need her to go on, and she does.

We have five headnets for the six of us. We misplaced one somewhere. Monica and I take turns walking exposed.

A wave of passing northbound hikers reports, "We've been walking through them for four hundred miles."

On day three of mosquitoes, Henry concedes at last, "I take it all back. These are a lot worse than Florida mosquitoes."

Near lunchtime, I wave him to me, "Go and see if we can set up down by that lake."

We follow him off the trail. He is lost to us for twenty minutes. We are thirty miles from any road in any direction. In my search, I cover and re-cover ground, betraying my panic to Monica's quiet queries with curt responses, "It's fine, it's fine. We will find him." But I have already unlocked the SOS button on the Garmin three times. Five minutes later I find him over a ridge where he has followed an elk herd.

"Look at them," he says. "Isn't that cool?"

I demand explanations.

"I never heard you, Dad."

Around a bend the next day, I see Aiden off-trail down a steep bank. She is holding her hip with tears in her eyes. I scramble down to her, and she shows me the scrape. The bleeding stops when we hold pressure on it. "That's going to bruise, Aiden. What happened?"

She looks up and points. "That stupid ice patch in the shade. I couldn't decide if I should go over it on the uphill side, but it looked too steep there, so I tried to pass on the downhill side." She looks down at her feet where we are standing. "I'm glad this log was here, 'cause it slowed me down." She looks up at me and shakes her head laughing. "We walked through so much snow, and now that there's almost none of it left, this happens."

In the late afternoon, we pause at a junction, where two hikers redirect us. "Not that way," they say. "Come to the right." They had walked nine miles toward the left to Lake Waptus.

We tell them we are sick of false summits. "Dad calls them high school boyfriends," June says. "They'll tell you they love you, but if you commit, they just disappear. Especially Deception Pass. I hated that one."

"But," Aiden says, "at least it was well named."

The next day, when they catch us, we greet each other with a, "What the Waptus!"

We are early into a long climb and a passing hiker says, "You're almost there." Before he is out of earshot, Georgie turns back to me. "I hate that, Dad." Why would he say that when it isn't true?"

Over the summit, we are descending when a northbound thru-hiker climbs toward us with wide, unrelenting strides. When he passes, Georgie says, "I think he is going up the hill faster than we are going down it." He hears her and turns, so she says again, "You're faster than us, and you are going uphill."

"Just wait," he says, until you get your trail legs."

We reach the bottom and wade for miles in ankle-deep water. A man with a long white beard passes us for a second time. His name is Tock and he is sixty-eight years old with over thirty thousand trail miles under his feet. "I can't walk as fast as I used to could, I go two miles an hour uphill and two miles an hour downhill for thirteen hours a day."

"Do you have any advice for us?" I say.

"I'll tell you one thing I've learned. You can spend money in town, just don't spend time."

"And you are called Tock? Why is that?"

"I'm as steady as a clock," he laughs. "In every way."

Several northbounders marvel that Georgie is only eleven. We walk in silence for a few miles after we pass them until she muses, "Dad, it seems to me that it isn't the youngest that is most impressive. It's really the oldest, I think. I hope I am as lively as Tock when I get to be that age."

Paige is perched cross-legged atop a wide stump. She shows us one of her tiny clay pots she has made. "I am placing them in picturesque locations and taking pictures for an album to save. I have given away two to trail angels."

She says she has blisters.

"We've been walking without socks after our shoes get wet, just until they dry, and that seems to help. Don't we Georgie?"

"Good idea, I might try that," she says, and as we stand to go, adds, "By the way, I have been gifted a trail name. It's Potter. Mad Max named me."

Thigh deep, in one swift stream crossing, somewhere in the unmaintained Suiattle Basin, Georgie spots a flash of white chord flung about in the current. Aiden traces it to a submerged phone. I stuff it in her pack to carry to the next town.

We walk through a cold mist into the night on an endless traverse. We sleep on the first flat we find under the pines without pitching our tents. We pray that it doesn't rain.

I walk behind Georgie on the narrow Kendall Katwalk. It had been dynamite blasted and cut from walls of sheer granite for miles. I see that Georgie will not look down. "This was the most expensive section of trail to build, Georgie. That's according to John Smith." I step nearer the edge and look down.

Georgie touches the rock wall and turns past her hand to look over her shoulder. "Get away from the edge, Dad. I don't like that."

Our hunger increases. We rename passes for food on our descent to Snoqualmie. We descend through a forest of fir. Monica waits for me on a long switchback. "This feels like the longest five miles we've walked."

We surprise the Royal Family when we catch them in town, and one of them mentions that Sassafras has lost her phone. "She is one day behind."

Aiden runs to her pack and passes the phone over the counter at the Aardvark. "Every hiker stops here at my food truck," the cook says. "I'll pass it along."

We order six bowls of rice from him. Two times.

We meet a hiker named Oh Lordy when we sit down. He has ice wrapped around his quad and reaches into what looks like a daypack. "I'm injured," he says. "I may take a few days here. We'll see."

"How much does your pack weigh?" I say.

He laughs. "Six pounds."

After we sort out our resupply, we set out not too far behind the Royal Family. They are surprised when we catch them in camp.

Bluebear and Columbus share our night fire and stories. We commiserate over our hatred for hanging bear bags. "There is one thing I don't like about America," Columbus says. "Why would they call those tiny little Snickers 'fun size'? If anything, they should be called 'disappointing size.' Why not call the thing what it is?"

Henry trails off to sleep with an, "I like Columbus and Blue Bear a lot."

We are all of us taking off shoes at a stream when Oh Lordy steps to the top of the bank behind us in full throated song. He stomps right through, and, for a moment stops on the far side of the stream. "Don't bother with stopping at water. Just walk your shoes dry."

"I thought you were injured," I say.

"I mean, I'm here anyway. I'll hit as many forties as I can until it's time for my flight. I can rest when I'm home."

"You aren't walking the whole thing?"

"I'm only here because I got bored with the AT after six hundred miles. I can walk that trail anytime. I'm a teacher back east." As soon as he passes from our sight, we hear him burst again into song.

Aiden's skin begins to separate into a large blister two inches by four inches on the sole of her right foot. We tape it down tight with Lukotape. "Don't take it off 'til we get to the Browns."

For two days we leapfrog with the Royal Family. Each overlap, our conversation concerns the twelve-mile water carry to come.

On a high windy pine bluff, we pause to let The King pass. We step three to each side and raise our trekking poles to form a makeshift arch. As he passes beneath, we pay homage to his majesty. He takes a bow. "Be sure you load up at the next water. There is a twelve-mile carry beyond."

Henry bows low. "Thank you, my liege."

Fourteen miles through the Norse Creek Fire burn section. Sixty thousand acres had been claimed the previous year. We walk through a forest of dead giants. Each of our steps kicks up ash.

June stands on a ledge overlooking the burn. "This is sad."

"I don't see what's so sad about it," Henry says.

We sleep through a chorus of cracked, cracking voices of the drying, dead trees.

In the morning I wake before everyone and sit not far from the tents. The sun rises through the black remnant of trees, and all through the creek bottom beside us, small, yellow flowers lift their faces to the sun.

An unsullied and unhurried, uphill hiker named Brazil Nut steps off the trail to let Henry pass. After she's gone, we argue at length about which direction should have the right of way. He will not relent. In town, we confirm that Henry is wrong and discover that Brazil Nut is on pace to break the fastest known time for an unsupported thru-hike of the PCT, sixty days.

Another northbounder asks where we are headed. I say,
"We are thru-hikers."

He asks me what trail we have finished. When I answer, "None," he says, "You aren't a thru-hiker yet. Don't get ahead of yourself."

We catch Emily and Ryan before they finish lunch beside a wide lake. "We didn't expect to see you again," she says. "We have received our names now."

"What are they?"

"I am Vamp." She touches her arm. "The arm sleeves. I have a sun allergy. Ryan is now Swarm."

"Why is that?" I say.

"These mosquitoes," he says. "No matter who we are with, I am the target of their attention."

He joins me in singing "You'll Never Walk Alone" as a goodbye. When they are gone, I say, "This time for sure. This will be the last time we will be seeing them."

On the twelfth day, in the mid-afternoon, we descend to Sheep Lake, just two miles from Chinook Pass. We have time to kill and fish to catch. Aiden wants to swim without tape on her foot, so she says to Georgie, "Rip it loose fast, so it won't hurt." Georgie obeys. The tape comes off, blister and all, and she bleeds, and she bleeds, and she bleeds.

Henry eats his first fish over our evening fire.

We sit around it well into the dark, for only the second time since we've begun. One hundred seventy-eight miles from Red Pass leaves one sleep and two miles between us and our friends.

"I hope Aiden's foot heals quickly," I whisper.

"Me too," Monica says. "I'll wrap it up again in the morning."

328.7

Jamie,

I won't stop long enough to write this letter. On-trail, power is too precious to keep my screen on for long. In town it's all flurry to prepare for the next section. If I had paper and pencil I could do it, I suppose, but I would never carry the weight. So, here is the letter I will meant to have sent.

When you squealed your tires from the parking lot toward your seven hundred and fifty mile day, I chuckled at the relative equivalence of your and our ambition, despite so disparate a number. You, planning to cover an entire state, and me just twenty plus miles after such a late start.

When I was halfway up the grassy slope above Chinook Pass, I turned to watch the white speck of your full-sized passenger van round a final bend of the winding mountain road. Though I could not see the cluster of stickers across the back doors, I could picture them. Each, an Ebenezer to commemorate a destination in this natural world where you have taken your family adventuring. We hold a claim to memories with you for a handful of those stickers. Your family, you surely know, struck the spark that would become this hike.

You taught us to camp. We could afford little else at the time.

Remember when Georgie and Porter raced back to camp on that twelve-mile day hike in Shining Rock Wilderness? You edged us out with a shortcut from that old road bed at the top of the last rise. We ate pancakes over the cast iron stove we "packed in" a mile and a half that night. Remember that early morning downpour in Panthertown when Porter crawled under the vestibule of our tent when his tent collapsed? Remember the "shortcut" we took up that bouldery wash from the west fork of the Gila Wilderness? Remember when Creigh scolded me for cutting down that standing dead tree for firewood? These are long walking days with hours of mind space to fill. I have time to remember here.

We would not be here, but for you.

Your van was out of sight, but I swear I caught a waft of your burnt rubber. A fleeting, floating thread of reconnection.

All day the kids said, and repeated, "That was so much fun."

I tried to tease more from them, because I know "fun" cannot be the whole of it. They only shrugged and smiled. I can't say exactly what they mean, but I can guess.

Yours has always been the eye for the itinerary. Somewhere back in May, before I had planned our food drops, you said, "July 18th we will meet you at the pass with pizza, if all goes as planned."

I remember asking, "Whose plan?"

For each waking moment of these last two hundred miles you have been our target, our pinned point on the map. You have been the math I calculate at night when I wake in the dark. I have learned and relearned that ten days of walking is not the same as the tenth day of walking. I'm embarrassed to admit how many times I had to relearn it. In fact, we pushed for a week at nearly twenty miles per day when seventeen would have done just as well.

One night, after coercing a climb up just-one-more-hill, in order that "we won't have to do it in the morning," Henry fell into a pine bush. When I pulled him to his feet, he had a steady stream of tears clearing a clean line down his dirty cheek. I wiped them with the heel of my hand. When I said, "At least we're one hill closer to the Browns," he smiled.

Another day I stood inside some trees off-trail. June passed by me on a climb, and I overheard her say, "Come on legs, you can do it. Don't give up before you get to the Browns."

I don't know if you've read the book Moonwalking with Einstein. Aiden and I listened to it the other day. It is a book on memory and memorizing. In the book he talks about reducing an unmanageable string of numbers into manageable chunks of three and four and nine. When we began, Mexico was 2,650 trail miles away. From the first, that has been inconceivable. And were the sum of it on our mind, we would have been overwhelmed. It has not been on our mind. We had three hundred thirty-four miles to make it to our friends, and each day brought us a marked percentage closer.

At the pizza place in Packwood, Creigh asked if I had seen your recent posts. I hadn't. She scrolled to them and reached her phone across the sticky, checkered tablecloth. She showed me three pictures of your family on the Pacific Crest Trail in playful poses. "It's a picture challenge," she said. "When you get there, you'll have to take one just like it."

The first was at a road crossing in Oregon. "Above a lake," she said.

The next beside a sign in the Sierra.

The last in the desert in California.

"Don't confuse me," I told her, "just tell me where the first one is."

She wouldn't say.

"If it's in Oregon, I think we can make it," I said.

"You have done so much already," she said. "If you didn't make it past today, you'd already be heroes in my book."

I've thought of that a lot today. We have done so much already.

I've found the first location. It is near Odell Lake and Shelter Cove. It is just over 400 miles away. We've done nearly that already, surely we can do it one more time. And, in a way, you will be there waiting for us, a thread of a connection back toward home.

After the smell of your tires disappeared this morning, I stepped into the trees with the shovel. I told Monica I would catch her. When I caught her an hour later, she turned and smiled. "It's nice to have friends."

By now you are a full state away, but you are with us in more ways than remembering.

See you again, soon enough.

365

The last of the sun's light pierced the tops of the juvenile pines and fell in dappled patches on the floor of the small clearing. I lay flat on my back in the dust between an old fire ring and the log where Georgie was seated. The light made a halo in the frizzy ends of her hair as it played its way through. The outermost strands diffused into the light. She wiped her face with a dirt-stained hand. At her feet, her food for the long section lay in a cluttered pile.

"You've got to pack all that up, kid."

"I'm so tired." She sighed and leaned forward to wrap her arms around her legs. She looked at me. "Eight days?"

"Eight days."

She sighed again. "My shoulders hurt."

"It was a long day. I think I could fall asleep right here."

"Me too. I could probably sleep sitting up. Is this our longest section?"

"The longest on the whole trail. I could have made it a little shorter. There was one option to stop, but it would have required a hitch, so I just figured we'd skip it." I picked up a stick and turned it in my hands. "You know what tomorrow is?"

She looked at me. "Tomorrow?" Georgie sighed again. She didn't say anything for a long time.

I cracked the stick in half and continued cracking the halves into halves.

"Knife's Edge?" she said.

"I still have your drawing on my phone."

"What drawing?"

"The one that you drew on the chalkboard. I took a picture of it. 'God will protect us on the PCT' you said, and you drew a little trail sign toward Knife's Edge. I don't think you need to be worried. Every northbounder we ask says Knife's Edge was their favorite part of the trail."

"I bet they aren't as scared of heights as I am."

"Do you remember how nervous we were about that creek crossing?" I scooped the small pile of broken sticks into my hand. "Why would this be any different?" I tossed the sticks into the fire ring. "Either way, once we are past it, there will be nothing left to scare you all the way to Mexico."

"Are you going to carry me across Knife's Edge?"

"If you need me to."

She stretched her arm out to pinch her empty food bag and pull it toward her.

"Start with your tortillas, and lay them flat against the side of your food bag," I said. "That way you don't end up with all tortilla crumbles."

"I like the crumbles. They are tortilla chips."

We climbed all morning, but the last stretch of the climb was the steepest. It was as though they had abandoned the idea of switchbacks altogether in favor of one last push for the top. At the higher level the trail cut a traverse across a mix of talus field and cut rock.

I rounded a bend to find Georgie waiting for me. She was looking down with her back to the trail. I adjusted my feet on the loose stone and looked up again, laughing. "How bad is it, kid? What do you think?"

"It looks like God dropped a giant stegosaurus right on top of a ridge."

"Let me come look." I stepped up beside her. Down either side, wide glacial bowls swept far away. A dinosaur was a fair description if the dinosaur were made of extrusive igneous rock and had been dropped longways along a high smooth saddle to form a craggy bridge between two mountain tops. "You know what I think, Georgie?" I offered up an alternate proposal. "I think it looks like God was late to turn in an art project and grabbed some brown playdough from the wrong jar, and just smashed it in here."

"If he used spiky play-dough, yeah." She laughed. "And then he was like, 'Oh well, that kinda looks cool, I guess I'll leave it.'"

Fifteen minutes later, Georgie stood less than eighteen inches from the long drop. She reached a toe toward the edge and nudged a pebble from it. She looked up at me and smiled. "Did you hear that, Dad? So far down."

"Knife's Edge, Georgie," I said. "We are finally here."

Georgie looked back at me. "Dad, I'm a teensy bit scared, but not as scared as I thought I would be." She stepped toward the edge and looked down. She turned to me again with wide eyes. "It is a long way down, though."

Aiden reached back for Georgie's hand. With her opposite hand, she pointed our gaze below and into the valley. "Look at that."

"What am I looking at?" I said.

"It's an eagle flying in big circles. It's easier to see against the white."

I scanned for movement against the green, against the dotted snow patches, and against the islands of boulder piles topped with pine trees. From there, I traced the creek down and down, then looked up toward the horizon. Mount Rainier towered there, dominant.

Georgie released Aiden's hand and turned to step toward me. After a first faltering step she found her balance and looked over the steep drop to her left. She scooched toward it and raised up on her toes to peer down. "It's just as steep on this side."

She reached for my hand and pulled herself up beside me. "Follow my finger, do you see it?"

A speck against a snow laden gully on the far side of the valley dipped and swooped into a wide circle below. Behind me, Monica touched my elbow. She tilted her head up to look at me from under the brim of her hat. She whispered, "It doesn't seem like any of this can be real."

I sat down on the rock. They both sat beside me. Thirty feet downtrail over a drop, Henry leaned against a rock. "What are we waiting on?"

"We are resting, but we still have to decide whether we are going to take that cut across the snow, or climb up and around it," I said. "It doesn't look too bad from here."

He slumped his shoulders and kicked the ground.

"What do you think?"

"I can't tell from here," Monica said.

"Do you care if I send him, as long as Aiden is with him?"

She shrugged.

"You can go, Henry. Just make sure you guys stay together, and if you get to that traverse and it looks sketchy, wait for us." I picked up my pack and swung it on. When I looked up, they were gone. "Alright Georgie, lead on."

Georgie bent beside Monica on the last rise of the spine of Knife's Edge. She turned to me and pointed toward Monica's hand. I leaned in beside them to see between Monica's long fingers, the head of a flower of soft pinks, and washed-out yellows, cloverlike. Monica turned to me and smiled. She said with a soft voice, "Something so gentle, so beautiful, and in such a hard place."

387.9

Aiden lay on her back on her dirty groundsheet opposite me with her hand on the top of her hat. She rolled her head to the side and reached with her other hand toward the outer door of her tent. She dropped her arm back down and sighed. All three of our tents were tucked tight together just off the bend in the trail opposite the grassy approach to the lake.

Henry tilted his head and dropped the last crumbly bite of his tortilla into his open mouth. He wiped the back of his hand on his mouth and then scraped it a couple of times on the grass beside him.

I groaned and rolled over to my knees and crawled to my pack to loose my water bottles from my side pouches. "Does anyone need me to fill them up? I am going to fill up tonight, so I don't have to do it in the morning."

"Take mine, please," Aiden said, "but first can you hand it to me so I can take a sip. It's just under my tent flap. I was trying to reach for it a second ago, but I didn't feel like getting up."

"Henry, come over here and take your shoes off," Monica said. "I need to look at your toes."

"June's are worse than mine," he said. "Why don't you look at hers first?"

"Mine are not bad at all anymore. Dad popped my only blister at lunch yesterday, and it's not bothering me now."

The high grass reached almost to my knees as soon as I stepped to the far side of the trail, and the low-lying ground became soggy. I came to a short canal-like strip that ran from where I stood toward the glassy lake. When I knelt, a cloud of white flies flitted from the grass and swarmed around my face. I blew them away from my mouth and dipped my dirty bottle into the clear pool.

Georgie tapped me on the shoulder. "Do you need any help, Daddy?"

"I didn't hear you come up. Nah, I can do it."

"I am surprised there are no mosquitoes by this lake."

"They would have been swarming us like crazy a hundred miles back. I think we have passed the worst of them now."

"If you want to stick around, you can help me carry these bottles back over after I'm done filling them up."

Monica was hunched over Henry's extended foot when we returned. She turned at the sound of my approach. "Look at this, Vince. What do you think?"

I dropped to my knees beside her and put a hand on her shoulder. "What is it?"

"Do you think we need to pop this blister on his middle toe?"

Every toe on Henry's foot was covered in tape, but the one. "What do you think, Henry?" I pinched his toe between my finger and thumb.

"Don't squeeze it, Vince," Monica said. "I don't want it to get infected."

"My fingers aren't as dirty as his toes. Does it hurt, Henry?"

Henry shrugged his shoulders and reached his hands behind his neck. "Mom taped them all up at lunch."

"You didn't answer my question."

"They don't hurt that bad when I'm lying down."

She tapped his exposed toe, and then lifted it for me to look beneath. "Can you grab the bacitracin from the med kit? I want to put some more on this thing before I tape it again. I don't want it to get infected. It may be that his shoes are too small. Could we order him a new pair a full size larger?"

"You need to quit growing so fast, Henry," Aiden said.

"You are one to talk, Aiden," he said.

"What are you talking about? I haven't gotten any taller for at least a year."

"Yeah, but you are growing more and more annoying."

"Oh, pfft. You are the one that's annoying." She sat up to her elbows. "What is the name of this lake, Dad?"

"It's called Lake Walupt."

Aiden laughed. "That's appropriate, 'cause you're gonna be walloped by the time you make it this far." She watched Monica stand and take a few hobbling steps. "Mom, are you okay?"

"My feet are killing me tonight," Monica said.

Aiden sighed and sat up. "Lie down in your tent, and I'll come rub out your feet for you."

409.1

It is 1 a.m. I am awake. June is snoring beside me. Tonight we share a tent. She argued for it at lunch. "Henry always gets to because no one wants to be in a tent with him, but that's just because he's annoying. Why should he be rewarded?" In the end, Aiden agreed to take him in for the night. Georgie is happy to be with her mom.

We call June the furnace, because she heats up a tent. I slide away from her and press my face to the cool side of the tent. Every day she is stronger. We say it together at the top of each climb. On the way up she coaches herself in my earshot. "Come on legs, don't give up."

Right before she had fallen asleep, I said, "What was your hi-low today?"

"I don't have a low today. My high ..."

"June, wait ... what? Monica, did you hear this? June said she didn't have a low today."

Aiden cheered.

"Listen up guys, June is going to tell us her high."

"My high was probably my blackberry snow cone at lunch. That was good. Or maybe all those goats we saw after Knife's Edge."

"How many were there?" I said.

"Twenty-five," she said. "And, good it's called Goat Rocks Wilderness, huh?"

"There were twenty-eight goats," Henry said. "You didn't see those other three on the far snow patch."

"No, Henry! I counted those too. Now can everybody just be quiet. I'm going to sleep."

After staring at the tent for an hour, I fumble about for my Garmin. While it is powering up, I rerun the numbers back to Cascade Locks. I text my cousin Nathan. He will be coming from Portland and has asked for a target. I text him to expect us the fifth day, and then follow up quickly. "I mean the fifth day from tomorrow."

I am awake again. It is 3 a.m.

"Hey, Daddo," June whispers, "I just thought of something."

"I thought you were asleep."

"Do you think the mountain lions just don't like it up here?"

"I would think they would like it up here. Why?"

"Well, because that was a big herd of goats, and they didn't seem scared at all." She rolls to her side, and I stare at the roof of the tent for a long time. She speaks again into the dark. "Daddo, I just thought of something. Good Maggie and Boots didn't come with us like we thought about."

"You don't think they could handle it?"

"Well, you know how you said today that the mountain goats have a tough time surviving out here. If Maggie and Boots got separated from us, I just wouldn't want them to be alone."

"You love your goats, don't you?"

She is quiet again for a long time. "I miss them. But I'm glad they didn't come. Maggie wouldn't have liked walking this far."

I wake again in a half dream, with the face of a northbound hiker before me. He is bearded and pale, vacuous. He wears an expression of elsewhere. He is elsewhere than here. Elsewhere than our conversation. He is emaciated and empty. Pushing north to the border, as if with his last ounce of life. Monica asks him, "How are you?"

He says, "I'm tired," and floats on.

He is one type, a representation, of three types of male northbound thru-hikers that pass. The second, and more common, is the one that has stopped looking around. Ambitious and driven, he is eager to close out his hike.

The last, and most rare, is the one that is smiling. Smiling whether he's seen you or not. He leans in when he talks. He gesticulates in big sweeping motions. He is breathing the last of it in. He is joyful and jealous for you to see what he has already seen, and he tells you stories of what not to miss.

"Everyone has said Goat Rocks is their favorite," I tell him, "so there may be something good ahead for you yet."

"Something new every day," he says. "Enjoy every minute."

We are walking through waves of northbound hikers now. We are as dirty as they are and nearly as strong. I begin to feel less like an imposter. Less like one that is hoping to make it. It's now closer to "we are going to make it if all goes as planned." I am confused to discover that we are already known to them.

They ask, "Are you the family we've heard so much about?" After the first few hikers recognize us, I feel a deep pride. By the fourth and subsequent hikers, I ask how they've heard of us, and each of them say, "Sassafras." It seems we have her to thank for all of our trail fame, such as
it is.

422.8

For most of the cool part of the morning, I fell into a trance watching my feet fall on the dirt and pine straw path through the low valley forest. By mid-morning, we climbed our way up to wide, wildflower slopes that stretched out through tree stands. Near the top of our climb, the trail cut a long, flat traverse. Monica paused for a moment in front of me and looked over the valley below us. "That view is so pretty. Why don't we stop for lunch at pretty places like this?"

"We could," I said. "I just don't like having to carry that much water up the climbs. Water is heavy. 2.2 pounds a liter is a lot to carry uphill."

She laughed. "I think you're becoming a weight weenie."

"There is no question about that," I said. I stepped closer to her and looked out. We stood that way for a while. "I could be talked into taking our lunches up high," I said. "If you can promise a view like this at the end of the climb."

Along the high ridge, we spread out, each into our own separate paces for a few miles. Before the trail began its descent, Aiden and Henry sat waiting. "Dad, can we go ahead?"

"Why are you in such a hurry?"

"There is trail magic down at the road junction."

"Trail magic?"

"Yeah, that northbounder that just passed said there was a man grilling hamburgers for hikers down by the road crossing at the bottom of the hill."

I looked at Monica. "Do you mind if they go?"

"If you think they will be okay."

"Go ahead then, you guys." I said, and placed a hand on the top of Georgie's head. "Do you want to go with them?"

She nodded.

As the three of them dropped off into the trees on the other side, I called out. "Make sure Georgie stays with you." I turned to Monica. "You could, too. June and I can bring up the rear."

She shook her head. "I'll stay with you. My feet hurt on the downhills."

When Monica and I reached the road junction a few miles later, we stopped to wait for June. She lifted her left foot to her right knee and squatted to stretch. "I don't see anyone." She turned her head to look up the road. "There are a few cars up that way. Do you think that's where they went?"

I shrugged. "June should be here soon."

"I just hope nothing bad happened," she said.

"Like an abduction?"

"That isn't funny. Why would you even joke about that?"

"Let's ask this guy."

"Ask me what?" The hiker smiled and pulled off his cap. He wiped his forehead with the back of his sleeve and fitted his cap back on his head. "Ahh, you are the parents of those three kids. They are up there under the tent." He laughed. "And they found the food. They sure can put the food away."

"You're a northbounder," I said. "Almost there."

"I'm getting close," he said. "They'll be glad to see you."

"Who's that?"

"The couple doing the trail magic. I guess they heard you were coming."

"This will be our first trail magic," I said.

"Wow! Really?"

"Is that surprising? Have you had a lot?"

"Oh yeah," he said. "Especially at the beginning, down in Southern California."

"Why would northbounders get more trail magic?" Monica said.

"There aren't that many of you coming this direction," he said. "I'm guessing that has something to do with it. If you were trying to do trail magic for hikers, you wouldn't want to set up to cook and risk having only a few people come by."

"I could see that." I shrugged.

He nodded and turned his head up the hill to where the trail disappeared into the trees. "I wish my parents had done something like this with us when I was little. My sister would have hated it though." He paused. "Enjoy every minute. This is something they'll never forget."

"How did you like Oregon?" I said.

"I loved it. The water carries are pretty rough the further south you get, but it's been great."

"How bad are the bugs?"

"I walked through some black flies around Timberline Lodge, but no mosquitoes."

Monica waved a hand in front of her face as if shooing a bug. "They were the worst for us around the lakes near Snoqualmie, especially the boggy ponds, but they may be gone when you get there."

"How was Washington?"

"Amazing." Monica turned to me and smiled. "The flowers on Mount Adams were beautiful."

"Goat Rocks seems to be everyone's favorite," I said. "We loved it."

After we stood in silence for a little while, he pinched the brim of his cap. "You guys better hurry, they are shutting down."

"We are waiting on the last of our kids," I said. "If you see her up there, tell her to hurry."

We approached a white canopy tent, walled about by mosquito netting. It was boxed in by several backed-in vehicles. I peered inside the tent to see Shivers in a folding chair opposite Georgie. She waved to us and then caught the attention of the man behind the charcoal grill.

"Ah, the rest of The Family! We've been expecting you," he said.

Monica touched my hand and said, "I'm going to check on Georgie. She said her backpack was rubbing her back."

"Is it bad?"

"I haven't seen it yet."

Henry stood on the open tailgate of a red truck leaning over an open cooler. "Want one, Dad?" He held out a Coke.

"No," the man said, "he'll want a beer." He wiped his hands on his apron and walked around the far side of the truck. "Is an IPA good?"

"Anything," I said. "She'll take one too." I nodded toward Monica. When he handed me the two beers, I held one of the cold cans to the side of my face.

"Feel good?" he said.

I nodded. "What is all this?"

"Out doing a little trail magic," he said.

"Are you a hiker? Have you hiked the PCT?"

"Nope," he laughed. "My wife and I," he nodded toward the tent, "we come up to Trout Lake every year for vacation. A few years ago, on our way in we saw a van with a roll out canopy parked on the side of the road with a bunch of scruffy looking hikers sitting around in folding chairs. My wife made me pull over, and we ended up hanging out for three hours. The guy on the grill told us he was a trail angel and does it for thru-hikers. We didn't even know that the trail came through here, much less what a thru-hiker was, so we went home and went down a YouTube rabbit hole. We just got obsessed with the whole thing. So now whenever we come out here, we load up the coolers and set up a grill on the front and back side of our vacation. And, to be honest, it's our favorite part of our vacation now."

"This is our first trail magic experience so far," I said.

"It's an honor." He made a motion as if to doff his hat and bowed. "You should start seeing more, now that you are walking into the northbound bubbles. We weren't far from breaking everything down. I'm glad you were able to make it in time. We were hoping you would."

I turned and scanned the tent.
"Grab a burger, and whatever else you want," he said.

I carried a plate loaded down with three cheeseburgers into the tent. "Monica, did you want me to get you something?"

She held up a finger and continued talking to Shivers, "I thought you were with the Royal Family," she said.

"I plan to meet up with them again soon. I'm just going to walk a few days with a friend."

After we had eaten our fill, the couple rejected our offer to help break down the tent, so we hit the trail again. My feet fairly floated along as though they were independent of me.

Henry skipped up behind me. "You think we'll have any more trail magic, Dad?"

"Northbounders get a lot more. What do you think, Aiden?"

"It kind of stinks to be a southbounder," she said, "we hardly get any trail magic."

I heard the fizz of a Coke cracking open and looked over my shoulder. "What are you doing, Henry? You realize you have to carry that trash all the way to town."

"It's worth it."

"Don't let it cut your backpack."

"Can Aiden and I get by, Dad?" he said.

We were nearing another trail junction thirty minutes later, when Aiden came running back up the trail toward us. "Mom! Junie! More trail magic. It's Skybird's parents. She is there with her sister and Spatz. Come on guys."

One half hour later, we made our goodbyes and walked into the forest on the far side of the road. Monica looked back at me. "Me too," she said, "I can't stop smiling."

"You guys," I said, "this is the best day."

Behind me, I heard the crack and the fizz from another Coke can. "Henry! Are you kidding me?"

503.2

"Careful, Dad." Aiden tapped the side of the 4x4 post.

I traced my fingers in the letters that formed a faded commemoration to a Boy Scout project from long ago. "Thanks, kid. That would have been bad." I bent to insert a finger into its rotten base, six inches from the ground. "That's worse than I thought." I straightened up and rested a hand on her head.

She looked up the trail. "I bet there will be a perfect tentsite just around the corner. The perfect spot is always just around the corner from wherever we stop."

"I didn't mind stealth camping here."

"Not so 'stealth camping' if we are only 10 feet from the trail," she said. "We are pretty obvious."

"I just mean that it's not a designated camping spot. That's all."

I shuffled over the trail through the thick layer of brown leaves and around a few new growth fir trees toward the last standing tent. Henry was inside, cocooned in his quilt. Georgie stood at the door balling up the rainfly. "He won't move," she said.

I gripped her shoulders while I passed behind her. At the door of the tent, I turned. "June, hurry up, we've got to get moving." I turned and called up to Aiden, "Would you come give her a hand?"

"Sure, no problem," she said.

"Why are you rushing me?" June thrust an arm in our direction. "Henry hasn't even gotten out of his tent."

"You worry about yourself," I said. "I'll take care of Henry."

I squatted down to unzip the door to the tent. Only a small circle of Henry's face was visible through his cinched-down sleeping quilt. I shook him, but he still didn't move, so I leaned in close and whispered, "I cannot believe you are going to pretend you're asleep?" I tapped his forehead.

He shuddered and cracked his eyes open a sliver. "What?"

"Nice try, Dude. Your acting skills need some improvement. Pack up. I told Nathan we'd be there by 4:30 this afternoon."

"You said it's only nineteen miles to town. It's not even all the way light."

"It's 19.8," I said. "I guess you are wanting to walk right through lunch?"

"Wait? What?" Monica said. "Last night you told us it was only nineteen miles."

I looked up at her through the tent mesh. "I said nineteen when we were still planning to reach that designated tentsite."

"Why don't you ever just tell us the real number?" she said. "Georgie's feet were killing her, we had to stop here."

"You're in trouble, Dad," Henry whispered.

"Come on, bud. There's ice cream in Cascade Locks," I said. "The best on the trail, supposedly."

"Why should I even get out of my bag yet? It takes them forever to pack up."

Henry sat up and swept a hand through his coarse hair and knocked a dirty band-aid loose to his lap. I backed out of the tent and brushed my hands together. "You pigpens need to clean out that tent."

He pinched the band-aid and held it up to the light. "This is Georgie's, not mine."

Ten minutes later, Henry was lying on top of Aiden and Monica's packs. He pointed across the trail. I followed his finger to where Monica and Aiden were helping June and Georgie close up their packs.

***

We sat for a while at the first water stop. Aiden nudged my elbow and held out a Ziploc filled with blueberries. "Try some, Dad."

"Where'd you get these?"

"They're everywhere along the trail. You haven't seen them?"

Georgie looked over from where she stood filling her bottle. "Do I have time to pull out a bag?"

"Why not? You guys are walking fast this morning."

"It's a town day," June said. "We are always fast on a town day. Town days are fun days."

"You call this fun?" Henry said.

"Nathan says we can stay three nights at his house," I told them. "Well, he said we could stay longer, if we wanted, but three should be enough."

"Three nights under a roof," Monica said. "Have we been under a roof since we started? Or had a real shower?"

"Oh my goodness." Aiden pulled her water bottle from her lips. "This will be our first time."

"You guys go ahead. Georgie and I will catch up."

I stopped in the middle of a clearcut hillside in the shade of a solo, scarred tree. In the distance, a chainsaw motor screamed. The downhill slope fell away toward the Columbia Gorge. Over the near rim of the gorge, I could see the slim shimmering line of the far side of the river. I tossed my Garmin up from the trail so that it would have full exposure to the sky. I looked down at my phone: 4.6 miles to the Bridge of the Gods. And Nathan. And Oregon.

On a whim, I switched my phone out of airplane mode and was met with a deluge of notifications. I forced a first text to Nathan before looking at anything else. I am not sure how long I sat there on my phone.

Georgie didn't see me under the tree. She was watching her feet scuffing dust from the path and swinging a loaded Ziploc bag between two fingers. With her opposite hand, she dug in for another fistful of blueberries. When she saw me, she extended the bag. "Want some?"

"You gave me so many at lunch, I don't want to take all your blueberries."

"I have three more bags in my back pouch."

"Full of blueberries? I thought you only found one baggie."

"June gave me one of hers, and then back there I went through my pack and found more."

"No wonder it took you so long to catch up," I said. "I was worried. Here, bend down." I pulled out one of the bags and held it up for her to see. "These aren't blueberries in this one."

"Those are wild raspberries, like in North Carolina."

"They aren't really raspberries, you know. They're thimbleberries."

"Wild raspberries to me, and look in this one, I finally found some ripe huckleberries. They are so good, Dad. You have to try them."

I scooped up the Garmin and clipped it in place on my shoulder strap. "If I had known you'd be the slow one today, I wouldn't have sent them ahead."

"I'll go faster," she said, "as long as I don't see any more berries."

When we were nearing a dirt road crossing, Aiden ran toward us with both palms extended, each finger stained purple. "Dad, these blackberries are amazing," she said, and grabbed Georgie's wrist. "Come on, Georgie, you've got to see this."

Monica pulled two purple-stained fingers from her lips and smiled.

"Good?"

"They are so ripe they dissolve in your mouth. Here, try one."

I looked past her to where all four of the kids were leaning into the bushes to their armpits. "Henry," I said, "don't spoil your ice cream."

When we left, Aiden held out her arms to show me her scratches. "It was worth it. That was so good."

When we reached the next road junction, Aiden stopped again. "Look at these, I think they grow even better here in the full sun."

"Five minutes, Aiden," I said. "We are going to be late."

After we crossed the road toward the square, steel frame of the wide cantilever bridge, Georgie turned back and glared at me. She motioned me close and pointed up to the sign. "Bridge of the Gods?"

I shrugged. "Yeah? What about it?"

"Why didn't you tell me?"

As we passed from the pavement to the open metal grating it was as if the earth disappeared beneath us. Georgie inched forward ahead of me. "This is worse than Knife's Edge by a long way."

After a few more steps, the trees that had been blocking our view to the side fell behind us and the wide gorge opened up. Sheer cut walls on either side of the river dropped two hundred feet straight down to the water. A wind gust knocked us sideways. I reached an arm out for Georgie. As we began walking again, I looked past my toes to the river below. It took a moment for me to orient myself to what I was seeing. "Those little whitecaps that look like ripples down there, Georgie, I think those are waves."

She looked back and glared at me.

"I promise you, I didn't know."

"Come on, Georgie." Aiden extended her hand. "Don't tell me you're scared after everything you've done. Let's hold hands so these wind gusts don't knock us over."

I looked down past my toes and held my arms out wide to help with my balance. "It's probably 200 feet at least, Georgie."

"And you've jumped from this high?"

"No way. The highest I've ever jumped from is probably 85 feet or so. You might not live if you jumped from this height."

"You're making it worse."

"These cars make it worse," Aiden said. "You can feel the whole bridge move when they pass."

A box truck passed and shook the bridge, and I looked left to the guardrail. It looked shorter than I knew it to be, but I couldn't shake the disorientation. I pictured a gust of wind pushing me to the guardrail and me tumbling over the top.

Henry bumped into me from behind. "Get it moving there, Dad."

At the end of the bridge, we all turned and waved. "All right, everyone," I said. "Say goodbye to Washington."

"Which way is the ice cream?" Henry said. I pointed down the hill.

I pulled Monica to the side. "Did that bridge freak you out? I had a moment where I almost freaked out. I've never had that happen to me before. That was weird."

She shook her head, and we crossed the road holding hands.

505.4.1

I slid the chair to the dining room table and drew a slow sip of coffee in the pre-dawn quiet of my cousin's Portland home. I found two spaces for my elbows among the scattered ruins of last night's game of Code Names. His daughter Grey beat us at the wire with a clever misdirection. I placed Nathan's laptop on top of the pile and lifted the screen. I stared at it and sipped the first cup down. I sat down again with a second cup. Before everyone stirred I hoped to have written a reflection on Washington. It seemed to have happened in a blink. But if I slowed down and looked inside that blink, I could find innumerable hours, excruciating and glorious, long hours, slow hours. So many steps. I lifted my fingers to the keys and felt apprehension.

A weight falls to the teller, to codify into words a remembrance of the essence of a thing, as fully, truly, wholly as can be done. Each word robs all the other words of their place. A wrongful omission detracts. A wrongful inclusion distracts. I couldn't see through all of my children's eyes. And I didn't do any of it for them. I couldn't do it for them. It fell to their feet to step. Each step was theirs. If I forget to remember the horses that came by just at the right moment for June, will she remember?

Still, an approximation is better than nothing, and maybe my words would capture a place enough to wake in them the remembering. Remembering a challenge overcome. Of a long slog endured. A bird. An elk. An Aiden feathering fingers through fields of wildflowers. A fear. A joy. Something.

I knew that in two or so hours, all would be flurry. Town stops are busy, busy with resupply. But this resupply would be harder than any before. From home we had mailed resupply boxes through to Portland, so each stop had only consisted of gathering boxes we'd mailed ahead. Dumping out trash and replacing supplies, food and otherwise. Those boxes had been prepared with all the convenience of home over the space of two weeks. We have only one day to prepare the boxes for the next five hundred miles and get them mailed off. Nathan had offered us his car and made a few shopping suggestions. All the same, I was dreading the day. "I can't wait to get back on the trail, so I can rest," I said aloud.

My phone buzzed with a text notification.

It was Jamie. "You need to pick up the pace."

"I know, right? We killed it in Washington."

My phone rang. I spilled my coffee in the scramble to silence it. I put it to my ear and whispered, "Hello."

"I'm not joking. You need to pick up the pace."

"What?"

"You need to pick up the pace, or you won't make it through the Sierra on time."

"What are you talking about?" I dabbed a dishrag over the spill. "We flew through Washington. We averaged over eighteen miles a day. We were only shooting for fifteen."

"Well, your math sucks," he laughed.

"Wait," I whispered, "everyone is sleeping. Let me step outside." I held the phone to my chest and felt my pulse quicken. When I turned the door handle and pressed the door shut again, I sat down on the stairs off the front porch. I lifted the phone slowly to my ear. "What are you talking about?"

"I have the map pulled up right here. You have to be through the Sierra Nevada range by the end of the first week of October. I was working out the mileage this morning. It's gonna have to be a lot more than eighteen. What mile does your map say you're at?"

"I've got you on speaker so I can look at the map. It'll take a minute to switch to California. Cascade Locks, where we are, is mile 505. I'm looking for Kennedy Meadows South. Once we are there, we don't have to worry about winter."

"Yeah, I've got it at mile 1950 or so. Let me know what your map says."

"I show 1951.8."

"That's the same thing." he said. "You are back on the trail tomorrow, right? So you start walking on August 3rd to make Kennedy Meadows South by October 7th. That's 21.9 miles a day average with no rest days."

"I don't see how we can do that."

"You'd kill yourselves that way. What do you think you need? A full day off every seven days? Eight days? What do you think?"

"We could probably do it every eighth day. We haven't taken any full zeroes so far."

"Vince, you're looking at just over twenty-six miles a day. Think they're up for that?"

"Ugh. Our biggest day yet was twenty-three miles, and we were wrecked the next day. Are you sure we have to make Kennedy Meadows by the seventh?"

"That's their one hundred percent, you'll-be-good date. Mid-October is likely-to-get-through. Beyond that, they say you're pushing your luck."

"Alright, what do we have to do if we say mid-October?"

"If you add in the rest days, it's just over twenty-five."

"Ugh."

"What? Is that too much?"

"Maybe not. But …"

"But how are you gonna tell Monica?"

"And the kids. It's a lot to ask. Only one rest out of eight. The furthest we've made on the same day as a resupply has been fifteen miles, so we can't make it up that way. And when we get to Etna for that resupply, we are going to have to make packages all the way through to South Lake Tahoe like we're doing here. No way it takes less than a day and a half there. When we get there, we'll have to buy and ship through to the other side of the Sierra. Together, that's three days at least. I guess those days are rest for some of us, but Aiden, Monica, and I work harder on those days than any on-trail. That leaves, what, six days of rest? Probably half days by the time you factor in resupply, washing clothes, and all that."

"Georgie's got this, man. You guys will be fine."

"It's not as much Georgie I'm worried about. Her feet have stopped hurting and she's a much stronger walker than June. It's gonna be hardest for June. But I don't know, man, Monica's feet have never quit hurting. She rubs them out, but they aren't getting better. I don't know what to think. I'm pretty sure pushing harder isn't the answer."

"Well."

"Yeah, exactly. Well." I paused for a long time. "Thanks for working that out."

"Yep. Talk to you later."

A man walking his dog on the sidewalk paused in front of the house. "How's it going?" I said.

"Good. Beautiful morning out. How about you?"

"Great. Just great."

I pulled myself up by the railing with a grunt. I turned the knob slowly and moved with careful footsteps across the living room to sit back down at the table. I tapped the spacebar to wake up the screen, and to write about the triumph of Washington.

505.4.2

It is early in the morning in Portland, and the house sleeps, as it should. I am up early with resupply thoughts racing through my head. Did we forget something for the stretch between here and Etna? Etna is five-hundred-eighty trail miles away from here. Before the early afternoon, we will have packed over thirty boxes full of Knorr rice meals, couscous, instant mashed potatoes, tuna, shelf-stable bacon, pepperoni, sausage, Clif bars, Snickers bars, every other bar you can think of, seaweed, cereal, Pop-Tarts, hot chocolate (to make cereal milk), Jolly Ranchers, electrolytes drink flavoring, leukotape (for blisters), duct tape, batteries, replacement plastic bags ...

It has been a month since we piled into John Smith's fifteen-passenger van in Yakima, Washington, and were greeted with snacks and treats enough for a whole troop of Boy Scouts. He drove us five hours one way to Hart's Pass, just because.

My brother, Stephen, and his son, Silas, joined us for the first stretch. Nearly one hundred miles. It is nice to have your youngest brother step out of the van with you into a cold snowy day at the top of a pass headed into the wilds. And if you are an older sibling, you know why. You can't look at your youngest brother and say, "I have made a horrible mistake, let's get out of here." Oh no, you have to look at him and say, "Once more into the breach, my friends," or, "To Narnia, and the North." You have to pretend you know exactly what you are doing. And so I did, and so we did.

We got our wires crossed, and Stephen needed to be home to Denver a day earlier than I had originally planned, which meant we had to push. "Push" here means, that at the end of the day, you have to drag two hours more from your tired legs and feet than you think they can go.

I am glad Stephen came. He carried us through the first section of the trail.

I kept telling myself what I had read. Three weeks. Three awful weeks, and then it gets better. Eighteen miles is miserable at first. Terrible.

June, you will get stronger on the climb, you will get faster, remember ... three weeks.

Henry, I know you hate it here, and you want to be playing FIFA at the Ewerts' ... three weeks.

Georgie, I know your knees hurt, I know you miss the cousins ... three weeks.

Aiden, I know you are feeling impatient to go faster, that's your three weeks of suffering ... be patient.

Monica, I thought there were going to be more opportunities to shower ... three weeks.

We passed hikers, and hikers passed us, and they showered the kids with praise.

Gentleman overlapped us for days and said, "It just makes me so happy, every time I see you guys."

Sassafras would pass and say, "Every time I come to a scary spot, I say, 'Georgie is doing this, come on, Sass, you can do it!'"

And to pull us the rest of the way there, the rest of the way through the pain of the start, stood the Browns. The Browns would be at Chinook Pass on the 24th, and there would be pizza. "Kids, we have to make it twenty miles a day to get there, can you do it?"

And they did it.

Here I sit in Portland, one hundred eighty odd miles from Chinook Pass in the house of my cousin Nathan and his wife, Jodi. We had packed out of

White Pass with eight days of food, and we made it in six and a half. We have found our legs. Nathan took the day to play host to us yesterday. His younger brother, Owen, also has taken time to chauffeur us around. They have fed us and allowed six stinky hikers to foul their showers, clean their gear, and resupply in comfort.

If I am typing incoherently, please forgive me. There is an unfulfilled Portland promise that I have to keep. You see, we stopped here on the way North to see Monica's vacationing parents. And Grampy treated us to Blue Star Donuts. For the last hundred miles Georgie has traced their logo on her palm with a pen. They only keep the doors open until they sell the batch they've made for the day. You get one shot. So, as soon as the house stirs, I am out of time.

It's the people, you see. This trail is hard. It is beautiful. It is painful. It is wonderful. There have been moments with my kids that are the best that I've known. I have sat with June and cried with her through her despair at the base of a hill. I have sat with Georgie and prayed with her at the top of an excruciatingly beautiful pass, a prayer of confession. With both of us too busy in the work-of-it to see all the beauty at hand. She, missing it for longing for home. I, missing it for my obsession with miles before dark. Confession. Time. So much time. So much slow time. Time for so much.

Thank you, Washington.

505.5

June and I stopped at the bend of the first switchback just fifty feet up from the trailhead. We turned to wave our goodbyes through the trees. Nathan, Jodi, Grey, and Catch waved back. "It's not too late, come with us," I said. "It'll be fun."

"I wish," Nathan said, and it seemed to me as if he meant it.

Though we had taken our place in the rear, June marched out with purpose, leaned hard on her trekking poles. "Woah, June, ease up on the toddle-boosters there. I don't know how far we'll have to go before we find a place to camp."

"I know, Dad. I'm fine."

Crossing an outcropping of volcanic boulders, I called her attention to a flower that was new to me. "I've seen those before," she said without stopping.

"These orange ones?"

She did not look back. "They were everywhere on Mount Adams."

I turned to look back over the Gorge. We had walked out of sight of the bridge. Would this be my last look at Washington too? I took a picture with my phone and set it to airplane mode. I tapped my shoulder strap to turn on my Garmin, and finding it missing, dropped my pack and pulled everything out. When I found it, I clipped it to my pack and powered it up. It beeped with a text from my dad. "How far are you planning to go today?"

When I finally caught June, I said, "Tell me something new that you are learning out here?"

"That I'm stronger every day."

I laughed and said, "Good thing."

***

In the tent, Monica resituated her groundpad. "I can't find a place where I don't have a giant rock poking into my back."

"It's not a very good place to camp, is it?" I leaned out the door to our tent. "At least we aren't right on the edge like Henry and Aiden."

"Oregon isn't off to a great start with me," she said.

"June did great on that climb. How'd you guys do?"

"We did fine."

"This three miles gives us a good jump on tomorrow. We'll make it to Timberline Lodge the night after."

"Tell me again why we are in such a hurry to get there."

Aiden interrupted. "Dad, didn't you say Timberline Lodge was where some scary movie was filmed?"

"It's called *The Shining*, and it is not just scary. It is very scary. Jack Nicholson is in it."

"Who's he?"

"He is the voice of the president in that funny alien movie you guys like, *Mars Attacks*. But in *The Shining* he plays a writer that is shut up with his family all winter in a hotel. He goes crazy and tries to kill them, all because he is trying to finish writing a book."

"Aren't we supposed to be there tomorrow?"

"We were fifty miles from it at the trailhead when we left Cascade Locks. You want to go for forty-seven tomorrow?"

"I'm good," she said. "Dad, isn't that cool waterfall somewhere around here?"

"Uh, yeah, we aren't going to see that. We would have seen it this morning, but that alternate is closed. Remember me telling you about the Eagle Creek fire?" I said.

"That stinks. That was one of the things I was looking forward to seeing."

"Sorry for the inconvenience," I said. I rolled onto my side and found a nice groove between two rocks near my hips.

"I like being back out here," Monica said, and shifted again on her pad.

"Me too," I said and then called out to everyone, "So, guys, forty-seven miles tomorrow?"

"You trying to kill us, Dad?" June said.

I fell asleep with a smile on my face and woke up once in the night to adjust my position. Before the sun rose in the morning, we had made 1.8 miles and kept up a good pace throughout the day.

***

With a few minutes 'til dusk, June ran the final few steps downhill to the junction beyond the long glade. We turned down the narrow overgrown spur. We stepped over a log to join the others where they stood behind a kneeling Aiden. "We saw you guys from the trail," June said.

Aiden reached a hand toward her. "Give me your dirty bottle. I'll fill it up for you."

Monica motioned for silence and pointed toward two tents tucked in the trees under a mound.

"I think they took the only two spots," she said.

"We'll find something if we push back up into that glade," I said. "I could see plenty of flat space from the trail."

"Can you and Henry go look? We can fill up your water."

In less than forty-five minutes, Monica and I lay in the tent. I pulled out my phone to plan for water in the morning. "It just says, 'Spring and Tentsite' for this one. I think it's funny that they don't put a name for the spring."

"Look in the description, Dad," June said from her tent. "It's right there in the comments."

"Salvation Spring. That's a great name. You know there has to be a story there."

"Give me back my phone, June," Aiden said. "You're right, Dad, it is called Salvation Spring. It's probably called that because …"

I smiled at Monica and whispered, "Here we go."

"... this guy probably was hiking up an old mine road from the Columbia Gorge, but he got all turned around and started wandering around in the mountains. I'm sure it was a low snow year, because there wasn't much water. I mean, there isn't as much water on this side of the Gorge anyway, but that year it was a particularly bad year. So, his donkey probably got lost in a thunderstorm or something, like *in Man from Snowy River*. Wait, that couldn't have happened, 'cause then he'd have had water. So it was just a big wind storm. Yeah, and a tree fell on his donkey, and he narrowly escaped. But by that time he was so far beyond help that he couldn't get back without water. Just as he decided he wasn't going to make it, a little jay started hopping on the ground in front of him, and looking back every few hops, like it wanted the man to follow. So he did with the last of his strength. He came upon that long flat that we saw walking in and walked along it. There were lots of trees down from the wind, so it took him forever, but finally he made it to the water and fell into it, face first.

I forgot to tell you that he didn't believe in all that church and God stuff. But he had prayed that day for the first time since he was a little boy. See, because when he was a little boy, he stopped praying, because when a mountain lion attacked his dog to save his life, he prayed that God wouldn't let the dog die. It did though, so he stopped praying.

Well, anyway, when his thirst was all quenched, he rolled over and looked up. He saw the sun setting behind a tree down that hill. It was like one of those 'Y' trees and a big branch had fallen into the crook and was perfectly horizontal, so that it made a cross. That's when he named it Salvation Spring."

"There's at least one problem with your story," I said.

"What?"

"The sun is setting on the other side. Up the hill."

"No, 'cause last night remember at that camping spot over the gorge?" she said. "It set to our left."

"Look at your map."

"Okay fine, Dad," Aiden said. "The cross tree was probably just up the hill above where we are. Or maybe it was morning when he found the spring. I don't know for sure, but I'm sure it was something like that."

"I'm sure you're right," I said.

"How far 'til water in the morning?" Henry said.

"You won't even need a liter," I said.

"Georgie," Monica said, "did you hang up your food bag?"

"No."

"Georgie, you need to do it, kiddo."

"She's just going to use it for a pillow tonight, Mom," Aiden said. "She'll be fine. She's in here with me."

"I don't like it that they are doing that," Monica said. She blew up her inflatable pillow. "I'm too tired to argue though."

"Big day tomorrow," I said. "Twenty-five miles."

"Tell me again why we are in such a rush to get to Timberline Lodge."

"My cousin Brian is hoping to meet us there. Plus, there's a breakfast buffet."

The sounds of the night settled around us, amplified by the lack of wind. The last of the light faded into a soft glow from the moon. I rolled to my back and said, "Goodnight John-boy."

"Goodnight, Beav," Henry said.

When I next opened my eyes, it was to the glow of our tent all lit up like a pink princess castle. "Wake up, everyone. We overslept."

544.0.1

By mid-morning we had dropped a long mild downhill and tightroped across a tricky log crossing to crest a bank. Beyond the bank, the trail widened and snaked its lazy way through the basin. We dodged day hikers for the first time in a long time. "Was it Snoqualmie Pass, the last time we ran into day hikers?" I asked Monica.

"Did you get reception?" she said.

"No."

"What time do we have to be there?"

"It's not a big deal. I'd just like to resupply tonight, so we don't have to worry about it in the morning. The gift shop closes at 6. How far ahead are the kids?"

"Not far. Will you run up and tell them to turn down the speaker?"

"You think it's that big a deal? It seems like every other person is listening to music."

"That doesn't mean we should."

The trail tightened again and dropped toward another river crossing. We picked our way through river rock toward a narrow log. Aiden said, "That doesn't look stable," and sat down to take off her shoes.

"I don't see why you would bother to take off your shoes," June said, and stomped through without stopping.

The trail, when we found it, followed the shoulder of a precarious sandy embankment that seemed almost eager to break away.

Aiden fell in line behind Georgie before the final climb and turned back toward me. "Dad, can we turn the speaker on again now? It really helps Junie, and we are right in the middle of a book."

"Sure, but keep an eye out for people. What are you listening to?"

"*Unbroken*."

"That should help on the uphill. What part are you on?"

"They just got picked up by that boat and taken to the island with the rats."

"I thought you passed that part."

"We finished the whole thing a few days ago. This is our second time through," she said. "Every time I am tempted to whine, I think about how he lived on a handful of rice every day."

Georgie stepped to the side and hitched her thumbs under her shoulder straps. She nodded everyone past. Before I reached her, I stopped. She unhitched one hand to wave me by. "Go ahead, I feel like walking in the back," she said.

"You don't want to listen to the book?"

"I just want quiet today."

"I'm happy to walk with you. I almost never get to anymore. You are too fast for me."

"Yeah, right. Are you really going to let me walk in the back?"

"Why not?"

"You never let me."

"Never?"

"Almost never."

 She stopped and stepped to one side of the trail before pointing up the line of the lip. "It doesn't seem stable."

"This river bank? Not to me either." I stepped out toward the edge, peered over the drop and took a step back. With my feet spread wide apart, I stretched further forward. When I tapped it down a section of bank two feet across broke away and slid. I hopped back toward Georgie, "I'm not going to do that again."

"Yeah, you probably shouldn't," she said, then raised up on her tiptoes to look over the edge. "Why is the water so murky?"

"It's coming right out from under that glacier," I said.

"I would have thought that would make it clear."

"It's loaded with minerals."

"What kind?"

"I don't know."

"Look at that," and rolled her left hand and arm as if over a set of waves. "Look how roly that telephone line is. They usually just go straight up the mountain. Do you think that goes to the top of Mount Hood?"

"I don't know where anything goes. I'm just following wherever the trail leads."

"Do you think it would be easier or harder to put in those telephone lines here?"

"In this soft sand? Easier, I would think."

Further on, she diverted from the trail to dart out a short spur to an overlook. "It looks like a lot of erosion problems," she said. The drainage was no longer visible below us. The sound of crashing water from a cataract echoed up from below. In our sight there were other waterfalls higher up. They dropped into pools and dropped again as if down some multi-tiered wedding cake.

"It depends on how much rain they get."

"Or, if the snow melts too fast." She shielded her eyes. "The soil seems so soft that if there were a big melt it would flood and tear right through all of it and wash it out."

When we returned to the trail junction, she turned her face to me, "I think its cool to be halfway up a mountain we've been seeing in the distance for days."

The trail veered into a forest and we were swarmed by black flies. At the first water stop, I stamped my feet and begged her to hurry. She said, "It's not my fault you don't carry long pants."

After the water, the trail turned uphill again. June was sitting on a log around the bend of the second switchback with her dirty bottle dangling from her hand. She lifted her bottle and squeezed a trickle of water into her mouth.

Henry rolled his eyes, and fixed them on June.

She looked at me. "Daddo, I can feel myself giving up again," she said. "I can't make myself go."

"Well, now you've got us to cheer you on."

"That's not going to help," she said. "And Henry won't just leave me alone."

I turned to Henry. "Why aren't you walking with Aiden?"

"My leg hurts," Henry said.

"Where?"

He reached his hand back and touched high on his right hamstring.

"That's not your leg. That's your butt. Why don't you and Georgie go on
ahead? I can finish the hill with June."

"No," he said. "I want to walk in the back."

"Whatever we do, we have to go soon, these flies won't leave me alone."

Georgie blew her headnet away from her face and scraped the back of my
leg with her trekking pole. "You should have brought pants."

"I hate these flies," I said. "They are worse than the mosquitoes."

"At least they don't sting," Henry said. "Unless you let them sit on you too
long."

I tapped the sole of June's foot with my toe. "You ready, kid?" I reached into
my pocket. "Would it help to know how far we have to go?"

She turned her eyes up toward me. "It depends on how far."

"What if I tell you it's less than 0.8?" I paused and waited for the map to
load. "It isn't."

She started to cry.

I reached out my trekking pole and tapped Henry's leg. "Why don't you and
Georgie go ahead?"

"I'm walking in the back," he said.

"Do you care if I go, Dad?" Georgie said.

"No, go ahead. I'm sure they will wait at the top." I turned to June. "You've
been doing so great these last two days, and that hill isn't too bad. It's only a
little more than a mile 'til we reach a roly flat up top, and then it's a sleep
and a buffet."

"When you say 'roly flat,' you mean more hills."

"It doesn't mean that this time."

"It's just that," she reached her hand up to me, "it's just that I didn't want it to feel like this again. I thought maybe it wouldn't after Washington."

"I think it's always gonna have a little bit of "hard" in it no matter how strong you get."

544.0.2

June led the way, Henry walked out behind her, and I walked in the back. Something in his stride seemed off to me. "Is there something wrong, buddy?"

He shrugged his shoulders.

I watched his pack swing back and forth in a slow rhythm for a while. Once already on the hike, he had walked with blistered feet for days before he'd shown Monica. It had been late in the game to start treating them, and she'd had to tape every toe. I have long been impressed by his economy of word and action. He is clever and content to sit in the shadows and toss disruptive zingers into the fray. I remember walking around the corner into the great room on the way to the kitchen one morning when he was around ten years old, and he had been standing with his back to the wall around the blind corner. When I asked him what he was doing, he didn't answer. I made my coffee and sat down in the corner on the far side of the room. My entreaties for him to join me were met with almost imperceptible shakes of the head. It wasn't until Aiden's alarm sounded that I realized what he was up to. She had tripped him the day before, and he was plotting his careful revenge. The flip side of that is that when something is wrong, I have to dig it out of him.

"Henry, do you like it out here?"

"I'd rather be at home playing soccer."

"Do you like it out here?"

"It's okay."

"Certainly you can see some value in doing all this, can't you? I mean, anyone who has to wake up every day in the cold and force themselves to walk as far as they can all day long has to be growing in character to some degree, right? Or at least in courage?"

"It's not hard. It's just boring."

"It's not hard?"

"No."

"You think you could walk a lot further if we weren't slowing you down?"

"Yep."

"Like how far do you think you could walk?"

"If Aiden came with me, we could go at least thirty miles a day, and some days forty."

"Even with whatever you have going on now."

"It's my leg," He reached his hand up high on his hamstring. "And no, not when my leg hurts."

"Forty miles in a day, Henry, do you know what that would do to your body? I don't think you'd be able to keep that up."

"Sometimes, when you pick a lunch spot and let us meet you there, we get there before ten o' clock. That's sixteen extra miles in a day, if you'd let us keep walking."

"Would you ever do it? Would you go out ahead with Aiden and wait in the next town if we decided to let you?"

"Mom would never let us."

"But would you?"

"Sure, why not? But she wouldn't, so what does it matter?"

"I probably wouldn't either, not really. If there were no other people out here, maybe I would."

I laughed. "You know what I think? I think you like it out here a lot more than you let on."

He turned to look back at me over his shoulder and his lip curled up in the direction of a smile. "Maybe." He dropped his hand to his leg. "Just not today."

When we reached the top, Monica, Georgie, and Aiden lay tucked into a tight line of shade beneath a large boulder just off-trail. Henry stepped over a small spring and limped toward them. Monica lifted the pot from the stove and smiled. "I felt like an afternoon coffee. Want some?" I shook my head.

Aiden lifted the brim of her hat from her face and laughed. "Henry, where were you?"

"He has a little pain in the butt-butt," I said.

"More like a pain in the little butt-butt," Monica said.

Aiden lifted her hat again. "He is a little pain in the butt-butt."

Henry sat down on a rock and stretched.

"The flies aren't so bad up top, huh?" I said.

"There's just enough wind, I think," Monica said. "When do we have to get there again?"

"Six o' clock. If I get reception when we get closer, I'll call."

"We have to be getting close," Aiden said. "I'm seeing a lot of day hikers again."

555.6.1

In the winter, the wide hallway in the lower building on the grounds below
Timberline Lodge would be crowded with hard-booted skiers warming
themselves between runs. For us, it stood vacant and each footfall
reverberated throughout the hallway with a big hollow sound. The tables in
the wide cafeteria behind the glass were covered with upside down chairs,
gathering dust. Only the gift shop remained open. I met Monica there, as we
had arranged. "It's strange this place is abandoned, when the lodge is so
crowded. I'll grab our packages. We can take everything out back to the
loading dock. I don't think they want us resupplying here." I nodded toward
the bench. "His box didn't make it. You think we can offer him some of our
food?"

"Who is that?"

"Some northbounder. Look at the streaks of dirt on his shirt. Have a wee bit
of self-respect, man."

He stood from the bench and limped on worn shoes toward the vending
machine.

I walked toward him. "We will have some extra food after this resupply if
you want some. I wish I had some new shoes for you, from the looks of
those Altras. The soles on those things are paper thin."

"I think they will make it."

"How far have they been?"

"Thirteen hundred miles or so," he said, "so a pretty long way. Thanks for
the offer, but I don't mind resupplying out of the vending machine. It all
tastes the same to me now anyway."

Upstairs, after the resupply, I left the bar with my two hands filled with
overloaded pint glasses. I backed into large glass french doors to step
outside, confronted by the panorama of the towering Mount Hood as wide
as my view. I licked the froth from the back of my thumb and scanned the

large deck for Monica in one of the many wooden lounge chairs scattered about. She spotted me first and waved me to a vacant one beside her.

She reached for her beer and nodded to the people beside her. "This couple is from Indiana."

When the lady reached her hand toward me, her diamond bracelet clinked against her gold one. She raised her hand and shook them down her forearm before re-extending her hand. "We've been hearing about your hike. I've never heard of any such thing. What a great thing to do as a family."

"Is it?" I laughed. "I'm not sure your approach isn't better. You see all the same things"—I swept my arm toward the wide slope—"and you get to drive to it."

The man rattled the ice in his whiskey glass. "How are you able to leave work behind for so long?"

"I didn't have that much to leave behind. I managed to wind down most every construction project I had going before we left town."

"And what about school for your kids?" He eyed me over his whiskey.

"We homeschool," Monica said. "We're missing the fall semester, but they'll make it up in the summer. Except our oldest, she's in a regular high school. She will graduate a year later than the rest of her class."

"I can't believe she wanted to come."

"She came," I said.

Monica leaned forward. "I was really nervous about it all, but Vince agreed that it would be a one-time thing."

"A once in a lifetime thing," the woman said.

I reached a hand to Monica's knee. "Another round?"

"You're finished with yours already?" she said, then with a sudden movement, covered her mouth with her hand. "Oh my gosh! I forgot about the kids. Would you see if you can find them?"

I found Georgie sitting on the bottom step above the landing downstairs. I placed a hand on her head. She looked up at me and pointed me around the corner to a room filled with displays.

"Look at this." Aiden tapped a signboard and waved me over. "It says this hotel was one of those projects from the New Deal, like the dam project Joe Rantz worked on the summer before they went to the Olympics. They did stuff all over, huh?"

"Aiden!" I put my hand over my mouth. "Stop cussing."

She rolled her eyes.

Georgie stepped up behind me on the opposite side. "What dam project?"

"Oh, you guys haven't heard that book yet," Aiden said. "I listened on my headphones without you. They did all kinds of projects out here. But one of the characters, Joe Rantz, worked on the Hoover Dam one summer while he was in college."

"What are you talking about, Aiden?" Georgie said.

"It's just a book you are really going to like when we listen to it. It's called *Boys in the Boat*."

"Mom wants you guys upstairs," I said. "Did you find the ax from *The Shining*?"

Aiden pointed out the door without looking up.

I followed her finger, past a few columns and down a flight of stairs. A familiar phrase floated out from behind a pair of heavy double doors. It sounded like Chopin. It sounded like home. I pulled the handle and slipped in, enveloped in sound. The chords threaded me backward in time to my mother's piano, transported. I was there on my back with my feet pressed up underneath it, every vibrating note tickling my feet.

Though the ceiling impeded a full view of the piano on stage, I recognized the paper thin soles working its pedals. I tiptoed to a wide step, gripped the handrail, and sat. I listened for a long time.

555.6.2

I took a step back from the breakfast buffet line to wait for Henry. The rhythmic clatter of utensils and the clink of glass was intoxicating. He made his way to me from the corner of the dining room where the thru-hikers had been quarantined. I looked down at my new-to-me New Balance, size 16's, and turned up my toes against the fabric.

"New Balance, huh?" a hiker said. "How do you like them?"

"Yep. I used this pair for about a hundred miles at home before we left, but I'd prefer to be in Altras. The problem is, Altra isn't making any more in my size for this year's model. My last pair are down in the dumpster."

"What size do you wear?"

"Sixteen."

"Damn." He whistled. "Well, at least you are close to the end."

"We're southbounders."

"Okay, not so close at all then," he said. "You must be the dad of the family?"

"Yep, that's us." I nodded toward our table. "You're almost finished, though. You must be getting excited."

"Can't wait to get there. I'm about over it, to be honest. You think you guys will make it through the Sierra on time? It's still a long way from here. You might think about flipping down to Lone Pine and hitting the high elevation before it gets too cold." He pulled out his phone and danced his fingers on the screen. "Dude, you have to walk twenty miles a day, at least. Can your kids do that? They look pretty young."

"We have to pick it up a little bit. I haven't told them yet." I held a finger to my lips. "At this point we still want to do a true-thru, but we will see."

"No shame in a flip-flop, man, but you do you, hike your own hike and all that." He nodded to the line toward the food. "You're up."

"Oh no. I'm not in line. I'm just waiting for my son. I better go find him."

When Henry and I finished another pass through the line, I returned to the table and placed my plate beside Monica. She tapped my hand, almost without looking. "Listen to what happened to Surefoot last night."

The hiker across the table dropped her arm to the table. Her wrist was encircled by a faded, army green, threaded bracelet. With the opposite hand she tucked a rogue strand of hair behind her ear. She nodded and gave a half smile. "I was telling your wife. I did a twenty-four-hour challenge last night, and a mountain lion stalked me from Timothy Lake."

"How close was it to you?"

"It would wait in the middle of the switchback below me, and whenever I passed, it would walk almost straight up the hill. It followed me for several hours. Long enough that I," she paused, "I wouldn't say 'got used to it,' but close to that, anyway. My boyfriend had something similar happen last year."

"He walked the PCT last year?"

"Yes, he was stalked in Oregon too, around Mount Bachelor."

"Right where we are headed." I elbowed Monica. "But we won't be doing any twenty-four-hour challenge. How far did you hike?"

"It was about sixty-eight miles. I started on this side of Jefferson."

"The farthest we've gone," Monica said, "is twenty-five miles, and that was a one-time thing. I think twenty-two is about as ambitious as we want to be."

"We can do twenty-fives now, I think," I said. "You must be tired."

She nodded. "I'm going to sleep right after breakfast. Where did you camp?"

"Under a ski lift. I don't think it would be a good spot during the day; there was some construction going on there. It was pretty slopey. The youngest one," I nodded toward Georgie, "woke up on my son's groundpad, and he ended up on the grass."

When Surefoot left the table, Monica looked at me with wide eyes. "Mountain lions?"

I laughed. "It's the sixty-eight miles that gets me." I glanced toward the buffet line, then looked across the table at Henry. "Look, no line. Let's go for some more biscuits and gravy."

Henry grabbed his plate and pushed back his chair. "The biscuits are already gone."

"Who cares? We can just use waffles. That's what I did last round."

"Let's go." He scooched his way between the tight tables and around to our side.

Monica reached behind me and gripped Henry's wrist. "Get a new plate. They don't want you to reuse yours."

"I've used this one the last three times," he said, "and nobody's said anything."

"Henry, get a new plate." She pulled him toward her and wiped the side of his mouth with her thumb. She turned his head to the side. "How did you get chocolate in your hair?"

He shrugged.

When our turn came for the waffles, I held up two fingers to the man in the bowtie. He slipped a couple of waffles onto my plate and said, "Syrup?"

I shook my head, stepped left, and ladled out steamy sausage gravy until my waffles were no longer visible.

Monica inspected my plate as I sat down. "I can't believe I'm saying this, but that looks really good."

I pointed my knife and I mumbled, "Right over there."

"C'mon, can I just have one little bite?"

I leaned back. "If you want, I'll go get you one of your own."

Monica reached across me and picked up my knife and fork. "It's sad that Brian and Jana couldn't make it out. I would love to have seen them."

An hour later, we regrouped a quarter mile beyond the lodge in the shade of a few gnarled firs. I lifted my foot and watched the sand drain from the side of my shoe.

"I don't know why you didn't just order new ones," Monica said. "It looks like these are already worn out."

"These should have a good amount of miles left in them. I only used them for a hundred miles or so back home."

"But they already have a hole in them."

"We'll see." I shrugged. "June, will you find your gaiters? This sugar sand is going to be miserable on this long downhill."

"I don't need them. I'm fine."

"Look at me, kid. Right in the eye." I waited. "Right in the eye. Forgive me for framing that as though it were a question. What I meant was, sit down and put on your gaiters."

She slumped her shoulders. "They're in the bottom of my backpack."

"We can wait." I dropped my pack to the ground and sat on it.

"It's so weird how the sand just appeared on this side of the lodge," Aiden said. "It's probably because when the volcano erupted, it dropped more of the ash on this side. I mean, Mount St. Helens blew ash one thousand miles away. This is probably some of that ash."

"Scoot over, Dad," Georgie said.

"Jeesh, why can't you sit on your pack?"

"It's way over there."

"Oh, yeah," I waved my hand. "Way over there. How would you ever walk that far?"

"Want me to bring it to you?" Monica said.

"No," Georgie laughed, "Dad was just moving over."

"I guess I was just moving over. June, anytime now would be good." She groaned and stood up from her pack and unclipped it. I patted Georgie's knee. "Look at that." I pointed. "That's where we're headed."

"These mountains look a whole lot friendlier now, don't you think, Aiden?" Georgie said.

"Well, I wouldn't exactly say friendly."

"You left off the *e* and the *r*," I said. "'Friendlier,' not 'friendly'."

"Well, I guess if you put it like that."

“I did put it like that.”

“Come on you two. Cut it out.” I said. “They do look a lot more roly-poly all of a sudden. I think we can make better time on this stuff. Who knows what our mileage could be? Have you looked at the elevation, Monica?”

“A little bit. It didn’t look all that easy to me, but all I can think about is mountain lions. That will help me keep up the pace.”

“We have to pick up the pace.”

“What are you talking about?”

559

“We have to pick up the pace.”

“Are you trying to be funny?”

“No.”

“Vince, this isn't funny.”

"I don't think it is either."

"Kids, go ahead. Dad and I will catch up."

"I talked to Jamie about it, and we redid the math."

"When did you talk to Jamie?"

"That morning in Portland, when I was up before everyone else."

"And you are only bringing it up now? How much do we have to pick up the pace? You know twenty-two miles a day is about as far as we can go."

"We just did a twenty-five into the lodge."

"Wait, is that why you pushed for a twenty-five-mile day into the lodge? I knew it. I knew you were up to something."

"That was so we could make it for the buffet."

"Uh-huh."

"For real. Plus, Brian and Jana were trying to meet us there."

"How soon did you know they weren't able to make it?"

"Right when I told you."

"Well, it was too hard for June, and now you're wanting to do that again and again? How many miles a day are you saying we have to do now?"

"If we rest every eighth day, just over twenty-six … Wait, Monica, don't just walk away. If we want to risk an extra week into October, we can make it with twenty-five miles a day."

"Are you kidding me? That is not any different. You told me that we wouldn't increase our miles more than five to ten percent per week, and now you want to jump twenty percent."

"I don't want to up our miles at all. And I said we shouldn't jump the miles just based on what people recommend. I don't want to get to the Sierra too late to make it through, though."

"What did Jamie say?"

"He said that if we made it to Kennedy Meadows South by the first week in October we would be fine. If we make it by the second week, it's more likely than not that we would be fine. We figured out numbers based on that."

"Well, I think it's too many miles a day for us."

"Oregon looks pretty flat."

"Twenty-five-miles-every-day flat? This is going to ruin it. The whole point
is to be out here enjoying it. And now it's just going to be a constant push. It
ruins everything about it."

"I didn't do it on purpose."

"How did it happen?"

"I think I was figuring out miles to the Sierra and not through. It's a
difference of three to four hundred miles."

"Why didn't you tell me in Portland?"

"It's not exactly happy news, and everyone was enjoying their rest. Why
would I interrupt that? I felt embarrassed."

"I think it's more about that."

"We could just see what happens. But based on what I've seen, the kids
don't like to be cold. If we get there too late, it's going to be cold, cold."

"What time of year did we hike there with Chris and Savannah? That wasn't
too bad, was it?"

"Late October, but I think we got lucky."

"We had that one freezing night with them."

"Below Glen Pass? It was seventeen degrees, but cold isn't the biggest
problem, it's the snow. I don't think we want to be out there when the snow
comes. I mean, you have to go through high passes to get out of there, and
I'm not sure if you can still find the trail in the snow."

"That would be horrible not to make it after all we've been through."

"I think we can make it. Worst case, we could do what the guy at breakfast
suggested and flip down to do the Sierra before we finish northern
California."

"What would we do, get a ride back up to all that we missed? That's not a thru-hike. It wouldn't feel the same at all. I don't want to do that."

"Not if you are a purist, but technically, it would still count."

"I don't think I want to have to do that."

"I don't either, I'm just saying we can if we have to. To be a thru-hiker, you just have to walk all of the open miles of the trail in a calendar year. There are a few people out here flipping around. I just don't want to do it if I don't have to."

"Argh, I'm so annoyed. I wanted them to enjoy it. We were just beginning to enjoy it."

"I know."

She touched my elbow. "Are you going to tell them?"

"What do you want to do?"

"Does it even matter what I want now?"

"There might be more than one solution."

"But none of them sound good."

576

Your feet fall heavy ahead of me. Each ponderous footfall clears the previous only by inches. I pause to compare it against the footprints of Henry's wide and bounding stride. I restart a full minute later, and within twenty steps I recover the ground you have gained. How will we ever catch them? I am trapped behind you again. Why won't you go? You can. It is not strength that you lack. This loss is in your mind. It is late in the afternoon and my reserves are low. Too low to take an encouraging tone to sing you up the last bit of climb.

At each break today, you have thrown your head back and cried that you can't. At the base of each climb, we have re-assembled with a hope to set off together, but each new beginning finds you digging out some new excuse to stop and let the others trail off. I am left to breathe in the cloud of your hopelessness.

June, I don't always feel this way. As real as it seems, this is a lie-feeling. I know better than to trust it, because tonight when Monica crawls into the tent and the rest of us shake out our five groundsheets side by side, overlapping, you will say, "I'm next to Daddo," and I will smile. I will say, "I get the furnace." The same as I always say.

I lob a one-foot-in-front-of-the-other into the air, but it is just the wrong word at just the wrong time. You throw your trekking poles to the ground and collapse into the bank with a thud. You let your head fall over your pack. Stretching your neck back, you open your mouth into a long exhale and wail, "I'm done."

Why did I ever think we could do this? "June, it's going to be dark soon."

"I don't care. I'm not going anywhere."

"You aren't going anywhere?"

"I'm staying right here. Just leave me."

"You want me to leave you?"

"I can't, Dad. I can't do this anymore."

"You don't really believe that. You've said so before, and we have always made it."

It is cold here in the long shadow of the trees. I am seething. I am impatient. I am cold. I cannot ask you to take off your pack, or it will be an admission that we have stopped here. I slide my hand underneath you and lift. "Sit up for a second, so I can pull out your jacket."

"It's at the bottom of my pack."

Of course it is. "Let me see if I can get it."

"I'm not cold."

"You will be if we sit here any longer."

You shuffle your way out of your shoulder straps. Clever. You work your pack around to your stomach. Without looking, you crawl your fingers to each clip. You unfold the top and fish around for your jacket. In several separate attempts you tug parts of your sleeping bag into view and say, "Come on, jacket, I know you're in here somewhere."

"Give it to me." I yank your bag from you and jump to my feet in one move. I throw everything onto the ground beside you. "You're right, June. It was at the bottom." I toss your blue jacket over your face. "Where is your flashlight?"

You lay motionless underneath your jacket, speaking through it with a muffled voice. "You mean my headlamp? I lost it."

Of course you did. "You might have told me that, kid. There was one in the hiker box at Timberline Lodge. I could have grabbed it."

"I didn't know it was lost before we left."

I repack your bag and stand with it leaning against me. "Let's go."

You lift your jacket just enough to peek out. "I told you, I am not going anywhere. I am done," then drop it back down on your face.

I stand that way for a long time. The forest is silent. Today's dying light is lively in the trees. The front line of shadow marches past the midpoint of the wide valley below. The cold air now has a bite to it. I look at you. You are splayed out in a pose of exaggerated defeat. I toe tap the sole of your shoe. You move your foot and roll away from me to your side. I lay down beside you. I lift one corner of your jacket and slide my head underneath it, and tap you on the shoulder. "June, I love you." You roll to your back, and let your head fall toward me. I tap the tip of your nose with my finger. "I know it feels hard right now, but if you told me I could be anywhere else in the world without you, or right here with you, I'd rather be here with you."

You nod. And slide your jacket down from our faces. You find the sleeves and pull your arms into them backward. You look up at the sky. "Look," you point, "the first star." We lay like that for a while.

"Dad?"

"Yes."

"Do you think they'll be worried about us?"

"Yes."

"Dad?"

"Yes."

"I think I can make it. Can we just lie here a few more minutes?"

606.9

I pulled my sleeping bag down from over my head while my phone powered up. In the sky there was a slight glow, a hint of morning, new since the last time I'd been awake. "Is it finally time, this time?" If it were anywhere close to 5:30, I would wake them, though it would matter little if I did, we wouldn't be walking before light. If we could make 15 miles before lunch, our 25 miles would come easy. Yesterday we made 14 before lunch, and we didn't have to walk long after dark.

I pushed myself up to my elbows. My groundpad was flat again. Though, in truth, it wasn't my ground pad. I don't know whose it was. June claimed it was Henry's. Henry and I both thought it was June's. Either way, it had a hole in it. Two nights before, it had been flat on the ground within the half hour. At lunch the next day, I'd inflated it and dunked it into a pond to find all the holes. One of my four patches must have failed. I opened my map. "I'll dunk it in Timothy Lake unless I can find a good place in between."

In the middle of the morning, I caught up with Monica. "No wonder they do the twenty-four-hour challenge on this stretch."

'What do you mean?"

"It's so flat. We are making great time. At this rate we could make over 15 miles before lunch."

In the last of the afternoon hours, we walked a wide path parallel to Timothy Lake, Georgie turned a quick pirouette.

"It's not that kind of a song, Georgie," Aiden said. "It's more like this."

"You wish you could dance, Aiden." Henry imitated her movement.

I joined him in the imitation. "It's more like this, Henry, you have to be more jerky and throw your weight to the left side."

She scowled at us, then cast a long look across the wide lake. "Where on earth is that music coming from?"

"Music carries a long way across water," I said.

"But I can't even see where it could be coming from. It's not like there are any towns around here."

"It's a big lake, Aiden. Music carries a long way over the water."

After we finished our dinner on the wide dirt shelf where we made camp, I walked down to the lip of the sharp bank to drop to the water. I stood for a long time in the orange light of the evening. I hopped down to stand on the top of a wide rock that stood just out of the water and bent with my ground pad to submerge it. With a piece of charcoal from the fire pit, I marked each of the three places where I saw bubbles releasing. A trickle of dirt splashed in the water beside me.

"You think that will dry before dark, Dad?" Aiden said.

"No, but I don't mind. It isn't going to be very cold tonight."

Two hours into the night, I woke up flat on the ground. I popped open the valve to inflate the groundpad, but I thought better of it and lay back down on my side. When I opened my eyes again, June was standing above me in the faint light before dawn.

"Are you ready to get ready, Dad?"

"What time is it?"

"5:15."

"So early?"

"You said we could sneak out ahead of everyone if I got up early. You don't remember?"

I motioned her to me in order to whisper. "I'll tell your mom, so she won't worry."

Near the junction that led to the campground at Lake Olallie, June spotted a handwritten sign for trail magic.

"It's too early for that," she said. "They must have forgotten to take it down yesterday."

But before we made it to the first of the campsites, we heard the clatter of cookware. "Come back in a few minutes, and we will have eggs and bacon ready for you," the man said.

A sign on the door to the camp store said, "Hours, 7:30 to noon," so we walked toward the floating dock on the edge of the lake and dropped our backpacks on the ground to walk out. Small waves lapped against the floating dock beneath us. We sat down. "Look at that." I dipped my hand in the cold water and then pointed across the long lake toward the diffused outline of a mountain. "Do you know what that one is called?"

"You already told me, Dad. It's Mount Jefferson."

"Did I? Well, how about this? When do you think we will be there?"

"Maybe in two days."

"We will pass it today and be down the far side."

"It seems so far away."

"It is, but you're a big-walking-fool now, June Bug." I lay back and tucked my hands under my head.

"Dad, I just thought of something."

"Tell me, kid."

"We were the last to get hiker hunger. Do you think it's because we had more stored up before we came?"

"What makes you think of that?"

"Well. I'm starting to get hungry, and the others were a lot skinnier than us when we first came."

"You may be on to something."

"When the camp store is open, can we get some ice cream if they have it?"

"If you leave some room for eggs and bacon."

"That won't be a problem now." She smiled. "Remember, hiker hunger?"

Monica called to me from the shoreline, and I pushed myself to my feet with a groan. When I reached for my backpack, I noticed that my Garmin was flashing. I connected my phone and read: "Wow, you guys are flying. We need to come see you before you get too far down-trail. When will you cross Highway 20?"

"Tomorrow evening," I texted back.

"Who was that?" Monica said.

"My cousin Brian. He and Jana want to bring their kids out to meet us tomorrow night at Highway 20."

"How far is that?"

"Forty-five or forty-six miles. Let's not tell the kids though, it will be a fun surprise."

Monica held a finger to her lips and nodded. I felt a tug at my sleeve and looked back to see Henry looking up at me. "Dad, did you really tell June we could have ice cream for breakfast?"

628.8

Walking.

It's just walking.

Whatever I envisaged, this is the task. This is the activity. This is it. All of it. Just walking.

The pace matters. Fast enough to make miles, but not so fast that we wear ourselves out.

Every day we wake up and grab something for the go. Some other hikers boil water, but that would add at least a half an hour to our already slow morning routine. "Grab the Pop-Tarts and walk" takes an hour, at least. We now hurry our stops for water. Dip the dirty bottle and don't stop to filter it. Dip and dash, and get back to walking. Unless there is a long carry coming, and there have been more long carries now that we are in Oregon. In that case, we "camel up" as it's called. We drink as much as we can to carry as far as we can. I check the next water stop; if it's an off-trail water source, we try to carry past it to the next one. Off-trail water takes extra time. Anytime we drop our packs to the ground it takes time, because it becomes a rest, and we don't have time to rest.

If we need big afternoon miles, we eat a short lunch. On days that we get good miles early, we take a long lunch to recover, up to three hours. We walk into camp as late as we can. We walk to a target and then start looking for a flat place to sleep. Usually an established tentsite; there are plenty of those. But on occasion, we sleep on steep downslopes against logs or tree trunks.

Step by step, each step eats a tiny chunk of the 2650 miles. These miles don't walk themselves. But these steps are beginning to add up.

Other hikers walk fast and stop longer in town. We aren't fast; we just keep walking, and we are catching up to people we thought we'd never see again.

We have three gears:

Toddleberry - Inspired by Tim Conway's sketch, Mr. Toddleberry, this is the slow slow. It is excruciating to endure these hours. It is inspired by pain, tiredness, difficult terrain, or protest. Anything under 1.5 miles per hour qualifies. To walk behind June here is a study in patience.

Toddlebooster - This is a slow walk approaching an acceptable pace. It's like a Toddleberry with the anchor unstuck. It feels like it could be fast, 'til you glance at your watch and realize you aren't anywhere near your objective. Anything between 1.8 and 2.2 mph qualifies for this category.

Making Hay - Make hay while the sun shines! Ahh. This is when you are cruising, gobbling up the miles, the wind at your back and a song in your heart. You look at your watch, and there is still so much time. At this rate, you'll make thirty miles easily! It is anything over 2.7mph.

There are culprits for each category. We all have our own preferred pace, our own sense—or lack of a sense—of urgency.

Henry is bored. He stands on top of a couple of toothpicks and would effortlessly maintain above 3 mph if we'd get out of his way. He marches to the music. He kicks his toes out and swings them in just to have something to do. He refuses to use trekking poles and hunches over to lean into the climbs. His hands are always on his shoulder straps, so he wears a dirt triangle at his elbows.

Aiden is no less speedy, though she is more patient. Her stride is quick, calm, and assured. She prances a little, but it is relaxed enough that it says, "I can do this all day."

Georgie has a lazy looking stride. She's a bit knock-kneed. She's all over the path, right to left. Partly to blame are the flowers, the berries, and the views. She stumbles a lot, twists her ankles, and will not learn the lesson. Georgie has every bit the look of being out for a stroll.

Monica has a careful and determined walk. She is walking with almost constant foot pain and assuredly has some degree of plantar fasciitis. Most of her stride is defined by the awareness of pain, but she has also to be wary of falling. Let's just say, she is not a near relation to "sure footed."

June is a plodder. She walks like a stocky Irish coal miner. I think you must know what I mean. The trouble is, her walk has a bit of a poker face. She can be in the Toddleberry zone and it looks and feels exactly like her Making Hay. One day, in great frustration, I asked her to speed up. She looked at me as if devastated. I checked my watch and we had been going 2.5 mph, uphill.

It's 5:15 now, time to wake them up for the walk.

645.4

The dusty, brown path cut a sharp line on its traverse through the green meadow. I paused and looked behind me for Georgie. She was on her knees and pressing her nose against a flower stalk. I turned and watched her for a while. When she stood, she saw me looking and smiled. "What are those purple ones called, Dad?"

"Your mom said they are Lupines."

"I like them. They smell sweet, but not too strong. Do you care if I pick some?"

"I wouldn't mind, but then you'd have to carry them. Some people might get upset with you for picking them though, because they'd say you were disturbing the ecosystem. I guess if there were a lot more people that came through here, it might be of concern."

"What do you think about that?"

"I think, in a way, you'd be helping the flowers out. Most of these seem to have gone to seed, so you'd just be carrying seeds to a new place and dropping them. And the way I see it, those flowers ought to thank you for helping them find new soil. Everything out here has one goal."

"What's that?"

"Replication … No, multiplication." I waved her by me. "Let's get moving, Georgie, we are long way behind them by now." When we rounded the bend, a wide bowl opened before us, all craggy and glacial-cut. I asked Georgie to wait and pointed her gaze toward a sharp ridge line. "That's gotta be one of the Three Sisters, eh, Georgie?"

"Dad, why don't you just pull out your phone?"

"I'm saving the battery." I looked again at the jagged ridge line. "Besides, it won't change what we have to do for the next hour. It looks to me like the trail goes just to the right of that triple-peak part, but you're right, it's too interesting-looking not to have a name."

"Look at that trail coming down off the left side of it all the way down to that lake."

"This is all glacial, kid. You see how that rock piles up alongside the lake and then runs down toward the end of the bowl. That's called a moraine. It's formed when the glacier breaks up the granite into smaller pieces and traps them in the ice. When the ice melts away, it leaves the rocks piled up like that. I can't say what type of moraine it is. I would think that stuff alongside the lake would have to be lateral, but there's rock piled up on the end too. I'm not sure what that would be called."

"Let me guess. We can look it up when we get to town?"

"Exactly."

"Only we won't. Will we?"

I laughed. "No, we probably won't." We walked in silence for a few minutes.

"You know what I think? I'm too tired to think in this heat anyway. I'm really glad we aren't trying to do school on the trail like you and mom were threatening."

"I'll remind you of that next summer when we are back home and all the other kids are playing outside and having fun."

Georgie stopped to smirk at me, then turned up the hill. "Maybe you can ask this northbounder since you don't know what it is."

"Ask her what?"

"The name of that peak."

"How about you ask her?"

The northbounder smiled in response to Georgie's query. "That's Three-Fingered Jack."

"So, not one of the sisters?" I said. "We are not the most aware PCT hikers."

"Don't feel bad. I only looked it up myself a few minutes ago."

Georgie pulled my sleeve and whispered, "Tell her about the dead horse crossing."

"Why don't you tell her?" I said.

"There's a stream crossing coming up for you that has a dead horse trapped in it," Georgie said.

"An actual dead horse?"

"Yes, but it's downstream from the crossing, so it's not quite too bad."

"Thank you for the warning." She tilted her head and looked at Georgie. "Can I ask how old you are?"

"Eleven."

"Wow, you are brave to do this."

Georgie looked up at me and tightened her lips. "It's not like I had much of a choice."

"It's so hot," I said. "Is there any shade over the other side? This climb has been miserable."

"It's worse than this on the other side," she said. "At least here you've got a breeze, and there is a big burn section coming up. On the far side of it though there is a pond you can swim in. That is, if you make it that far. How far are you going today?"

"At least to Highway 20," I said.

"That far? You'll pass the pond then."

I turned my head and nodded down the hill. "It's mostly fast walking and flat for you for a while. You're lucky too, 'cause we won't be there blaring our music on our speaker."

"Ah, you are one of those? Don't worry, me too, when no one is around." She paused for a second. "After Big Lake Youth Camp, the lava is pretty awful. You can see the heat coming off the rocks. Look, the soles of my shoes are practically melted off. I shipped a new pair to Timberline. I hope these last all the way there."

"Those are pretty bad." I whistled. "Did you stop at the camp?"

"Yes, it's amazing. They have a separate cabin for hikers. You can eat for free in their cafeteria too. If you want meat, though, you're out of luck, they are Seventh Day Adventist. Keep in mind, they're shutting down the day after tomorrow for a staff trip or something. They said the hikers are welcome to stay, but the kitchen will be closed."

"We should be there tomorrow around lunch or so, and we were planning to take a full zero."

After we said our goodbyes, the northbounder set off down the hill. Georgie turned to me and said, "What do you mean 'were planning', Dad?"

"I mean, we will have to see," I said. "I didn't know they were going to be closing the kitchen. I was counting on those meals when I calculated our food for this section. I just hope we have enough food to make it to Crater Lake with an extra day off-trail."

"We are taking that zero. You told June we would."

"Hey, look at that." I pointed to a figure far away on the ridgeline. "Is that Henry?" I bent down to guide Georgie's gaze.

"He's so annoying," she said.

"He's so fast, but at least we always know where he is. He's the only one out here wearing the New Balance Fresh Foams. Look at his track."

"I thought Columbus was wearing those too," she said.

"Columbus' tracks are covered up by now," I said. "He's at least three days ahead, and there are so many northbounders right now."

"Forty-six," she said. "I counted seventy-five yesterday, and today I'm already up to forty-six."

"You're counting all the northbounders?"

"What else am I going to do all day?"

"We had fun yesterday, didn't we?"

"Well, yeah, 'cause we were all walking together and dancing to music."

"Do you have a favorite to dance to?"

"Just one song or a whole album? 'Cause that would be different answers. Something from the Gypsy Kings for a song, maybe "Volare," but for an album it's probably *The Greatest Showman*."

"We haven't listened much today."

"We're all spread out today."

"You don't like it, being spread out?"

"Actually, I don't mind," she said. "I zone out after a while, and if I get bored, I watch movies."

"You watch movies?"

"I watched *Man from Snowy River* yesterday. I'm saving *Tombstone* for tomorrow. Aiden and I already talked about watching it together."

"On her phone?"

"No, in our heads. If one of us can't remember, the other takes a turn telling the scenes."

My Garmin beeped.

"Who was that?" Georgie said.

"Nobody," I said. "Just a beep."

652.1

Georgie tiptoed with bare feet across the tricky rocks to test the temperature at the edge of the pond. Before she made it to the water's edge she cried out, "These rocks are burning my feet off."

Aiden invited her into the water. "It's cool once you are in here but try not to stir up the bottom. It's really mucky."

"Or just float on your back like I'm doing," June said.

Georgie dipped her toes into the water. "The mud is hot. Gross."

"Keep coming," Aiden said. "Further out to the middle. It's better out here. Henry, what are you doing over there? Why don't you come to the middle with me and Junie."

Henry was twenty feet farther up the shoreline, bending over a pile of rocks. Without looking up, he said, "No, I just saw a snake go under this rock. Dad, want to come help me catch him?"

"Oh, no, I'm gonna stay right here and enjoy the shade with your mom."

"More like you are enjoying Mom's shade," Aiden said. "

"What's a-matter, Dad," June said. "Are you afraid of a little cool water?"

"You know I don't feel the cold, I only feel its power." I shielded my eyes, and dropped my head back. "I will come out there again in a little while."

I tossed the Garmin a few feet from me.

"Who are you texting?"

"Brian," I whispered. "He wanted to know if there was anything special you wanted?"

"I think what people mean when they say 'want' is more like the extra stuff beyond the basics. I think need is more like the essential stuff. You know how we are always joking about the 'if onlies'?"

"If only it weren't so hot." I laughed.

"If only we had cloud cover."

"Or if only it would rain."

"Just a little bit." She held her fingers a fraction apart.

"Yeah, not too much."

"If only there were no uphills."

"If only the downhills were not too downhill."

"If only there were a view."

"If only these kids would quit complaining."

"If only I could quit complaining." Monica laughed. "I'll tell you what I want: a bed, a shower, an air conditioner, and something to make my feet stop hurting."

"Would you settle for a Diet Coke?"

Monica sighed and smiled. "Oh, a fountain drink would be so nice right now."

"You want a fountain drink? For real? I'll ask him." I reached for my phone. "Now, would you say you want a fountain drink, or you need a fountain drink?"

"I would have said want before you mentioned it, but I think now it has elevated to the level of need." She laughed and tapped my elbow. "With lots of ice. Can you ask him to bring the ice on the side?"

"I have submitted your request, your royal highness."

"Oh, and toilet paper. We need toilet paper."

"Need? Is that really a need?"

Monica was quiet for a minute, as if elsewhere. "Wait, you don't think toilet paper is a need? That's disgusting."

"Backcountry bidet." I raised my right hand and shook it. "You just have to remember which hand to eat with. Oh, look at that." I pointed. "Henry, hold up that snake so we can see." He had one hand pinched high on the neck of the snake and the other near its tail. He held it high in the air and walked toward us.

"Henry, not on the groundsheets," Monica said and began brushing the sand from the corner of her Tyvek. "Walk around them." Henry jumped over my groundsheet and held the snake forward for me to see.

Monica leaned in and tilted her head. "Are you sure it isn't venomous?"

"I think it's a garter snake," I said, "or at least it's just like one. All the markings are the same, and it sure stinks like one."

Henry nodded his head back toward the water. "There are tons of tadpoles and salamanders everywhere. He's got everything he needs here. Are we staying here much longer?"

I reached a hand to Monica's side. "What do you think about trying to go all the way to Big Lake tonight?"

"How much further is it?"

"It's around five miles past Highway 20," I said. "I think we'll all catch a second wind after the dinner."

"Did he say what he was bringing for dinner?"

"What did who say?" Henry said.

"Henry," I said. "See if you can sneak up on Aiden and dunk her."

He looked at me with wide eyes and then to the snake in his hands. "I have a better idea. Watch this," he said and tiptoed off toward the water.

Monica looked at me and whispered, "Oops, do you think we're busted?"

"I doubt Henry will put it together," I said.

"What did Brian say he was bringing for dinner?"

"He asked if we were alright with chicken."

"Okay."

"I told him you would want something salad-like if possible, and he said he would try."

"Oh, are you serious? That would be nice. I miss vegetables."

"You can have as much salad as you want at Big Lake Youth Camp, as long as we get there in time. That's kind of why I want to keep going tonight. We could have a full zero, three good meals, and as much salad as you want."

"Let's just play it by ear. I don't want us to push so hard that someone gets hurt."

"I've been surprised by these bigger miles, haven't you? I expected to miss more of the scenery, but you can take in a lot at a walking pace. Remember how we were saying that all those big mile walkers were missing out on the good stuff? I don't feel that way anymore. I don't see much difference between twenty and twenty-five miles."

"I know what you are saying, but when my feet start to hurt, it's hard to think about anything else."

"Are they hurting that bad today?"

"Yes, terrible." She looked toward the pond. "I should have soaked them here. Did Creigh say when my next pair of shoes will arrive?"

I reached one hand to her arm and covered my mouth with the other. "Oh no, do we need to order you some new ones?"

"Vince, we talked about this in Portland."

"I'm joking." I patted her arm. "They are coming to Shelter Cove. They should be there by now. She sent me a tracking number. Do you want me to text her and ask her to check it?"

"I'm sure it's fine."

I stood to my feet. "Do you want to soak your feet? I'm sure we have time."

"No."

I turned back. "Would you care if I went ahead with Henry when we take off from here?"

"And leave us?"

"It's ten miles to the road, but it's all downhill."

"Why don't you wait 'til we're five miles out?" She paused for a minute, tilted her head to one side and squinted her eyes. "Wait, hold on a minute. That means we're still fifteen miles from Big Lake?"

653.6

Henry and I lay in the grass on our backs near the bottom of the swale, near the highway. I looked at my phone. "Maybe we missed them," I said.

"We've been on the trail the whole time." He picked an M&M from his trail mix and popped it in his mouth. "Found one."

"You only eat the M&M's out of the trail mix?"

"Pretty much."

"Maybe the girls accidentally went to the parking lot at that junction. We've been here a long time. Let's walk up that driveway and check."

"Shouldn't we stay on the trail? They might pass us if we go off trail."

"It runs right by the parking lot. Besides, they wouldn't go past the road without us."

The driveway flattened out onto a wide parking lot. Across the parking lot under a few pines, we saw the girls sitting at a picnic table. A blue minivan with its back door open was parked right beside it. My cousin Brian turned and came bounding toward us with one of his two sons in his arms.

"Oh, I get it now." Henry squinted at me and turned up his chin. "That's what you and Mom were talking about."

I embraced Brian in a big bear hug, released him, and patted his son on the head. "Sorry about that, Jack," I said. "I didn't mean to squish you."

We turned together toward the picnic table. Georgie swiveled on the bench and lifted a chicken breast high in the air. "I guess they beat us here," I said.

"Did you guys miss the turn?" Brian said.

"We've been waiting down by the road for forty-five minutes. I'm not sure how we missed you. Thank you so much for coming to see us."

"I was afraid we wouldn't catch you." Brian reached up his hand and clapped me on the shoulder. "You guys are flying. I thought you'd be in Oregon at least another week and a half."

"We've picked up the pace," I said. "Go on, Henry." Henry ran toward the table, and I nodded after him. "You ought to see that boy walk. I couldn't keep up. I had to jump in front of him on the downhill to slow him down.

He's walking four miles per hour like it's nothing." I stretched down and pressed my thumb to my shin and winced.

"Something wrong with your leg?"

"I don't think so. It just felt funny on the way down the hill … probably nothing."

On our way to the table, Jana waved at us from behind the van.

"Let's go help her." Monica encircled my wrist with her hand and swung one leg over the bench. "Jana, what can we do to help?"

"Please, stay seated, you've been walking all day, just relax." She turned toward me with one arm looped through the handle of a large picnic basket, and a sheet in the other.

"Jana," Monica shook her head. "This is so amazing."

Jana smiled and looked toward Brian. "Would you hold this?" She handed him the basket and unfolded the sheet. "Lean back for a second," she said, and unfurled the sheet wide onto the table on her first attempt.

"Who's up for some more chicken?" Brian said and lifted the wicker basket high and placed it in the center of the table. "There is wine and cheese in there too ... for the adults."

Back at the highway, their van tires buzzed on the worn asphalt as they drove away. We stepped into the unpainted center of the quiet road. Georgie rubbed her belly. "That was some good food," she said. After we waved them over the far horizon, we stood for a long time until we heard another car approaching.

Monica dropped her pack in the grass. "Just in time," she said, shaking the roll of toilet paper in one hand. "I'll be quick."

"We'll wait here," I said. With my open pack at my feet, I looked down the line of the four of them. "Get out your flashlights," I said.

Georgie grabbed my hand, and I looked at her. She nodded toward the road. "Dad, I didn't even know I had an Uncle Brian and Jana, and they just decided to drive three hours to come see us and bring us chicken." She paused. "That's really nice of them."

I knelt beside her and with a hand on the outside of each of her arms, I looked her in the eye. "It really is. Isn't it?"

"And she brought a tablecloth and everything, Dad. It's just really nice."

I pulled her to me and hugged her. "Let's remember to thank them when we get a chance."

Aiden tapped me on the shoulder. "How much farther are we going tonight?"

"Five miles or so," I said, "but it's all more or less flat."

"More or less?" June clipped her pack, cinched it down tight, and sat down with a thud. "You know we don't believe you when you say that."

"Come here, I'll show you on the map."

June took my phone and began to scroll. "Oh wow, he's actually telling the truth. It does look easy."

"You still need your flashlights out," I said. "It will be dark soon. And check the batteries if you have one of the pen lights. They don't last very long."

"I think I heard Mom everybody." Aiden swung her pack onto her back. "Let's go."

When the darkness began to settle around us, Henry and I dropped off the pace a few steps. He turned off his flashlight behind me. "I can see better without one," he said.

"You're using their lights and memorizing where the rocks and roots are," I said.

"If you need to go walk with the light, go ahead. I'm fine in the dark."

"I could probably do it with my eyes closed, but I still say you're using their light."

"Fine, I'll drop further back," he said. "You can too, if you think you can handle it."

"Good by me, however far you want to let them get ahead, I'll do it too." I stopped, and we stood with eyes locked, unblinking. He hitched his thumbs under his shoulder straps. I hitched mine too in deliberate imitation. We stared each other in the eye while we waited for the girls to stretch their lead. Without a word, I waved him forward, and we started again. I lifted my feet high and stepped with care. A loose rock rolled underneath me, and I nearly fell.

"You okay back there, Dad?"

"Oh, I'm good. I thought I saw a mountain lion, so I jumped in that bush to grab him by the tail."

"Uh huh," he said.

We walked a while longer, and my eyes adjusted. "It's cold all of a sudden," I said. "That was weird.

It seems to happen at random. It's just these little cold pockets. Whenever I reach for my jacket, I warm up again."

At that moment, I heard Georgie cry out. I snapped my light on and ran to her. She was pushing herself up from the trail, and a stranger was kneeling beside her. "Oh, sweetheart, are you okay?" the stranger said.

Georgie nodded and rolled to a seated position. She dropped her head between her knees. Georgie took a deep breath and wiped her cheek. "Yes ma'am," she said.

I reached out my hand and placed it with care on the top of Georgie's head. "Looks like we had a bit of a fall." I bent close to her ear and whispered, "Are you okay?"

"I hate that," the stranger said. "It happens to me all the time. In fact, my trail name is Faceplant, because I do it so much. I do like to walk at night, so maybe that's why. What are you guys doing out here this late?"

"Walking to Mexico," I said.

"But we don't like to walk at night anymore," Georgie said. "Not after that fall. Right Dad?"

"Did you see anyone else pass?"

"They're not far ahead of you," Faceplant said.
I turned back to Henry. "We can walk with a light now, Henry."

He coughed.
"For Georgie," I said. "Have a great hike, Faceplant. It was nice to meet you."

The others were huddled together in a grassy open area when we caught them. Monica extended her arm toward Georgie. "What happened to you guys?"

"I fell," Georgie said.

"Oh no, how did you fall?"

"I tripped on a root and I face-planted right in the middle of the trail.

Monica pulled Georgie in and hugged her. "Did you hurt yourself?"

"I dropped my flashlight. I hate these roots and rocks when I can't see them. But Mom, this lady named Faceplant was there."

"Let me look at you." Monica stepped back and knelt in front of Georgie. "Someone shine a light on her." She scraped the knees of Georgie's pants and turned each of her hands over. "Oh, sweet kid, you scraped them up pretty good." Monica looked up at me. "Which is this Faceplant?"

 "Isn't it cool that her name was Faceplant, Mom?" Georgie said. "She said she falls all the time, 'cause she walks at night a lot."

Monica pulled Georgie in tight, looked up again at me, shook her head, and smiled.

"Hey, were you guys feeling all those cold pockets?" Aiden said.

"I did," Georgie said, "so I just wore my jacket backward."

"Maybe that's why you fell on your face."

"That's not funny, Aiden," Monica said and looked at me. "I hate walking at night. Let's make this an exception."

A wispy cloud moved away from between us and the bright moon, and a cool glow lit the dry grass. I looked down at my hands, pale in the moonlight. I opened and closed each fist. I reached one hand out for Monica, and she reached a hand back. "This is nice," she said, and looked up.

Georgie slipped her hand into mine on the opposite side. "Daddy, have you ever seen so many stars?"

"The only place I can remember like this was in Minnesota one summer. I guess I was about your age."

"My neck hurts from looking up," June said. "But I can't make myself stop looking."

"I bet they were like this in Washington," Aiden said. "It's just that we were in our tents before dark. What time is it anyway?"

"It's after ten. We should be there soon." I dropped Monica's hand and reached into my pocket for my phone. "One mile to go."

"Let me look," June said. "Dad, can I see your phone?"

"It's time to get moving. I'm getting cold. Maybe I'll let you look after we get a little way further on. Does everyone still have their flashlights out?"

"It's so nice here," Aiden said. "I wish we could just lie down here."

"We could," I said, "but then tomorrow wouldn't be a full zero."

Monica waited beside me 'til all the kids filed out singing "Stars" from *Les Mis*. "Why wouldn't you show June your phone?" she said.

"I missed the first turn to Big Lake," I told her. "It would have saved us about a mile of walking."

"You missed the turn?"

"Yep."

"It's probably best that you didn't show her," Monica said. "How far have we gone?"

"If you count the alternate," I said, "today is our first thirty-mile day."

"But we don't count off-trail miles, do we?"

659.1.1

I woke up with my head jammed beneath the lowest branches of a thick bush. One in a long hedge that bordered the beach along Big Lake. I parted the branches above me in order to sit up on my deflated groundpad. During the night, the wind had shifted to blow toward us and kicked up a good chop. For a long time, I stared at the small whitecaps crashing not far from my feet against the black sand.

Henry, Aiden, and June lay packed together beside me across the path that led back to the trail through the bushes. Having promised to let them sleep in, I took my time packing up. I walked to the water with my groundpad, and stepped in, up to my ankles. After blowing into the valve of my groundpad twice, I remembered that my patch kit was deep in my pack, so I left the repair for later. I attempted a tricky tiptoe between the sleepers. On the way past, I stumbled and bumped into Aiden.

"Dad," she said, "what are you doing?"

I held my fingers to my lips. "I want to check this place out. Careful not to wake the others."

As we tiptoed past Henry and June, June stirred. "Where are you going?" she said.

"To check out the camp. Want to come?"

"I'm going back to sleep," she said and turned her head away from us.

Aiden pointed to where Monica's tent stood, all cattywampus and leaning into a hole in the direction of two pine trees. "That cannot be comfortable. I don't know why they don't just cowboy camp with us. Especially now that there is no dew in the mornings." She pointed at my feet. "Why are you taking your shoes off?"

"I feel like walking barefoot on this pinestraw."

We followed the soft path parallel to the lake for a few hundred feet, and came to a sign that read, "No camping beyond this point."

"Oh, that's why we had to camp back down there?" Aiden said.

We crossed a road and turned up through sparse stands of pines and followed the slope of the hill up toward an A-frame where a few other early risers had assembled. We mingled among the gathering crowd, until a man stepped onto the deck and pulled out a keyring on a retractable cord. He turned and saluted the crowd. "Sorry folks, I got a bit of a late start this morning. We'll get you in here. Let me know if you need anything, should be plenty of laundry soap, I topped it up last night before I locked up. If I'm not around, look for someone in the mail room." He pointed to another outbuilding. "They should be up right after breakfast, somewhere around nine."

Someone behind us said, "Excuse me, can I squeeze past you? I just have some clothes in the dryer. I'm trying to get back on-trail early."

"No problem." I pulled Aiden out of her way. "You're skipping breakfast?"

"Everyone is saying the lava is terrible in the heat of the day, so I'm trying to get there before it gets too bad."

"We're taking a full zero," I said. "So we aren't in a rush. You're the first new southbounder we've seen in a while. When did you start?"

"June twenty-fifth."

The man with the keys swung the front door open, and said, "Come on in."

"Excuse me," she said again, and we stepped aside to let her pass.

After a quick tour of the A-frame, we followed the crowd down the hill as people trickled from every part of the property toward the dining hall where they formed a single, long line. Hikers, campers, and staff all mixed in together.

"I should probably go get my shoes," I said. "You wanna hold a place for us?"

"Nah, I'll come with you."

We stepped from the path to make way for breakfast bound hikers and bowed from the waist.

"You're going the wrong way," one of them said.

When we reached our camp, June was seated on top of her backpack. Her lips tightened when she saw me. "I looked all over for you guys."

"We were up at the hiker hut. I didn't know you were coming."

"I changed my mind, but you were already gone."

"It's almost time for breakfast. Are they awake?"

She shook her head.

"Do you want to be the one to wake Henry up?"

She smiled.

Later that morning, after three helpings of food, I stepped into the crowded A-frame and found Aiden on a far bench reading a book. As I was shimmying by a hiker, I bumped his knee. He pulled his earbud from his ear and looked up. "What's up?"

"Sorry, I was just trying to squeeze past to talk to my daughter." I nodded toward Aiden. He replaced his earbud and looked back to his phone.

"Have you seen your mom?"

"I'm in here." Monica peeked her head around the door to the laundry. "What's up?"

"Are you ready to do our resupply?" I walked to Aiden. "Take Henry and the others down to the mailroom to grab the boxes? See if you can set them up on the side of the building so we can do our resupply there. I want to get it out of the way, so we can just relax the rest of the day." Aiden nodded. I stepped back to the laundry room. "What do you think about us doing resupply now?"

"I have to wait for this load to dry. I'm sharing it with someone else."

"Okay, we can get started without you." I picked my way through the room again to the front door and bumped into Aiden on the deck. She was empty handed. "Where are the boxes, kid?"

She pointed past me back into the A-frame. "They told us there's a back room in here on the right." On her way by the hiker boxes, she dug out a canister of Isobutane. "I'll hold onto this until I make sure we have some in one of our boxes."

The back room had shelves to the ceiling, and all of them full. I touched both Aiden and Henry on their shoulder. "Do either of you remember how many we shipped here?"

"There should be a total number written on all of them for each stop," Aiden said.

"That was a great idea."

"It was Mom's."

"Look at this," Henry popped the side of a box with the back of his hand. "I found one of ours, but someone wrote on it." He read, "What the Waptus? I bet that's from Salty."

"Look, here is Potter," Aiden said. "She signed this box. Columbus and Bluebear signed too. He wrote, 'Catch us if you can,' under his. I wonder how long ago they came through here. We aren't going to be catching them anytime soon. At least not the Royal Family. Do you think they are still walking together?"

"At least a few of them are," Henry said.

Aiden shook her head. "How would you even know that?"

"I read the log books. They sign on the same date."

"Let's get these out of here," I said, tapping the top of the stack of six boxes. "You guys grab two boxes each and find a good place nearby. I'll be out there soon. I'm going to talk to your mom for a second."

"I'm coming too," Aiden said.

As if she had anticipated our approach, Monica leaned out the door with a stack of folded clothes in her hands. "Can you take this to the kids?" I straightened my arms, stepped toward her, and eyed the top of the box. She dropped the pile on top. "Did you find the package from home?"

"I didn't know to look for it."

"Creigh sent one that people from church got together." Monica rounded the corner of the A-frame with a neat stack of clothes in her hands.

"Mom, wait 'til you hear what we're doing," Aiden said.

"What is it?"

"Dad looked it up, and there is a stop in the middle of this section. So instead of carrying food for seven days, we are going to split everything up and ship half of it to someplace in the middle. That way we can be super light when we cross the lava tomorrow."

"What is the place called?" Monica said.

"Shelter Cove."

"It sounds good to cut our food weight in half, but will it get there in time?"

"The lady said it would," Aiden said. "I guess FedEx picks up today."

"In that case, it sounds good to me."

659.1.2

Along the back wall, between the storage room and the laundry, a man wearing rolled up black pants sat with both legs propped on a box. He had a bag of ice on each leg wrapped inside a few tight layers of cellophane.

"What happened," I said.

"It's shin splints," he said. "I pushed it too hard in all this volcanic rock."

"It looks painful."

"It is." He pointed to the one on the left. "This one feels like someone is sticking a knife in my shin every step I take, but this one feels like there's a hot iron against it even when I'm sitting still." He put his hand on the leg, and didn't move his eyes from his hand.

"It isn't the ice burning?"

"Oh no, it's been like that for two days. Since Elk Lake, at least. I pushed too hard. I started doing thirty-mile days when I crossed into Oregon."

"Are you …?"

Without moving his head, he turned his eyes up toward me. "Am I done?" He half smiled and looked back toward his hand. "No, I'm finishing this damn thing, if it kills me, but you can bet I'll be dialing it back."

"I'm really sorry, man." I shuffled around him.

"Take it easy on those rocks," he said. "Try to hit it early. You don't want to be on those rocks when it's hot. Trust me."

659.1.3

Down by the lake, in the midafternoon, Henry and I lay drying in the sun on our groundsheets on a nice strip of grass near the water's edge. The girls were standing waist deep in the water watching sailboarders pass back and forth.

Monica dunked her head under and came up smiling. She walked toward us, wringing out her hair. "Don't you love this place?"

Two hikers, a couple, stepped into the clearing, and patted dust clouds from their shirts. "Hello," they said as they walked toward us. "You mind if we join you? This is such a great spot."

"Not a problem," I said.

"Which way are you headed?" Henry said.

"We are northbounders, and you?"

"Southbounders," I said.

"All of these kids are yours?"

"So she tells me. I'm not so sure about the redhead."

"You're the family then," said the woman. "I wondered if we would run into you."

"You just came through the rocks, then," I said. "How was it?"

The man looked over at the woman. "It's worse," he said, "than whatever you've heard."

"How far is it," I said, "from here to the rocks?"

"It can't be more than five miles," she said.

Aiden plunked down on her Tyvek and unwrapped the bundle of cards from back home. "Want to hear some, Dad?"

"I'm sorry," I said. "We just got a care package from our church back home."

"Oh, don't apologize," the woman said. "I'd love to hear."

"Aiden, read her that one joke from Maryfran," I said.

"Maryfran is their cousin." Monica touched her fingers to the woman's forearm. "She is Aiden's age."

"Okay, okay, here it is." Aiden shifted on her groundpad and cleared her throat. "What is green and has wheels?" She looked up.

The woman looked at the man, and said, "Okay, we give up."

"Grass," Aiden said. "I was just kidding about the wheels."

Monica leaned toward her again. "I'm sorry, it's so dumb."

After dinner that evening, with Monica sitting beside me on a picnic table bench with my emptied burrito plate in front of me, I looked toward the lawn where our four kids sat in a circle with the couple from the lake. I elbowed Monica and nodded.

"I know what you're thinking," she said.

"What am I thinking?"

"You are thinking of hiking out tonight to get close to the rocks, so we can cross in the cool of the morning."

"I had thought of it, yes," I said, "but I wasn't going to mention it."

She sighed. "June isn't going to like it."

663

It was four in the morning when we woke in a forest not far from the lava field. We walked fast through the silent mist of the morning, and through a cool fog over the alien rock that was sharp edged, porous, and uncomfortable under our feet. But the mist kept us cool. The high-pitched tone of the dark rock as it scraped and moved beneath our feet struck a note that held a hint of metallic. We wound between pockets and caves close at hand. The trail was subtle, an indentation, a subtle demarcation, but it was easy to follow just the same. My foot rolled on occasion and a sharp pain shot through my shin, but it faded when I righted my stride. Someone started singing, I think it was Aiden, and we danced our way through the fog.

Not once did we stop, and before nine in the morning, we sat in lawn chairs around Coppertone's van on the far side of the lava.

"You picked a good day for it," he said. "Yesterday was a scorcher."

"Wait, was that it?" I said. "Was that all of it?"

"That was the worst of it. You gain elevation from here, so it will be cooler the higher you climb."

He offered us the last of all that he had, and we sat for a long time and talked. Monica tapped the side of my leg, and said, "We should get going before it gets too hot."

"That was it, Monica," I said. "That was the lava. That was all of the flow from the Belknap Crater that everyone warned us about. I'm sorry. We could've stayed longer at Big Lake."

"Well, we are here now, with a nice start to the day."

683

High in the Sisters Wilderness, June and I sat in the dead center of the dusty trail 4.2 miles from camp. "Look at me," I said.

She shook her head hard to one side.

"Look at me. Right in the eye. You punched her. It's not okay that you punched her."

"She knows I hate that, Dad. Why would she do that? I don't do that when I see somebody's hurt, 'cause I know they don't want to be bothered. All she had to do was leave me alone. I told her to leave me alone, and she wouldn't."

"She's your mother, June. That's what mothers do. They move toward you when you are hurting. You want her to pretend not to care? You want her to act counter to her good inclination?"

"I just wanted her not to touch me, and I told her not to touch me."

"You hit her."

"I don't know why that happened. It was just a reaction."

"You punched her."

"It just happened."

"June, it doesn't just happen. Why don't you tell me what happened?"

"I tripped, and hurt my knee, so I just wanted to be left alone. I didn't want her to touch me or talk to me or anything, and I told her that, but she just kept trying to push. I don't even know why I did it, I didn't mean to hit her. Dad, I'm sick of talking about it. Would you please just stop talking about it?"

"No, we are going to talk about it. She's upset, and they've all left us and gone on to camp. It's just you and me here."

"I don't care."

"It's been a long day. Everyone is tired. It will be okay, but you have to see that you have to apologize to her."

"I'm not going anywhere, and I'm not apologizing."

"Again?"

"I'm sick of it. I don't want to walk anymore. I mean, what's the point anyway? I heard you talking to that guy earlier. He said we aren't going to make it before winter."

"What does he know?"

"Then why are you and Mom always talking about it? If we aren't going to make it, we should just go home and be with our friends and cousins. I hate it here."

"I hate it a few times every day too, but I don't hate it, hate it. Not really."

"Well, I do."

"I don't think you really do."

"You have a choice to be here. We don't, and you say we have to keep walking in the dark every day."

"It's getting dark earlier now, that's why we are walking in the dark. We are actually walking less hours than we used to."

"I hate it. All of it."

"June, until you fell down you were having a great day."

"No, I wasn't."

"I will remind you, because remembering can be like a good friend. Remember this morning that you and I woke up before anyone else. You were the first one ready, before five o'clock. Remember? And you chose the music, and we sang, all of us together walking in that crazy mist. You told me it looked like a graveyard. I thought it looked like a ghost world. Remember that? Then we got to the rocks that everyone told us would be so terrible, but they weren't bad at all. In fact, you even told me that you thought all those caves and everything were interesting."

"What about your leg hurting?"

"It stopped hurting right after the lava. Remember, the clouds that kept us cool the whole time we were walking over the lava flow. I also seem to remember a certain someone laughing at Aiden for what she said about the trees?"

"But, Dad, that's so dumb to think those dead trees were old enough to be killed by the volcano."

"And then we had trail magic, twice. There was Coppertone and the guy up at the road."

"We had three trail magics, because you didn't count the cooler at the end of the rocks."

"That's true, three trail magics in one day."

"Coppertone only had bananas."

"It's still trail magic, and he was almost done for the day, so he was out of everything else. Besides, he says bananas are the best thing you could have, and he should know, he's walked a lot more miles than any of us."

"I don't even care about that stuff."

"Well, the other trail magic had candy."

"Okay, that wasn't bad."

"And then we kept leapfrogging that old man and his dog."

"Roxy."

"Yep, and how cool was Roxy? She didn't even have to wear any pads on her feet."

"That's 'cause they walk on these rocks all the time, so Roxy is used to it."

"I kept thinking we'd never see that man again because he walked so slow. And then he kept passing us. Slow and steady wins the race. Then, we got to the top and saw all that obsidian. You made an arrowhead while you walked. Have you ever seen any rock like obsidian? It's so shiny and beautiful, and it's just lying around everywhere up here."

"My arrowhead cracked."

"Well, you had fun trying to make it."

"Georgie's was better."

"Georgie's cracked too."

"Why would that make me feel better?"

"I'm glad it doesn't. But June, this has been a great day. You even did your first spur off-trail to see the Middle Sister. Look at this picture." I held out my phone. "This is now one of my favorite pictures of you. It will make me smile and remember this day. It was such a great overlook. We could see all of those mountains behind us from there. Jefferson, Washington, and the crater, and all of them."

"Dad, you always get it wrong." She counted on her fingers. "It's the Belknap Crater, then Mount Washington, then Three Fingered Jack, and then Jefferson."

"Plus, we got to meet SoGood up there. She was nice."

"Mom already knew her."

"From where?"

"She's the one Mom shared the laundry load with yesterday."

"I didn't know that."

"And Henry wouldn't even come on the spur."

"Exactly, who would have thought you would do the spur and Henry wouldn't? You've gotten so much stronger. It's been a great day. Well, right up until now. I know your mom will forgive you. Don't let this one hard thing at the end ruin an otherwise good day."

June leaned forward and adjusted her pack. I stood to my feet and gave her my hand. We started walking.

"Why do you think you and your mom have trouble getting along sometimes?"

"I don't know. I don't really want to talk about it anymore."

"What else are we going to do out here?"

We walked on in silence for a while until we walked into a shaded meadow beneath a reddening peak off to the left. "I wonder if that's old Broken Top," I said. Isolated patches of snow near its top were dirty with the look of late season, but not so dirty that they failed to reflect the last of the afternoon sun.

"You could take out your phone and find out."

"My hands are too cold. I just want to get there."

When we entered the trees on the far side of the meadow, she said, "Dad, I think it's because of the car wreck. I think I'm still mad at her for breaking my arm. I just think maybe I haven't ever forgiven her all the way."

"You think you're still mad at her?"

"Maybe. I think about it a lot. And I notice that I think about it whenever I'm mad at her. I don't know why. I know she didn't mean to do it, but maybe she could have avoided it if she'd been paying better attention."

"It scared you a lot?"

"I was sleeping, and then I woke up with my arm broken."

"That was a terrible phone call. I remember. You were bleeding badly from that cut on your face." I stopped to pull out my phone. "It's important to talk about, it is good to talk about it."

"How much farther?"

"1.3 miles. We just have this one last hill."

As soon as I said it, she collapsed on the trail and wept. I knelt beside her.

"June, what happened? You were doing fine."

"I thought we were done climbing."

"It's only a small climb."

"You always say that."

"June, the climb is only three tenths of a mile, and it isn't that steep."

"You go, Dad. I'm done."

"You're done? Where on earth did this come from?"

"This time I'm really done."

"We can walk into camp as late as you want. I have a flashlight. You just need another rest before the last climb."

"I don't want any more climbs. I'm staying here."

I pulled out my jacket and lay with my back to the grass and stared at the darkening sky for a long time. I tried again. "How can I leave my fourteen-year-old daughter alone in the woods?"

"You can stay with me if you want, or you can go, I don't care."

"It wouldn't be fair to them. They will be scared something has happened."

In the course of our conversation, several hikers passed. Each said, "How are you doing?"

"Good, how about you?" I said each time.

When SoGood asked me, though, I answered in truth. "Not that great. June is having a tough day, how about you?"

"Your name is June?" SoGood jerked her hand to her mouth. "I love the name June." She clasped her hands, and knelt beside June, "Okay, you are going to have to forgive me, because some people might not take this as a compliment, but I truly do mean it that way. June is the name of my favorite goat of all time. When I had thirty-five milk goats, she was the Queen. Oh, she was a handful, but she was by far my favorite."

June sat up and turned to her face toward SoGood..

"Where are you planning to camp?" SoGood said.

"By the waypoint named Pond," I said. "Would you tell our family you've seen us?"

I didn't say anything after SoGood left us. We just sat. After a while, I pulled out my sleeping bag and lay back underneath it.

June looked up at me and wiped her eyes. "I can make it."

I nodded.

June's were the only words spoken before we reached camp. She said, "Dad, will you help me talk to Mom?"

687.7

After midnight, I lifted my head and looked past my feet down the slope toward the pond. I pulled a hand out and patted my quilt. It felt heavy and wet. I reached over to Henry and patted his quilt as well. Then Aiden's. Each was heavy with damp. While watching the moon's reflection on the water, I saw a shooting star flash behind it. It was cold outside of my quilt. The wet quilts concerned me. I considered waking them all to set up our tents, but we needed a good night of sleep. In the end, I decided to risk being wet, rolled over and fell back into sleep.

In the pre-dawn light I woke again and looked past my feet down the slope toward the pond. I pulled a hand out and brushed a layer of ice from my quilt. No wind disturbed the valley, so the ripple on the pond's surface confused me. My eye tracked the water's disturbance 'til it fixed on a swimmer's bobbing head. "Wim Hoff would be proud," I said aloud. I pulled my hand out again to brush off more ice, then propped myself up on my elbows. The swimmer completed two more wide circles, stepped out of the water, naked, and drifted across the rocks into the trees. For a moment, I half-considered a swim myself. I curled back into the warmth of my quilt, rolled onto my side and fell again into sleep.

714

Aiden stood beside Georgie holding her hand. "Dad, Georgie's freezing. Do you care if we start walking?"

"Wait for me," June said. "I'm almost packed up."

"As long as you all stay together. Do you have enough charge on your phone, Aiden?"

"We got this, Dad." Aiden and Georgie took a few steps toward the trail together. "June, we'll wait for you at the trail."

Late in the morning, a northbound family waved at us from a wide square of log rounds at the base of a hill. I nodded to Monica and walked toward them.

"Where are you all from? I can't place your accent."

"Austria," the father said and tossed a log round into the fire. He nodded toward his children. Both looked to be in their twenties. "These two have moved here to the United States for work. My wife and I are now retired, and they invited us to join them on their hike."

He pointed us toward the water cache by the dirt road. "Watch yourself, there are wasps all over the place."

After we filled up, June asked us to wait while she used the shovel. Monica handed it to her. June dropped her pack and ran ahead. We waited in the shade for a long time. "You know what? Why don't y'all go ahead?"

I woke up with June leaning over me. She laughed and shook my shoulders. "Wake up, Dad."

I sat up and stretched toward my toes, and noticed June's worn out shoe. "That's quite a blowout." I slipped a finger into the hole near her instep.

"It's the same place I got the holes last time." She switched her other foot forward. "This one's even worse."

"You have a new pair coming soon."

"They said they would wait for me. Why didn't they?"

"I told them to go. They didn't even ask."

"How far ahead do you think they are?"

"I was asleep, June. I don't even know for how long."

"I wasn't gone that long, and I wanted us all to walk together."

We walked for a long while in silence. "I think it helps me," she said, "when we all walk together."

"Yeah, but today I get to have you all to myself, Bug. And even though it's through this awful burn section, I don't mind, 'cause I get to be with you."

"How long is this supposed to be exposed like this?"

"The comments say it's not more than three miles," I said. "That's nothing to you, you've been doing so well. I think it helped to get it out of you."

"I talked to Mom some," she said, "and that helped." She stopped and looked up the trail. "How long do we have to climb?"

"I don't know."

"Look at your phone."

"1.1 miles"

"I don't understand why they just left me," she said.

"I'm going to use the shovel, June. I'll catch up."

At the top of the hill, two northbound hikers said they had spoken with her for a few minutes. "What a sweet kid you have there," one of them said. "She's so full of life."

"How long ago was it?"

"She says she rides horses?"

"That's her," I said.

A few minutes farther along the trail, I could hear June yelling. "I hate you! All of you." She threw down her pack and ran toward me, shouldering me to the ground as she passed.

"What is going on here?"

"She just started screaming at us, Dad," Aiden said.

"Where is she going?"

Aiden shrugged. "She just lost it and took off."

I dropped my pack and ran after her and might have run by her but for the crack from a stick that she stepped on. She was high stepping her feet through brambles away from the trail. I followed her at a distance. She didn't see me and turned toward a tight stand of trees. I didn't call out. When she sat down, I found a rock and sat down too.

She broke a stick and threw it at a tree. Then she broke another and started swinging it against the base of the same tree. I couldn't make out all of her words over the distance, but they were angry words. I waited there for a long time.

"Dad, you know I can see you."

"I'm not hiding."

"Why did you follow me?"

"Did you think I wouldn't?"

She gave no answer.

"Would it be okay if I came over there?"

"You can come," she said, "but I really don't feel like talking."

I ducked into the glade and sat down beside her on the ground. "This not talking is going to be hard for me, June, but I can try."

"Dad, I don't know why this happens to me. I get so mad at them. But, they left me."

"I told them to go. You should be mad at me and not them."

"It isn't just that."

"What else is it?"

"I think I thought it would get easier, and it's never going to. Not really. I think I thought I would be better at persevering, but I keep giving up. I keep getting mad."

"Would you like to go home?"

"You wouldn't let me go home."

"I wouldn't let you go home alone."

"You are saying we could all go home?"

"June, you know how much I want to finish this trail as a family, but I want to finish this trail as a family. I'm not staying here without you."

She reached an arm around me, and we sat for a long time like that. With her other hand she started tapping the ground with the stick. "Dad, I don't want to go home," she said. "Not really. I just want it to stop being so hard."

"June, as soon as your mom and I had kids, one of the strange things we would pray for you guys was that you would experience low-level suffering, so that we could go through it alongside you. So much growth comes from suffering. Of all of my kids, you suffer the most. I know it, and I know that you know it too." She leaned her head against me. "Did I ever tell you the story about my friend, Joel?"

I felt her head shake on my shoulder. "No."

"Joel, and I, and another friend named Dustin were driving in a car together past a house your grandfather built, and Dustin told us about a man who lived there that shot his wife, and then himself in front of his two daughters. Dustin and I had terrible responses, I don't even want to mention." I shook my head.

"What were your responses?"

"You want to know?"

She nodded.

"I found out that the man used to cut lawns, and I wondered how I might pick up his accounts. Dustin said his response was to think, 'Those girls are gonna end up strung out on drugs.' But Joel … I love what Joel said, and I think about it a lot. He said, "I pray that one day, through this experience, those girls will be able to identify with the sufferings of Christ, and come to know the love of God the Father."

"What do you mean?"

"June, your suffering can make you a better lover of people. You will walk into a room and see the one who feels out of place. When someone talks about hating the task that they have to do, you will know what that feels like more than Aiden or Henry or Georgie." I stopped. "Or me, for that matter. June …"

"Dad," June said. "Are you crying?"

I smiled at her. "June, if we had to go home today, it was all worth it, if only for this. I believe there is work going on inside you that will help you the rest of your life; we just don't know how yet. I love being here with you."

"Dad, why does God have to make it so hard for some people?"

I heard a voice from behind us. "Are you guys alright back there?"

I turned, and a hiker appeared through the trees. "Oh, it is you guys." He touched his hand to his chest. "Dahn. It's Dahn. I met you up near the border. I heard voices off-trail and just wanted to check."

"June is having a bad couple of days. She tried to turn into a northbounder, and I had to chase her down."

"Hey, I'm going northbound too, June."

She laughed and wiped her eyes. "I'm just really tired."

"Tired?"

"Tired of the whole thing," she said.

"Dad," Dahn said "would it be alright if I offered June some Skittles?"

"June? What do you say? You want some?"

"Are they melted?"

"Oh, don't you hate that? No, June, I keep them deep in my pack so they stay cool from the night before."

She smiled.

"Dahn, you don't have to pull everything out," I said, but by the time I got the words out, he was already dropping his sleeping quilt on the ground beside him.

He opened his food bag. "You know what's even better?" He nodded back toward the trail. "There was a guy setting up to do some trail magic at the bottom of the hill. I didn't wait around, but he said he was going to be making fajitas."

"Can we go now, Dad? Right after I eat these."

"Take them with you June."

"Thank you, Dahn," I said. "Your timing couldn't have been better." I reached a hand down for June. "Could it, June?"

About halfway down the hill, June said, "Dad, I was just thinking. Do you think maybe God put this trail magic here, 'cause he knew I was having such a bad day?"

744

It's shin splints, I know it. And it's going to end. This whole trip is going to end. If I can't get this pain in my shin to stop. Shut up, Vince. You are being dramatic. Just relax and walk deep in your stride. Don't flex your ankle. Turn your toe out. That seems to help.

Maybe down in Shelter Cove, massage it. It might not even be good for it, what the hell do you even know about shin splints?

All this way.

All this way, just to stop. All the blessings. All the fortuitous mishaps avoided.

What on earth? I'm such an idiot. I pushed too hard. I didn't do the things that needed to be done. I needed rest. We needed rest. I needed different shoes. I knew it the day I put these on. But they don't have any in my size, stupid Altra, don't they know how bad I needed them? And now it's done. It could be. I don't even know if shin splints are a big deal.

Why am I whining?

"Who is this that darkens my counsel with words without knowledge?"

I hardly know what you have for us, God. Why do I always think I'm the one in charge?

All along.

Every step, you have had us. You have kept us. Safe and walking. All of my fretting, all of my fear. All of it, nothing. For nothing. I didn't have nearly enough sympathy for that guy at Big Lake. Not if this is what he was feeling. Brother, I believe you now. Every word!

God, help that poor guy to make it to the end. God, help him endure. He won't be able to if it hurts like this.

I don't know how far ahead they are now. I told them to go on without me. Monica saw me wince and asked what was wrong. I brushed it off. Made pretense. But she knew. She always knows. I said there was "some" pain. I didn't want to be dramatic about it, especially if it is nothing.

It could be nothing. It could be nothing.

747.6.1

I stood with Monica overlooking a wide, grassy lawn that sloped away to the marina at Shelter Cove on Lake Odell. There was a slight breeze coming off the water that served less to cool us than to wrap the warmth of the day around us. A makeshift sign to our left pointed us toward the camp store and restaurant which stood among a jumble of buildings off to that side.

"It looks pretty crowded." Monica nodded toward the wide deck that wrapped below and beyond the buildings. "Let's take one of those picnic tables down there."

"Go ahead. I'll catch up." I limped forward with careful steps behind her. When I sat on the bench, I winced.

"Vince, I'm serious." She placed a firm hand on my shoulder. "Sit here. We can take care of everything."

I nodded and relaxed again onto the bench. "The packages will be at the camp store," I said. She tapped my shoulder once more and made her way to the steps, and I followed her with my gaze as she went. I reached down to rub my shin. It was warm in the sun—a good warm, like it would almost pulse its way into me. I sat that way for a long while.

Monica returned to the table with three drinks in her arms. She put one down in front of me and rested her fingers on my forearm, "Will you listen for them to call our name?" She turned to Henry. "Henry, if they call our name, go get the pizza for Dad, okay? I'm going to go help the girls with the boxes."

Henry shrugged.

Before she disappeared beyond the steps again, a hiker stepped out to the rail with a beer in one hand and a pizza box in the other. "Hey, fellas, you feel like eating some pizza?"

"I do," Henry said. "What kind is it?"

"It's Hawaiian. I couldn't eat all of it."

"We'll take it." Henry swung his feet over the bench. "I like Hawaiian."

Before Henry returned with the box, he pulled out a slice and took a big bite. He dropped the pizza box in front of me and then placed his slice in front of him onto the table.

"Dude, get a napkin," I said.

Henry spoke through his mouthful. "I think I'm acclimated to dirt by now." He lifted the pizza and inspected its bottom side. "Don't you think?"

"Just get a napkin."

He grumbled, but soon returned with a roll of paper towels. He slipped one under his piece and began picking off the pineapple.

"I thought you said you liked Hawaiian."

"I do. It's just that I don't like pineapple on it."

"Then you don't like Hawaiian pizza," I said.

Georgie skipped down the stairs to stand in front of me and thrust her foot forward. "Tada!"

"What is with those clown shoes?" I said.

"I found them in the hiker box." She bowed. "Do you like them?"

"Think you have enough room in the toe box?" I pressed a thumb to the toe of the shoe. "These have to be three sizes too big."

"I like the Lone Peaks better. Those Supremes were killing my feet."

"Are you sure you can walk in these? They look a little worn out."

"They feel so much better. You aren't going to make me take them back, are you?"

"You know your own feet." I turned back to the table. "Maybe I'm just jealous because I'm stuck with these awful New Balances."

Monica was shaking her head when she returned to the table empty-handed. June pushed past her to announce, "Dad, the boxes from Big Lake aren't here. They didn't come, so now we don't have any food for this section."

"She promised us they'd be here by Thursday morning," I said. "Did you ask if FedEx has delivered yet today?"

"I'll double check." June rushed off toward the camp store.

"What will we do if they don't make it?" Monica said.

"Here, Henry, help me up. I'll go talk to them." I lifted my leg over the bench and rocked forward. "Or you, Monica, can you give me a hand? I'm a little stiff."

She bent to touch my shin with a gentle hand and looked up. "How's it feeling?"

"It's good."

She tilted her head as if she would like to hear more.

"I ordered a new pair of shoes. They couldn't make it to Crater Lake on time, so I have to walk in this pair until at least Ashland."

"Altras?"

"No, they only had New Balance, but at least the new pair will have a wider toe box," I said. "Supposedly."

"I'm going to go up to the hiker box," she said. "We should go through it for food in case our boxes don't show. How many days do we have?"

"It should be three-ish days from here." I stood up with a groan. "If you see any size sixteen Altras up there, grab them."

"Oh, look," Monica called back from the top of the stairs. "It's SoGood. Have you talked to her yet?"

I shook my head.

After pizza, we spread our groundsheets at the bottom of the lawn near the lake, circled up, and piled our resupply between us. "Everyone, get your food bags from the last section and dump them into the middle, so we can see what we have." When she asked me for mine, I nodded to my backpack behind me. She tapped Aiden's leg. "Would you go grab Dad's, so he doesn't have to get up?"

Down at the water, a man moored his boat to the dock and began to crawl from it on his hands and knees. It took him a while and when he attempted to stand, it seemed to require great effort. He gathered his rods and turned toward us. He caught me staring, so I looked away. I could see from the corner of my eye that he continued his approach. He stopped in front of us. "What is this group?" he said.

"We're hiking the PCT," Aiden said in a cheery voice. "How about you?"

"I'm just coming off the water," he groaned, and reached one hand to his side.

"How'd you do?" I said.

He nodded toward the boat. "I have a couple of big lake trout in the cooler."

"Do you cast for them? Troll?"

"I mostly troll, really deep. Some people go around sixty feet, I try to stay in the twenty to thirty range."

"That seems deep to me."

"You fish where they feed." He nodded toward the water. "That's a deep lake. Nothing like Crater Lake, but it's deep."

"How deep?"

"This lake? Around 300 feet. Crater Lake is the deepest lake in the country."

"Crater is 1950 feet," June said. "We're going there next."

"Yeah, you did say you were on the PCT." He leaned in toward us to look at the pile of food. "That doesn't much look like trail food to me."

"This is not our normal fare," I said. "Our packages didn't make it on time."

"You shipped them here?" He pointed a crooked finger toward the camp store. "You aren't going to wait for them?"

"FedEx delivers on Tuesdays and Thursdays."

He looked at his watch. "It's Thursday today."

"Today's delivery came without them. They won't arrive 'til next Tuesday. You are welcome to them."

He shook his head and nodded up the hill. "We head out in the morning."

"Oh, are those boys throwing the frisbee yours?" Monica said.

"Yes, I'm here with my wife, our two grandkids, and my wife's sister. Send the kids up to throw the frisbee if they want to come." He paused. "You know what? I've got some extra snacks down in my boat. Can I bring you some?"

"I'm sure we wouldn't say no," I said. "Henry, run back down there and help him."

"Thank you," he said. "My back ain't doing so good today."

"No," I said. "We are the ones that should thank you."

When he walked away, Monica pointed to the pile in front of her. "I'm sorry about this. I bought all the tuna and peanut butter I could. And they didn't have tortillas, so I thought we could just use chips. They didn't have much to offer."

"Good thing I've been craving Dorito, peanut butter, and tuna sandwiches," I said.

"It can't be worse than your usual concoctions."

Henry and the fisherman returned with a large box of peanut butter crackers, and two bags of trail mix. "We're leaving tomorrow, so we won't need any of this stuff."

As we were watching him walk up the hill, SoGood caught our eye with a wave from the top deck. When we waved back, she jogged toward us across the lawn. She smiled when she reached us, breathless. "Look what I found in the hiker box." She held out a beer. "And these too." She dropped two cans of chicken and a box of macaroni into our pile.

I pressed the cold beer to my cheek and laughed, "So Good, this is not from the hiker box."

"Monica told me your boxes didn't make it from Big Lake."

"This is so sweet. Thank you." Monica stood up and hugged her. "Do you want to sit down with us?"

After I took a few sips, I handed the beer to Monica and lay on my back on the soft grass. A few sparse clouds passed overhead, everyone's voices began to blend into one, and I slept.

A while later, I woke to Monica's voice. "Where do you think you're going, Henry?" She reached up and grabbed him by the waistband.

He tugged a little against her, "I'm going to throw the frisbee with that kid."

"Okay," Monica said. "Are you sure you don't want a shower?"

He scrunched up his face as though he were offended. "What do you think, Mom?" He jerked himself free from her grip.

Monic turned to the rest of us. "Does anyone else want to come up to the bath house?"

We all shook our heads.

She looked around as if to take a full survey of the place and smiled. "Everyone has been so nice here." She pushed herself to her feet and made her way toward the bathhouse.

When the frisbee hit her, she stumbled. She stayed bent and took a few steps further up toward the asphalt where she sat down. I rushed up the hill, as fast as I was able. When I made it to her, she still hadn't looked up.

I placed a hand in the middle of her back and sat down beside her. "What happened?"

"You didn't see that kid hit me in the face with the frisbee?"

"I saw it." I suppressed a laugh.

"No, I'm serious." She lifted her tear-streaked face to me and swept her hand past her chin. A bright purple bump was already forming. I pressed to the side of it, and she winced. Her eyes welled.

"Oh," I wiped under her eye with my thumb. "I'm sorry, I didn't know it was this bad."

"Is it bad?" she said. "How does it look?"

I shook my head.

"I'm so annoyed. And on such a nice day too. What on earth?" He threw it so hard. I'm so mad at him."

"I'm just glad it wasn't Henry that threw it," I said.

Monica dropped her head. "What else can go wrong with today? The boxes didn't show. We have terrible food for this whole section. You have shin splints. My feet won't stop hurting." She pointed to her chin. "And now this."

"I don't know, you look more distinguished with this new prominent chin."

"Seriously, Vince, is it that bad?"

747.6.2

"Oh my gosh, Dad," Aiden said, "is this it?"

"Yep. This is where the Browns did that picture challenge."

"Our first one," she said. "Do you have it on your phone?"

I held it toward her. "I already had it pulled up, but there is one problem."

"Why would they do that to us?" Aiden tapped the phone's screen. "Why would they have an extra person in their picture? How are we supposed to get a park ranger to pose with us in our picture? Maybe you can send ours to Mr. Rob and he can photoshop a ranger into the picture."

I laughed. "That's a funny idea. Maybe. Let's wait to see what we can do when the others get here." I threw a stick toward the tree marked with the Pacific Crest Trail marker. "They shouldn't be too far behind us."

Aiden walked to the post marking the trailhead and rested her hand on it. "It is cool that they did that, the Browns. It makes it feel more like we aren't out here all by ourselves, knowing they have been here too."

Just then, a hiker appeared around the trail's bend. "Hey there," he said. "Is this the way down to Shelter Cove?"

"It sure is," I said. "Right down that way."

We talked for a few minutes, until he set off across the parking lot. When he turned back to us at the edge of the road, I called out to him, "Hold up. This might sound weird, but you wouldn't be willing to wait around a few minutes to be in a picture with us, would you?"

He laughed and walked back toward us. "What is all this about?"

I explained the picture challenge and told him that the rest of our family shouldn't be too far behind.

He took off his pack with a smile and sat down.

786

I felt in the dark above my head until my hand came to rest on my Garmin. After I powered it up and connected my phone, I texted my brother Ben.

V: What do you know about shin splints?

I dropped the Garmin and stared at the tent roof to wait for a reply.

B: Oh no! Who has shin splints?

V: Me. It's bad. It's like a knife in my shin even when I'm lying down in the tent. I can't sleep.

B: Do you have your leg elevated?

V: Yes, if you are thinking R.I.C.E., I only have the option for one of them. What do you know about this stuff?

B: Elevation?

V: Only at night. I meant compression. I have Georgie's ankle brace on it.

B: Isn't that a little tight?

V: My foot is purple and puffy, but it feels so much better than when it's off.

B: Take that thing off. That's too tight. You can't come off-trail?

V: In 50 miles, maybe. We're headed to Crater Lake.

B: Okay, I found a video for you. I sent a link to your phone.

V: I don't have reception.

B: It's a KT Tape and compression thing. Watch it when you have coverage. See if you can walk on your heels and say the alphabet.

V: Dude, that kills. I almost woke everyone up with a scream.

B: You've got to do it if you can. When you walk, you don't work out the muscles around your shin in both directions. Lifting your toes and walking on your heels will help with that.

V: Can I keep going? Am I done?

B: The danger with shin splints is they become stress fractures. Some say if you have shin splints you already have microfractures.

V: So we might be done?

B: I don't know what to tell you. It's more of a threat than Monica's plantar fasciitis.

V: How do you know she has Plantar Fasciitis?

B: Mom told me the symptoms. It sucks, but if she can walk through it, she'll be fine. Your shin splints though … By the way, I am not saying that shin splints hurt more than Plantar Fasciitis. But yours could shut you down if you aren't careful ... Can you get a compression sleeve and KT Tape? ... Can we ship it to you?

V: The nearest stop is 170 miles from here. Crater Lake has a gift shop and a camp store down the hill; there may be something there.

B: Don't push it too hard.

V: This sucks.

I tossed my Garmin over my head and checked to see if Monica was awake. I felt a great weight on my chest. I didn't bother to wipe the tears that ran down the side of my face.

Forty-five minutes later, my Garmin beeped. It wasn't Ben, it was my cousin Nathan.

N: Sorry to text late. We are in the area this weekend and Catch and Grey wanted to see your kids.

V: We aren't far from Crater Lake. We'll be there in two days.

N: We can do that. Can we bring you anything?

I breathed a deep breath in and let it out slowly. Tears came again. Hopeful tears.

V: If you can bring compression sleeves and KT tape, you'll be my hero.

833.3.1

We were all standing in a circle waiting for Aiden to finish stuffing her tent into her pack. Georgie blew into her hands. "Why did you do that, Georgie?" June said. "It's not even cold in the mornings anymore."

"You'll be warmed up soon, Georgie," I nodded through the trees to where the sun's first rays were making their way through the sparse trees and lifted my toes so that only my heels touched the ground. I shifted from one foot to the other.

Monica looked at me and sighed. "Are you still trying to do that?" Monica said.

I held up a finger, "D…E…F…G." When I made it to 'Z', I dropped my heels to the ground. "Ugh, that hurts!"

"Why are you doing it at all? It doesn't seem like it can be good."

"Ben told me to do it for the shin splints."

"Guys, Dad's in a mood this morning," Monica said. "I wouldn't cross him."

"What? What did I say?"

"It's not what you said, it's how you said it. We can leave you alone."

"You know what? That actually does sound pretty good. Maybe I just won't talk to anyone." I looked down at my phone. "There's only one stop for water today that isn't off trail. It's the cache right before the climb up to Crater Lake, so don't miss it if we get stretched out." I extended my hand. "Monica, will you take the GoPro today? I don't feel like filming, but I don't want to miss Crater Lake."

I walked myself into a dreary rhythm. With each step, I let the base of my left foot scrape the dirt. It lessened the pain. I concentrated on my stride, a step, drag, step and drag, step, drag. At lunch, I didn't bother to lay out my groundsheet and opted to lay in the dust. After lunch, I walked through the better part of the afternoon in a daze. We climbed up toward the lip of the crater above a wide plain parallel to a highway.

With the last of the hard elevation behind us, it would be flat to the Crater Lake Lodge, and I knew I could make it. I remembered the surprise that awaited Monica when we got to the lodge. Only June was in on the secret. I called her back to me, and together we texted my mother to thank her for the room reservation.

A whirlwind spun up in the sand near the lip of the crater, and Aiden ran toward it. "Come on, Georgie, it's the Tasmanian devil." A few times she closed in on it. Each time it dissipated. She gave up and walked to a rough-cut split rail fence and leaned over. She held her hat down against a wind gust until it passed, then opened her arms wide to the view. "Dad, hurry up, you've gotta see this."

"This is as fast as I go."

"It's the cleanest lake in the country, if you can believe what this sign says. And did you know you can hike down there? Dad, we totally should do that. How fun would it be to swim in that lake? Have you ever seen a lake so deep blue?"

"I'll wait up here for you if you want to go down there."

"That's right, I forgot about your leg."

We stood for a while at the overlook and read each of the sandwich board
signs. For the first few hundred yards from the overlook, the trail ran along
a sidewalk beside a parking lot. In the last available space there was a car
with an open trunk. A man pointed Inside the trunk toward two open
coolers. "Trail magic?"

"Yes, please," Aiden said. "Do you have any cold water?"

"I have soda too. And for the adults, I have beer." He plunged his hand into
the ice and held a cold can toward me. I sat down in one of the three folding
chairs. Between sips, I pressed the can against my shin.

Monica put a hand on my shoulder, and I looked up. "How is it feeling?"
she said.

"This beer makes it better."

We left the parking lot to walk the loopy, up-and-down track along the rim
of the crater. I dropped to the ground and propped my leg on my pack for a
rest each time the kids darted out a small finger, shoulder, or spur
overlooking the lake. We came to another long parking lot where the trail
bent off to the right. "It's up this way past this roundabout."

"But the trail runs this way," Monica said. "Why are you going that way?"

"We should at least look at the lobby of this old hotel." I winked at June.
"Shouldn't we? It's right here after all. It looks like it was built around the
same time as Timberline Lodge to me. Probably one of those New Deal
projects."

Inside the lobby, I invited Monica to follow me to the heavy, wooden front
desk. "I just want to see if they have any pamphlets on the history of the
place."

"What are you up to?" she said.

I tapped the top of the desk and said, "Pardon me, good sir. Do you have any reservation under the name Monica Strawbridge?"

Monica slapped my hand.

"Welcome, Mrs. Strawbridge," the clerk said. "We are happy to see that you've made it." He smiled. "We see a lot of thru-hikers, but not many families."

"Vince, what's going on?"

"My mom called in reservations for us for the night. What do you think?"

She spun around and looked up at the large timber rafters and she smiled. "I think I love your mom. How long have you known about this?"

"About a week or so. Nathan is driving up for dinner too.

"All the way from Portland?"

"No, they were in the area for the weekend. But they will be here soon, so we should get checked in and cleaned up."

I was still in the shower when I heard Aiden burst into the room to announce Nathan's arrival to Monica. "I'll go down and meet them, Monica," I called. "Just come when you are ready, and we can all walk over to the cafe together."

Nathan greeted me on the wide front steps of the hotel with a bear hug. He stepped back and held out a plastic grocery store bag. "I hope this helps. I know shin splints aren't any fun."

I put a hand on his shoulder and said, "You have no idea how grateful I am." His daughter stepped up behind him and touched his elbow. I leaned around him to say hello. She leaned away. "Hey there, Gray, I'm sorry we are so stinky."

Gray stepped behind Jodi, then peeked out from under her arm.

"You don't smell that bad." Jodi laughed.

"I'm glad you didn't have to smell us before we got showered."

The kids linked arms with their cousins and skipped side by side all the way to the cafe. For me, our time there was a blur of clinking cups, and stuffed bellies with a satisfied smile every time I reached down to touch the front of my shin. Nathan noticed my repetitive movement and said, "Does it feel any different?"

"I don't even know how to describe it. I bet the pain has dropped at least 80%. The reason I keep reaching for it is 'cause I can't believe that it's real."

That night, when Monica made her way again to the shower, I walked into the hall to check on the kids. I opened the door to Aiden and June's room to find Aiden sprawled across the big bed. "Dad," she said, without taking her gaze from the ceiling above her. "We have the best grandmommy in the world."

"There are a lot of best people around here. Nathan is pretty much the best too," I said and bent to touch the outside of my new calf sleeve.

"I don't know why I keep forgetting about your leg," she said. "I hope Uncle Benny's idea works for you."

833.3.2

In the morning, Monica backed into the room carrying a half-full laundry basket. "I split up the loads to try and get everything clean," she said. "Would you mind going down and grabbing the other load in a few minutes?"

"You're joking right?" I said.

"No. I could use the help."

"Oh yeah, no problem." I pointed to my shin.

Monica stuck out her tongue and turned to answer the knock at the door. Aiden leaned inside. "Mom, I can help with the laundry and get ice for Dad."

"You have some good ears," I said. "Thanks for doing that, Aiden."

Aiden smiled. "Where is the laundry room, Mom?"

"Why do you always have the kids do everything for you when I ask you to do something?"

"It's okay, Mom. I don't mind." Aiden said and backed out the door.

I pointed again at my shin. "How about just this once I'd like to be the one who isn't doing all the stuff. Honestly, Monica, sometimes I feel like I'm a single dad out here parenting my four kids, and that you're just some other solo thru-hiker who happens to be along. I know your foot hurts, but you aren't the only one hurting. Every time one of them falls apart, I have to deal with it. When there is a fight, I'm the one that has to sort it out. Whichever one is having a bad night, I sleep beside them. And you. You get to fall apart all the time. You get to say, 'I can't deal with this right now,' and go off and do whatever you have to do to recover. You get to take your time. When do I get any time? When do I get a chance to fall apart? When do I get to say, 'Take care of me,' huh?"

"Where is all this coming from?"

I lay back on the bed to watch the fan spin and let the words pass my lips in less than a whisper, "We don't have time for this. Would it be too much trouble for you to give me the slightest bit of acknowledgment for all that I do?"

Monica glared at me from across the room, with her hands on her hips.

We've always laughed about what we call the "bait and switch". When she married me, she said she'd thought of me as "Mr. Sensitive Ponytail Poetry Man." I always counter with what had been my expectation: "You were no laid-back, take everything in stride, flowy-skirt hippie girl, like you made me think you were." We were both deceived.

"Monica?"

She tilted her head.

"You know, the other day, when we were talking about how, if one of the kids is losing it, we just have to make them go on without the satisfaction of a full explanation. Like that day in the mosquitoes with Georgie, I caught myself trying to reason with her to help her understand that we needed to move, and she kept arguing with me and demanding to know why. I think, at some point, the thing that needs doing is more important than understanding the why."

Monica stared at me.

"Sometimes," I said, "'because I said so' is the best thing a parent can say."

"What does that have to do with this?"

"We are about to walk out of here and get back on-trail, and it is going to require everything from us. It will demand our cooperation. So, whatever we have going on here…" I slid to the edge of the bed and sat up before making a wide circle with my hands as if to envelop the room. "Not that it isn't important, but wherever we find ourselves in this whatever-it-is … maybe we'll work through it today, and maybe we won't. But it doesn't change the fact that we have to do the thing that's in front of us."

"What is it that you think is going on here?" She imitated the same circular motion that I had made.

I put my hands on my knees and spoke in a measured voice. "I think mostly what I'm asking is that you would consider that there's an imbalance of service to each other in certain ways, and I'm not even saying that it's something that has to change. I just want you to say thank you every once in a while."

"For what?"

"For carving out a wide space for you to fall apart whenever you need to."

"You said, 'above all.' What else you got in there that you're stewing on?"

"Maybe let's tackle one thing at a time."

"No, go on, let's hear it."

"Well, it's not something we haven't talked about before, but I think you undermine me when I tell the kids to do something. As though it's not within my rights as a dad to delegate tasks. It seems like whenever I do, you say, 'What are you doing?' or 'Why can't you do it?'"

"You don't think you pawn too much off on them?"

"No, I don't, but let's say I did have it a bit out of balance, I would still say I have the right to delegate tasks to them."

"It doesn't matter what I say. You're not listening to me, anyway."

"Oh, I'm listening, but I'm starting to think that I'll only get credit for listening if I do what you say."

She bit her tongue for a moment and bent to pick up a red shirt from the chair. With the shirt dangling from one hand, she pointed at me. "You seriously don't think I serve this family in ways that no one else does? Do you have any idea what I am going through to make this work? You think I walk separately from you guys because I want to frolic through the forest on my own? Are you seriously that blind? Do you even know that the pain in my foot is so bad that I cry for an hour every morning while it warms up? And you think I don't do anything? Who boils water every day for lunch? Oh yeah, that's right, you just lie down and sleep, so you wouldn't know. Would you?"

"My gosh, Monica, that is not what I am saying. I'm just saying let's be patient with these disagreements and work on this stuff as we go."

She dropped the shirt on the bed and turned toward the door.

"Monica, I swear, I didn't know you were crying every day for an hour." I couldn't be sure she heard the last thing I said. She had already shut the door behind her.

We stretched our stay to the last minute of a late checkout before convening downstairs on the front steps. I handed one of two medium sized watermelons to Aiden.

"What am I supposed to do with this?"

I nodded past the parking lot to a picnic table. "We can cut these up over there as soon as Mom joins us," I winked at her. "We wouldn't want them to go to waste."

"How are we supposed to cut them up?"

"I'll ask at the front desk. We could probably even make a plastic knife work if we have to."

A while later, with a belly full of watermelon, I slouched forward to rest my head on my arms. Monica put her hand on my shoulder and nodded toward the pile of watermelon rinds. "What are we going to do with all these?"

I pulled two plastic grocery bags from my pocket and began to sweep the rinds into it.

"Let me get those," she said. "You can rest." She nodded toward my shin. "Do you think you'll be okay to walk?"

"These calf sleeves seem to be helping. I guess it could be the KT tape." I patted the bench beside me, and she sat down with her legs facing away from the table. "I'm sorry about the way I talked to you last night. My shin has been killing me, but I think it's more than that. I think it's that I've been anxious that the trip might have to end because of me. That was messing with me."

"You think you're going to be able to make it?"

I shrugged my shoulders, "We'll see."

She leaned back against the table and turned her face toward the sun. "I don't agree with you all the way on that 'because I said so' stuff. Why do you think that is better?"

I turned my face toward her. "There have been a few times out here when I've thought that if they didn't do what I asked of them, right when I asked it of them, we could have ended up in a bad situation. What if we got caught in a storm, and they wouldn't go. Being out here on-trail is the first time in our lives we've lived so exposed to the elements. It's not even just in the dramatic scenarios, either. What if one of them refused to do the daily miles we need to do? We could end up stranded without any food. I don't know, but what do you not like about it?"

"It sounds like you're being a bully when you say it."

"I sound like a bully?"

"Not necessarily you," she said. "It just sounds like a thing a bully would say."

"Do you think a parent has the right to expect their kids to obey?"

"Yes, but 'because I said so' is what a parent says when they are exasperated, so it has a distancing element to it that I don't like. Plus, I think it's best if they know why you are asking to do something."

"Oh yeah. That's great. It's important for them to know why I'm saying, 'because I said so.'"

"You know that isn't what I am saying." She shook her head.

"Yeah, but what if it weren't just out of exasperation? What if it wasn't distancing? What if they knew it was for their own good? Ultimately, when our parenting job is done, I want them to be obedient to God, even when what he asks of them runs against their impulse or inclination. I think if I said something like, 'God's law is good, and sometimes it won't make any sense to follow it. I want to help you develop the muscles that will prepare you to obey him without question or hesitation, as if by instinct, even if obeying him is going to cost you. God gave me to you as your parent, so I have authority over you. Obeying me is good training for obeying him.' Every time I say, 'because I said so', and they obey, they're strengthening muscles that will prepare them to obey God throughout their whole lifetime."

"But what if the thing you're telling them to do is the wrong thing?"

"Well, that's even better, because the less it makes sense, the harder it is to obey ... as long as the thing isn't immoral. I'll give them that caveat." I reached out for the last slice of watermelon. "I guess if it has a high chance of maiming or killing someone, that'd be a reasonable excuse, too."

She shrugged.

"Listen, the whole reason I thought of it was because you and I were, or are, in the middle of a fight, but the thing that we have to do today is walk. The walk forward is the obedient act even though what we'd like to do is stop and make sure that we find our way to a perfect resolution. I guess, I mean it's okay for us to do the task in front of us, and be patient to work out the rest of it in its time.

860.5

"You all want to just go on ahead?" I said. "I can just get there when I get there."

Henry hopped up and put on his pack. "Come on, Aiden."

I waved my hand and lay back on my pack. "Go on if you want, guys."

"Are you sure you are okay if we all go?" Monica said.

"I'm staying with you, Daddo," June said.

"Oh, kid. That's sweet of you. You don't have to."

"But I want to, Daddo." We set out a few minutes behind them and walked under a high canopy of pines over gentle ups and downs. "Good it's been easy today, Dad. I feel like we needed an easy day."

"The trail is soft too with all these pine needles. I hope that's not the only reason my leg doesn't hurt as much."

"I don't think so. It was already easier for a few days even before we made it to Crater Lake."

"Other than the long water carries, I'd say I agree."

"Dad, I think I heard them. Don't you think these miles went by kind of fast?"

We stepped off-trail beside our three tents, and Monica walked toward me. "You made it," she said and looked toward the sky. "It looked like rain, so I had them set up the tents."

"Did anyone check how far to water in the morning?"

"Three miles," Aiden said. "I have plenty."

"I may get some before I go to bed. Have any of you been down to the water?"

Henry tossed me his dirty bottle.

"Vince, don't you think we should hang our food bags?" Monica said. "Have you seen all the fresh bear scat the last couple miles?"

"I don't think so, but if you want to, Henry can do it." I tossed my food bag at Henry's feet.

"You aren't eating tonight?"

"I ate while I walked."

I crossed the trail toward the spur to the water and sat down beside it for a few minutes. The spring was a small, clear pool that appeared beneath the roots of a tree. After I filled the bottles, I felt my leg. Beyond a little dull pressure, there was no pain. I sat there a few minutes more before heading back.

When I made it back to the trail, I saw a man slide from the door of his dyneema Zpacks Duplex tent and drag his kevlar food bag behind him. He swung it up forward and then back to catch it under his arm. He turned back to the tent. "Get the lead out," he said. "Hell." He turned back to me, rolled his eyes, and mouthed, "Women."

I stepped past him and walked to our tents. When I reached Monica, I whispered, "Do we know them?"

She shook her head. "They set up right after you left."

All of a sudden, the man was right behind me. "You don't mind, right?" He nodded to a nearby log and sat down on it. "You're southbound. Yeah, you're pretty much screwed. Just ask her." He nodded back toward his tent. "I ran into this one a hundred miles down-trail and convinced her to pretty much give up her southbound. At first, I tried to get her to drop down to Lone Pine and walk north, but she was too scared of the Sierra. Isn't that right? Scared to walk alone?"

The lady pulled back the tent flap and nodded.

"You aren't going to beat the snow at this rate. I mean, you'd have to make twenty miles a day on average. On average. You can't do that with these kids. Hell, I didn't go faster than nineteen miles a day, and that's after I got my trail legs. That's after I was walking better than thirty miles a day. I did a forty-one-mile day in NorCal. Yeah, you don't have a chance unless you flip down. You know that movie *Wild* right? She didn't finish the trail. She skipped the Sierra. There is no shame in quitting, man. You already did more than most."

"How far is it that you think we walk in a day?"

"Not more than twenty. I mean, how old is that kid?" He pointed toward Georgie.

June stepped beside me and slipped her hand inside my elbow. "She's eleven," she said.

"Yeah, ain't no way."

June squeezed my elbow. "We did a 30.1-mile day one time."

"One thirty-mile day isn't going to do it." He shook his head.

The lady called from the tent, "Let's let them get to bed."

"I'm just trying to help the man. Can't you see that?"

"Yes, I can see that."

I didn't sleep well. In the morning, as I walked past their tent before dawn broke, I said, "Have a good rest of your hike, you jackass."

"Dad?" Georgie said. "Watch your mouth."

"You weren't supposed to hear me."

"Did you mean that?"

"Mean what?"

"Have a good hike?"

"Whether I meant it or not, I don't see their hike being a whole lot of fun. Do you?"

"But you called him that word."

"He is one."

"But you tell us we can't say that word."

"Sometimes jackass is the only right word."

891

Georgie popped out from behind a fir tree, slid down the embankment to the trail, and placed her hand over her heart. "Oh my, Dad! That was so scary." She waved her hands wildly and pointed back up the hill. "I was back there with the shovel, and I kept kind of thinking I was hearing something behind me, but I decided I was just imagining things. When I stood up to bury everything, there was this deer, and it was only like ..." she held her arms out as wide as she could. "This far away from me!"

"What was it doing, do you think? Watching you poop?"

"I don't know, but it scared me half to death."

I rubbed her head and said, "You missed Green. He walked past while you were gone."

"Was Peach with him?" she said. "Where are they from, anyway?"

"I don't know, but they were friends in college. You know Peach just became a fireman. I like them a lot."

"Me too. What was it you were saying about them when you were talking to mom?"

"Oh." I laughed. "I just said they have the best bromance story ever, because they are so committed to doing this whole thing together even with all the times that Green has had to stop."

The rest of the girls walked up together, and Aiden asked Georgie for a turn with the shovel. When Georgie tossed it to her, Aiden said, "Can you all wait for me? I don't feel like walking alone in the back."

"Did Green already pass you, Dad," June said. "I like Peach and Green. They're nice. But, why do we still call him Peach when everyone else calls him DMV?" She paused and tapped her finger to her temple. "What is a DMV, anyway?"

"It stands for Department of Motor Vehicles. It's the place you go to register a car, or renew a license, that kind of thing. But it's mostly known for being inefficient." I leaned in as though I were sharing a secret. "It's run by the government, so what can you expect?"

"Why do they call Peach that, then?"

"Because he is always waiting in town for Green to catch up. Remember when we met him in Washington at the Dinsmores? Maybe you didn't meet him. He was sitting in the lawn chair over by the laundry room with his foot propped up. That time, it was blisters that were the problem too. Another time, it was a knee injury. They named him for his blister problems though, Green is short for gangrene. Apparently, his blisters were pretty nasty. I only saw them for a second." I shuddered to shake off the visual. "Your mom isn't bothered by that stuff."

"DMV is a lot faster than Green," she said. "I was thinking it seemed weird that Green passed us first this morning. It's usually Peach that passes us first."

"Green said he was trying to catch up to Bear Hair," I said. "I told him she was trying to make it to Ashland for breakfast tomorrow. At least, that's what she said last night."

Georgie looked up at me and shook her head. "Bear Hair wasn't camped with us last night."

"You were asleep when she came in, and she left before light. I bet she passed Peach and Green before they even woke up."

"Aren't we still fifty miles away from Ashland?" June said. "How could Bear Hair even make it there by breakfast?"

After declaring our target for lunch, we walked out at our own separate paces, but came together again before we arrived. When we got there, we found Green sitting with his back to a log and his legs splayed out in front of him.

Not far from his feet, there was a rectangular concrete trough with a plastic pipe secured to its lip. I reached my hand under the trickle and looked into the pool. "Clear and cool," I said. "That's nice." I looked toward Green. "Have you been here long?"

"I just finished eating," he said. "Did you guys want any candy? My mom sent some to me back at Crater Lake, so I didn't want to leave it behind. It's too much, I'm not going to eat it all."

"What have you got?" Henry said.

"I have lots of Skittles, and a few other things." He unclipped his pack and reached inside.

"I'll take the Skittles."

"Henry, don't be obnoxious." Aiden shook her head. "Green, if you have extra Skittles, I'd be happy to take some."

"I have enough Skittles for everyone."

"Is Peach ahead?" I said. "Normally, we see him first in the mornings."

"No, he isn't, because …" He paused. "I'm going to let him tell you when you see him."

Green had gone by the time Peach arrived. "Hey guys. You haven't seen Green, have you?"

"We've seen him," I said. "And, he says you have a story to tell us."

"Hah," he laughed. "You don't mind if I eat quick with you?"

"Sure," Monica said.

"Last night, Green and I stealthed just off-trail in some trees, around ..." He sat down. "You know where we were, because you passed us right after we set up. I usually bring my pack inside my tent, but it was nasty and sweaty after yesterday. I leaned it against a tree about ten feet away from my tent." He paused. "It was so hot yesterday, wasn't it? My shirt was so nasty I hung it on a branch too."

The kids nodded.

"You know it's bad when you offend yourself with your smell," Monica said.

"So, I wake up, a little disoriented, to some sound in the leaves. It took me a minute to figure out where I was. The first thing I thought was that it was a bear, because it was a big sound. Then I saw that the big sound was my backpack being dragged through the trees by two deer. I grabbed my flashlight and jumped out without anything on. I mean nothing." He looked at Monica. "In my defense, it was hot last night. Sorry, Mom." He held up his hand as if ready to throw something, "I picked up a rock and took off after the deer, but they didn't drop my pack for at least fifty yards."

"You were barefoot?" I said.

"Bare everything. Except for the headlamp. Finally, the deer dropped my pack, so I went to pick it up when I heard Green shout at me. It turns out that while those two deer were distracting me, a third deer grabbed my shirt from the tree. Now, I've got to prioritize. I've got an active situation with the shirt, but clearly the pack is more important. I decided to save the pack and take it back up and throw it in my tent. Meanwhile, the deer that has my shirt has made its way through the trees, so I take off after him."

"Green?"

"Green was no help at all. He was just laughing in his tent. I took off after the deer, and eventually he dropped it, but"—he flipped his pack over and pointed—"you can see what he did to my shirt." He pinched it with a finger and thumb and lifted it. As the tattered bits of fabric spread, streams of deer mucus remained attached to the various parts.

"Ugh," Monica said. "That's disgusting."

"I know, but it's my favorite hiking shirt. What can I do?"

"Are you going to try to wear it again?"

"If I can repair it in Ashland."

"Well, you'll probably have time," I said. "No telling what Green will be laid up with there."

907.3

Georgie and I walked in the back on the top of the rolling ridge line. We caught glimpses of the others when we topped the occasional knoll to roll through another high saddle. She invited me down each short spur trail to have a look out at each viewpoint. "I wish I had a camera, Dad. I don't know why Oregon gets such a bad rap."

"You like Oregon?"

"Well, the walking is easier, but it's still pretty. I know they say it's the Green Tunnel, because you have to walk so much in the trees, but I like the shade. The shade is nice especially now with the days being so hot. I don't know, maybe it's because Washington is so pretty, so they are just being hard on it."

"That could be."

"Do you like Oregon?"

"Sure. I have nothing against Oregon."

"I like it too, now that we are almost done. It feels like it went really fast."

"It's shorter, for one thing."

"Yeah, but it isn't just that."

"No?"

"No, it's because it's not as hard to walk all day anymore. Remember how hard it was in Washington, and my feet hurt all the time? And I would have a cry-thirty like three times a day. It's been three days since I've even had one. Actually, I can't even remember the last time I did."

"I can."

"That one doesn't count. That was because Henry was being a jerk." She stopped and pointed. "Look, Dad, a tent. We should be quiet."

In a small shady alcove between towering firs, a tent stood without its rainfly. I saw no movement inside, and we walked past in silence.

"Dad, don't you think this would be a hard trail to walk by yourself?"

"I think it would be a very different experience, but there are many people who do it."

"I think it would be scary. Especially at night."

"Okay. Here is one for you. If you could walk it by yourself, or just you and Henry, what would you do?"

"That's a tough one." She was quiet for a while. "I'd walk with Henry."

"Even though you think he's a jerk?"

"He isn't always a jerk. Would you want to walk it by yourself?"

"Maybe someday. If I could. I do wonder if it would be easier or harder to be out here alone. I spend so much time thinking about you guys, and what you need, if you are hurting, your food, your water … breaking up your fights. It's almost a nice distraction for me, so I don't ever get lost in my own head too much. I don't ever find myself in the middle of some existential crisis of meaning. I've thought being with you guys might make it even easier for me to finish because I have more of a defined job."

"I wouldn't want to do it alone."

"You are eleven."

"Do you think Bear Hair is okay?"

"Why do you ask?"

"That was her tent back there, and it's the middle of the day."

"She's probably just taking a nap. She said she wanted to make it all the way to Ashland for breakfast tomorrow morning."

"I don't think she's going to make it."

"It's almost noon now, and she still has over thirty-six miles to go."

The others were waiting at the junction to water. "I love how Gentleman leaves these arrows to guide the people behind them," Aiden said.

"You don't know if those are Gentleman's arrows," I said.

"He's the one that makes arrows out of sticks. I saw him doing it in Washington."

"You think he's the only one that leaves arrows?"

"Well, I'm pretty sure these are his."

"Did you guys already go down for water?" I said.

"No, we were waiting on you," Monica said. "Do we want to eat lunch here?"

"It's a long carry to the next water. I'd rather grab extra here and go a few miles further. Let's carry our packs down to the water, and then we can fill up whatever we need."

Henry dropped his pack to the ground and opened it up.

"What are you doing, Henry?"

"I'm going to leave my pack here. I'll take my food and my water bottles down. Why would I carry more weight than I have to?"

"That's a good idea," I said.

"What about animals?" Monica said.

"If we have our food, I don't think a bear is going to mess with it. As long as Georgie clears her food wrappers out of her junk drawer, we should be okay."

"What about deer?"

"I think Peach ran into a very special deer. I'm willing to risk it."

"Me too." Aiden reached into her pack and began tossing its contents on the ground beside her.

Monica looked at me and shook her head. "I give up. None of you people care about keeping anything clean."

"Oh, Mom," Aiden said. "What's the point anymore? Everything I have is so dirty. It's not like it could get any worse."

On the way toward the spring, I walked behind Monica. She stopped in front of me. "Did you talk to Bear Hair?"

"We didn't see any movement in her tent when we passed."

"She was still awake when we went by. I'm worried about her."

"What about?"

"She's walking forty miles one day, and fifteen the next, and I think her feet are a lot worse than she is saying. She says she wants to make it for breakfast in the morning in Ashland. That's too far to go on bad feet and no sleep."

"She was probably sleeping when Georgie and I were there."

"Still."

"If we see her again, you should talk to her. Maybe we could invite her to slow down and walk with us for a while."

"I might," Monica said. "I like her."

Near dusk, the trail turned to follow an overgrown forest road. We came to a small clearing, an old turnout, with a cluster of squat pines. We spread our groundsheets up against them ten feet from the trail and finished our food by flashlight.

"Tomorrow is Ashland, guys," I said. "Monica, did you find us a play?"

"It looks like the only one at the free festival is *Othello*."

"That's a bit morbid, but okay."

The stars grew brighter against the darkening sky.

"It's a good night for shooting stars," Aiden said, "don't you think, Junie?"

"I can never sleep the night before town," June said.

"You know I used to come to Ashland," I said, "when I worked at that camp in Northern California. They had some fun hippie shops all full of beads and stuff. Once, when I was left behind to work at the camp while the rest of the staff had a day off in Ashland, I asked another staff person to buy me some deodorant. She came back with a rock that you were supposed to just wet and rub on your armpit."

"Did it work?" Monica said.

"I think so."

"I bet it didn't. You probably just couldn't smell yourself. They were just too polite to complain."

A dim light lit the trail not far from us, and we heard footsteps, and one of us said, "Hello."

Bear Hair jumped and held a hand to her chest. "Oh, you scared me. I was looking at my phone to see how much further I have to go."

"It's 18.3 miles from here," June said.

"Are you going tonight?" Monica said.

"Yes, I want to have breakfast at Callahan's, so I will go the rest of the way through the night."

"Are you sure? You can stay here with us."

"I'm okay. I can make it."

"Do you have a flashlight?" I said.

"No, I'm fine. My phone has a light. The battery is not much more before dying, but I'll be fine."

"Bear Hair," Monica said. "You're crazy. You can't do this without a light. There's no moon tonight."

"It comes up around ten. I think I can make it 'til then."

I stood up and walked to my backpack. "Here, Bear Hair," I said. "Wait a second. I'll find my flashlight."

"I don't want to take that, you might need it."

"I can get it back from you in Ashland. We aren't going to be walking in the dark until after then. Besides, we have six flashlights between us."

"Okay, thank you. If you give it to me, I'll give it back to you in Ashland."

After Bear Hair left, Georgie rolled toward me and whispered in my ear, "Dad, was she going to walk all night without a flashlight?"

935.5

The woman leaned toward me across the coffee table in the crowded coffee shop in Ashland, Oregon. "You really do need to get masks on those kids," she said.

"Masks?" I shifted in my seat and leaned toward the woman in order to hear her better over the noise.

"This smoke is bad." She shot a glance backward toward her husband. "Especially for young children."

"Is it coming from the California fires? Everyone is talking about fires down the trail."

"No, this smoke is blowing in from Wyoming, but we could start to get smoke from the south too. It's bad this summer."

"Is this normal?"

"No, this summer's the worst we've had in a while."

Her husband cleared his throat and nodded toward the window. "If you read the latest tests for air quality here in Ashland, it's scary." He pulled his phone from his pocket and began typing.

"One hundred and sixty was it, on the AQI?" She looked at him.

"This morning was one hundred and eighty," he said. "That's way too high to be going out there." He scooted toward the front of his bench and held his phone out for me to see.

"AQI?"

"Air Quality Index," he said.

"I don't know what those numbers mean."

"One hundred and fifty is considered unhealthy, and people are discouraged from any strenuous activity." She tapped her husband's wrist as if to encourage him to put his phone down. "And that's down here in Ashland. It's worse in the mountains, I'm sure. You need a mask that will filter anything below 0.4 microns."

"I'm sorry, I don't know what those numbers mean either."

"It means you will need an N95 mask."

"Where would I get one?"

"There's an ACE Hardware just over on A street."

"Is it walking distance from here?"

"For you guys, for sure." She looked back at her husband. "But we'd be happy to give you a ride, once we are all finished here."

Monica waved at me from a nearby table where she sat with SoGood and Bear Hair and mouthed, "Do you want something to drink?"

"Excuse me," I said, and stood up to shuffle around the corner of the small couch and stepped high over the pile of backpacks. "I'll be back, kids. Don't get any ideas about running away with these nice people. You are still hiking with us."

"I'd steal any or all of them," the woman said. "You kids are delightful."

I stood beside Monica and placed a hand on her shoulder. "Can I get either of you anything?" Monica said to the table.

"I'm good," SoGood said, "thank you."

Bear Hair lifted her hand. "If you are going up there, would you ask for some water?"

I sat down. "How are you two feeling about the fires?"

"Oh, before I forget. Let me get your flashlight back to you." Bear Hair tapped her hands on the outside of her pockets and then looked toward her backpack. "Now, what fires are these?"

"Two fires in California affect us," SoGood said, "but they are a long way away. One has a trail closure now in Northern California south of Etna, and another one down in the Northern part of the Sierra is threatening to shut down some of the trail."

"How do you know all of these things?"

"Instagram," SoGood said. "I am following a lot of PCT Hikers."

"Show me some of their accounts," Bear Hair said.

"I just follow SoGood," I said. "She is the path to all knowledge." I smiled at SoGood. "We rely on you more than you know." I looked toward the couches. "I need to go save these people from my kids. They are very concerned about our kids walking through the smoke. But they said they would run me over to the hardware store after this. Do either of you need me to grab you a mask?"

"I have one," SoGood said.

"I would like to have one," Bear Hair said. "Would you mind getting me one?"

At the Ace Hardware store, I found my way to the shelf where the N95 masks should have been, but it was empty. The assistant manager found us some in the back. When I snapped my seatbelt on again, I said, "Thank you for doing this."

A roadside kiosk caught my attention. "When I used to come here a long time ago, there was an outdoor market that sold all sorts of cool stuff."

The man pointed behind us through the rear window. "That must be over the bridge, but Ashland has changed a lot in the last twenty years." He pointed out the side windows. "All of these shops are new. The whole city is pretty well gentrified now-a-days." He shook his head. "Good for home values, I guess."

A few minutes later, he turned into the parking lot of the post office. I pointed him toward the sidewalk where Monica sat with Bear Hair and the kids. We were waving our goodbyes when she rolled down the passenger window. "You are walking right into those fires."

I thanked her again.

She waved one last time. "Goodbye, kids. Be safe."

Monica held up a shoe box toward me and shook it.

"Yes! My new shoes," I said. When I slipped them on, I shifted back and forth testing the feel.

"Do you like them?" Monica said.

"I don't know, yet. Anything's better than that last pair." I lifted my toes. "I expected more room in the toe box. How do you like your new ones?"

"They are the same as my last pair, so I'm sure they will be fine. I think it helps me to get a new pair every four hundred miles or so."

"Not thirteen hundred miles?" I laughed. "Like that guy at Timberline?"

"Oh, Bear Hair, did you see that guy?" Monica tapped Bear Hair on the knee. "His shoes were like pancakes. I think they are the worst I've seen."

"No, but there was a guy up at Callahan's that had nearly fourteen hundred miles on his Hokas," Bear Hair said. "They looked like they had nothing left."

"My feet hurt just thinking about it," Monica said. "How are you liking your new shoes?"

Bear Hair lifted her leg and turned her foot from side to side. "Have any of you tried the Altra Lone Peaks?"

"Vince loved his, but they don't have any in his size until September."

"I am very jealous of you right now," I said.

"Oh, Bear Hair," Monica said. "I forgot to tell you. Aiden and I went to the outdoor store to trade out some socks. The guy at the store started telling us about your feet."

"He was talking about me?"

"He said he didn't know how you were even walking still. He said he's never seen feet so torn up. Are you sure you're okay to keep walking?"

"This guy!" she said. "I think I will need to go talk with his manager."

Monica and Bear Hair moved under the deep shade of a sprawling cypress, and I stood up to help Aiden throw away all of the trash from our resupply. When I stepped outside again, I made my way to them and lay down beside Monica. She tapped me on the chest and said, "We were just talking about some of the people we've both hiked around."

"Oh, Bear Hair," I said, "I never asked you about Survivor Man. He told me you guys had hiked together for a few days up in Washington."

"A few days? Is that what he said to you?" She shook her head. "I leapfrogged with him for one afternoon, but I walked really fast to get ahead of him. That crazy guy walked until late at night to make it to where I camped. For the next two days I hiked thirty-five miles each day just to make sure he couldn't catch up. And, you know what else? I had plans to stay in Steven's Pass for a full zero, but I changed it to a quick stop, just so he wouldn't catch me. He gave me the creeps."

"I think I would have called him Pemmican," I said. "If he hadn't already named himself Survivor Man."

Bear Hair moved her hand to her mouth and laughed. "Oh yes, I am sure that he made himself sick eating that very gross food. Sassafras told me he was behind us now, so I won't have to see him again."

960.2

"What is that up there?" Henry said.

"It's a UFO," I said.

"What's a UFO?"

"It's an unidentified flying object, or a you-figure-it-out, or a do-you-really-want-to-know-what-it-is?"

"Yeah, what is it?"

It's the top of a ski lift. There is a ski resort on the backside of that mountain."

"It looks more like a spaceship."

"Okay, let's go with that."

Henry looked back toward the top of the ridge one last time before we entered the trees. "I like it better, this side of Ashland."

"Me too. It's almost like it has different trail designers. And the vegetation has definitely changed. It's greener, and there's more water. It also helped to have trail magic right away. How do you think they dragged those coolers all the way to the trail? I didn't see any roads around there."

"Well, they couldn't spell, however they did it."

"I'm not going to hold it against them. That root beer was good, and cold too. Plus, maybe they did mean 'lone distance hikers' like they wrote on the cooler, and not long distance hikers."

"Dad, let me see your phone again, I want to show Aiden."

"Show her what?"

"How stupid this trail is."

I turned with my phone. He walked for a while looking down and scrolling around on the screen. "Aiden, come look at this. Look what the trail does. It goes west all the way this way, and does this big circle to the south and goes all the way back east to the other side of California again, almost to Nevada. It's stupid." He traced a straight line out toward the horizon. "We could seriously just go that way."

"Hand me my phone back. My Garmin just beeped. I think it was Jamie texting me about the fires." I held out my hand. When Henry put my phone in my hand, I opened the app.

J: The Hirz fire is the one to watch for. It's mostly contained, and those numbers are dropping, so you should be good.

V: We are seeing more smoke, that's why I was asking. Thanks for keeping an eye on it.

J: The CalFire site is extremely informative. There is one that has just started in the Sierra, the Donnell fire, so I'll keep an eye on that too. The one in Redding won't affect you, but it was nasty.

V: We have masks, just in case, but so far it's not bad. Thanks for staying on it.

***

"What did Jamie say?" Monica said.

"Basically, the same thing as SoGood. I guess we'll just see when we get there."

"I'm getting my mask out," Aiden said. "Can you guys wait up a second?"

Henry bumped into her. "Why, Aiden?"

"You can't smell that smoke in the air?"

"I mean, why do you want us to wait? You can just catch up."

"I don't feel like catching up. It'll only be a second."

After Aiden put on her mask, I reached for Monica's sleeve and held it. She turned to me and said, "We never get to walk together. Want to walk in the back with me?"

"Sure. How are your feet?"

"Alright, the rest was good, but I think we need to go back to long lunches. They are always better after a long rest and it gives me a chance to rub them out."

"I like a long lunch. I don't know why we couldn't." I held up my fingers and pinched them almost together. "We just have to walk a little bit into the dark."

"I hate walking in the dark."

"But the Sierra."

"I thought we were still on track."

"We're one day behind where Jamie said we needed to be, but I don't think a day more or less is a big deal. The hard part is trying to figure out where to tell Dax and the guys to meet us when they come out to hike a few days with us."

"Why not just play it by ear?"

"What if they fly out here and we're in the middle of a section somewhere. I need to time it so we're in a town, or at least a road crossing somewhere."

"Isn't it a long time 'til they get here?"

"They get here on September 20th."

"What is the date today?"

"August 23rd."

"What's the problem then?"

"Honestly, the problem is your feet."

"My feet?"

"It doesn't seem like they are getting better. The days are getting shorter. We are trying to make ourselves take more rest days. It's hard to calculate where we will be because I can't tell how many miles you can make it in a day. Plus, you guys won't walk at night."

"We walk every night," she said.

"Forty-five minutes after dark doesn't add much in the way of miles. I don't mean it as a complaint. It just makes it hard to figure out. That's all. One day we walk twenty-eight miles and the next we walk twenty-two."

"I'm doing all I can."

"I'm not saying you aren't. I'm worrying about it before I need to, I'm sure. We can worry about it once we get past Etna."

We walked for a while in silence. The gold grass reflected the afternoon light. Rustles of shadow and sound. The path wound upward across the long field toward a pass. I pointed toward it. "Let's start looking for a place to camp, as soon as we make it over the top."

Monica looked toward it and tripped on a rock. She threw her foot out to catch herself.

"Nice move," I laughed. "Did you not see that rock?"

"No. How could I see it? I was looking up there toward the pass?

"You don't look where you step?"

"You look at every step?"

"Every single one." I looked down at my feet in the fading light. "It's not direct maybe, but I always know exactly where my foot is going to land. I usually know the next few steps in advance. You are saying you don't look at all?"

"Not when I'm looking around."

I shook my head and watched her feet for a while.

She stopped at the first switchback of the climb. "You are telling me, every step, you know where you are going to put your foot?"

"Every single one. This might explain why you trip all the time."

"You think everyone does that? How do you even look at anything we are walking through, if you are looking down at the trail the whole time?"

"I can't wait to tell Henry about this. We have laughed about your foot placement. I had no idea it was so haphazard."

"Well, I don't know what to tell you."

I bent over to pull a pebble from my shoe, but I couldn't isolate it with my finger. "I'll catch up to you," I said and sat to slip off my shoe. Monica stopped and turned her head toward the valley. She stood that way for a long time. With my shoe in my hand, I watched her walk forward again. She stopped in the path and stood in the swaying grass with her head up-tilted toward the mountainside. In every way, she fit into the scene. When she walked again after a backward glance toward me, I smiled. I tapped the heel of my shoe, drained the sand and debris to the ground, and slipped it back on.

970.1

"Gross, Henry, get up from there." Monica said. "What are you doing?"

"Mom, look at all these Skittles someone dropped. It's like trail magic."

Georgie wiped a Skittle on her shirt and held it up for us to see, then popped it into her mouth. "Trail magic already, and we are only two steps into California."

"That's gross, you guys have no idea what you are eating."

"It's Skittles, Mom," Henry said. "Relax."

"You have no idea what is on those Skittles."

"We're wiping them off." He popped another one into his mouth.

I tapped Henry with my trekking pole and nodded down the trail toward two approaching hikers. "Hop up, bud. Let them pass."

"No, no. Don't get up," one of them said. "We're taking a break here too. Finally finished our first state."

"At least you're over halfway," I said. "We may have only one state, but we're a long way from halfway."

Georgie tugged on my sleeve and whispered in my ear. "Mom wants to know if they could take our picture."

One of them smiled and reached out his hand. "Where do you want to stand?"

Monica pointed toward the tree. "Let's use this one."

After he took our picture and handed my phone back to me, we set off down the trail. I opened my map. "Guys, we get to switch maps for the second time."

The map for Northern California took a long time to load. I checked it again and bumped into Georgie. "Dad, watch where you're going," she said.

"Watch where you're stopping."

"I was waiting to find out what you saw on the map."

I looked down again. "There's a lot more water here than in Oregon. That will be good."

Georgie pointed my attention behind us. I turned back to see that Monica was pushing herself up from the trail.

"Dad, we aren't even five minutes into California, and Mom already fell."

Monica brushed her hands off and walked toward us. "I'm such an idiot. Go on, you guys. Please, just go."

"Hey everybody," I said. "When you come to a cabin just off trail, wait there, and we'll have lunch."

"How far ahead is it?" Aiden said.

"You won't miss it. Just keep your eyes open."

When I leaned my chair back on the front porch of the Donomore cabin forty-five minutes later, the sun fell warm on my face. Aiden sat beside me on its wide planks to read out the history of the place. Her words flitted in and out and around me like so many buzzing flies, never landing, almost musical, and entirely unimportant. The story was something about some ranchers. I peeled my compression sleeve down to let my leg breathe.

"California, Aiden."

"Yep, Dad. California."

"Two thirds of the states are done and dusted. Feels pretty good."

"It feels like we should be more than halfway, but we aren't."

"How does that make you feel?"

She shrugged her shoulders.

"As in, do you feel like we can do this, or as in, do you feel like giving up?"

"I know we can do it. It's just that now I know how hard it can be, so in a way, that makes it harder."

I looked toward the trees. Monica sat cross-legged on a groundsheet just this side of the shade with Georgie lying back in her lap. She held a clump of Georgie's hair in one hand and brushed it out with the other.

"Other than the Sierra," I said, "I think all the hard stuff is behind us."

981.3

Georgie pressed her fingers into the outer rim of the footprint and moved closer and blew softly into the dust. She turned to look up at Henry. "You don't know that they are hers."

"You think there is more than one person wearing sandals out here?" Henry said. "Look at the zigzags in the middle of the print. Those couldn't be anyone but Trouble's footprints."

"It's not even for sure that they are sandals." Georgie shook her head.

"You two need to quit fighting," I said. "Have you seen Rogue's footprints?"

"Dad," Georgie said. "We don't even know if Rogue and Trouble are walking together, and we've never even met him."

Henry rolled his eyes, "I know they are hiking together, because in that last trail log, they wrote their names 'Trouble' and 'Rogue.' And, anyway, after that rain the other day they were the only footprints ahead of us, so I know we are getting closer to them."

"He doesn't know what shoes Rogue is wearing. He probably thinks he knows, though."

"He's wearing boots." Henry looked at me. "And Trouble wears sandals like these." He tapped the print with his trekking pole.

"Henry's pretty good with recognizing footprints, Georgie. I'm not sure I'd bet against him. Why don't you wait with me while June catches up? Henry, you go ahead and catch Aiden."

We walked a western exposure in the cool of the morning until we came to a pass where we crossed over to the east side where we lost our shield from the sun. At the junction to the water, we came upon Henry where he sat on his pack in the shade of a tall pine tree.

I stepped into the shade line beside him and wiped the sweat from my forehead. "You didn't go down for water?"

"I've got enough."

"We may not make it to the next water before lunch. You need to go down and fill up."

"I can make it on this." He lifted his quarter-filled dirty bottle and shook it.

"Henry, just get down there, and do what I say. You don't have enough water for lunch. We are about to walk in full exposure uphill for a couple miles, and we have no way to tell how far your mom can walk before her feet give out."

He sighed.

"Look, Dad," Georgie said and pointed her trekking pole toward a gray Gossamer Gear pack. "It's SoGood."

"That's like Henry's pack, only she's kept hers in a lot better shape."

Aiden knelt in front of a bush that she held to the side with her left arm. Between her two feet, a narrow line of water ran across the trail. I leaned around behind her. "Oh, good, they have a pipe for us."

She looked up at me. "It's pretty cool how they have it just jammed into the side of the hill and the water trickles out right from the pipe. You think that it's bad for you that it's rusted? Still, it's pretty cool, even if it is a bit slow."

"It looks cold and clear to me. I wouldn't worry about a little rust on the pipe, but you are filtering anyway." I scooched past her to where Monica and SoGood sat with their backs to the bank.

Monica made a space for me to sit down. "SoGood said there's a cafe down in Seiad Valley."

I pressed my hand to my stomach. "I could use a good meal," I said.

"You didn't let me finish. They close at two today."

"What is it from here?" I looked at my phone. "Seven miles. We could make that, maybe. For sure, if we skip lunch." I nodded at Monica's feet. "You think you could make it?"

"I feel okay now." She rolled her foot toward the inside. "We'll see."

"I'm going to try to call them if I can get reception up top," SoGood said. "If you'll adopt me, I'll tell them we have a family coming. Seven hungry thru-hikers might make it worth it to them to stay open. I'll text you on your Garmin and let you know."

"Yes, SoGood, please join the family," Monica said.

I laughed. "For sure. We will call you Aunt SoGood. Kids, we are adopting SoGood. Although, I feel like we ought to call you by your real name if you are family, and I don't think I know what it is."

"I don't think you do either. It's Katie."

"Aunt Katie it is."

At a certain elevation the trees died away and left us in the open beneath bluebird skies. We weaved our way through a chest-high prickly scrub that offered no relief from the sun. I rejected several how-far-to-the-top entreaties until the question plagued me as well. "Not much farther," I told them.

None of the boulders up top were large enough to cast shade, and all of them hot to the touch. Monica said she could go no further. We found the thickest of the frail clumps of scrub and tied the corners of our groundsheets above us like a series of tarps that served only to trap the heat.

"Did SoGood text?"

"Yes," I tossed my Garmin away. "They will be closed when we get there, because of this stop."

"I hear what you are saying."

"You do, huh?"

"I needed to stop, Vince. I'm not sure what you expect me to do. My feet are killing me."

"I'm going to see what Aiden is up to." I pointed up to the overlook and pushed myself out from under the makeshift shade.

"It's hot out there, too," she said. "I'm going to take a nap."

"Do what you like." I sat up and crawled over June,out from under the tarp, and muttered, "You are going to anyway."

"What was that?"

"Nothing."

I leaned on the rock beside Aiden where she sat on the topmost point of the ridgeline. I picked up pebbles and tossed them toward a small, disassembled rock cairn not too far away.

"It's amazing, isn't it, Dad?"

"It's hot."

"Look how far you can see from here is that where we're headed?"

I pointed toward a jagged ridgeline. "We walk downhill just below it on this side. You see the trail? Then we take that cut and drop over into Seiad Valley on the other side."

"Into that cloud?"

"That's not a cloud. It's smoke."

"Now that you say it, I smell it."

I scooped up another handful of pebbles to toss them. One of the pebbles I tossed made a "tink." I stepped over to inspect it and found an old wine bottle in pieces. I moved the largest piece and pulled the rounded bottom piece out.

"How old is that thing?"

I felt the lettering on the glass and held it up to the light. "It doesn't have a date on it."

"It's funny to think about people sitting up here a long time ago drinking from that bottle. I wonder what time of year it was."

"I doubt they were up here on as hot a day as this."

"It's still better than cold."

I sat beside her again and looked down toward the others. I shook my head and pulled out my phone. "We can't go on this way."

"What do you mean?"

I motioned down toward our lunch spot. "It's such a bad place to stop."

"So?"

"So, what are we going to do if we run into a real situation that requires us to push?"

"This isn't that."

"This is an indication of how we will do when we have to deal with that, though."

"I think when the time comes, we will be able to push. Mom's feet were hurting, and you are making too big a deal of this."

"Oh, I am, huh?" I nodded toward the nappers. "I'm gonna head down there. Are you coming?"

I tiptoed around the furthest overhanging tent fly and squatted to look underneath it. Georgie lay on the far side with her head sideways in the dirt, her hair caught in the brambles of the bush above her. I thumbed a bead of sweat from my nose and reached across June to touch Monica on the hand. She stirred.

"Are you ready?" I said.

She rubbed her eyes. "What time is it?"

"1:45. Are you ready to go?"

She nodded. "But I don't think we can go on like this."

I looked at her.

"We need to take long lunches, and not push so hard in the mornings. Every morning you are angry because we haven't started early enough. It's never early enough for you. We never get enough miles before lunch. You always want to go a little bit further. I need these lunches to recover and rub out my feet."

I did not respond.

"I know you are mad, but if you keep this up, everyone's going to want to quit, and I won't be able to keep going. You need to quit pushing."

"You think I'm pushing too hard?"

Aiden said, "You've been pretty impatient lately."

Henry nodded beside her.

June rubbed her eyes. "I'm tired, Dad."

"Well, I guess that leaves Georgie. Georgie, what do you think?"

Without moving her head, she said, "Don't try to involve me in this."

990

When the trail dropped over the jagged ridge above Seiad Valley, Georgie and I stopped to wait for the others with our masks on. I pinched mine to snug it up tighter to the bridge of my nose and reached a hand out and patted Georgie's blue hat. She brushed my hand away.

"You can't tell anything about what a person is thinking from their eyes alone," I said. "I don't care what the songs say."

"Can you tell what I'm thinking?"

"You are thinking that you are delighted to be walking out in front with your favorite dad."

"Nope, not even close. I'm thinking how cool these reddish, barkless-looking trees are."

"They're called Madrones."

"Aiden said they were Manzanitas."

"They are similar, for sure."

"Is there water between here and town? I'm almost out."

"About halfway downhill there's something."

The others rounded the corner, and Georgie and I waved them past. Monica walked in the back of the line. I reached out to her as she passed. "Can you turn around for a second?"

She turned.

"I'm sorry," I said.

"I can't tell if you're being sincere."

"It's the mask, isn't it?"

"Yes."

"I am being sincere. I've been all caught up in planning out where we will meet Dax and them, and I'm a little nervous about the Sierra Nevada."

"Well, we can't ruin our trip just to try to make their trip work out exactly as planned."

"I know. You're right. I always default to the only option being us speeding up, when we could also slow down."

"That doesn't mess us up for the Sierra?"

"We are already two days behind schedule. I doubt a day or two more would make that much of a difference."

Georgie nudged me from behind. "Can I get by?"

"We are done. Stay in the back with me, kid. I never get to walk with you anymore. You're too fast these days."

Monica took a sip from her water bottle and then handed it to me. "Will you stuff this?"

We walked for a few hundred feet without talking. "Monica, Georgie and I were talking about how you can't tell much from a person's eyes. Can you imagine if we had to wear masks everywhere?"

"I wouldn't do it," Georgie said. "I hate these things."

We dropped below the smoke cloud and out onto a road. When we stepped out beside it, I couldn't see any of the kids.

Monica stood with her hands on her hips looking both directions. "It bothers me that they wouldn't wait here for us. I don't like being separated when we get to towns."

"There they are, Mom." Georgie pointed toward a thick clump of shrubs.

Aiden stepped backward into view and cupped a hand to her mouth to call, "Blackberries!"

Without looking to her right or her left, Georgie said, "Oh yeah!" and sprinted across the street.

Twenty minutes later, I tapped Georgie on the shoulder. "Should we catch them?"

"I'm in no rush."

"I think these are just about as good as the ones near the Bridge of the Gods. What about you?"

"They taste as good, but I know they can't really be as good. These are covered in dust, and those others were clean."

"Context is important."

"What's that supposed to mean?"

"I mean it's so hot and dry. We haven't had any for so long, and these blackberries were a complete surprise. So, they benefit from being in the right place at the right time. It's like this one burger stand at the boat ramp on Lake Kissimmee. It's called Dottie's. I'd still say they have the best burgers I've ever eaten. My mouth is watering just thinking about it. But I bet it isn't even that great a burger. It's just a burger in the right place at the right time."

"Dad?" Georgie's lips tightened and she held up a finger. "I think I just ate a stink bug."

"Maybe pick a few more, so you don't have to end on a sour note, and then we'll go."

When we reached the parking lot, I pointed toward the General Store and Georgie angled off toward two crowded picnic tables. "I'll grab you something," I said.

Cold droplets ran down the side of the three bottles of Elysian that I placed on the counter. "How much are these?"

"Two dollars per bottle," the clerk said.

"Wow, how much is a six pack?"

"Nine-fifty for a six pack."

I turned and walked with the three bottles back over to the refrigerator and switched them out for a six-pack.

As I approached the picnic table Monica said, "A six pack?"

"It was cheaper. Well, almost the same price. I figure someone here might want one."

"Really?" Trouble raised her hand. "If you're passing them out. I'll take one."

"Oh my gosh, Trouble. It is you."

I passed out the beer and looked over at Henry. He smirked and nodded.

Georgie glared across the table at him. "Don't even say it, Henry."

He pointed beneath the table and mouthed, "Sandals."

SoGood and Monica talked at the far end of the table. I heard Monica say, "State of Jefferson."

"What is with that?" I said. "I saw a bunch of signs on the way in."

"It's some kind of secession movement," she said. "Not secession from the U.S., of course, but parts of Southern Oregon and Northern California want to become a separate state."

I looked at SoGood.

"It's not the first time they've tried it." SoGood turned her phone to face me. "I looked it up on the wifi. They almost brought it to a vote in the forties, but World War II killed it that time."

"That's interesting. I'll have to read more about it. How was the cafe?"

"I missed it too. Everyone did. They were closed up today for a town festival."

A local came to the table, and we talked with her for a while. As she left, she invited us to a potluck down the street.

As we walked past a few minutes later, Aiden said, "Why are we passing this up? That BBQ smells so good."

We crossed the road and passed a fenced-in front yard that housed a one-horned goat. It walked straight to June, and she stopped to feed it some grass and scratch its head through the fence. On the far side of the bridge, we passed a few more State of Jefferson signs before reaching some rocks on the side of the road that were laid out in the number "1000."

"You guys," I said. "One thousand miles. Let's take a picture. Come on, Aunt Katie, get in here with us."

1002

Good morning
Good morning
It's great to stay up late
Good morning
Good morning to you

"Dad, cut it out!" June said.

"Let's get to it, guys, we have a big day ahead. Just a quick morning hop to the top, and then it's all cruising to Etna."

"I'm sick of Pop-Tarts," Aiden said, "When we are done with this trail, I will never eat one again as long as I live. Does anyone have cinnamon that they would trade me for a strawberry? C'mon, Henry."

"You really think anyone is going to give up their cinnamon?"

"I'll give you a s'mores flavor," Georgie said. "They're disgusting."

"I hate how badly we eat out here," Monica said. "What do you eat, SoGood?"

"Calories," she said. "Calories are good. I have an extra cinnamon roll from the Seiad store, if anyone wants it."

"Henry," Monica said, "sit down, you aren't taking the food she carried out of town for herself."

"Come here, Henry." SoGood reached out of her tent for her food bag, "I already split it up for you guys. "Sorry, Monica, it's too late to say no. But, to answer your question, I think that with all the work your body is doing out here, it is going to be pretty efficient at converting whatever you eat into what it needs. When I go to town, I pack out pastries, avocados, and big bags of chips. Honestly, whatever I'm craving."

"Dad sent everything ahead," June said, "So we are stuck with the same things over and over and over again."

"Maybe you and I can do some trading, June," SoGood said. "If we end up at the same place for lunch today."

"That's some good motivation, eh, June?" I said. "It's a race to the top of the hill."

Across the creek from the campground the trail turned uphill and wound along the wash. We crossed a bridge together, and SoGood left to carry on at her own pace. We came to a note pinned down by a rock. "Warning! Rattlesnake in the area!" and "Atención serpiente cascabel venanosa en la zona."

Thirty yards later another note, with the same words under a rock for northbound traffic.

"I wonder if that was SoGood," Georgie said.

"That's not her handwriting," Henry said.

"How do you know?"

"From the logbooks."

"It's funny," June said, "whoever left that note had to walk past the snake two extra times to leave the note. That was pretty nice of them."

"I don't see any snakes though," Aiden said. "So what was the point anyway?"

I leaned over Monica's shoulder. "Do you care if Henry and I walk ahead to the last water right before the trail leaves the creek? He and Georgie are winding each other up today. It's not bad yet, but it seems like it might go that way."

Henry and I were a long way in front of the others when he saw the yellow jackets, but by the time he saw them, we were already too close. He squealed, and I jumped when the first one hit my left calf. "Run boy! Just go!" We sprinted until the last of them peeled away from the chase.

"How many you got, Dad?"

"At least four, let me count again. Three on the leg and one up the shorts."

"On the …?"

"Nope, thank goodness, but pretty close."

We sat down on our packs. I pulled a Snickers from my back pouch and leaned back on the bank. "That was not fun."

Henry pulled out his water bottle. "You think we should go warn them?"

"Holy … Henry, I'm an idiot. Thank you for thinking of that. I hope they aren't there yet."

"We could leave a note, too, for other people that are coming. Like those people did about the snake."

"You got any paper?"

"Mom does."

"You wanna be the one to run back through them? For your sisters."

"Let's flip for it," he said. "Heads, I win, and tails, you lose."

I met Monica on the far side of the yellow jackets, scratching the back of my left arm. "I only got one on the way back through, but it's the worst one yet."

"Do you know where they're coming from?"

"Out of the base of that log there. You just have to run." I put my hand on her pack and spun her around. "Can I get that little notebook out, so I can leave a note? Is it in your back pocket?"

Georgie peered over my hand as I wrote. "Dad, shouldn't you write it in Spanish too, like that note down there about the snake?"

"I don't know how to spell the word for wasp in Spanish."

"I could draw a picture."

"Okay, I'll just write 'Cuidado' and you can draw an arrow to your wasp when you're done."

When we were all gathered again on the far side of the yellow jackets, Aiden reached out a hand to help Henry up. He looked at me and shook his head. "None of them got a single sting?"

"Nope."

I stepped around Monica to Henry. "Why don't you and I walk in the back?"

"Why would I do that? I don't like to be in the back."

"June and Georgie seem to be doing better when they aren't walking with you today for some reason."

"Well, come walk with me in the front."

"It's best if I stay in the back in case someone needs me."

The trail made diversions around outcroppings and returned to the creek. It continued back and forth in this way for a long time, until at last it left the creek for the climb. The vegetation changed from rough scrub to big leafy deciduous trees. When we crossed another creek, Georgie was waiting.

"Where are the others?" I said.

"They left. I felt like walking with you."

"And Henry too? Maybe I should walk between you?"

Soon after we began walking together, Georgie said, "Henry, are you really that dumb, or are you just trying to be annoying? Dad, tell him."

"I'm not getting involved. You two can sort it out."

"He won't listen. I know he knows I'm right."

"No," Henry said, "I don't know that you are right. I'm right."

"You aren't right. That's not how you say the word crustacean."

"Wait," I said. "Which way are you saying it's pronounced, Georgie?"

The trail switchbacked through knee high grass meadows and linked up with a forest road where it hugged the outer edge, juvenile pines having crowded the inner part of the flat. The air cooled a little, and the forest thickened. We passed several inquisitive deer. And still they argued.

"You know that word could be pronounced either way," I said.

"We aren't arguing about proper pronunciation. We are talking about how it's pronounced in the song," Georgie said.

"Oh, in that case," I said, "Georgie is right."

"No," Henry said. "You are both wrong."

"How about we just take a vote with everyone when we get to lunch. Would that satisfy you both?"

"It won't matter what anyone else says," Georgie said. "He won't accept the results unless they agree with him."

I turned back to look at him. "Is that true, Henry?"

"Yeah, that's probably true."

1017.2

I shifted on my Tyvek and looked past my feet up the trunk of the gnarled shade tree not far from the spring. "This is about as perfect a lunch spot as anyone could hope for."

June stepped over me on her way to the water. I grabbed her ankle and reached for my water bottle. I tapped her foot with it.

She laughed. "Dad, let me go."

When she'd gone, I said, "Dadgummit, my phone is running low on battery, and I forgot to set out the solar charger. I'll give someone one million dollars to do it for me."

"If I thought you had it," said Henry, "I would."

"Kill me." I rolled to my side and pushed myself to my feet.

Monica leaned over the stove and smiled at me. "Coffee?"

"Oh, yes, please. I'll have some when I get back."

I propped the solar charger against the trail sign at the junction, then pressed a hand to the solar cell panel while shielding my eyes with the other. When I confirmed that my phone and battery charger had begun charging, I looked down the path toward the water where June hopped across the outlet beneath a shallow pool. I walked to her and peeked into the pool. Tadpoles darted away from the edges.

June dropped to her knees to lay parallel to the trickling outflow just below the pool. I placed a hand on her hair.

"Hey, kiddo."

"Daddo, I just thought of something. It's good I didn't quit in Oregon."

"Why is that, June?"

"If I quit in Oregon, we wouldn't have made it home in time for North Carolina anyway, so we would have missed the vacation with the cousins."

"Is that the hardest thing you've had to miss while we've been out here?"

"I think so. That, and horseback riding lessons."

"Which horse do you miss the most from the barn?"

"Probably Frankie. That's who Ms. Shannon has me ride the most.

"Even though Frankie refuses the jumps?"

"Miss Shannon says that's the rider's fault."

"Is it your fault when Frankie stops? What are you doing wrong?"

"Sometimes, when I get nervous, I look at the jump and that communicates to him that it's a big, scary monster."

"Is that what Ms. Shannon says?"

"Yep."

"I bet you'll be better at it when we get home."

"I'll have to get back in horseback riding shape. It's a lot different muscles, 'cause you have to squeeze with your knees all the time."

"You'll be a lot braver, I bet." I reached out a hand to her. "Here, hand me that bottle. I'll filter it for you."

"Don't filter that one, I was catching tadpoles in that one."

I leaned over her to look past her into the pool. "I thought you were over here filtering water."

"No, I've just been playing around. How do you think tadpoles make it through the winter here?"

"Frogs hibernate, so maybe tadpoles can too."

She tilted her head. "You don't think they could have just been frozen eggs in the mud or something?"

"My guess is that these would have hatched out earlier this summer."

"How would a frog even find this tiny, little spring in the middle of nowhere?"

"That's a good question. The fact that they are here at all seems like a miracle to me."

"Look, Dad." June laughed and pointed up the hill toward the trail. "It's Aunt Katie. How did we get ahead of her? Aunt Katie," she called. SoGood waved. June pushed up onto her elbows and pointed her toward the shade. "Mom's over there under the tree. We stopped here for lunch."

SoGood dropped her backpack at the trail junction and came down the path toward us. "I need to grab some water for lunch. Do you mind if I join you?" She pulled out both of her water bottles. "I'm glad I caught you. Do you think any of you would like some muffins? I carried way too much food out of Seiad."

***

I woke to the sound of Monica's titanium cook pot with my legs crossed and propped on the tree. I stared up past my feet through the thick canopy to the blue sky. "Is it time to go already?"

"You've been asleep for over an hour."

"Is SoGood gone?"

"She left a while ago."

I lifted my head and turned. Henry stood with his pack leaning against his leg.

"Oh, I'm sorry, guys. You're all packed up." I stood up and reached down for my groundsheet. "On second thought, Monica, do you have the shovel?"

"Georgie has it. Are you serious? You are going to use it now?"

"That coffee finally hit me. You guys can go on ahead. I will catch up."

I leaned my pack against the shade tree and ducked under a few low hanging branches.

When I swung my pack onto my back and stepped back onto the trail a while later, I smiled for the joy of walking alone into the golden warmth of the early afternoon with all of us stretched out in a long flowing line through the mountains.

I stopped to text Dax, Dustin, and Grandy that we were on pace to meet them, but to play it by ear as to location. They would be joining us for a four-to-five-day section somewhere, depending on how far we made it before their arrival. "We can play it by ear," I texted, and I meant it, too. We could play it by ear. Who could control fires and weather and fate? What of my worry could shape or shift outcomes? We would walk as we were able, as far as we were able. And oh my, weren't we walkers? Not that we no longer grew weary, but that we woke up renewed in the morning. No tightness, no soreness, nothing.

June stood in the shade of a tree near the top of the last rise looking back toward me. I looked at my phone. It had been less than thirty minutes.

"Hey, Dad," she said. "I just thought of something."

I put my hand on her elbow and nudged her forward. "Tell me while we are walking. We have a long way to go tonight. You know Mrs. Lloyd is meeting us first thing in the morning. Just under twenty-eight miles, if we make it." We turned through a sparse stand of firs and out onto a long, flat, white slab of granite beneath a broad granite surround. "June, look at that."

"There are already shadows under it, Dad, and it's only the middle of the afternoon."

"It's dark by 6:30 now."

"6:42, last night. I checked on Aiden's phone."

The field of gold was interspersed with shades of pink and green and blue, colored by subtle wildflowers across the wide span. June walked on, and I stood for a long time. When I restarted, it took me a long time to catch her.

"June, what was it you were trying to tell me earlier?"

"I forgot." We walked in silence for a long time. "Oh, I remember, now. How much do you think Mom is thinking about mountain lions through here."

"It looks a lot like mountain lion country to me."

"Plus, we saw all those mountain lion tracks right on top of the hikers' footprints. So we know it came through here today."

"You should ask her, if we can ever catch up."

1024

Not long after we walked out from last-water, June stopped at the entrance to a small stand of trees and bent back a branch that overhung the trail to peer into the shady alcove. She waved me to her.

"What is that, June?" Between the trees, I saw dark shapes of large animals.

She turned to me. "I told you."

I looked over her shoulder again. The man leaned against one of the trees with his legs crossed at the ankles. He offered a slow nod in our direction, spun the piece of grass between his lips, then tipped the brim of his ball cap.

There were countless children around him on scattered piles of saddles and blankets. The large, dark animal shapes turned out to be horses. Seven in all were parked between trees and tied about.

I counted the children. The youngest could not have been four years old. "Ten kids?" I said. "You have them all out here by yourself?"

He pulled the culm of grass from his mouth and dropped it to the ground. He threw a nod away from me. "Me and my wife." His wife raised her hand.

"Oops, I thought you were one of the kids. I'm sorry."

The woman smiled and dropped her eyes.

"That's exactly what I thought too," Monica said and reached her hand toward me. I stepped past June toward Monica.

"Okay, I gotta hear this story," I said. "What are you guys doing?"

"We live down in Scott Valley, just come up for a few days. We run cows up here, so we do a little checkin' on 'em while we are up here. We don't round them up 'til the fall."

"I bet you know these hills like the back of your hands."

He nodded.

"The kids too?"

He added a smile to his nod.

"It's free range here, isn't it?"

He nodded again.

"We have seen a lot more cattle lately, so I wondered. You don't happen to know Tim Lloyd, do you?"

"He's a good man. I do some work with him from time to time."

"What kind of work?"

"Me and the kids shoe horses for him, and a few other things now and again. How do you know Tim?"

"I love Tim. He's one of my heroes. I worked for him for three summers at JH Ranch. My kids are sick of hearing me talk about him." I waved my hand toward the valley below. "Y'all live in Scott Valley?"

He nodded.

"Have you ever thought about doing the PCT on horseback? We pass a lot of people on horseback, and there are separate campsites in most of these parks we pass through. We haven't met a thru-packer yet, but I bet you could do this trail a whole lot faster on a horse."

"That all depends. How far are you all walking a day," he nodded toward Georgie, "with the kids?"

"Today we will go 28, but we are walking at least 25 miles a day when it's not a rest day."

"You couldn't go a whole lot faster than that with a horse without them going lame. I guess if you took a pack horse and one extra you could rotate them out, and rest them, but I couldn't see going farther than 30 miles with any kind of regularity."

"I would have thought horses would be a lot better than people."

"Over a few days, maybe." He shrugged his shoulders. "But there is nothing like a human for walking."

"What do you think about that, June?" I said.

"I'd rather be on a horse." She huffed and then turned to the man. "I jump horses at home at a barn near our house."

He nodded and swung a slow look toward his wife. She waved him to her. He bent low. A slight smile crossed his face. "Do any of you want a lemon cucumber from our garden?"

"Oh, I do," Monica said as if without thinking. "Are you sure you can spare it?"

The woman nodded and extended her hand.

"I miss vegetables so much out here. You grew this?"

"She and the kids keep a good garden at the house. You all ought to come by if you're stopping in Etna. We're the Bishops."

"We will be with Tim for a couple of days," I said.

"He'll know how to find us. How much farther are you going tonight?"

"I'd love to get over the top of this next climb," I said.
"There's good camping at the cabin if you stop there."

"Cabin?"

"There's an old rancher's cabin just off-trail coming up with plenty of flat ground and a firepit."

"Can you stay in it?" I said.

"It's usually locked, but I probably wouldn't."

Monica shot me a look as if to say, "What is that all about?"

I looked up through the canopy of the tall pines to the darkening sky. "We'd better get going if we don't want to walk in the dark."

The sharp angle of the gable end of the cabin caught my eye over the embankment that bordered the trail. Henry scrambled up a shortcut to survey the area. "It isn't that bad. At least it is flat."

Monica looked up at him and then toward me. "Are you sure we want to stay here?"

"If we get up early, we can be to the road at Etna Summit before nine." I pointed my trekking pole toward the roof. "It's funny, isn't it, how obvious man-made lines are when you encounter them in nature? I always wonder what the story is with places like this."

"It's just kind of creeps me out, but if there is nothing else nearby, let's just stay."

After Aiden dropped her pack onto her groundsheet a few minutes later, she said, "Come check out the cabin with me, Dad."

"In the morning, if I feel like it."

"Come on, Dad, just real quick."

I held up my finger. "As soon as I get set up, I'll come over there."

When I joined her, Aiden had her arms draped over the bottom half of the wooden dutch door at the front of the cabin. She waved her small pen light up and down toward the far corner of the room. "It's a mess in here. I wonder why someone would leave it so trashed like this. But look, there is even a refrigerator. It could be gas, I guess, huh? 'Cause I don't see any power lines for electricity. How would they even get that thing way up here?"

She turned off the light and tapped my elbow. She stepped away from under the soffit and pointed up at the eave. "And look, it has numbers for an address. You think someone actually delivered mail up here? There isn't even a road into this place, and it's not like you could get here with a car anyway."

"There isn't a road now, but did you not notice that we were walking on an old roadbed for the last little bit before we turned in here? Someone drove a car up here at one time." I leaned my head into the room and looked down the wall. "I do wonder about places like this. People don't come out here, much less build in a remote place like this for no reason. It's funny, whenever we've been out here for a few days, I'll catch myself thinking of us as walking through places that have rarely been seen. Sometimes, I even think of myself as an explorer. But then we come to a cabin with a refrigerator in it, I remember that we are not really trailblazing. Shoot, Ben Bishop's kids know their way around every inch of this place."

I stepped back toward the front door and tapped the top of the lower half of the Dutch door. "In some ways I like thinking about who was here before and why. I default to assuming it was for mining, but who knows?" I tapped the door harder than I intended, and it made a boom that resonated in the room. "Hand me your flashlight for a second, Aido." I shined the light to the left down the long wall. I reached in and flicked the light switch up and down.

"Why would you think that would work?"

"I didn't think it would, but at one point it did, and someone's fingers flicked that thing up and down the same as mine. It's kind of weird to think about that. I can picture a kid coming in from a cold rainstorm to dry off by that old cast iron stove over there." I stepped back from the door. "It doesn't feel creepy at all to me, though, like these old places sometimes do. Did you know that when you were a baby we used to go camping on the south fork of the American River? The trail down to the river was an old mining supply route. There was a mining town back in there somewhere, but we never found it. A lot of the stuff that's in here is left over from that same era."

"Did you look?"

"A little, but it was harder to camp with a baby than we expected, so we usually just hung around the water where we base-camped."

"I don't remember that."

"We will cross the headwaters of the American River before we get to the Sierra Nevada, so you'll get to see some of your old stomping grounds."

Aiden nodded into the cabin. "Did you expect it to feel creepy?"

"I'll tell you something that may sound a bit strange. I think old stories get locked into a place. Almost like residue, a whisper from the past. Maybe it's more like timelines overlapping. Either way, I think sometimes we can pick up on it. You know, like in Genesis when Abel's blood cries out from the ground. I don't mean to say it is only the bad stories that get locked in, but those tend to be the ones people notice. Sometimes, I feel a weird vibe in a place. I think there is something to it."

Aiden tugged on the brim of her hat. "That's kinda weird, Dad."

"Oh, I know. I don't say that out loud very much. I know I can't prove it. Remember when we were doing our training hikes before the trip? Every time we went to Lakeland Highlands Scrub, I'd get this kind of icky feeling."

"Oh man, Dad. Now that you say it, I did too … in the scrub."

"Oh great, I may regret saying any of this to you, kid. As given to conjecture as I know you are, I have no idea where something like this could lead." I put my arm around her shoulder, and we took a step back toward the others. "Are you about ready to go to sleep?"

She looked over her shoulder toward the cabin. "I don't feel anything weird about this place at all."

I made an attempt at producing a ghostly sound, laughed and then dropped into a mock-serious tone. "Maybe it just keeps its dark secrets from strangers."

1030.0.2

I dropped my fly to the surface with minimal splash in the shade of the giant inflatable slide in the dead center of the camp's swimming pond. The trout sucked in the fly and pulled hard. With the fixed-line Tenkara, I had no way to offer the fish any slack, so I followed him into the water. The cold water took my breath away. After a while, the fish made one final run and gave out. I backed my way up to the shore, scooped him up, and lifted him high for Henry to see. "Take that, sucka."

"It took you long enough, Dad. I've caught three already."

"Nothing this big."

Tim Lloyd stuck his head out of the outbuilding bordering the pond. "You should have used my spinning rods. You wouldn't lose so many fish."

"We carried these Tenkara rods the whole trail," I said. "We may as well put them to use."

"It's okay with me if you want to do it the hard way." He walked back into the shed.

"You need help up there? That's what lackeys are for."

I heard Tim laugh inside the shed, and I looked at Henry. "That's what he used to call me when I worked for him."

"You already told me that."

"Hey, come take my picture with this thing." I reached for my phone in the grass and tossed it to the sand at Henry's feet.

"One more cast."

"No, now. We get a bite on every cast. Take the picture first, but make sure you keep all the buildings and that inflatable slide thing out of the background. We have to make it look like we actually caught some big fish on the trail."

"We caught a bunch of fish in Washington."

"And not a single one in Oregon."

"I caught a salamander."

"I should have shipped them ahead to South Lake Tahoe. We could have saved ourselves the weight. Oh well, next time."

"What do you mean 'next time'?"

"You don't want to hike this trail again sometime?"

"Dad, I'm never hiking again after we are done with this one."

I pointed toward our towels in the shade, and Henry nodded. We sat for a while there without talking. I lay down and looked up past the fluttering leaves of the apple tree toward the blue sky. I reached a hand out to the soft, cool rye grass and brushed my hand across the tips.

"Before we leave for the trail, you and Georgie need to go through your packs and get all the trash out. You two are pigpens."

"Everything but my Coke can."

"What?"

"Everything but my Coke can. I'm carrying that all the way to Mexico."

"Get rid of that thing, Henry. It's extra weight for nothing, and it will cut everything up. No wonder your pack is so ripped up."

"It's my first trail magic though."

"I thought it was from your second, with Skybird's parents."

"No, I saved the can from the first one."

I nodded toward the pond. "This place is alright. Do you think you'd ever want to come out and work a summer here?"

"June says she wants to. And that was even before Ms. Dana took her on that horse ride."

"I loved working for Tim at that other summer camp."

"Why did he leave?"

"A horse fell on his leg, and they let him go."

"A horse fell on his leg?"

"He was rounding all of the other horses up in the winter, and his horse slipped on some ice."

"And they fired him?"

"Yes," I said and nodded across the road toward the shed. "It took three people to replace him. I've never met anyone who can do what he does."

Tim backed out of the shed in a waddle with two large tupperware bins stacked one on the other. "Lackey? More like slack-ey."

I jumped up and jogged across the grass to the road. I picked my way across the sharp gravel to Tim. "I'm coming, boss. Sorry about that."

"Go back there and relax. I'm just giving you a hard time."

"Here, give me one of those. You aren't as young as you used to be."

"You're sounding like my wife now." He paused with the bins facing me, and I lifted the top one. I set them one at a time on the tailgate and slid them in. "It is true though," he said. "I am slowing down." He leaned the box back toward him and stood there with it for a few seconds as if thinking. He nodded and laughed. "We get old. It's happening to you too, you know."

I put my hand on the tailgate and turned. "I like your new place. Nice to have your own orchard and all."

"Oh yeah, the squirrels do love all the apples. But I'm not sure why you would call it new? I've been here fifteen years." He paused. "But I guess it's new to you. Are you going to take the kids up Mount Shasta while you're here?"

"I've been to the top once, a long time ago."

"I know, you took my son with you, and you bailed on him on the way down."

"I had altitude sickness. Plus, my snowboard broke on me, so I didn't see the point in sticking around."

He laughed. "Excuses."

I clapped a hand to Tim's back. "It's good to see you, Tim. You have no idea." Tim flashed a broad smile, threw his head back, and laughed. The same smile he'd given me from the cab of his truck more than twenty years before. I had been angry with the director of the summer camp, but I couldn't put my finger on the exact reason. It was something about the way he caused division among the staff. There were those who were "on board" with every last thing. They were the ones that would join him at six-thirty every morning to pray for a new idea that he had, a dream for a traveling high school revival show. It sounded hokey to me, spurious at best, deceptive at worst, but either way, I slept in until breakfast each day. Throughout the summer I had noticed a growing separation in his valuation of the particular groups. But, when one day the camp director had tossed me the beginnings of one of his banal platitudes, in hopes that I would complete it, I had left him disappointed. His response was to say, "It's no wonder you can't get with the program, Vince. You never attended our camps in high school, did you?"

Tim could tell that I was in a foul mood as he'd driven past, so he'd called me over to his truck. My bellyaching to Tim had left him laughing. For hours he'd asked me the same question. "Is it a matter of personality or character? If it is an issue of character, you have an obligation to confront him. If it's personality, you have to let it go."

Near the end of that day, we had driven with him to check on an outbuilding my friend, Genie had been instructed to paint. It had not been a good effort on her part. "Let's go get her from dinner," he sighed as though he were sad to have to do it. On our way back to the outbuilding, she sat between us in the cab of his truck. No one spoke. When he stopped in front of the building, he said, "Genie, the quality of your work is a reflection of your character."

She had put her hands to her face and cried, "Oh, Tim."

Tim and I worked alongside her until after dark to redo it.

Tim snapped his fingers in front of my face. "You with me, Lackey? You were spacing out on me again."

I clapped my hand to his shoulder again and said, "You were never a man for excuses, were you, boss?"

"Speaking of excuses," he said, "Don't let me forget to stop by the store on the way home. Marcia needs something for the dinner she's putting together for you guys tonight."

"You wouldn't happen to still have those homemade ice cream makers, would you?" I don't want to hear any excuses."

Tim's lips tightened and spread into a wry grin.

"Henry," I called across the street. "Tim is making us some of his famous homemade ice cream tonight."

Henry stayed on his back and didn't turn to look at us, but he held up his arm and gave us a thumbs up.

Tim laughed. "There is something I have been meaning to ask you." He nodded in Henry's direction. "How did you come up with his name?"

"Oh, that's easy. We were down to three names. It was going to be Paul, Atticus, or Henry, so I walked out the front door and screamed each of them as loud as I could, and there was a clear winner. Check this out," I said, and yelled, "Henry!"

"What do you want, Dad?" Henry called.

1040

Walking out from Etna Summit the following day, we were greeted with the intermittent clanking of the cattle's kettlebells through the trees. Once, June stopped and searched the downslope. "There are three calves with that group."

"We're in the Bishops' free-range lands now. You think those are their cows?" I said.

"Maybe."

"You kind of wish you were a Bishop, don't you, June?"

"It would be fun to have a horse."

"And a place like this to ride it?"

Henry came up behind me.

"Where have you been?"

"I had to use the bathroom. Can I pass?"

"Walk with us in the back for a bit. Have you noticed how different the trail is on this side of Etna?"

"Yeah."

"What do you see that is different?"

"Back there they just wanted to take you up to the top and back down to every lake along the way. Over here," he made a sweeping motion with his arm, "they just cut it even."

"You like this better, I bet."

"Why would I want to see every lake? A trail is supposed to get you there, not loop all around."

I called ahead to Monica. "Let's just stop here." I pointed down the slope to an old forest road. "I don't know if we're going to find a flat before dark."

"Mom, did you hear that?" Aiden said. "Dad is asking to stop. Am I in a dream?"

"You don't think we can find a better place than that, Vince?" Monica said. "I don't want to have to scramble to get back to the trail in the morning."

"There hasn't been anything flat for a long time now, and I've looked at the map. The contours don't make it look like it will get any better."

"How far is the saddle?"

"1.2 miles."

"Oh, that's okay." Monica flipped her hand as if to brush aside my concern. "It won't be dark for a while."

"You kids go on ahead," I said, "but keep your eye out for something flat."

Monica and I dropped to the back.

"I like walking on pinestraw," she said. "And this is my favorite time of day."

"The golden hour."

"It's everything. The light in the trees, everything gets kind of quiet." She stopped in front of me. "Listen."

She sees it better, fuller, deeper. Hears inside the conversation on the canvas in front of her, the orchestral interplay. When we were first married, we had sat on the sand on the Florida Gulf near where she grew up. She had said, "I love all the colors." I hadn't seen them. I'd only seen green, blue, and pink. "Look for the purple. See the orange, and the yellow."

She moved another hundred feet up the trail and turned to look up the hill into the trees. She reached back into her side pocket for her water bottle, took a sip, and smiled. We stood that way for a while. "Are you coming?" she said.

When I stopped beside her, I pointed past her. "Uh-oh."

"What?" She turned her head to follow my finger. The tall trees swayed ahead of us, and a few pine needles drifted down.

"It's going to be windy at the pass."

She looked back at me.

"Do you think we can camp there?"

"I don't know. If we can find a flat place on this side, out of the wind, it would be better."

When Georgie stepped up beside Henry and Aiden, she turned into the wind and spread her arms out wide. The wind ripped her hat from her head and carried it thirty feet through the air.

"Henry, run down there and get Georgie's hat for her." I looked at Monica and then scanned the saddle. "This is going to be interesting." One step from the trail, in the flat of the saddle, there was a single spot flat enough for a tent. "Aiden, take out your tent for Mom tonight. Your tent is better in the wind than ours. June, help her set it up."

"You sure there isn't anything better nearby?" Monica said.

"Aiden, you and Georgie run up around the corner and look."

"I guess there is that, at least." I pointed to a make-shift wall of stacked stones. "But it's pretty slopey."

"Henry, let's get some stones to run along the bottom here for our feet to keep us from sliding down the mountain."

He dropped his pack and bent to pick up a rock.

"Pull out your rain jacket to block the wind. We are going to get cold fast." I opened my pack and pulled out my groundsheet and stepped toward the wall. After we dropped a last stone for our feet, I said, "Lie down and see if that is going to work."

"It's tall enough that we'll be out of the wind over the top, but there's a lot coming through the holes between the rocks. It's gonna be cold for whoever is lying here against them."

"That's gonna be you, so let's figure something out."

Henry tapped a finger to his lip a few times, ran to his pack, and came back with his groundsheet. He wrapped it over the wall, longways. "Grab some rocks, Dad. That way, we can pin it, so it won't blow away."

"Nice thinking, Henry."

As he lay down to test it, I heard a guttural outburst from Monica. "What's going on down there?" I said.

"These stakes keep popping out. Can you help me do it?"

"Let's go, Henry."

Henry raised his arms, tucked them under his head, and then crossed his legs in a deliberate motion. "I think I'll stay here and test this out some more."

I rolled my eyes, and jogged a few steps down to Monica, and the wind kicked up even more. She said something to me that I couldn't hear over the popping sound from my wind-whipped rain jacket. When I pounded the final stake into the hard ground, I stood up to inspect it. I hadn't heard Aiden come up behind me, so I jumped when she spoke into my ear. I asked her to repeat what she'd said. "I guess you are going to go ahead and set up here."

I almost had to shout so that she could hear me. She nodded when I said, "It seems like you're frustrated."

"What if we had found something better?"

"I was pretty sure you wouldn't. That trail looks like it dives off that side pretty fast."

She steadied the hood of her jacket with her hand. "Then why on earth would you send us?"

"You never know what's around the corner."

We ate a hurried dinner, huddled below our makeshift windbreak, and lay down to sleep. Their laughter mixed into the howl of the wind as I drifted off.

In the earliest orange of the pre-dawn light, I propped myself to my elbow to peer over the wall. The wind had subsided in the night. They were all tucked in tight, like so many sardines, and it took careful movements for me to extricate myself without waking them up. When I freed myself, I tiptoed toward the saddle to sit on a large and flat rock overlooking the valley. I heard a rock shift behind me.

"It's just me," Monica whispered.

I inched to one side to make room, and she sat beside me. I nodded toward the horizon. She smiled and draped an arm around my shoulder.

"That's Shasta," I pointed.

"It's so pretty."

I turned to look at her.

"There are so many colors."

"What do you see?"

1130

It is dark tonight. There is no moon in the sky. Beyond the silhouettes of my kids, the Hirz fire throws a red glow against a dark sky. We are, all of us, cowboy-camped tonight, save Monica. She is tucked away into the only off-trail flat space, tight between the young trees. I begged her to join us. She refused.

I heard a whisper. "That fire isn't going to get us, is it, Dad?"

"Is that you, Georgie?"

"You can't see me?"

"Only when the fire flares up over that ridge."

"Are we okay to sleep here? It won't come over that ridge, will it?"

"I think we are okay." I said.

I turn my head once more toward the fire. Then rolled away and pulled my sleeping bag over my head.

I know it won't jump the ridge. Tim said it wouldn't. But it's so close. It is burning trees across parts of this trail where we would have been walking tomorrow. Dropping them down, reducing them to ash. They would be just like the trees in that section we'd walked through in Washington, just before we met up with the Browns. Next year's PCT hikers will wonder what it would have been like to have been here, same as I wandered back there. Would they feel the same eeriness ghosting through cracking trees? Would they feel as if they were walking through a graveyard? Before a fire on this scale, I feel small. I wonder if some person on the edge of some fire in some time now long gone lay on the ground thinking about the ones who would come behind them.

I must have been whispering aloud, because Monica said, "What was that you said?"

"Just thinking about this fire. I'm bummed we have to skip miles. Did you know that Peach and Green are walking around it?"

"Georgie told me."

"You aren't at all tempted?"

"I thought they told you there would be dangerous road walks."

"But still. I am wondering if this might change the way I think about the trail. Remember that guy, Dahn, that we met coming back from the border? You know how he is skipping all over the trail. It's such a clear task when you get out of the car on one end and walk to the other. All that bouncing around might make it harder to stay motivated to finish the whole thing."

"Why are you thinking about that?"

"We have to skip this section. I guess I'm just wondering if it will always sort of feel like we didn't complete the trail in some sort of way. Will it nag at you? And will that make it easier to skip again further on?"

"Not for me."

"I don't know why it bugs me so badly. You are usually the perfectionist of the two of us."

"Maybe you are more of a perfectionist than you know."

"Maybe." I rolled back onto my back. "I can sleep on my back out here now. Isn't that weird?"

Monica didn't respond.

"I guess you're asleep."

I wriggled my toes in my quilt and reached down to feel them. The three outer toes on each foot had gone numb on the way down from Castle Crags. My new New Balance shoes were supposed to have a much wider toe box. They had felt good walking around in Etna, but the six miles of sustained downhill at the end of the day had been a better test. I needed Altras, but Altra still had not released any more size sixteens for the year.

I kicked June's foot beside me. Her feet had taken every step mine had. But each of her steps belonged to her. Without any help from me or from her mythical magic shoes. This walking thing is consistent with the way we are made. Closer to the essence of human power, stripped of technology. Well, subsequent technology, anyway. It would be reasonable to assert that these engineered wide toe box shoes sewn over some specialized compound rubber soles are downstream from sophisticated advancements in technology.

I roll to my side and look at Henry's face. Still, it's good, right? Good to have done this.

What's that Cormac McCarthy line? "Man's a creature to build a machine, and a machine to make an evil machine to run itself a thousand years."

It's coming, if it's not already here. Henry isn't trapped by it yet. He's not trapped by the crap. But it's not through some grand foresight in personal development that Monica and I dreamed up. Nope, going bust in the housing market debacle had been a gift.

"Can I have an iPad?"

"We can't afford it."

"Can I have a game system?"

"We can't afford it."

So, if a friend says, "Your kids are so unspoiled," how disingenuous, how
presumptuous am I if I take credit?

Still, I am glad that it's become true.

I look at each of them sleeping, faces glowing red in the faint light.
Sleeping comfortably one ridgeline away from a wildfire. Tomorrow we
will walk into church dirty and stinking, and we will walk out of town a few
hours after. And they will not complain. And being here is doing that. Is
making them. And I don't know if I ever want to go back there again.

I had been annoyed with Henry when he first laughed about the fire closure,
as though skipping thirty miles wouldn't water down our thru-hike at all, as
though he didn't care a bit how it would affect anyone else. I pulled Henry's
quilt up to his chin. "You've earned a skip."

1153

Georgie slipped her hand in mine. "Is that where we are going for lunch?"
She pointed up the street.

I nodded.

"The place with the milkshake on the sign?" She squeezed my hand and
started skipping again.

"We have to hurry though. We're meeting that guy for a ride around the
Hirz fire."

***

I lifted a tentative hand toward the driver of the passing truck. He slowed and tipped his cap through his open window as if to indicate recognition and spun the steering wheel to park in front of us. I pressed a hand to Henry's shoulder to rise to my feet and walk past the growling diesel engine. As I passed, the engine fell silent. "You're the ones that need a ride around the fire?"

"That's us."

"Is this everyone? I thought you said six."

"My wife is in the checkout line; we needed a few extra things for this section."

He turned his thumb up.

"How close did you all come to that fire?"

I nodded toward Georgie. "I've got a picture of it glowing red just over the next ridge behind her head. Thank you for the ride."

***

He did not roll up his window when we merged onto the interstate, so I rolled mine down a few inches. The growl of the knobby tires on the asphalt overpowered our conversation.

When we left the main highway, he spoke. "I was on duty and kept seeing these hikers walking along the interstate. I'm not an asshole kind of highway patrolman, but that was dangerous. I picked one of them up, and I've been giving people rides to town ever since."

"It's a great service to hikers."

"It's a moral obligation for me. I've pulled bodies from cars you wouldn't know were human. You have to be careful, and it's just getting worse. People can't put their damn phones down long enough to drive."

"It's a tough hitch down there. I had to hike uphill to get any coverage."

"It's worse with the fire. They've evacuated all the communities up the road from there, so there aren't any cars coming down this way from that exit. All the hikers have been coming up to the interstate now to catch a hitch." He shook his head. "I have seen some bad stuff on I-5."

"We thought about road-walking around the fire, but we couldn't figure out how to connect it up on forest roads."

We pulled to a stop at an intersection. He lifted his pointer finger from the steering wheel. "This is McLeod. It's your last town if you all need anything. They have ice cream here in the general store." He turned to look toward the kids in the back seat. "What do you think? Should we stop?"

"We would love some ice cream," June said. "Can we get some, Dad?"

"More ice cream? We just had milkshakes at lunch." I paused. "You know what? Let's do it. Why not?"

While everyone else was in the store, I leaned against the truck beside our driver. "So it's been getting a lot worse, you say?"

"Dunsmuir has gone to hell," he said. "It's a crack town now."

"We went to church there. It was kinda strange."

"The church?"

"That too. I love Jesus, and I love America, but I am not used to singing about them both in the same song."

"Be glad you live in Florida. If it weren't so hot, I'd move there. I'm getting out of here as soon as I retire. My son lives in Tennessee, so, most likely, I will end up there."

"It's that bad?"

"If I bust someone for cocaine possession in California, they won't spend a single night in jail. Not one. There is no enforcement mechanism in place anymore. No consequence. Nothing. It's not even a misdemeanor charge. Drugs are killing these communities. And Dunsmuir is about the worst. You saw it."

"The area is beautiful though."

"That's the worst of it. This climate is so nice you can be a vagrant and move up and down the state milking the system, and nobody will do anything about it."

"We are kind of vagrants ourselves, in a way."

He shook his head.

On the other side of Mcleod, the road narrowed and wound around tight turns through dense forest. He pointed into the overgrown brush. "You see that. These hippie types, no offense, they won't let the forest service come through here and thin that stuff out. It's a powder keg waiting to go off. Did you see what happened in Redding?"

I nodded.

"It's a matter of time 'til all of this burns."

We rounded a turn and Henry said, "Peach and Green, Dad. Look!"

"Dammit. You see? That's what I'm talking about." He shook his head. "They are going to get themselves killed. I'll stop on the way back and offer a ride."

"They won't accept it," I said. "Peach is a purist."

He looked over at me.

"He is going to walk every mile. Last time we saw him, he was studying paper maps for forest roads to walk around this fire. I guess he didn't find any if he's on the main highway."

Our driver shook his head.

I stared ahead for a while. "He's a fireman."

He thumped the heel of his hand against the steering wheel and mumbled, "He damn well ought to know better then."

The asphalt ended and we dropped onto a dirt road to wind up along a long canyon. He pointed out several mines along the river. At an intersection, he slowed to a stop and pointed up the road. "That takes you up to the dam at the end of Lake Mcleod." He pointed a finger over the steering wheel. Ash Camp is just up here."

Troubadour was sprawled under a tree in the shade, strumming on his guitar at the far end of the parking area. I jumped out of the truck. "Troubadour, what are you doing here?"

"Just waiting for someone to show up. I left my phone back in the hostel in Shasta. There was a music festival there, so I lost track of everything."

"You need a ride back to town?" our driver said.

"If you don't mind."

"What was your plan otherwise?"

"Wait until someone else comes along. Someone always comes along, if you are patient."

"Throw that bag in the back. I'll run you down the hill."

"Yeah," I said. "Maybe you can help him talk Peach and Green into taking a ride back up here to avoid the rest of that road walk. What do you think, Troubador?"

"I think Peach isn't going to skip anything."

"Hang on, Dax." I pulled the phone from my ear. "What was that, Georgie?"

"It's Troubadour!" She gestured toward the bridge below us. "We caught up to him again."

"Henry has been seeing his footprints for a while."

I put the phone to my ear again. "I'll call you back, Dax, if I ever get reception. But yeah, the gist is that I am not sure exactly where we will meet you guys, but we will be somewhere accessible on that date … Yes, it's Monica's feet. Some days she's fine, and some days we have to stop early … No, stopping early is more like between 23 and 25 miles … Looking forward to seeing you too."

Georgie and I peered down the short drop of the rock wall bank. Monica brushed dust from her hip and laughed, but her laugh held a hint of a cry.

"What happened?"

"I slid down and banged my hip."

"How bad is it?"

"I don't know. There's a little scrape, but it hurts."

"How are your feet?"

"This is distracting me," she pointed to her hip, "but I think they are okay."

"You ought to soak in the water while we're here." I nodded toward the creek.

"I'm going in, for sure."

"Sorry to disturb your tranquility, Troubadour. Do we get a concert?"

"You don't mind if I play?"

"Mind? Are you kidding? We'd love it."

Monica tiptoed with bare feet across the rocks toward the pool at the base
of the bridge. She sat beside the water and reached a toe in. She looked over
her shoulder and made a face. "It's so cold."

She turned to June. "June, how are you just sitting there in that water?"

"What? It's not that cold, Mom."

"I think you might be the Polar Bear again, kid."

June laughed. "I hadn't thought of that. Yeah, I guess I am." She slid over to
the far side of the pool.

Monica held her breath and sat down in the water up to her waist. "Oh my
gosh," she gasped and put two hands over her face before lying down into
the water. She was standing on the bank within a few seconds. "Oh my
gosh, it's so cold."

Troubadour began to strum his guitar. I turned to him and made a motion as
if to turn up the volume. I moved out into the sun in time with the music.
The rock slab burned my bare feet, so I lifted my knees high. I spun toward
Monica and said, "Come on girl, get with the beat." I spun a 360 and held
my arms toward her and sang. "Get your shoes though, ooh, ooh, 'cause it's
hot, too hot on the hot rock."

Troubadour laughed and hit the strings harder.

Aiden joined me first with her arm dangling, left-leaning drop with a twist
on the half-beat style. I mimicked her movement back to her and passed my
hands back and forth over my face. Aiden laughed and threw it right back.
Then we both turned toward the bank and begged Monica to join us.

By then, Monica came into the fray with her own mix of rhythmic reckless
abandon and grace, ever self-effacing, but playful and smooth.

I'd no sooner grabbed her hand to spin her into a dip, than June tapped me hard on the shoulder, her hands on her hips. "When's it my turn?"

"Get out here, Henry, "Monica said. "Let's see your moves."

For some reason, Henry's deep connection to music doesn't translate into motion. He's a herky-jerky robot at best. His contribution of twiggy appendages was all wild and out of time. It demanded my full attention, but I didn't want to enjoy it alone. I tapped Monica's shoulder and pointed. She spun around and continued to dance, but when she turned her face toward him, she covered her laugh with her hands. "We never taught him to dance."

I dropped my head into my hand. "We've failed him."

For a few minutes, that felt like an hour, it was all laughter and flailing limbs and colliding bodies, more mosh pit than ballroom dance. Every so often I caught a glimpse of Troubadour's smile as his head bobbed in time with the beat.

I bowed out first and raced with my sore feet to the cold creek to soak them and watch the dancing wind down. One by one they each joined me, breathless. We all dunked in the creek one more time. Like some minstrel lost in some epic ballad, Troubadour continued to play. It wasn't until we all stood before him in a wide semicircle that he looked up and hit the strings one last time.. He lifted his hand away and let the guitar ring. "What you Strawbridges lack in rhythm, you make up for with enthusiasm."

When we topped the rocks again a few minutes later, I hugged Monica and wiped a bead of sweat from her cheek.

"I'm not sure why I bothered to get in the creek." She lifted her arm and waved her hand under her armpit. "I'm already dripping with sweat."

"We'll cross a big dam soon, so wait for us there." I called to the kids, "Hey, Monica, wait up a sec." When I reached her, I said, "I think we have pretty good rhythm, do you not?"

She laughed. "Trail rhythm, maybe."

Henry worked his way over the chipped keys of the out-of-tune, banged-up upright piano in the dining hall at Burney Mountain Guest Ranch. The flattened tink of the high notes slipped into the room under the clank of the dishes, and the low conversation. Lunch was still two hours away, but I was already hungry again.

"Is that from La La Land?" Skybird leaned across the table toward Monica. "Does he take lessons?"

"He takes lessons from Vince's mom, but that's not one of the songs that they've worked on. He just likes that one. He still won't read music."

"He learned that by ear?"

Monica slid toward me. "He has always been into music, ever since he was little. The first time we noticed was when we got up from the couch after watching *The Last of the Mohicans*. I'm sure he was way too young for that movie. I came back from the kitchen, and he was just sitting there watching the credits with tears running down his face. I asked him what was wrong, and he said, 'This music. I didn't know music could do this.'"

After Skybird left the table, Monica turned to me. "I can't believe you guys all left me there under the trees last night. I woke up and everyone was gone."

"We thought you'd want to sleep in."

"By the road on someone's property?"

"I doubt they'd care."

"Yeah, but those sounds in the bushes last night. What was that? You and Henry were freaking out."

"I have no idea what it was. Every time I shined a light toward the sound it was gone." I snapped my hand to her wrist. "Wait a minute! Did you see the sign on the way in?"

"What sign?"

"The yellow sandwich board sign out front."

"Oh! Yes." She turned and opened her eyes wide. "You think it was a mountain lion?"

I nodded.

"It was a big animal. Last night, I thought it was a coyote or something, but a coyote would have made more noise."

"You think it might have been?"

I nodded toward a neighboring table and leaned in close. "That guy said that there's a problem lion in the area that has acclimated to people. Apparently, two hikers came in yesterday saying it had followed fifty feet behind them for a few miles on Hat Creek Rim. He told the kids that if we see fawns around though, that there are no lions nearby."

"Do you know where the kids are?"

"I told them to go clean their filters and get ready to resupply."

"Oh, did you grab our boxes already? Will you go find them?

"Yes," I pointed. "And the boxes are out on the front porch by the corner." When I hopped from the front porch and my feet hit the red clay, they kicked up a cloud of dust.

Skybird laughed and shook her head.

I coughed. "That did not go as planned."

She nodded toward a shed to the side of the property. "They are over there if you're looking for your kids."

Aiden was hunched over at the waist beside the running water spigot. The water splashed into a ring of rocks below. She banged her filter on the side of one of them, twisted it in her hand, and banged it on the rock again.

I leaned over her. "What are you doing?"

"Dad, you gotta see this." She held up her filter. "I already did mine. This is Georgie's. Watch how much dirt comes out." She reversed the filter and fitted it to the top of her Smart Water bottle. "Look at this." She squeezed.

Jet black filth poured out the bottom end of the filter. "That's the second time I've done it. Skybird showed us how to do this. You bang the filter on the side and it shakes all the nasty stuff loose. Wait 'til you see how fast mine is flowing again."

She flipped the filter around and threaded it to her bottle the right way around. She squeezed it between her knees. "Can you believe that? Mine hasn't been this good since Washington."

"Are you sure it's okay, banging it against a rock like that?"

"I'm sure it's fine, Dad. Where's Mom?"

"She said she was going to do the laundry." I nodded toward the shed. "You didn't see her come by?"

She shook her head.

"I'll check on her." I slipped into the tight utility shed to find Monica leaning over the open washing machine. "They don't have a dryer?"

She shook her head.

"I don't think we have enough time to stick around and let everything hang dry."

"I know. I am just washing the socks and underwear. We can let everything hang on our packs if it doesn't dry in time."

"Okay." I looked out the window. "I'd like to get out of here pretty soon. They said to be careful around the fish hatchery. The mountain lion hangs around there around dusk."

"How far is it from here?"

"Only a couple miles. Not far."

"It's so hot. You sure you don't want to wait 'til later when it cools off?"

"I want to get a close as we can to that water cache on the rim, so we don't walk too far without water in the heat of the day tomorrow."

"How far is the cache?"

"If we get five miles tonight, we would have just eight miles to the cache in the morning. The rim is supposed to be pretty miserable in this heat. After the cache, it's sixteen miles to the next water. Unless we want to go off-trail for water in the middle somewhere."

"I'd rather not."

1255

"Give me a second, Georgie." I cut through the sparse scrub down the side trail and stood on the edge of the rim to look down to the floor of the valley below.

Georgie stepped out beside me and pointed away, toward the far range of mountains opposite the valley. "The traffic is backed up on that highway. It doesn't seem like that big a road."

"It's just a two-lane highway."

"Why is it so busy this early in the morning?"

"You see that?" I bent and pointed. "Just between those two peaks."

She nodded and stared out across the valley. The plume of smoke that rose between the two peaks was shaped like a malformed mushroom. The top flumes and billows were broken up by a cross wind that carried the smoke off to the north.

"I wonder how far that smoke will travel, Georgie. I bet people in Ashland will have to wear their masks again from this one."

"What fire is that?"

"That's the Delta fire. It just started yesterday. I heard some people talking about it at lunch."

"Is it bad?"

"I don't think they know yet how bad it is, but it's bad enough that they are rerouting all the traffic off interstate 5. I am sure they are already trying to contain it. They've already had one fire jump the interstate this summer down in Redding."

"How do they contain it?"

"Tim was telling me about it the other day. Remember those uneven forest roads we were crisscrossing on the way into Ashland? Those were all fire breaks, apparently. Tim said they will get bulldozers and just cut firebreaks all over the mountain, sometimes they will back burn the fires, to starve it of fuel as the fire comes across. It all depends on who is fighting the fires."

"What do you mean?"

"CalFire and the federal firefighters have different ideas about how to fight the fires. One prefers complete eradication and suppression and the other takes a "let it all burn as long as there isn't too much threat to life and property" approach. But California has big problems with fires all the time. Tim used to tell me that the problem was that they had used such a strict eradication policy that they put out every little fire as it flared up. They ended up with all the underbrush grown so thick that when they would have a fire it would have crazy amounts of fuel, so, if there is ever a spark on a dry windy day here, there would be so much fuel from the overgrown brush that it would destroy the whole forest. Did I ever tell you about the time I almost started a fire at the JH Ranch?"

"Did you really?"

"Oh yeah. Tim set me up to cut some metal for a trailer out back by the woodshed. It was really hot in the sun, so I moved the saw over to the shade. I cut my first piece of rebar, and the sparks caught some pinestraw on fire. By the time I turned around, it was already burning about fifteen feet wide and straight up the hill."

"Dad!"

"Thankfully a bunch of other staff people were nearby splitting wood, so I screamed at them, and they came running with shovels to help me put it out."

"What would have happened?"

"I probably would have spent my whole life paying off fines."

"You got lucky." Georgie turned back toward the valley and pointed south. "What is that mountain called?"

"That's Mount Shasta; we were looking at it from the other side the other day. Did I tell you I climbed it a long time ago, when I was just out of college? I carried my snowboard to the top and rode it down."

"Was it scary?"

"No, I cracked the tail of my snowboard messing around the night before, so I took it easy on the way down. I had altitude sickness anyway, so I didn't care. It's over fourteen thousand feet at the summit."

"Is that higher than Whitney?"

"No, Whitney is taller. Does that make you nervous?"

"I don't want to get sick like I did in the Gila that time with the Browns."
She paused for a while before speaking again. "But I want to if I can." She
turned in the other direction to look toward the northern end of the valley.
"What about that mountain? What is that one?"

"That's Mount Lassen. It's a part of that volcanic spine we've been walking
since Washington. Adams, Hood, Jefferson, the Sisters. Shasta is a part of it
too. It's been really fun for me to bring you all out here to see this part of
the country, since I spent so much time out here. California is a beautiful
place. When your mom and I lived in San Francisco, we would always say
that we wished we could have all our Florida people live out here."

"Why did you leave San Francisco?"

"We left right before June was born. When I first took a job out here as a
youth pastor, my boss told me he hoped we weren't planning to have kids
right away. I told him we weren't. The truth is, we thought we couldn't.
Your mom had had a procedure on her spinal cord when she was young, and
the doctor said it was possible that she might never have kids. Two weeks
after I started that job, I had to tell him we were pregnant with Aiden."

"But why would he say you couldn't have kids?"

"San Francisco is a very expensive place to live. It wasn't easy to make
ends meet when it was just us and Aiden. When we found out June was
coming, we knew we would most likely have to leave."

"You said you didn't leave until right before she was born."

"That's right. I had started to interview for new jobs, and one looked like it
might be good enough that we could afford to stay. We loved a lot of things
about San Francisco, but in the end we decided to go home and be with
family."

"You didn't get offered the job?"

I laughed. "Yes, I was offered the job, but it was a job building houses and I
had gone out there to work in the church. If I wanted to build homes, I
could do that at home." I pointed again to Lassen. "It would have been

crazy to have stood here when all of these volcanoes were active. Don't you think?"

Georgie nodded and walked around me to head back to the trail. After we walked again for a while, she stopped and looked up at me. "I can't believe we've walked all the way back here from Canada."

The sun was high when we caught Monica. I lacked the energy to acknowledge her with more than a nod, and we walked together in silence. When the trail left the edge of the Hat Creek Rim, Monica said, "How far do you want to go past the cache before we stop and eat lunch?"

"Do you think they will stop?"

"It's starting to get hot."

"It's been hot. But the more we get done before lunch, the less we leave for the hottest part of the day."

"Let's get as far as we can then."

From a cluster of Coulter pines not far from the trail we heard the twang of a guitar. Without turning to check with us, Georgie veered from the path. The others were already gathered around Troubadour with their Tyveks spread out in the shade. He picked up his guitar and began to play. He played for a long time, and no one spoke.

When he set down his guitar, I said, "Do you have plans to do music professionally?"

"I plan to give my life to music, however it plays out," he said. "Music can take you places nothing else can." He swung his guitar to lay it on the ground beside him, and with his picking hand made a sweep toward the trail. "Not even this."

"I might offer if it's not an offence. This place does seem to inspire you to play."

"It's everywhere, man, if you listen for it," he said.

"He who has ears let him here," I said. "How did you get into it?"

"Once upon a time there was a song," he laughed. "No, my grandfather had a guitar, and he was always playing records when we would visit. I wasn't joking about the song though, because there was one song, man. That song was home."

When we left the trees after lunch, Georgie found her way to me again.

"That song is about home, isn't it? The one you were talking about."

"Almost every good song is about home," I said. "In one way or another."

"Troubadour knows a lot about music."

"A lot more than me. I tend to attend more to the lyrics. But, if you know how to hear it, you can hear home, and away, and home again even in the notes. There are notes that resonate … I don't know how to say it … maybe you'd say with resolve. Others that have a dissonance to them."

"Dissonance?"

"Yes, like a note that can almost make you feel irritable or sad or unsettled. I should have asked him if there was something like that happening in 'Come on Up to the House'."

"That's the Tom Waits song you were talking about?"

"Yes."

Georgie stepped from the trail to scoop up a giant pinecone in the shade of a lone tree, then jogged to catch up to me. "If you like songs about home so much, why did you drag us all the way out here?"

"You think it means I don't love home, because I would leave it?"

"Yeah, doesn't it?"

"The best homes might be the ones that are so secure that you know you can always return," I said. "Think about that Tom Waits song, and where home really is for him."

"What is the line?"

"Sing it to yourself. I bet you'll find it."

"Just tell me."

"We have time for you to figure it out on your own, but I'll give you a hint. You know how we were talking about the ways that music can make you feel unsettled, and then resolve in the end. The lyrics can do that too. And you'll find that Tom Waits does that sort of thing as well as anyone. Probably, and this is only my opinion—he never talked to me about it or anything—but probably because he has not only a clear hope in the good that is coming, but also a deep experience of the brokenness of the in-between."

"What does that mean?"

"It means, I think he's had a pretty hard life in some ways, but that he knows there is a purpose to the suffering. Or at least he looks forward with some expectation toward a relief from the suffering. But again, he never talked to me about it, so I can't be sure." I started to sing:

Well the moon is broken and the sky is cracked
Come on up to the house
The only thing you can see, is all that you lack

Georgie joined me, and we sang the last line of the verse together.

Come on up to the house

As we finished the line, the trail entered a pine glade, and we heard a noise in the trees over our singing. Georgie darted into the trees and came back with a large pinecone. "There are no mountain lions around here."

"What do you mean?"

"You didn't see that fawn run off from those trees?"

"I missed it, Georgie. All I saw was that giant pinecone you found."

"You should see the one June has."

1276

"Are you sure you want to go off-trail?" Monica said.

"He said the Subway caves were amazing, and cool," I said.

Henry rolled his eyes. "I've seen plenty of cool things."

"Not that kind of cool, you turd. Come on, I want to check them out. Plus, there might be a water spigot in the parking area, and I'm running low." I pointed. "There it is you guys, let's wait for June to catch up at the top of the stairs. She knew we were coming down here, right?"

I dropped onto my pack beneath a shady cottonwood and turned to keep an eye on the junction. June swaggered into view and turned my direction without breaking stride. She was swinging a giant pinecone in one of her hands.

When she stood above me, I asked, "Why are you still carrying this pinecone?"

She dropped the pinecone into my hand. "It's huge, Dad. It's the biggest I've ever seen. Do you know what kind it is?"

"I think it's a Coulter Pine, but why are you still carrying it?" I handed it back to her.

"I want to mail it to the cousins."

"You are going to carry it 'til the next town?"

"Whenever I carry it, I remember to think about the cousins."

"At least let me strap it to your pack."

A few minutes later we stood on the wide steps above the mouth of the cave. "Can I leave my backpack here?" she said.

"I wouldn't." I tapped her hand. "Look, kid, they are all down in the cave already. Let's go."

We bounded down the stairs together and crossed the uneven, guano-covered floor of the cave past the shade line to where the others stood hunched over a sign.

Aiden tapped the sign with her finger and looked back at me. "Dad, it goes all the way through. Can we go?"

I turned to June. "Uh-oh, Bug, you'd better run up and grab your backpack. Guys, let's wait for June."

"This is all natural?" Georgie said. "That's crazy."

"When she gets back," Henry said, "let's see how far we can make it without our flashlights."

Deep into the dark tunnel, I spoke in a spooky voice: "The only way out is through."

"It's so cool here." Georgie searched in the dark for my hand. When she found it, she said, "I think I could live here."

1304

Aiden rolled her fingers alternately into the grid pattern of the powder coated patio table on the deck outside the restaurant of the Drakesbad Guest Ranch. She nodded toward the door. "That sign in there said we were past the halfway point."

"I saw it."

"We aren't though, are we?"

"Not yet, but that must have been true at some point."

"How would that work? It's not like the land could change." She rested her chin on the table and raised her eyes to me. I looked back at her, turned my head to the side, and smiled. She turned her eyes toward the water glass in front of her, reached a hand toward its rim and spun it one quarter turn. "Oh, pfft," she said. "They changed the route, didn't they?"

I nodded.

"How come everyone besides us gets interesting trail names?" She nodded toward Troubadour.

"He carries a guitar and plays music everywhere he goes."

"Yeah, but why don't we have names?"

"You want a name?"

"Kind of." She sighed. "Yeah, I think it would be cool to have a trail name."

"Trail names are given for something distinctive about the person."

"So?"

"We are always together, and we are a family, so the most distinctive thing about us is that. That's why everyone just calls us The Family."

"I know, but wouldn't you rather have one of your own?"

"I like my real name."

Aiden dragged a finger across the plate to scrape up the last of the chocolate syrup. "It was nice of Mr. Brown to get us donuts. How did he even know we would be here?"

"A few days ago he texted me on the Garmin to ask when we would be here. Then this morning he texted me again. I should have known he was up to something."

"So, he just called them and paid for it over the phone? You have to remind me to thank him, because those donuts were so good."

"The wine too, but not quite enough of either one, eh?" I crossed my arms in front of me on the table and laid my head down. "I could probably have eaten at least a dozen more donuts all by myself."

Aiden picked up June's pinecone and spun it in her hand. "I thought she was going to mail this to the cousins."

"There's no post office here, it's just a …" I sat up and leaned back in my chair to look around at the cluster of buildings across the street from the store. "I was going to say resort, but it's more of a cross between a resort and a campground. Either way, they won't let us send any packages out from here, you can only receive them, so June Bug will just have to carry her pinecone to the next town."

After a few minutes, Aiden said, "Why can't we just give each other trail names?"

"It doesn't work that way. You don't get to name yourself, you have to be given a name."

"What trail name do you think I would get?"

"If I were naming you, I'd call you Nondescript."

Monica walked toward us with Troubadour behind her. "Hey Vince, who did you get our boxes from? Troubadour hasn't found his packages. Who did you talk to about ours?"

"The guy that just went in the restaurant." I nodded toward the door. "They keep them upstairs. I talked to the bartender, and he sent someone up for them."

Troubadour half turned, tapped the top of the chair and said, "I'll run in there and check again." A few minutes later he returned to the table empty-handed.

"How far are you carrying?" I said.

"I was planning on going through Belden, but I could get off in Chester if I had to."

"Let me gather up the kids," I said. "I'm sure we have extra, if you don't mind the castoffs." I slid back my chair and leaned forward.

"You sure?" That would be awesome. It would save me a hitch out of here."

Monica pressed her hand down on my shoulder. "Stay here with Troubadour. I'll go get them. I was going to use the restroom anyway."

"I'll come with you, Mom," Aiden said.

I presented an empty chair to Troubadour with a sweep of my hand. "Have you heard anything about the fire?"

"What? There are more fires ahead?"

"I know there is at least one coming up in the Sierra called the Donnell Fire. I'm not sure how bad it is, but it's threatening to close a highway over there that would mess up our resupply."

"What town is that?"

"Sorry, we aren't resupplying in town for the first part of the Sierra," I said. "We went for a four day trip down in Lassen with some cousins before we started the trail, and some random lady we met in the parking lot offered to resupply us through the Sierra. She messaged me that Highway 108 might be closed, so she's saying that she isn't sure she will be able to get to us."

"I hadn't heard anything about that fire yet, but I kinda just roll with this thing one day at a time."

I felt Monica's hand on my shoulder again. She leaned in to whisper, "You might want to talk to Aiden. You hurt her feelings."

I leaned away and turned my head to look back at her.

"The trail name," she mouthed.

1305

The trail wound away from Drakesbad Guest Ranch on a long boardwalk that straddled a marsh. We shared the boardwalk with resort dwellers and day hikers and stepped to the side several times. At one junction Henry led us the wrong way, and we hit a dead end at a sandwich board sign. I reached in my pack for my phone. "You all go on," I said. "I want to get a few pictures. This reminds me of Florida, a little bit."

'Yeah," June said. "It's like Florida if you squint your eyes, so you don't see the mountains in the background."

When I turned away from the swamp, I reached toward my hip belt pocket to put away my phone and caught my toe on an uneven board. My phone flew from my hands and over the side. I caught my fall with the heel of my hands and lay face down for a moment. I heard a voice say, "You alright there?"

I did two quick pushups without looking up, and said, "Oh, yeah, just getting in a quick workout before I head back out into the woods."

When I was standing again, I brushed off my hands and took a few steps up the boardwalk before bending to my knees to reach into the bog and pull out my phone.

"Oh, man," the man said. "Is it ruined?"

I shook the phone and rubbed it against my shirt. "We bought waterproof phones for the hike. Water resistant anyway, I'm not sure anything is really waterproof."

"I assume that was your family that just passed. Are you heading out for a few days?"

"What about you?" I said. "What brings you to Drakesbad?"

"I'm a fire liaison." He nodded toward the other end of the boardwalk. "My wife and I are spending a few days here to finish up a few things before I head back to my next rotation down in the Sierra."

"Are you working the Boots fire?"

He jerked his head back. "I was, but they are assigning me to the Delta fire for a few days to get them off to a good start."

"What does a fire liaison do?"

He laughed. "I'm fairly essential to the enterprise, to be honest. I have to help all these different departments work with each other. Local, state, and federal, they all have different ideas about how to deal with the fires."

"My friend was telling me about that. Which is the one that wants to just let it burn?" I said.

"Federal."

"Do you have a preference?"

"I'm not gonna weigh in on that." He smiled. "Not with you or anybody."

I laughed. "Fair enough. My friend says the problem started when they went full suppression and allowed all this undergrowth to come in so thick."

"I could see how a person might draw that conclusion. Controlled burns would have been, at one time, an option. Thinning the forest might be an option, but that isn't the most economical proposition in areas where forestry is restricted. California is in a bad spot."

"You aren't from here?"

"Oh no. I'm from back east. This," he pointed at his feet. "This is a nice place to visit."

1306.6

"What is a geyser?" Georgie said.

"You've never heard of a geyser?"

She shook her head.

"It's like an underground hot spring that erupts from time to time."

"Like a volcano?"

"Only it spurts up water and not lava. There are a bunch in Wyoming in Yellowstone Park. There is one called Old Faithful that erupts on a perfect schedule. I went to see it when I was about your age."

"Does this one erupt?"

"The notes in Guthooks say it just spurts a little bit here and there, so this is about as much as it does, I would guess."

She pulled the brim of her hat back toward her forehead and looked at me. "We should go see Old Faithful sometime."

"I would love to." I swept a hand forward inviting her to lead the way out. "This stuff is interesting, isn't it?"

Georgie stopped in front of me and placed her hand on a waist-high, jagged rock bordering the trail. She turned her face toward the rising steam and stared into it for a while as if in a trance. "I've never seen anything like it, Dad. I wish Mom had come down."

"Her feet were hurting. I think she just wanted to massage her calves and rest."

"If we were here at night, we could camp down by the creek. I bet that air coming off of the that water would keep us warm all night."

"I wonder if you're allowed to camp here. They might not like that." I turned to look back toward the creek. "Henry, don't touch that water."

"It's not that hot even." He pulled his hand from the water and stuck his finger in his mouth. "It tastes good too."

"How far is it back up to the junction?" Georgie said.

"Not far." I reached a hand past Georgie to pinch Aiden's shirt at the elbow. "Wait up, kid. Would you walk up with me?"

She sighed and nodded.

We dragged behind the others, and I filled several minutes with poor direct explanations and even poorer analogies, until I stumbled my way toward a, "You know you are really important to me, right? Nondescript was just a joke."

"It's not that," Aiden said. "It's just that I don't understand why you would even call me that."

"I'm sorry. I shouldn't have said it."

"Yeah, but you thought it, so …"

"Would you give me a chance to amend the observation?"

"You can try, I guess."

"Permission to ramble?"

She shrugged.

"I may have to weave my way toward my meaning. In fact, why don't we walk together after the junction."

She and I waited at the junction 'til everyone else was out of eyesight and earshot. I waved a hand for her to walk in front of me.

"You know how Uncle Tim-o says he loves his job because he gets to be the number two? And the job of the number two is always to make the number one great. I asked him about it one time, because it struck me as odd. Odd, as in, counter to culture, counter to what nearly everyone seems to strive for. You know what he said? He said, 'Why would I hate being given the same job Jesus was given? Jesus' only job was to do the will of the Father, to bring glory to the Father. So, when I think about what my job is, I have the best role model.'

"You are like that. You have always been the best guest at a birthday party, because I swear, there was never a birthday girl as excited about opening her gifts as you were excited for her to open them. You are always willing to help without a complaint. You see the right thing, and you just do it. I always told your mom that self-righteousness or pride was a far more likely besetting sin for you than any more common vice. I can tell you, there is no way I'd have turned classmates in for cheating, but you didn't even have to give it a thought. 'Oh well, doo-be-doo, it's just what I do.'

"I guess, in some way I take you for granted. If I ask you to help Georgie pack up when she's cold, you do it. Shoot, you do it without me asking. You spot the need and seek it out. All of my focus ends up on the ones who have need, and that is almost never you. So, I don't see you. Not like I'd like.

"And with Mom's feet hurting, you have stepped up to fill some of that role for the others. Rubbing their feet, shopping in towns, all of it.

"Servant-of-all would have been a better trail name for you. And for the love of all that's holy, don't hear that in some diminishing way. 'Whoever would be greatest among you,' and all that.

"Kid, what I am trying to say is that you are far from nondescript, you are a faithful servant, and there is no greater thing."

Aiden didn't respond.

"Do you hear me?"

She nodded.

"Does any of that make sense?"

She nodded again.

"You know that doesn't mean I see you as less than in any way, right?"

She turned and gave me a big hug.

I pulled her head tight to my chest.

She looked up at me. "Servant-of-all would be a stupid trail name."

"If you want to take off and catch up, you can."

"No, it's good, Dad. You and I don't walk together very much."

After a while, I said, "Aiden, I don't know how you will be able to navigate this world. If someone heard me say all that stuff to you, they would tell you I was holding you back or limiting your potential. It's not as though it's anything new. Not really. Grandpa, your grandpa, used to sing a song 'Nobody wants to play rhythm guitar behind Jesus, everyone wants to be the lead singer in the band.' But Aido, something feels different these days. It's unapologetic, overt. Like selfishness is a virtue to be celebrated. Self-love before anything. Can you imagine being in one of your classes at school and quoting that verse ... How does it go? 'Do nothing out of selfish ambition or vain conceit, but in humility consider others more important than yourself.' But that's it, Taters. That's the calling. That's what love looks like. I guess, Aido ... that's all I'm trying to say. You are good at putting other people first. You are good at loving."

She turned to me and smiled. "Hey, Dad?"

"Yeah, kid?"

"Do you care if I run to catch up to Henry?"

I nodded, and she jogged away. After she had put about fifty feet of distance between us, she turned and waved. "Thanks, Dad," she said, and turned away again.

1326

I rested my hand on the top of the concrete pylon and read aloud, "PCT Midpoint."

"Halfway, guys," Monica said. "We did it."

I patted the top of the pylon and stepped back. "Halfway. It is so weird to be standing here with thirteen hundred and twenty-five miles behind us."

"Yeah, and thirteen hundred and twenty-five miles ahead of us," June said. "And it's worse now, 'cause now we know how hard it's going to be."

"That's exactly what I mean, June. What about you, Henry? What do you think?"

He stretched his legs, one on either side of the pylon. "One leg is past halfway, and one leg is before."

"Which leg do you like better?"

"The right leg. It's going home."

"See you later," I said. "Actually, home is either way. Just as close."

"Yeah, but Chester is right down the hill. I could always get off here."

"I'll take the one that has less snow," Aiden said.

"Monica," I said. "How about you? Thoughts on halfway?"

"Uhm." She stretched her arms back. "I'm exhausted."

"No. Seriously?"

"Seriously. I am completely exhausted." She laughed. "I'm happy we are here. Proud of us. It's a long way."

"Georgie?"

"I really like my 3 Musketeer bars."

"Or as you like to call them, Chocolate Push Pops."

"That"—she pointed the candy bar at me—"that is only when they are melty."

"Troubadour," I said. "We get to be with you at the midpoint. Do we get to hear a song?"

He reached for his guitar. "Will play for Skittles," he said. "What do y'all wanna hear?"

1368

I heard a faint rustle beyond the warmth of my sleeping bag and slid my hand forward to where the edge of my quilt draped to the ground, breaking the seal with a finger. When I pulled my hand back from the cold, I tucked it into my armpit again, rolled to my left shoulder facing June, and resituated my quilt over me. In my pocket, my flashlight pressed into my leg, so I pulled it out and clicked it on. Diffusing its light with my hand, I pulled back both mine and June's quilts, just a little. In the light her rounded nose was pockmarked with dark pores filled with trapped dirt. Her whole face was a canvas for an abstract artist whose medium was dirt. In Washington, Georgie had called June dirtface, and, though the name had not stuck, it had become even more true. There were darkened places under the crease of her nose, and dirt caked into her eyebrows. She reached a hand to the flap of her quilt and pulled it toward her neck. I smiled and reached for one of her fingers. There was dirt deep beneath her untrimmed fingernails. Even her cuticles were outlined in black.

"Ready to walk, June?"

"No."

"You don't want to wake up yet?"

"No."

"Are we going to fight about it again this morning?"

"No, I'm going back to sleep."

I bonked her on the nose, and she rolled away from me. I rolled away too and wriggled backward to tuck my back tighter against her for warmth.

I woke again to a clank and a woosh of lit gas. I lifted my quilt and peeked through the sliver of separation. Monica sat cross-legged with her hands encircling the flame. She pulled them away and blew into them. I parted the quilt a bit more, and she looked up. She mouthed, "Coffee?"

I flipped open my quilt, suppressed a gasp from the cold, and dug around for my shirt.

"You're up early." I whispered when I sat beside her. "What's up?"

She smiled. "It feels good today. I feel like we are going to make it." She pulled her hands back and slipped one in behind my elbow before clasping them together again.

I picked up a small stick and cracked it in half, then in half again. I tossed the pieces onto the kids' quilts.

"Let them sleep," she said. "I don't think we need to be in too big a rush today. Do we?" She slid her hands apart and pressed one to the back of my shoulder. "Your shirt is disgusting. Have you seen these streaks?" She traced a hand down my back.

I pulled my shirt off. "You know what's terrible. My shirt looks just like that guy at Timberline Lodge."

"What guy?"

"The northbounder with the flat Altras that we met outside the gift shop." I laughed.

"What?"

"I don't know if I said it out loud, but I was thinking that he needed to have a little more self-respect. Now, look at me. I'm the same. Although," I nodded toward June, "Take a long look at June when she wakes up."

"I hate how disgusting we are, and I'm sure we stink too." She lifted the collar of her shirt to her nose and sniffed. "You know it's bad when, after you've stopped smelling yourself for a while, you start to smell yourself again. I think if it weren't for the stinkiness and dirt, I would love everything about being out here."

"I'm more or less used to it."

She reached for my phone. "How far are we going today? What's the terrain like coming up?"

"We have that big climb out of Belden tomorrow, so I just want to be close to the start of it when we camp tonight. I think we can let them sleep a little while longer."

"How bad is the climb?"

"It's about six thousand feet in six miles." I nodded toward the kids. "I was thinking we could let June pick the music and lead us. If I tell her this afternoon, it will give her something to look forward to, so she doesn't dread it all night."

"I don't like playing music on the speaker."

"We haven't seen many people lately."

She reached for the valve on the stove, twisted it closed to kill the flame, and shook two packets of instant coffee into the pot. Then she lifted it by the handles to her lips and blew softly into it. She smiled a faint smile and looked at me over the pot. "The birds are back."

"I hadn't noticed they'd gone."

Before the sun broke through the trees, we had walked more than a mile. Henry and I dropped to the back. "Why so slow this morning?"

He shrugged. "I don't see the point of rushing."

"June is walking strong today. I wonder what has gotten into her."

He shrugged again. "Can we listen to something on your phone?"

"I have to save my battery."

The sun played a dance along the crest of the hill we ascended. Flashing in and out of view. We caught the girls before we turned a blind corner, and the sun came fully in front of us. I squinted over Aiden's silhouette. To the left of the turn, a hiker leaned over trekking poles, his head framed by the sun, as if by a halo. I could not see his face.

"The King!" June and Aiden cried out at the same moment.

"What in the holy hell?" he said. "I never thought I would see you again."

During a long lunch, we marveled at having caught The King. Georgie took my phone to search the map for road crossings and trailheads that might have a trail log. "Do you think we might get to see the whole Royal Family again, Dad?"

"I never thought we would see The King again, Georgie, so who knows? But I don't get the feeling the Royal Family is together anymore."

"They are lucky. We are stuck with each other."

In the last hour of daylight, Georgie turned back toward me with her mouth agape. "Are you kidding me? Look!" She pointed off-trail toward two tents. In front of the tent sat two hikers. The light-haired one sat cross-legged, flipping his shirt in his lap. He flipped it open at the base and pulled it over his head before turning. She called out to them. "Hey, Peach and Green."

In the dark that night, we lay side by side on our groundsheets and stared through the high canopy of the trees into the darkening sky as the first of the stars came out. We giggled. "What on earth is happening?" Aiden said. "How are we catching these people?"

1369

Monica brushed the dark dust from her hand and slid around the round corner booth to the back side. The server approached our corner booth table and tipped her coffee pot toward Monica's cup. "Can I top you off, honey?"

With a quick movement of her hand, Monica covered her coffee cup and shook her head. "Thank you, no." When the server turned away from our table, Monica whispered, "This stuff is awful." She leaned closer toward me and added, "I don't think I like Belden."

"It does feel sketchy." I lifted my cup and extended my pinky. "But at least they have coffee."

Henry elbowed me in the side of my ribs. "Let me out."

"Why? You gonna jump off of that bridge?" I reached past him to separate two horizontal slats of the dust covered blinds, then tapped the window and pointed through the opaque window toward the blurred shape of the red metal bridge spanning the North Fork of the Feather River. "Come on buddy, there are easier ways to get out of walking. Besides, I think it is only about a forty foot drop to the water, and the landing looked plenty deep to me. It might hurt, but you won't injure yourself badly enough to go home if you jump."

"Dad," Henry rolled his eyes, "I just have to go to the bathroom."

After he had gone, June said, "You wouldn't jump off of that bridge, would you, Dad?"

"I've jumped from a lot higher. Haven't I shown you the pictures?" I reached for my phone.

"Only a million times," Aiden said.

"I only meant …" June said.

"What did you only meant?"

"Ugh, Dad, why don't you ever let me finish?" She slapped the table and huffed. "I only meant you wouldn't do that while we are on-trail 'cause you might hurt yourself or something."

"That's true, June. I probably wouldn't," I said and slid toward the edge of the bench. "I want to see if they have some tuna packets. You need anything?"

June shook her head.

"See if they have any cinnamon Pop-Tarts," Aiden said. "I only have the gross fruit kind left."

I was standing in front of the Pop-Tarts when The King buzzed by me and grabbed a packet of ramen noodles and was gone from the aisle before I could even say hi. I blew the dust from the top of the box of cinnamon Pop-Tarts and followed him toward the counter. When I stopped behind him at the counter, he turned around.

"Any idea if someone is working the register?"

"The lady told us she wouldn't be long, but that was right before we sat down to breakfast." I pointed toward the dining room. "I can go ask our server."

By the time I returned, the cashier was back, and The King was gone. "Did you check out the guy with the Ramen noodles?"

The cashier nodded and started ringing me up. "Are you all planning on staying in town for the night?"

"No, ma'am, we are hitting the trail in a few minutes."

She leaned toward me and whispered, "Good, I wouldn't recommend anyone stick around Belden any longer than they have to."

A few minutes later, June and I were crossing the parking lot with our packs on. She slipped her hand into mine, and I nodded toward an old phone booth, "Need to make your one last phone call?"

"What do you mean?"

"Wait, have you ever even seen a phone booth like that?"

"In movies. I have."

"Wow," Monica said, "that makes me feel old."

June squeezed my hand. "Hey, Daddo. I think I'm ready for the climb. You said I get to pick the music, right?"

"Let me guess, Disney?"

She laughed. "How did you know?"

A third of the way up the hill, I stopped to scan the trail above us to catch a glimpse of Monica. She had pushed ahead to listen to music of her own. It took a while, but I spotted her as she was passing another hiker on the trail above us.

"June," I called ahead, but she didn't hear me. I didn't call a second time. She was walking strong, and whatever the trail etiquette surrounding speakers may be, I didn't dare disrupt her momentum.

After catching The King on a switchback, we continued our ascent. It wasn't until we were crossing above the treeline that he passed us again. We saw him pause briefly in the distance to talk to Monica by a large boulder, and then he was gone.

June heard voices in the pines beyond a large log that blocked the horse camp from our view. She cocked her ear toward it and looked back at me. "That's not Mom's voice." She listened again. "It's the others, but Shivers and The King are with them."

When she saw us, Monica said, "Oh my gosh, Vince, did you know that Shivers is getting off-trail to sit for her medical boards?"

"It's not that big a deal," Shivers said, holding up a stack of well worn three-by-five cards held together at the corner by a binder ring. "I just flip through these while I walk."

When I squeezed the last of my hot sauce into my tuna pouch, I offered an apology to The King for the music.

"Yeah, what was that? It was horrible."

"I told June if she'd climb without any complaining that she could play whatever she wanted on the speaker. She chose Disney. Trust me, I feel the same way about it. I am genuinely sorry."

"Oh, I didn't know you guys saw each other out there," Shivers said.

"Yeah, they passed me on a switchback."

"Wait!" Shivers snapped a look to The King. "They caught you on the way uphill?" She held a hand to her mouth. "I changed my mind. I don't think they owe you any kind of apology for the music. If you get caught climbing a hill by an eleven-year-old, I think you should have to listen to whatever music they want to listen to."

1405.4

"Dad, come look at this," Aiden said. "It's the dumbest thing."

"What is it?"

"Look at this sign. It says, 'A-tree 29 miles'."

"That's hilarious. I don't even know what A-tree means. Imagine if they had a tree sign for every single tree out here." I reached in my pocket. "There are a lot of 'A-trees' out here. I've got to get the GoPro out, so we can commemorate this historic occasion."

"Dad, what's wrong?"

"Give me a minute." I dropped my pack to the ground.

"What's wrong?"

"Oh my." I tapped both of my pockets again. "I know right where it is. The GoPro fell out of my pocket at camp."

"Are you sure?"

"Yes, I went up the hill to use the bathroom. When I squatted down, my phone fell from this pocket. The GoPro must have fallen out of the other pocket at the same time and I didn't notice."

"How far back is it?"

"Five miles."

"Can you get another GoPro?"

"It isn't that. It's all the footage on the SD card. Everything since Tim Lloyd's is on there. Otherwise, I might consider leaving it. I can't believe this. Where are the others?"

"They are just up on that bridge."

"Alright, you go ahead, and I'll catch up."

"Are you sure, Dad? Are you sure you don't want me to go with you?"

"I'll leave my pack here and pick it back up on the way by. Tell the others. I'll catch up to you at lunch."

It took me less than two miles to rethink the idea of leaving my pack. Peach had his pack dragged away in the night by camp deer. I'd stuffed my emptied tuna pack from my snack into my right hip belt pocket. A bear would smell it from miles away. I sat down for a minute to decide.

"Hey, Vince, you okay?"

"Troubadour?"

"Dude, are you okay? Where is your pack, and your family?"

I told him.

"I'm so sorry, good luck," he said.

"If you see them, tell them I loved them." I waved.

Ten extra miles today for some video. Ten miles. I couldn't even be sure what I'd captured since we left Lloyds'. I was sure of when I'd last changed out the SD card. Short clip after short clip of our time, to capture moments of singing or some breathtaking view. I couldn't remember anything in particular I might forget, but wasn't that the point? To mark down a moment in time with a capture, so that it could enliven all the other surrounding moments. "Capture the moment," I laughed to remember.

"Put the camera down, cowboy, it's not about capturing the moment, it's about living it." That's what that guy had said from the top of that party bus at Burning Man Festival seventeen years ago. My friend Doug had been standing with a giant camcorder on his shoulder as the bus made a wide circle around us on the hard packed desert floor in Nevada. Oh, how we laughed at that guy. And we laughed again about that guy when we plugged the VHS tape into the VCR after we got home, because had we obeyed him, we'd not have been bent over the television with such excitement. I'd called

Monica to come in from the other room. We told her the story of the guy on the bus and said, "But when you see this, Monica, you are going to have to agree that it's about capturing the moment too."

Doug had flown to San Francisco unannounced and coaxed me into joining him for a few days at Burning Man. His express intention was to hand out pamphlets he'd printed up at his church. He'd said, "Man, this Burning Man thing is flipping going off." None of his plans to talk about Jesus came to fruition as most of the festival's attendees spent the week stoned out of their minds. But when I hit play on the VCR, Doug could hardly contain himself. He jumped up from the couch, "Mon, mon, you are about to see the most amazing thing ever captured on film. This man," he tapped the screen, "is about to retract all of his man parts into his body. Can you believe we caught it on film?"

Monica had turned her back to the TV. "You guys are disgusting. I'm not watching this. Vince, did you actually see this happen?"

"I can vouch for him, Monica. It happened. After he found the guy, Doug came running to find me in the tent where I was taking an afternoon nap. He dragged me over there to witness it happen in person."

***

My GoPro was right on the ground where I had dropped it in the morning, beside my cat hole up the hill from the camp. "At least it's all downhill back to my pack," I said aloud, and pressed the power button. I sat down on the pinestraw beside the trail. One by one, I scrolled through the video files, and smiled. There were four video clips in a row of the kids singing songs. In another, Georgie had laughed at the camera and said, "I can't tell if the dirt is on the inside or the outside of my bottle." The clip after that one was cut short. I had been filming her walking with Monica when Georgie had fallen, but I'd stopped recording to run to her. She'd cut her knee open, though not badly.

I lay on my back and selected the next clip. "I had forgotten some of this stuff … some of it, I would have forgotten forever. You know what, Cowboy? I'm not saying don't live the moment, but sometimes it's good to capture it too."

I stood up and jogged back to the trail. In one hour and twenty minutes I was standing over my backpack again. After filming the trail sign for A-tree, I crossed the bridge where I'd last seen them to push on to lunch.

Georgie spotted me first from a trailhead. She jumped up from a log and ran toward me. "You did that fast!" she said and hugged me. "That's 20.3 miles."

"That's how far I walked?"

She looked at her watch. "Two o'clock."

I didn't bother to take out my groundsheet and collapsed at Monica's feet.

"Are you tired?" she said. "I guess you would be."

"Just a few minutes should be all that I need." I fell asleep.

"Thirty-six miles," Monica told me that night. "That's a record."

"Nope," Henry said, "doesn't count."

They were still talking that night when I rolled to my side and pulled my quilt over me. Within minutes I was asleep, and I did not stir until morning. I was standing by the time my phone powered up. I tested my weight on each foot.

"You okay?" Monica said.

"I feel fine. I can hardly believe it. I was sure I'd be dead."

"Are you serious? What time is it, anyway?"

"I feel good. Are you up for another thirty-six?" I picked up my phone from the ground. "It's five-thirty."

Henry rubbed his eyes and coughed, "Doesn't count."

"What doesn't count, boy?"

"You don't get to count thirty-six miles." He raised his eyebrow and scrunched up the side of his mouth. "You wouldn't count our thirty-mile day that time we walked an extra mile off-trail to Big Lake, so you don't get to have these miles either."

I reached out my hand and tousled his hair. "Got me there. In that case, yesterday was the hardest twenty-six-mile day I've ever done. Are you guys feeling it too?"

Around mid-morning, he asked me for some of my drink flavoring.

"I warned you, you were gonna run out."

He said, "Please," but still I persisted. "What if I trade you something?"

After a while, I offered him a deal. "Henry, if you'll take a big, big, through-your-nose whiff of my stinky armpits, I'll give you enough for a liter."

He tapped his lip and said, "Do I choose the amount?"

"What do you think?"

"I think," he tapped his lip, "I think I'll pass."

1408

I left lunch last and found Georgie waiting. "Are you feeling okay today?" she said.

"I am. My feet ache a little. Well, everything aches a little, but I'm surprised at how good I feel after yesterday. What about you?"

"I feel fine, but I was thinking. I think I figured out what you were saying about home in that Tom Waits song the other day."

"That was over a hundred miles ago, Georgie. What made you think about it today?"

"I don't know. I guess I was just thinking."

"Well? What about home?"

"You know how he says, 'This world is not my home, I'm just passing through.' That's the part you were thinking about, right? When he says home, he's talking about heaven, isn't he?"

"Wow, that's it, exactly. Heaven is home, because it's the only place that all the wrong things can be made right, and all the hardships can end."

"Like in the beginning how he says the sky is cracked."

"Because nature itself is not as it should be. At first, he even says the moon is broken and there is nothing you can do to make it right. Not right, right, anyway. In some ways he is saying that you just gotta hold on 'til you can get to the other side, you know?"

"But I don't think Uncle Ted would agree with all that 'just a' passin' through' stuff, would he? I've overheard you talking to him about this kind of thing."

"Oh, no, he doesn't think that way at all, and neither do I. He would say heaven is the place where there will be no more fear, no more crying, and that the location of heaven itself will be right here." I pointed at the ground. "Actually, here. It is called the new heavens and new earth for a reason. This earth, these very hills where we are walking, will all be remade, as it was meant to be. The cool thing about that is that something of what we do here gets pulled through the fire after the refining at the end of all things. Your life and your work matters. When you do good work, you lay a fingerprint on the planet that will be recorded for all time. When Christ returns, he will come with the fire of judgment. You know how people talk about this world and say, 'it's all gonna burn'?"

"I've heard you say that."

"If you've heard me say it, I was probably making fun of the people who say it. I don't mean to say that it isn't going to burn at all. It just isn't going to burn in the way they mean it."

"What do you mean?"

"Fire has more than one quality. It doesn't only destroy, it also purifies. You know that verse that talks about God's words being pure words, refined in the fire seven times? I'm sure I've quoted it to you more than seven times."

"What does it mean though?"

"Remember that one burn section up in Washington where it looked like everything was dead and burned to ash. But then we camped near that spring, and the green there was so beautiful, and the flowers were so amazing. I think that the fire of judgment will be a fire that is more a refining, than a consuming fire. God will burn up all that is wrong and set all things right. All things new, right?"

"It's kinda weird. Does everyone think that?"

"Not even the majority of Christians think that," I said, then leaned in close to whisper, "I don't even think your mom thinks that. Most Christians think that the ones who are in Christ will be whisked away to some happy cloud in the sky while the whole earth is burning behind them ... But I guess we will find out someday if Uncle Ted and I are right or not. You want to know what else I think?"

"What's that?"

"I think he will set the blaze with his words. The same way that he made the world in the beginning. He spoke, and it was so. 'And God said' is what it says. God spoke and it was."

After walking in silence for another mile, we came to a rocky outcropping near the top of the climb. Georgie walked out to stand on the edge of a large rock. I joined her and looked out over the long valley. I squinted my eyes, and the rocks, lakes and forests altogether blurred into a dusty, gray green.

Georgie said, "Dad, I could see how if someone had a really hard life, they might be mad enough that they would want the whole earth to just burn up, or at least maybe think of it as if it were a place they were just passing through, couldn't you?"

1458

Before anyone else was awake, I stepped from my tent in my bare feet. I rubbed my arms and reached back into the tent for my down jacket. The night before we had pitched our tents in a rush, fearing rain. June and Aiden's tent was pressed against the trail sign on the one side and straddling the trail on the other.

I looked up toward the clear sky and held my phone above my head. My phone showed no reception, so I walked along the ridge away from the tents until it showed two bars.

On the third ring, I heard Dax pick up. "Hello."

"Real quick," I said, "in case I lose you. If we can make the miles I'm expecting, we'll have finished our resupply before you get there. So we will see you in South Lake Tahoe, Dax…I know, it's soon, right?"

We talked a few minutes more, until I lost reception. I pulled my beanie from my pocket and sat on a nearby rock. The high-pitched wail of a two-stroke motor resonated through the valley below me. I tried, without success, to locate the origin of the sound. It grew faint and faded to the point of disappearing, when a wispy line of dust emerged from distant trees. I had mistaken the cut in the trees for a river. Above the cut, the rising sun lit the line of the far ridge. I reached for the zipper of my down jacket and stood up from the rock.

As I neared the intersection of the trail on my return, I stopped to brush the sand from the bottoms of my feet. Two hikers, a woman and a man, surprised me. "Yikes, you're up early," I said.

"We camped down at the lake and wanted to get an early start."

"I don't blame you a bit," I said. "I'd like that too." I nodded in the direction of Aiden's tent. "Although I'm not alone, so I don't always get my way."

We spoke in whispers for a while. "Maybe we'll see you in Sierra City later this afternoon," I said. I waved them goodbye, and they tiptoed around Aiden's tent.

Sometime around mid-morning, Georgie waited for me on a long traverse. "Hey, Dad, whatcha doing back here? Having a good walk this morning?"

"This is great, isn't it? Did you see that big tower up there?" I pointed to the ridge.

"June showed me from the other side. Is that a ladder coming down off of it?"

"I think so."

"Oh, that's cool." She waved me by. "You can go first."

I held the GoPro in my right hand and pointed it backward to film her. I tried to cover the beep with a cough, but she laughed. "Are you making faces at the camera?" I said.

"Can I hold that camera for a minute?"

I handed it to her.

Two trail miles above Sierra City, we crossed paths with two backpackers climbing the switchbacks. "Are those two kids down there with you?" one said. "We told them they should wait for their parents. We saw two bears down there."

I smiled.

"They acted like they were excited about it and took off down the hill like they wanted to find them."

"Your other kids don't seem to be afraid of bears," the other said. "What about you two?" She nodded toward June and Aiden.

"We aren't either," June said.

"We've been out here a while," I said.

"How long?"

"A little over two months."

"And you haven't seen a bear the whole way from Canada?"

"Those two in front haven't. The rest of us have seen several. All of us saw a bear today. My wife had one run down that wide open slope. It came from the top and barreled right across the trail in front of her. What, Monica, thirty feet from you?"

"I could see it coming from a long way away."

"Yeah, and then in the trees just back there, one darted across the trail in front of us." I nodded downhill, "Those two were right there with us, but by the time they looked up, the bear was gone in the trees."

The trail threaded through forest and skirted a busy campground before dropping over a final sharp outcropping down to the road. Georgie and Henry were waiting there, so I dropped my pack beside them to sit down on it. When I did, something sharp stuck me in the backside, and I jumped up. "What is this?"

Georgie giggled.

I reached into the back pouch and pulled out thirteen small rocks. "That's why you asked for my camera. You were filming yourself filling my pack with rocks, weren't you, you turd?"

1488

Georgie stood with her hand on Aiden's backpack. Aiden bent at the waist, breathless.

"Dad, Aiden just saw a bear."

"You saw a bear?"

She nodded her head without looking up and lifted her pointer finger. She caught her breath. When she looked up, she smiled and pointed down-trail. "I was walking up here listening to my headphones. I was looking down at my feet, and Henry was ahead of me. When I kind of glanced up and saw this flash of blonde hair, I just thought it was Henry. Well, it took a second to register that it wasn't him. When I looked up again, I realized it was this huge bear."

She lifted up both arms above her head.

"How big was it?" I said.

She adjusted her hand to a height just below her shoulders. "It was this tall on all fours. It stood there for, like, half a second and then took off up the trail that way. I was shaking, but then I remembered that Henry was out ahead of me, so I kind of freaked out and took off up the trail after the bear and screamed for Henry, 'cause I was scared the bear might have trucked him."

"Did you see him?"

"Not yet, but the bear's footprints left the trail after about 200 yards or so, and I heard him crashing through the bushes down the hill, so …"

"Have you seen any of Henry's footprints since then?"

"No, but I didn't really look."

Georgie scanned the ground and took a few steps up the trail. "Here's one right here."

We turned down into a long valley stretched under a steep bluff and walked into the cool of the late afternoon. I walked alone in the back. Weary walking. It's a weary walk that elicits a smile. It's a thing that you know if you've known it. I stopped at a small spring that trickled out from the embankment just above the trail. I reached my hands through the foliage and waited for my bottle to fill. The sun felt warm on my neck, the good kind of warm. A lone bead of sweat fell against it, cool, and I smiled. They are going to read with the light of a new understanding. They'll trace a finger across an otherwise dead line of text to see it enlivened. They'll feel something, a flash of memory of this. I spoke aloud, "This is what we meant. This is it."

***

Aiden stood at the top of a stair in front of the door near the peak of the A-frame building. Above her head a sign read "Peter Grubb Hut."

"Dad, check this out. The entrance is up here for when it's covered with snow in the winter. Have you seen the snowline on the trees? It was like fifteen feet high in the forest back there. I wouldn't want to get caught out here in the winter."

"What is this place?"

"It's some sort of ski lodge. Ms. McGuyver is here too. There's this big loft we can sleep in."

"We met her a while back, didn't we? Isn't she from Sweden?"

"She's from Finland, Dad. You think every blonde European is from Sweden. Come on, Mom's boiling water. She said she wants to eat something hot tonight." She paused. "Why are you smiling?"

"I love being out here."

She descended the stairs and stood on the step right above me. I gave her a hug.

"Me too, Dad. I'm glad we decided to come."

"Let's go inside. You want to?"

I placed my hand on the front door handle, and Aiden tapped me on the elbow. "Oh, you know what tomorrow is, Dad?" I turned. "It's Donner Pass." When she stepped into the dark interior of the hut, she announced, "Hey guys, guess what? Tomorrow is Donner Pass."

I heard Henry chuckle. "You're the only one that has to worry about that, Dad."

"What is this 'Donner Pass'?" Ms. McGuyver said.

"A party of settlers were trapped there for a winter," Monica said. "When they found the survivors, they discovered that they had eaten the people that froze to death."

"Oh, yeah, Ms. McGuyver," Aiden said, "there was even one guy that preferred to eat human flesh. When they found him, he had an untouched deer leg sitting right by the fire. Supposedly, it was only after someone died that they would eat them, but some historians say that they weren't always waiting for the people to die."

"But why does Henry say your dad has to worry?"

"If we get trapped for the winter," Henry said, "he has the most meat to go around, so we are probably gonna eat him first."

"Oh, that is terrible."

"Oh, you think that's bad," I dropped my food bag on the table and straddled the bench, "before we left home, we had them all pick a Bible verse to laminate and carry with them on the trail. Go ahead, Henry, tell her yours."

"Mine goes, 'For my father and my mother have forsaken me, but the Lord will take me in.'"

Monica lifted the stove and canister and shook them. "I can't get this thing to work. The clip that you turn for the gas broke."

I reached for it. "Henry, shine your light on this thing." A small piece of the metal clasp had broken off in the housing. "If we carried a leatherman we could just use that to twist it."

"Do you mind if I have a look?" Ms. McGuyver said. "I have a paper clip and some copper wire."

Aiden laughed. "Because who doesn't carry copper wire when they hike?"

Within a few minutes, Ms. McGuyver lit the stove and placed it on the picnic table with a smile. Monica thanked her and balanced the pot over the flame.

After we ate, Monica called Georgie to her so she could look at her back.

Ms. McGuyver nodded toward her and whispered to me, "What's going on there?"

"Her pack rubbed a raw place on her back a couple of weeks ago, so we've been keeping it bandaged up. It was rough for a week or so, and we even considered coming off trail to let it heal. It's getting better now, isn't it, Georgie?"

Monica looked over at us. "It's stopped getting worse is more like it. I wouldn't say it's healing up yet."

"I think maybe I've just gotten used to it by now, Dad."

Monica shook the tube of bacitracin. "We need to remember to buy more of this stuff when we get to South Lake Tahoe."

I pulled out my phone and tapped the screen. "I'll put it on the list."

1514

We heard the guitar as we rounded the turn. June looked back at me, laughed, and began to run. "Troubadour!" His feet hung over the trail and his legs disappeared into the shade behind a cluster of bushes. Beyond him a small trickling creek ran past the trail.

"I thought you said we were coming up to the American River?" Monica said.

"I did, but maybe headwaters means it's not quite a river yet."

"American River?" Aiden said. "Dad, didn't you say you used to take me camping there when I was a baby?"

"We did, but a good way downstream. I thought that we would have seen something a little more substantial than this."

"Remember how hot those rocks were?" Monica said. "We couldn't even let you out of your pack-and-play, Aiden."

"Was it before I could even walk?"

"The first time we went, yes. We couldn't even let you crawl around in the shade, because the tree was dropping a sap that was so sticky"—Monica interrupted herself with laughing—"that you had sand and leaves stuck all over you. It took me forever to get you cleaned off."

June, Henry, and Georgie were sitting in the shade beside Troubadour when we arrived. I leaned over them to wave a hello. "I hope it's okay that we interrupt your session."

"Man, come on in."

"We'll just grab some water and get out of your hair." Forty-five minutes later, we still hadn't moved. "Does this happen to you a lot?"

"You mean get stuck in a place?"

"Yeah, you just sit down and start playing, and all of a sudden an hour has gone."

"I love to sit and play by the water," Troubadour said. "Sometimes, it will give you the rhythm. And when it does, you can't stop 'til it's over."

"Can we just stay here and eat?" Aiden said. "I mean, we might as well, now."

"No, we'd better keep moving." I stood and pulled them one by one to their feet. After they started off down the hill, I returned. "Hey, man, my brother is surprising the kids at a trailhead coming up in a bit, if you want to join us. He's in town for some sort of race, but he's coming out to the trailhead to meet us with food. We'd love to share."

"Right on." He stopped strumming. "I'm gonna play here a bit longer, and then maybe I'll catch up."

Georgie sat beside Monica on the edge of the picnic table and three women gathered around. One lifted her boot and tapped the sole with a trekking pole. "Our fourth should be here soon. It was a loop hike, and her first time to come with us."

"Oh," Georgie said, "that's neat."

"So, your uncle brought food out here to surprise you?"

Georgie looked up at me. "It's not the first time Dad's kept it a secret."

The woman laughed. "Do you not like the surprises?"

"I like them, but sometimes I think it would be better motivation if we knew about the thing that was coming, and then we could look forward to it to get through the hard stuff."

"Has this part of the trail been hard?"

"A few friends from home are coming out to walk with us for a few days, so I've had to ask a bit more of them lately than maybe they would have liked."

Georgie elbowed me. "Yeah, and then we get to slow down. Right, Dad?"

"How many miles do you walk every day?"

"We walk at least twenty-six"—Georgie swung her trekking pole toward Monica—"unless Mom's feet are hurting too bad, so sometimes we stop around twenty-five."

"That's incredible." The women exchanged glances. "Do you ever wake up and say, 'Nope, sorry parents, not today?' I think if I were eleven, I would have revolted if my parents asked me to walk twenty-six miles a day."

"Well, it isn't like they aren't walking twenty-six-mile days too, and it's not any easier for them than it is for us. But we have to beat the winter to the Sierra, so it's not like we don't get to not do it."

Lee moved away from the conversation at the far end of the picnic table and rested his hand on Georgie's shoulder. He lifted a bag with a whole rotisserie chicken inside. "Anyone want some of this before it's all gone? We have plenty."

"No, we are headed down the hill to a restaurant, and these kids look hungry. I'm not sure you have enough. Do you live near here?"

"No, I'm from Florida. The same place they are from. I'm here for a race down in the South Lake Tahoe." He pointed toward his van. "I sell running shoes." He flashed them a smile. "Ever heard of Newton Running? I could sell you a pair."

"He also has a skin slather." I pulled a small tube from my hip belt pocket. "Skinstrong. This stuff is a life saver."

"What is it?" She reached for the tube.

When I said, "It makes your monkey butt disappear," she pulled her hand back.

"Dad!" June said. "That's gross."

"Hey, this is hiking, June Bug. You gotta embrace the gross stuff. Am I right, ladies?"

I pulled my credit card bundle from my pack and slid some cash out from under the rubber band. I excused myself from the conversation and tapped Lee on the shoulder. We embraced, and I thanked him for coming to meet us. "I'm sure it was out of your way."

"No, it wasn't too bad." He waved away my offer for cash. "I got this," he said.

When we put our packs on to leave, all four ladies were standing beside the picnic table in a semi-circle around Troubadour.

"Do we get a concert?" one of them said. "Do you have time?"

"Oh, yes ma'am," he said. "I ain't got nothing but time. What do you wanna hear?"

Monica tapped me on the shoulder. "Are you coming?"

"I think I'm gonna listen for a few minutes," I said. "I'll catch up."

Ten minutes later, I said goodbye to Lee again and set off to catch up to the others. Ten minutes after that, I heard an unfamiliar voice from behind me and was shocked to find Ms. Macgyver waving her hand in the air.

"I had no idea you had caught up to us," I said. "What is that you have in your hand?"

"I thought you might need these," she said, and dropped something into my hand. "I'm glad I caught you."

"Oh my, thank you." I shook the banded bundle of credit cards in my hand. "I wouldn't have gotten far without these." With my other hand I inverted my pocket and pointed at the exposed inner lining. "I forgot that this pocket had a big hole."

She pointed at the bundle. "I replaced the rubber band with one that I had. Yours looked like it was beginning to fray."

1561

"Dad!" Aiden shouted with her face pressed to the glass.

June jumped from the hotel bed. "What is it?"

"It's Mr. Gibson! Come on guys, let's go!"

The door shut behind them, and Monica ran to it. "Henry, are you seriously going to leave without your rain jacket?" She threw it into the hall behind him and turned back into the room. She shook her head. "That boy."

I walked to the window and pressed my forehead against it to look down. Dax was leaning over the trunk, and all four of the kids raced across the parking lot toward him. Before he could stand up, they hugged him. He turned and flashed them a familiar smile and rubbed his bald head. Dustin and Grandy stepped around the side of the car and gave the kids each a hug too. I stepped back from the window. "This is going to be great to have them all here."

"How did Dax talk Grandy into it?" Monica said.

"Grandy is a big hiker, apparently. He has hiked the Rim to Rim trail at the Grand Canyon several times." I glanced back down to the parking lot. "Wow, Dustin has a big camera attached to his pack. I figured he'd bring one, but that thing looks heavy."

"Yeah, his wife told me that he was bringing it when I talked to her."

"Are you about ready?"

"You go ahead, I need to repack my pack." Before I reached the door, she said, "What do you know about this section? Is it supposed to be bad?"

"It's not the Sierra, so how bad can it be?"

By the time the sliding doors opened in front of me, there was a boisterous seven-person conversation taking place under the porte cochere. All giggles. All smiles. I made it eight, and hugged Dax. "Be glad you met us after two days in a hotel. This would have been a stinky group hug on-trail."

"You guys," Dax said, "it's so good to see you."

I was at the end of the asking of travels, when Bear Hair spotted us and crossed the parking lot with hurried strides. "Oh, Strawbridges, you are heading back to the trail today, yes?"

Dax pointed back and forth between us. "You guys know each other?"

"Dax, this is our good friend, Bear Hair."

He leaned closer and pushed his glasses further up on his nose. "Bear Hair?"

"It's her trail name."

"Okay." He leaned back and crossed his arms. "It's nice to meet you, Bear Hair."

"Bear Hair, we are headed to trail in about thirty minutes, if you need a ride. We have room, don't we, Dax?" I tapped his arm. "I think we will have to take two trips anyway, before we can shuttle the car around."

"Oh, it's Bear Hair!" Monica skipped across the sidewalk with her arms open. "And Dax, I need a hug from you too. How's Michele?"

"I want to go with you guys for the shuttle," Henry said.

I patted him on the back. "Let me text Anne to see if she has room."

"How do you know this Anne?" Dax said.

"I don't know that you'd have any reason to know this, but we did a prep hike in Lassen before we started in Washington. We met her in a parking lot and she said she would help to support us through the Sierra Nevada."

"What is it with these people? That's so nice."

"She's a trail angel. It's mind blowing how nice these people are. We have met so many, right, Henry? This kid loves trail magic."

"Trail magic?"

"Mr. Dax, trail magic is awesome. It's when these people just set up by the trail and cook you stuff. And they almost always have Coke and candy."

"Tell him about your Coke can, Henry."

"I still have a Coke can from Washington."

"Isn't that unnecessary extra weight?" Dax said. "Why not drink it?"

"I drank it already. I'm just carrying the can for a keepsake."

I shook my head and turned to call Aiden over. She hopped to a stop in front of me, and said, "Yeah, Dad?"

"Why don't you go with the first group? You guys can wait with them up by the lake for the second carload. After that, Dax and I will drive to meet our ride for the shuttle."

Henry tugged at my sleeve. "Remember, I want to go with you guys."

"I forgot. Let me text Anne one more time."

When Henry, Dax, and I dropped the second group near the trailhead, I checked my phone for the time. "We better hurry, we'll be lucky to be back before dark."

Monica waved us to a stop, ran across the parking lot to the car, and tapped on the window. "How will you find us?"

"Just find a good spot not far off the trail, and we will find you."

"In the dark?"

"Oh, you're right. You know what? Take the Garmin, and text me a mile marker when you find a spot."

"How will you be able to see it?"

"We're driving for four hours, I'm sure somewhere in there we'll get reception."

"Let's hope."

"Stay close to the trail, just in case."

It was six and a half hours later when I tiptoed over sleeping bags in the dark, shimmied around Grandy's small one-man tent, and knelt in front of Monica's tent to scratch on the door. "You didn't text me."

"Shh. Keep it down," she whispered as she unzipped the door from the inside. "You guys made it."

"You didn't text me."

She gave a quick wave toward a pile of gear in the corner of the tent. "Oh, I couldn't figure that thing out."

"Georgie didn't want to sleep in the tent?"

Monica nodded past me. "She wanted to sleep out with the girls."

"Good, I'm coming in." After a while I said, "It's fun to have friends come and join us. June was excited."

"You should have seen her. She led the way up the hill. How was your drive?"

"Henry got sick and puked all over the place."

"In the car?"

"Yes, it was nasty."

"Why didn't he puke out the window?"

"He tried. He just didn't make it."

"That's so gross."

"We pulled over and took everything out. She had a towel in the car, and there was a creek nearby so we had water to wash everything down. She didn't seem all that upset by it, and Dax was great with her. He apologized enough for all of us, and he talked to Anne the whole way back while I slept."

I groped my way to my clothes bag and laid it under my head in the dark. "This thing isn't as comfortable anymore, now that I'm having to wear more clothes at night to stay warm." I put my arm over her and closed my eyes and smiled. "Fun that they are here."

After a few minutes, she whispered, "Did you download the Sierra section?"

"Oof."

"Aiden and I have it on our phones."

"That's good. Maybe I can get enough reception in the morning when we get up a little higher."

1563

Henry reached a hand up toward a low flying helicopter and called out, "Give me a ride!"

"What do you think they are looking for?" Dax said.

Aiden looked up as she walked. "Oh man, Mr. Gibson. Did Dad tell you about the people that got rescued right near us one night?"

"No, where was this?"

"I was the only one that got out of the tent to see it, but there was this big helicopter flying right beside us. It turned out, it was searching for these people who fell off the side of a cliff."

Having heard Aiden tell the story several times before, I stepped off the trail to wait for Grandy. After he passed by me, I followed him across the wide flat to where the trail turned a few scrambly switchbacks up a steep bank. He paused, and I passed him to start up the short hill. Halfway up, I turned to look back to find Grandy at the base looking up.

I waved.

He shook his head and leaned on a tree.

I pulled out my phone and held it high in the air. It showed two bars of reception. I started the slow download. "Thirty percent," I said when Grandy reached me. "At this rate it might take until tomorrow to download this section. Are you doing okay?"

"Altitude." He held a hand to his chest. "The altitude is getting to me. I can't believe your kids, man. You guys are machines. Dax warned me I needed to prepare for this, and I knew I should. I wish I hadn't blown it off. I just kept thinking, 'If June can do it …'"

"You were her first ever soccer coach," I laughed, "so you know how 'athletic' she is."

"Yeah, but out here, she's like Secretariat, and I'm Eeyore. I'm sure I'll be fine. I just gotta move at my own pace. You go ahead, I'll get there, eventually."

"Nah. I'll walk with you. I like to walk in the back."

During our long lunch by a lake, June lay down beside me and whispered, "Do you think Grandy's okay?"

"Remember what he used to say to you when you played soccer for him?"

She shook her head. "What was it?"

"Shh, not so loud. Later on today when you are with him, you should say, 'Come on Grandy, you walk like you're swimming in peanut butter.'"

"Oh yeah, I remember he used to say that." She smiled. "But that was about running, and I'm not gonna say that to him."

I nodded toward Dustin at the water's edge. "He's going to get some great pictures out here." I called over to him. "Make sure you get some rest, Dustin. It's a little hilly this afternoon."

"That wasn't hilly this morning?" Grandy said.

Monica laughed. "Don't ever believe him when he says 'hilly.' He always makes it sound easier than it is."

"Yeah, like," Aiden deepened the tone in her voice, "'It's just a little pop, kids.'"

"Or, 'Just one more little bump to the top,'" June said. "It's always a lot harder."

"Come on, you guys, it's not my fault I can't read a map," I said.

"You can read it just fine, Dad," Aiden said. "You just try to trick us into going more and more."

"Hey, there are a lot of high school boyfriends out here."

"High school boyfriends?" Dax scratched his head. "What's all this about?"

Aiden lowered her voice again. "They tell you they love you, but as soon as you believe it, they dump you flat."

"What does that have to do with anything?"

"Oh, you know," Aiden said. "All these disappearing horizons. As soon as you think you are at the top, you find out there is a lot more you have to go."

Dax shook his head and laughed. "I'm not sure I quite understand, Aiden."

"Well, it makes sense to us."

Dax pulled his sleeping bag from his backpack and placed it carefully between his feet. He looked over to where Henry and June sat. "Henry," he said. "You just dump all of your food out on the ground?"

"We all do," Henry said. "It's easy to stuff it all back in before we leave."

"Can I see the famous Coke can?"

Henry picked his way through his things and lifted the crumpled can with a smile.

Dax laughed.

"I'm not sure how they keep all of their stuff separate when they dump it in one pile like that, though," I said. "Henry, how are you and June going to be able to tell whose is whose?"

"We can tell," he said. "I'm gonna pack up first anyway, 'cause I want to go fish and swim a little while we're here."

"Oh, come on, Henry," Aiden said. "I thought you said we were going to go climb those rocks?"

We walked all afternoon through steady and rolling climbs, and across a wide field with a weathered wood cabin. At last, near dark, we stepped off-trail into a small glade of Aspens. The glade straddled a minefield of tent-sized granite boulders patched in between with flat spaces of dirt and pinestraw.

June offered to help Grandy set up his tent. He held up his finger and sat down on a rock with a groan. "I'm not too proud." Leaning to the right, he reached his two hands under his knee, lifted up and winced as he straightened his leg. "Thank you, June."

"Come on, Grandy," Dax said. "Cowboy camp with us. It's a part of the experience."

"You will never catch me doing that. You have no idea what's out here."

"That's what I always say when they try to get me to do it," Monica said. "I'm not sure what a thin tent is going to do to protect me, but it just makes me feel better."

After we ate our food, I stretched out on my back and looked into the canopy above me. Their talking and laughing surrounded me, but felt somehow distant, as if filtered.

All of a sudden, they grew quiet, and a man appeared above me as if out of nowhere. I glanced toward his heavy leather boots beside me and looked into his slanted and steely eyes. He leveled an even gaze at me, and when he spoke, his deep voice had a harmonic rumble to it. "I'm looking for a level spot of ground with an eastern facing aspect."

I sat up. "Through there, out past the rocks." I pointed toward a tight path between two boulders. "We didn't use it because we were concerned about the wind."

"My concern for the wind does not outweigh my desire for sun in the morning." He looked at each of us in turn. "Tell me, what is this group?"

I told him, and then asked his name.

"I do not carry a trail name. People will sometimes call me NTN. No Trail Name. I began hiking long before you kids began coming up with these so-silly trail names."

When I cracked my eyes open in the morning, he was standing above me looking down with the same steady gaze from the night before. "I cannot tell you how much I admire what you have chosen to do with your family."

"It was her idea." I pointed at Monica.

"Son, speak true words. I'm sure you had no small part in this." With a few even steps, he was gone from the glade.

1591

Aiden stepped to the side of the trail to let the rest of our group pass her. When I stopped beside her, she grabbed my elbow and whispered, "Mr. Gibson has blisters."

"How bad?"

"He's limping pretty badly."

"Can we work on it at lunch, or do you think it's bad enough that we need to stop now?"

"How long 'til lunch?"

"Less than a mile, maybe a mile and a half."

When we all settled in our groundsheets a half an hour later, Aiden pointed toward him. I nodded. "Dax, how are your feet?"

"Not bad."

"Not bad is not good. Do you feel a hot spot?"

He pulled his sock past his heel and winced. "A little bit."

"Let Aiden have a look," I said.

"Monica said you were having trouble with your shoes." He nodded toward my feet as Aiden knelt beside him.

"They aren't unbearably bad, and they've turned out to be durable. It's just that I can't feel a few of my toes."

He pulled back as though he'd smelled something bad.

I laughed. "After a while these things stop bothering you."

"Pfft," Aiden said and turned to me. "This isn't too bad, Mr. Dax, you should've seen mine when Georgie…"

Georgie jumped up and rushed to put a hand over Aiden's mouth. "Don't tell him. I hate that story."

Aiden pulled her hand away. "She doesn't want me to tell you about how she ripped all of my skin off of the bottom of my foot." She stood up, brushed off her knees, and jogged toward Monica. "Hey, Mom, don't worry about that, I'll boil the water, so you can help Mr. Gibson tape his blisters."

Monica held up the stove and shook it. "Who has the med kit?" Before the words came out of her mouth, a plastic bag had intersected my view in mid-air. It landed hard on Monica's leg. "Henry, what on earth?"

"Don't forget about Georgie's back, Mom," Aiden said.

Dax waved a hand up as Monica approached him. No, Monica," Dax said. "Take care of Georgie first. I can wait. What is the deal with your back, Georgie?"

"It's almost gone now, but my pack rubbed a big rash on my back that wouldn't go away for a long time."

"We've been dealing with it for a few weeks now, I guess," I said. "Right, Georgie? At least it didn't ever get infected."

In the afternoon we stepped out onto a wide meadow, blanketed under various shades of golden grass. Aiden stopped me and pointed behind us up to the far end of the valley where two lines of pines met at the end of a shallow rise. "Those trees look like they were planted to me, or at least cut back that way." She held a hand to her brow and squinted her eyes. "And that could be part of a wall of an old cabin. I bet someone lived here. Do you think they farmed all this? Or just ran cattle and sheep?"

"The season would be short up here, but they would have pushed sheep up here in the summer."

From that meadow we climbed to others through forests with long, slow switchbacks, until we traversed beneath a high and rocky ridge. After a late afternoon stop, we picked a target for camp.

I tapped Dax's pack, and he stopped. "I'll drop to the back with Grandy. We should be there a little after dark."

"No, we'll stick together," Dax said. He turned and looked up the trail for a moment, then nodded toward Henry, who was hopping back and forth over the trail from one rock to another. Georgie copied his steps.

"It's a game they play," I said. "Whenever one of them says, 'The trail is lava,' they aren't allowed to step on the dirt."

"Ahh, the floor is lava. They used to play that at our house with our kids when you guys would come over." He turned to continue up the trail. "I'm amazed they have the energy for that?"

At the last water stop I sat on a rock beside Dustin while he finished refilling his water. He pointed toward my water bottle. "You don't need to filter any water?"

"I filled up at that last little stream we crossed."

"Without stopping?" He shook his head and turned away from me. I followed his gaze and saw Monica and Grandy talking with a northbound hiker.

"Oof, Dustin, that guy is late if he's hiking through."

"What do you mean?"

"If a northbounder hasn't finished California by now, they'll never make it."

"Remember that German northbounder about a week ago?" Aiden said.

I nodded and pushed myself up from the rock where I sat and screwed my filter onto my dirty bottle. "Ready, guys? It's the last push of the day. Although, we'll be walking well into the dark, so maybe we should call it the last push before the last push of the day ..."

"Dad," Aiden tapped my elbow and pointed, "I think that's Dahn talking to Mom."

I buckled my chest strap and looked up to follow her finger. "Cool, let's go see them."

 Dahn waved as I approached and flashed a broad smile. "Hey there, Dad. You've been making great time." He reached up his hand to wipe the side of his nose and half turned.

"Your pack is so small," I said. "It looks like a daypack."

He reached his hand back and patted it. "I'm not carrying a tent now, so I have saved some weight."

"He says there is a storm coming in the Sierra," Monica said. "Did you know anything about that?"

"I thought we only had the fire to worry about. They opened up the 108, so I thought that meant we were good."

"Unless this wind picks up," Dahn looked over his shoulder, "the fire shouldn't be anything of a problem. I camped not far from it last night."

I looked at Monica. "Bear Hair mentioned something about a storm this morning."

"They are calling for snow next week at high elevation," Dahn said.

I nodded toward his small pack. "Is that not a concern for you?"

"I'll be back up to Oregon by the time it hits." He tilted his head side to side with a slight motion. "Keep an eye on it, you don't want to get caught up high in the Sierra this time of year. Plus, the parks are all closing soon."

"Red's Meadow?"

"They are open a little while longer, but Vermillion, Tuolumne, and Muir Trail Ranch are already closed. Where do you resupply?"

"We met a lady in Lassen before the trip. She's bringing it to us at Red's."

"I don't need to bother you with all this stuff, you know what you're doing. You guys are pros by now."

"I don't feel like a pro, all of a sudden."

"The Sierra is intimidating." He looked around, and then up at the sky. "It has a different feel to it." He pointed behind him up the trail." The rest of the kids seem well. They were all out front just dancing along to the music."

"Oh no," Monica said.

He laughed. "Let them enjoy themselves. They've earned the right to listen to whatever they want as loud as they want. Besides, there's almost no one out here this late in the season." He paused. "June seems like she is doing well."

"Much better than the last time you saw us. You're about finished, right?"

"Not really, I mixed in a long trail in between."

"What does that mean?"

"I got off the PCT to do the Arizona Trail, and then came back."

I looked at Monica and then back to Dahn. "That's eight hundred miles, isn't it?"

He smiled.

"It wasn't that bad." He nodded north. "I've got some miles to get between here and Washington, then I'll flip down to Kennedy Meadows South."

Dax stepped up behind me. "Dahn, this is Dax, one of our pastors from our church in Lakeland. Dax, this is Dahn. He spent some time in Lakeland, on the north side of town."

"What a small world."

"I don't think he's coming back to Lakeland again," I said. "Unless it's for a visit."

"How did you get to know these guys?"

"It's not a wide path," Dahn said. "We've run into each other a few times now."

We talked for a while before making our departures. I waved and said, "Will we see you again?"

"I hope so," Dahn said and waved back.

In the late afternoon, my Garmin beeped and I dropped to the rear. I stopped to send a reply.

After I caught her again, Monica said, "What's wrong?"

"Anne."

"What? Can she not bring our resupply?"

"She is saying she won't."

"She won't?"

"She says this storm coming in is bad, and she doesn't want to be responsible for enabling us to take the kids out into it."

"I thought you said it wouldn't be that bad."

"I don't think it will be. I told her we would resupply at the camp store in Red's Meadow if she decides not to come."

"Do you think she will come?"

I shrugged. "I hope she does." I tapped my instep. "Otherwise, I'm stuck in these horrible shoes 'til who knows when."

After sunset, the moon reflected grayish red against the high cliff wall to our right, casting dark shadows in its vertical cuts. Between us, large boulders cast their own long shadows up toward it across the wide slope. Our path was lit. Almost white against the moonlight.

"How much farther, do you think?" June said.

"Are you tired?"

"No. I was thinking of Grandy."

"He'll be okay. He's just walking steady and slow."

"Remember, you used to always have to say that to me, Daddo?"

"What's that?"

"Slow steps. Steady steps."

Grandy didn't speak when he shuffled into the camp. He made it almost to Dustin and dropped to his knees, then lay down on his stomach. Right in the dirt.

Dax laughed. "Grandy, are you okay there?"

"Somebody pull this pack off of me."

"You want me to set up your tent for you?" June said.

"I don't care what happens, I'm not moving from this spot."

I motioned for Aiden's attention and then pointed to Grandy. I mouthed, "Food," and tapped my fingers to my lips. "Before he goes to sleep."

She nodded.

"I guess you're cowboy camping tonight, eh, coach?" Henry said.

Grandy groaned. "Isn't there a road crossing first thing in the morning?"

1594

We stopped early in the morning on Highway 4, where it intersects the trail at Ebbetts Pass. Grandy sat down on a wall near the road. "This is it for me. I don't care how long it takes for me to find a ride." He turned toward me. "Which way am I going?"

"I don't know." I pulled out my phone. "Let me look." I heard a door slam and looked up. "There must be a pull out nearby, let me go down and check."

As I approached the man from across the parking lot, I noticed that he was reaching into his trunk and pulling out a small daypack. I coughed to announce myself. After a few pleasantries, I said, "Would you be able to give our friend a ride down the hill to the main road? Ultimately, he is trying to make it to their car at Sonora Pass, so he is going to need more than one hitch."

"If he doesn't mind waiting an hour or two. I'm only planning to do a few miles today."

We found Grandy splayed out on his Tyvek. He said he was happy to wait. "Just shake me if I'm sleeping when you get back." He tilted his hat down over his eyes and leaned his head back on his pack.

1612

Aiden waited for me on the far side of the cattle gate. The fabric of my rain shell snapped and popped in the wind whipping over the top of the knoll. She shouted something. I shook my head. "Wait 'til we get into the trees."

She shrugged her shoulders as if she didn't understand, so I pointed.

When we reached the windbreak, she said, "Did you see it?"

"I did."

"Are you worried?"

"Only a little, because of this wind."

"It wasn't very much smoke, I guess. Did Mom see it?"

I shrugged.

Throughout the afternoon there was laughter. There were songs and stories. Monica let her hands glide through golden leafed aspen. Henry parkoured across grand granite faces marked with ancient striations. Georgie took guided turns behind the lens of Dustin's camera. And we talked. And we walked. And we talked.

At the crest of a rise near dusk, Georgie stopped and held up her hands. "I think I felt a raindrop."

"Is that a big deal? Should I be worried?" Dax said. "You do feel pretty vulnerable out here, don't you?"

"Not so much here." I pointed toward the horizon. "But when we get back in there, it'll feel that way."

We stood silent for a long time beneath the broad panorama of mountains as it was slowly enveloped by the deepening evening shadow. These were not rounded and rolling peaks as in Oregon, nor wooded, green and alive as in Washington. These mountains felt youthful and violent, as if in some geological adolescence with lines all jagged and sharp.

"It seems like everything could change in an instant," he said.

I bent over and rested my chin on my trekking pole. "There are plenty of scary moments, but out here there is so much time, so much grind. You wake up dirty and stinking and eat on the walk. You walk and walk until lunch, then you calculate your remaining miles until camp. And you do it all at this pace that is strange at first, really strange. I remember waking up one morning before a town stop with 6.5 miles to go, more or less three hours of walking. At home, if I woke up knowing I had to drive three hours to Jacksonville, I would be annoyed by how far away it was. But something shifts here. This trail life pace makes you patient."

"And dirt," Georgie said, "and food, and walking, and more and more walking."

"It's true, Georgie," I said. "I'm just saying that the stories we are tempted to tell are almost always about the few scary moments."

"That's 'cause that's the interesting stuff, Dad. Nobody wants to hear all that boring stuff."

"Yeah, but if you don't tell about the stink, and the dirt, and weary hours of walking, you don't really do it justice. At least that's what I think."

"I'm getting a sense of that already," Dax said. "Of that slower pace. Just being off of my phone for a few days with you has made my mind less frantic."

We fell into silence for a long time. Georgie pointed, without speaking, toward the moon as it rose over a dark peak southeast of us. It seemed as if a sacred spell had been cast over the three of us, and that we might stand that way forever, so I offered words far less than fitting for the moment, "Well, they aren't the Appalachians, are they?"

Georgie opened her mouth and tilted her head upward. "I just got a drop of rain in my mouth."

"It's okay, kid, I don't think it's going to rain, but let's get moving."

"What is the Lord up to?" she said.

Dax laughed and looked back at me. "What's that all about?"

"You know my Uncle Timo. It's a thing that he says all the time. But he's funny about it, if you ask me. He says it when things aren't going right. A guy walked into his office one weekday to tell him his wife had been running around town with other men. Timo asked him to sit down. Then he said what Georgie just quoted. He said, 'Surely, the Lord must love you, to give you such a chance to share in this suffering.' He thinks, 'Why do we only see it as God's hand when things are going well?'"

Georgie glanced over her shoulder and said, "Dad always makes fun of us when we say 'if only' because it's like, whatever is happening, we wish something else was happening."

"What do you mean?" Dax said.

"Well, you know, like when it's hot and sunny, we say we wish we had clouds. But when there are clouds, we are chilly, so we say we wish it were sunny."

"I don't just make fun of you guys," I said. "I make fun of myself too. I'm just as discontented as all of you."

Georgie lowered her voice. "In everything, give thanks."

"Is that supposed to be your dad's voice?" Dax laughed.

"Oh, yeah. He says that to us all the time." She pointed, "Look Dad you see that flashlight on the ridge. Someone is waiting for us, I guess."

We found June sitting on a large rock just off-trail with her feet a few feet off the ground. "Dad, I'm tired," she said. "Can we be done walking soon?"

You've been pushing it hard these last few days." I reached an arm around her and pulled her to me. "We will stop as soon as we find a good place. Maybe the others have found something already."

As we rounded a turn onto a grassy knoll, we heard them call us from a glade of pines. All of the trees were still living but burned to twelve feet up their trunks. Monica stood up and walked toward me.

"Can you give me the tent? It's in your pack." She paused as if to reconsider. "You know what? I think I'll sleep outside with you guys tonight."

"Mom?" June said. "Did I hear you right?"

"Monica!" Dax said. "Cowboy camping. Here we go!"

"Well, it's partly that," and she pointed past us down the hill. "But I don't like the look of that smoke, and if we have to get out of here quickly, I don't want to have to pack up the tent."

"You see, Dad," Aiden said. "I told you she saw it."

"When did you see it?" I said.

"You weren't with us at the time, I guess. There were two hunters on horseback passing us earlier today. They pointed it out. They were leaving because they were nervous about it."

"And you never mentioned it?" I said.

"Dahn didn't seem worried about it, so I thought they might be making too much of it."

We watched stars come out one by one and called out the shooting stars. Henry kept count of how many he saw first. Aiden disputed his claims.

"What's our day like tomorrow?" June said.

"We drop into a ravine, and then slow steady climb over the top, and then down to Sonora Pass. It shouldn't be too bad."

"Yeah, right, Dad. Slow and steady."

I rolled on my groundsheet to reach my Garmin. "Did you hear it beep, June?" I turned it over. "Hey everybody, it's Grandy. Want me to read it? 'Made it to the car. Waiting on a second cheeseburger and a third beer. Cheers. See you tomorrow at Sonora Pass.'"

"He's the best," Dax said. "Good night, Strawbridges. Good night, Dustin."

My Garmin beeped again. "Check this out, that guy that gave him a ride from Ebbetts Pass took him all the way around to Sonora Pass."

"That's pretty nice," Aiden said.

"Pretty nice?" I said. "Grandy said it was about four hours out of the way."

1634

I pressed my cheek into the unfriendly fragments of stone so that I could look her in the eye. "June, this came out of nowhere. You were doing so well."

She let her tears fall unhindered, sideways over the bridge of her nose. "I give up, Dad. I can't do it."

I looked at her. "Me too, June."

She cried and did not respond for a long time. "Are you serious?"

"Yes."

"So we can go home?"

"We can go home."

June sat up and looked toward the pass. I turned my eyes to follow hers. The final bit of the climb was visible from where we'd stopped. I traced the faint indentation of the trail through heavy brush as it weaved its way back and forth up switchbacks of varied length and steepness. The last of the others stood, a silhouette against the sky along the ridge, but only for a moment, then disappeared from sight. Only the two of us remained.

"You think they will be mad at me?"

"Not Henry."

She laughed. "Henry will be happy about it." She wiped her eyes with the heels of her hands.

I sat up and slid back to lean against a rock. I thought about how each of them might react if I told them we would be going home.

"I bet Aiden will be mad about it; she never wants to quit anything once she's started. What about you, Dad? Will you be upset?"

"No, June," I said, then I paused. "No, that's not true. I will be upset. I won't blame you, but I will be upset. Of course, I want to finish. You know that, and there is no use pretending. But I won't love you any less." I traced my fingers through the pebbles beside me. "From the first day, you have had to work harder than anyone else, and we have had to push hard to get here on time. That's my fault. Me and my stupid math." I reached the heel of my hand to my eye. "Come here, June Bug."

June didn't move. "How did you mess up that bad, Dad?"

"I don't know, kid. Pretty dumb, huh?" I rolled my head back against the rock.

She pushed herself to a seated position and sat beside me. "Why do you want to do it so bad?"

"I can't explain it, June. I don't know that I can, anyway. It's a quest. It's a pull. It's a dream. I mean, Canada to Mexico, and all the way on foot. The whole thing seemed impossible, even though I hadn't a clue what it would take. I mean, not fully. Then when I got a taste of what it would take, it seemed even more impossible." I threw another small rock. "Now, it seems almost within reach." I looked toward the pass. "So yeah. I would be upset."

"How far ahead do you think the others are now?"

"I don't know that I care at this point." I reached out my arm and she scooched in to lean against me. "I pushed us too hard, June. You know how I complain about all the fear mongering? And I say we will just see when we get there? But about this, I couldn't make myself mean it. I got worked up about getting to the Sierra … I just couldn't let it be what it would be. I couldn't trust. I had to get us here. I pushed you too hard, and I'm sorry. And if the cost of that is going home, it is my fault completely. I do not … I will not, blame you."

We were quiet again for a long time.

"So I think it's my fault. Not yours."

"Daddo? Do you think we could take it easier, if we kept going? A little bit?"

I shook my head. "Kid, I want to keep going. I want to finish, but that stuff …" I pointed up the trail. "That next three hundred miles is going to be harder than anything we've done yet, and I am not going to take you in there under false pretenses."

"Could we back down the miles at least?"

"We are not going to do twenty-fives in those mountains, if that's what you mean."

"How about we keep it around twenty?"

1639

Dax groaned when he lifted Monica's bear canister from the car. "How far do you have to carry these things?"

"Three hundred miles or so," I said. "We can turn them in when we get to Kennedy Meadows South."

"How much weight does it add?"

"The bear canister alone is an extra two and a half pounds. The worst part is that I've seen videos of bears breaking into them anyway, so it's really annoying to have to carry something that might not even work."

He tapped the hard plastic top. "How far will this resupply have to go?"

"Anne is meeting us at Red's Meadow in one hundred and ten miles," I said. "But it is what it is. I can't tell you how great it was to have you guys join us. Especially right before this part." I looked across the road toward the ridgeline to the south.

He placed a hand on my shoulder and turned to look with me. He exhaled with an, "Oof" and dropped his head. "It looks like it's about to get a lot harder for you guys. I can't say I wish I was going with you. I hope we didn't slow you down too much. I know you have a schedule to keep."

"No, it was great. Perfect timing. That section was no joke that you guys just did, and we needed a bit of a break." I nodded toward Georgie. She and Dustin were bent over his camera with attention. She twisted the lens and looked up at him as if to ask him if she'd understood. "I think that kid may have found a new interest," I said. "She already angling for me to get her a nice camera someday."

Monica and I stood on the hill and called for the kids. "Come on. We have to get a picture before they leave, guys. Let's go!"

She looked over her shoulder at the mountain behind. "The Sierra," she said.

I turned around and looked too. "And now we have to carry these heavy bear canisters."

The golden glow of the afternoon gave way to the sharp, pre-dark cold. We stopped long enough to add a layer and offer a last wave to the taillights fading flare-like. Monica stepped close to me. "It was nice to have them."

I put my arm around her. "We've got to keep moving. The temperature is dropping. Let's only go until we find a flat enough spot."

"How far are we going tonight, Dad?" Aiden said.

"Until we find a good spot."

"We should start another book," Monica said.

"I'm sick of books," June said. "I don't want another boring book."

"It's *Boys in the Boat*. It's Mrs. Linder's suggestion, June. You've liked every book she's suggested."

"Oh, Junie. You'll like that one," Aiden said. "I've listened to it already. It's good."

"It sounds boring," June said. "I'm not going to listen." She stomped away up the hill, bumping Henry on the way past.

Aiden looked at me and threw up her hands. "She'd like the book, Dad. I don't know what her problem is."

Henry hooked his thumbs under his straps and rolled his eyes.

"June, stop!" I said. "Get back down here." I looked at the others. "Give us a minute."

When I reached her, she had her hands clenched by her side. "I know, Dad. I know."

"Look at me, kid." I put a hand on her shoulder. "Look at me, right in the eye."

When she did, she softened.

I looked down toward the road. "It isn't too late."

"Yes, it is. I can't go back on it now."

"It isn't too late." I pointed up the hill, then down the hill and away down the road. "Either way you want to go, I will go with you."

She stood for a while, as if undecided. Her hand tightened on the grip of her trekking pole, and she stabbed it into the dirt, before taking a determined step up the hill. She turned back to me. "Well, what are you waiting for?"

The steep ascent from the road soon flattened into a gentle slope along the spine of the rise toward the ridge. A sharp wind whipped across the cold rocks below and cut through us. We pulled our hoods over our heads and walked on. A mile further up the trail, we came to two small clumps of gnarled brush offered a windbreak.

"You kids set up behind those bushes, and Mom and I will use this smaller set to block the wind."

"Are we in tents tonight?"

Monica looked at the sky. "It doesn't look great."

"Let's set up the tents tonight, guys, just in case."

When I finally zipped the tent closed, Monica whispered, "How bad was it with June?"

"This afternoon? That climb up along the river didn't look bad on the map. But all that up-and-down off the river, and so many tricky steps. I think it all just wrecked her."

"You don't think she burned herself out the first couple of days with them?"

"What do you mean?"

"She was practically running up the hill the first day with Dax and Dustin. You were in the back with Grandy, so you didn't see. She was giddy to have people here. Probably didn't want to miss out. I think today it finally caught up with her."

"I bet you are right."

I rolled to my side and lifted the flap of my quilt over Monica, and she lifted hers. "Oh, you are warm," I said and reached a finger to touch the tip of her nose.

"What are you doing?"

"It's gotten colder out here all of a sudden."

"It's been cold."

"I mean cold, cold."

We lay quiet in the deepening dark of the tent, until a pittering sound broke the silence. I covered Monica's ears.

"What are you doing?"

"There's something I don't want you to hear."

"What?"

"Nothing."

"What is it? Did you fart?"

"I don't fart." I laughed.

"Seriously, I'm getting annoyed. What is it?"

"Mice."

"Gross, where?"

"In the bushes."

"Daddo," June said, "are you hearing these mice?"

"Yes, June, go to sleep."

"They probably found Georgie's junk drawer."

"Oh my gosh," Georgie said. "My Snickers. I left them in my backpack."

"They aren't your Snickers anymore," Henry said. "Those Snickers belong to the mice."

1641

There was a cracking when I touched the tent wall. A thin layer of ice broke free and slid down in sheets. I pulled my hand back into my quilt and turned to Monica. "It's going to be another cold start."

She pulled her quilt down to her chin and said, "Let's just stay warm a little while longer. It's not even light."

"Thirty minutes? I'll set an alarm." I listened to Monica's breathing beside me and waited. I watched my breath for a while, thinking of my conversation with June the previous day. At home, I wouldn't have attended to the subtle transformation. She would be one of four surrounded by the constant distraction of life, but here, she has all of me. Here she has special attention, because she walks in the back, and it's my job to walk in the back with whoever is struggling the most. I get so much of her. She gets so much of me. There is enough time here for me to see—to really see—her. I rolled to my side and pulled my quilt over my head.

"Okay, everyone. Let's go together and move fast, so no one has to be standing around. Henry, you switch up and help Georgie with that tent, Aiden you stay where you are, and Junie can come help you."

A blast of cold wind met me in the face when I swung wide the tent door. "Come on guys, let's go." I blew into my hands and tucked them under my armpits. I danced on my toes. I bent down and looked in the door. "Monica, are you coming? I need to shake the ice off the tent. Hurry."

Georgie tossed her bag clear of the door and sat on it. She wrapped her sleeping quilt around her legs and leaned into it.

"Georgie, stuff your quilt, and Henry, you help her out. There's no warmth for us now, but for walking. The faster we pack up, the faster we move."

"I can't, Dad." Georgie shook her hands and tucked them under her armpits. "It's too cold. I can't use my hands."

"June won't help either," Aiden said.

I looked up the treeless climb behind me. "June, stuff your pack fast and you and Georgie start walking toward the ridge, toward the sun."

"Dad, no," Georgie said. "It will be so much worse up high in the wind."

"Walk to the far side of that big rock up top there and put your back to it. Do you see the sliver of sun on the ridgeline? That rock will block the wind, and you'll be in the full sun."

"But I'll freeze to death before I get there," she said.

"You'll walk yourself warm, kid. You two, get moving."

Monica parted the tent flap with her jacket sleeve. "You're going to send them alone?"

"You can go with them. We'll come behind with the tents, won't we, Henry?"

"Oh, sure, so now I get to carry the tent, and the rain fly too, while Georgie gets to carry nothing."

"Just 'til we catch up and get warm."

Ten minutes later, Aiden and Henry and I fell into a nice stride together. "It kind of stinks we have to carry the whole tent," Aiden said. "Especially now that we're stuck with these heavy bear canisters."

"We only have to carry the canisters through the Sierra."

"It's frustrating that it's in the place that is hardest—where you'd like to be the lightest—that you have to be the heaviest because of that rule. Plus, it's not like we can carry less clothes. It's so much colder."

"Yeah," said Henry, "and now I'm stuck with the whole tent too."

"You know what, though, you guys? If we did this every morning, if we sent the girls on and packed up the tents, there would be a lot less crying. They could pack up inside the tent and just get out and start walking. We would get to sleep in for an extra fifteen minutes and catch up."

"Fifteen minutes more sleep doesn't sound bad," Aiden said.

"It's not like they're gonna help anyway," Henry said.

"You think we could give their part of the tent back to them when we catch up in the mornings?"

"How about this, Aiden? As soon as everyone is good and warm, we can stop and swap out everything."

"I could go for that. How about you, Henry?"

At our faster pace, it seemed like it took no time at all to crest the mountain and drop down to the valley on the far side. We caught them there and stopped to rebalance the load. I fell in line behind June. "Kid, you're walking funny. Are you okay?"

"No, I'm not."

"It's like a waddleberry, not a toddleberry."

"Dad, please stop," she said. "Don't call it that."

A few minutes later, she dropped back. "Dad, do you have any of Uncle Lee's slather?" I think I have a rash, I just didn't want you to talk about it in front of everyone."

I fished out a tube from my hip belt pocket. "Jump behind that rock and spread some of it wherever it burns."

"Will you wait?" She looked over her shoulder as she walked off-trail.

"I'll wait on the far side. You should know that it's going to hurt, really bad, but after two or three minutes it will stop, and you won't feel it again."

"How bad is it going to hurt?"

"Enough to make you cry, but it will be worth it."

I turned my face toward the sun for a moment and called out, "June?"

"Yeah?"

"I'm proud of you for telling me about the problem. I know you don't like to talk about embarrassing things, but this kind of thing is important to catch early. If something like this gets infected, it can end a hike."

"I know," she said, before cutting in front of me and onto the trail. For her first few steps she seemed to be sorting out a limp, but soon lengthened her stride. She turned with a laugh and said, "Try and keep up, will you, Dad?"

"Shush, stop moving around on your Tyveks, guys," Aiden said and cupped her hands around her mouth. "Echo, echo."

Henry interrupted her echo with a, "Hello, hello."

"Henry, cut it out." She slapped his ribs and laughed. "I'm trying to hear my echo, you big dummy."

Henry, himself, could not speak for laughing until he managed to say, "You think I don't know that?"

I ran my fingers in the golden grass that bordered my groundsheet and propped myself to my elbows to look across the meadow. "What a day!"

"How much farther are we going today?" Georgie said.

"We can play it by ear."

"I know what that means."

"No, we are past the big push now, so it's just a matter of having enough food 'til we get to the next stop."

"It feels like we're a long way from everything out here," Monica said.

"That's because we are, Mom," Aiden said.

"It doesn't help that everything is closed for the season," I said. "I checked the comments, just in case, and both Muir Trail Ranch and Vermillion are closed."

"Good we didn't send packages there, Dad," June said.

"No kidding. I didn't even think of that. I wonder if anyone behind us sent food there." I lay down again and looked up. "Look," I pointed to a white speck against a blue sky. "If you were in that plane looking down, would you ever dream that a family was lying down in a high Sierra meadow, looking back up at you? Those people on that plane could have had breakfast in LA, and they might have dinner in New York."

"That seems so strange that people can travel that fast," Aiden said.

"Big deal, your twenty-five hundred miles," Henry yelled. "We're doing twenty-five."

"We are not doing twenty-five," June said. "Mom's feet, Henry."

"It was just a number, June. Chill out."

"Dad, tell him."

"We'll only go as far as we go, June. Don't let it bother you." I held out an arm toward her. She shuffled over and lay beside me with her head on my arm. "Is the rash okay?" I whispered.

"Yes."

"You were walking a little funny just then."

"It's not that. I'm just stiff when I first stand up. How far are we going tonight, Dad?"

"We'll see." I kissed the side of her forehead, then whispered in her ear, "I wouldn't mind catching a ride on that plane though."

She made a motion as if to lasso it.

"Oh, that reminds me. Stephen is going to send out some new Tyvek, and I'm getting rid of my groundpad. Does anyone else want to swap out for a piece of that reflective bubble wrap?"

"Would it be a lot lighter?" Aiden said.

"A lot lighter, and because it's made of that mylar material, it reflects heat."

"In that case, I'll do it."

"Not me," Monica said. "I'll never give up my groundpad. You guys are crazy. That stuff would be so uncomfortable."

"It's got little bubbles, Mom, so it's a little bit padded," Henry said. "So," I said, "everyone but Mom?"

Aiden cupped her hands to her mouth again. "Echo, echo."

And Henry called, "Echo, echo."

"Daddo, did you remember to send that picture to the Browns?" June said. "From the picture challenge."

"I didn't have any coverage. I'll do it when we get wifi somewhere."

"That was a good picture challenge," Monica said. "It was definitely more fun than the first one."

"It didn't feel like as big a deal to me this time," said Aiden, "but that's probably because we are in so much more of a hurry now. Or maybe it's because it doesn't seem like such a big deal to be out here anymore."

"Two down," Henry said. "One to go."

1699

The kids are all grouped up and waiting when the sun burns the cold out of the morning the next day. Henry is a few feet off-trail, standing in the first rays of sunlight and barking across the wide, golden meadow.

"What are you doing?" I say.

"Shh, Dad. It's a coyote family," Aiden says. "They've been talking to Henry all morning."

"What do you mean?"

She points across the meadow. "They started howling way back there at the start of the valley, and they've been walking along with us just inside that far tree line over there. They stay just a little behind us and talk back to him whenever he barks."

Monica steps close to me. "Shouldn't we be nervous?"

"I don't think coyotes would give us a problem," I say. "It's kind of cool though, isn't it?"

In the late morning, I stand atop a drop, above the gaping mouth of a gorge with its bottom well out of my sight. Switchbacks hacked and blasted into hard stone, steps held fast with iron impaled into granite.

"If we go down there, we have to come up and out. If we got lost, we can't follow just any creek into river, into meadow, into town. Most of these creeks will cliff out, impassible. This cut trail, down, up, up and down again, and all of it again and again, is our only way through. We do not belong here in this alien landscape this late in the year, Monica. It feels eerie."

"Are you nervous?"

"However I feel," I say, "the only way out is through."

"Do we get to see any of those big trees?" Aiden says.

"Not this trip. I'm sorry, kid."

"Can we have a fire?"

"Not this high, there are different rules here."

"Why should it be so different?"

"When you get up this high in elevation, the conditions are harsh, and it is harder for anything to survive. No matter if you are a plant or an animal or anything alive, it is harder."

"Why would the animals want to live up here, if it's so hard then?" she says. "It doesn't make any sense."

"I guess it's a matter of priorities, isn't it? If I am a marmot, maybe I want to get up this high and try to survive, because there are fewer predators than down in the lowlands. Also, with fewer trees in the way, I could see danger coming from further away. You remember in Washington how all those pika would start warning each other whenever they would see us?"

The trail follows a creek for a mile, and Henry sees several trout rise. "Dad, can we stop?"

We catch seven brook trout and one golden before we decide we should catch up to the girls. Before long, he asks for the shovel kit, and I wait on the trail while he darts off in the trees to take care of some business. While I am waiting, a ranger happens upon me. "Let me have a look at your bear can." She reaches inside my bag and taps the plastic top and says, "Pull it out, all the way."

"Didn't you feel it through the bag?"

"People carry just the tops of the bear canisters to try and fool us sometimes."

"You can just go right inside my pack? Isn't that some sort of fourth amendment violation?" I laugh.

"You'd be amazed how far a park ranger's jurisdiction extends," she says without breaking a smile.

I am packing everything up when Henry returns from the trees, a roll of toilet paper behind his back, as if to disguise what he has been doing.

"You guys are packing everything out, right?"

"Everything, everything?" I say. "Like even our feces? Because we haven't been doing that."

"That's not a requirement here, though we would appreciate it. But you are taking your used toilet paper with you, right?"

Henry glances away.

"We will now," I say as we leave her. "That was a close one."

"Did you know we had to pack out our toilet paper?"

"I do now."

1710.8

Monica and I lay in the shade of an island of boulders topped by a few defiant scrub pines. She reached her hand toward the Tyvek behind her and fished out Georgie's food bag from under the pile. I touched her arm. "Leave that for her to take care of when she comes back."

"It drives me crazy, the way they leave a mess."

"Just don't look at it. Look out this way instead, and you won't have to see it." I pointed across the field of knee-high golden grass bending in various ways with the wind gusts, each angle reflecting a different shade of gold.

"It's so pretty here," she smiled. "I'm so glad we get to do this." She turned her head and looked across the field to where Henry and Georgie stood beside one of the wide, connected ponds the creek formed as it flowed through the meadow's basin. Henry jerked his rod backward and threw it down, and then stamped his feet.

"What is he doing?" Monica said.

"Looks like he had a bite and missed it."

Monica laughed and lay back to prop herself on her elbows, crossed her leg, and pressed her calf down into the corkball. "I like this better."

"Is that thing helping?"

"It does seem to help. Moreso than rubbing my feet."

"That was good of Grandy to ask his podiatrist friend, and then find you that ball."

"Did you ask him to do that?"

I shook my head.

"It makes sense that the calf is important, since plantar fasciitis involves the achilles. It's all connected. I love the way the body works." She touched the top of her calf. "When this muscle stays too tight, it engages the achilles, and the achilles is what causes the pain in the bottom of the foot. It's amazing how often we focus on the pain, and the solution is elsewhere." She paused. "By the way, I wasn't talking about my leg when I said I liked it better. I meant that I like not pushing so hard." She nodded across the meadow. "I don't think I'm alone in that either."

"It seems Georgie has claimed my Tenkara rod as her own. You think she'll let me take a turn with it? It's like shooting fish in a barrel in that pool. They're everywhere. And hungry too."

"Why haven't they caught many?"

"You have to sneak up on them. If they see you, they won't take the fly." I pushed myself to my feet. "I'll go show them real quick."

"Take your time. I need a nap after last night."

"That ranger was a jerk last night, wasn't she?"

"We were set up right on top of Soda Springs. She was just doing her job. What was she supposed to do?"

I intoned the ranger's voice, "You are camped illegally!"

"Well, we were camped illegally."

"I know, but she maybe could have shown a little compassion. It's not like we knew where we were when we set up. It was so dark, and then she recommended we stay in that campground nearby, illegally. I was about to ask her why it would be any different to stay in a closed campground than where we were."

"You might have gotten us kicked out of there too."

"It was eleven o'clock, and she made an eleven-year-old pack up and walk an extra mile in the dark. Poor Georgie."

She smiled and nodded again across the meadow. "Looks to me like she's forgotten the whole thing."

Georgie lifted her feet high as she ran across the grass toward us, carrying a small trout in her hand.

I hopped up and jogged to meet her in the middle. "That's a pretty one, Georgie. Let me get a picture. Then I'll take a turn."

When I bent to my knees and pulled out my phone, she took two steps to the left. "Dad, get the mountain in the background. It will make a better picture."

The wide glacial bowl that served as her backdrop was topped by impassible snow fields. Various drainages leaked out from below the snow and into a large pond at the base. "You are a regular Ansel Adams, kid. This will be a much better background."

"Who is Ansel Adams?"

"He's a famous nature photographer, and his pictures of Yosemite are his most well-known."

"That wouldn't be a bad job to have," she said.

I pointed to the fish in her hand. "Let's get this little guy back in the water, quick."

"They are so high up here, and they seem like they would eat anything. They must be feeding up for the winter. Do you think trout stay all the way up here when it's all covered in snow? What's our elevation?"

"Hang on, I'll pull it up. Ten thousand four hundred seventy-seven."

"Which way do we go out?"

I pointed. "Right up that way, Donahue Pass."

She put a hand on the top of her hat and squinted to follow my finger. "I'm glad you didn't say we were going up into those snowfields."

"Oh shoot, come on kid, let's get that fish back in the water." We walked toward the pool together. I put a hand on the middle of her back and leaned down. "Did you see that old road cut into the sluff yesterday morning?"

"Maybe, was it about halfway up the slope and running along beside us for a while?"

"Yeah, I read a comment that said it was the Emigrant Trail, an old passage through the Sierra. We aren't the first to pass through here. However alone we may feel."

"I don't understand why you feel that way. I love the Sierra so far. The granite cliffs are so cool, and you can see all the striations in the rocks from when the glaciers moved over them. And there's so much fishing."

"Just wait 'til we get to Rae Lakes. If we're on schedule, we might spend a whole day. The fish there are this long." I held up my hands.

"Dad, that's at least two feet. You think we can get them to bite?"

"When your mom and I were here last time, I had them chasing twigs they were so hungry, and it was this same time of year."

"When do we get there?"

"It's in the next section. After we resupply at Red's Meadows."

1737

"I'll catch up to you guys," I said. "Stay together so you don't miss the junction for Red's." I turned to Anne. "I can't thank you enough for bringing our resupply," I looked down at my new Altras and wriggled my toes. "And these shoes. You have no idea."

She shook her head. "Vince, I am going to say it again. You shouldn't take those children out into this storm."

"I appreciate your concern." I motioned toward her car with my hand.

She nodded and, with the use of my arm, lowered herself into the driver's seat. As I shut the door, she sighed.

After I watched Anne drive away, I set off down the trail behind the others. It took me fifteen minutes to catch Monica.

She heard me coming and looked behind her. "I don't think I understand why Anne met us back at that parking lot. Wasn't the plan for her to meet us up here at Red's Meadow?"

"That was the plan, originally. I'm not sure why she changed it. She just texted me to switch it up yesterday. Maybe this is a more convenient road to access the trail. I didn't ask her. It could have been that she had to be somewhere this afternoon later. It's a bummer to have to carry all this food for eight extra miles."

"That's how far it is to Red's?"

"Yes. Eight miles from that parking lot back there, so we will be eating in a restaurant tonight."

When I stepped out of the camp store, SoGood caught my eye with a wave and beckoned me toward the picnic table where she was sitting on the bench at the feet of an older man. She swept her hand up toward him. "This is Golden." She swept the same hand toward me. "This is the dad of the family I was telling you about. I've been trying to catch up to them for a couple hundred miles. They've agreed to adopt me into the family for this next section."

Golden hung his head for a moment. He gathered his white beard to a point and turned to me. "It could be completely fine when you get out there, but I'm telling you, son, I wouldn't try it. Not with these kids."

I fumbled in my pocket for my Garmin. "My friend just sent the mountain forecast, and he said that, at most, we should expect an afternoon of rain."

Golden leaned back and adjusted his torn khaki shorts. His unzipped, down jacket fell open to reveal his gaunt and leatherbound frame. "This is the Sierra." He adjusted himself forward with deliberate motion, replaced his elbows on his thigh, and shook his head. "Forecasts don't count for nothing around here. I have my car. I can take you to town if you like, and run you back out when the storm passes." He looked down at SoGood. "That goes for you too."

Monica, SoGood, and I stood in a huddle behind the outbuilding that housed the laundry. We huddled as though we were some kind of secret high council.

"That section was hard," I said.

"Well," SoGood laughed, "they do call it the 'meat grinder'."

"Wait." I tilted my head to the side. "What?"

"Yeah, that stretch outside of South Lake Tahoe. They say that's the testing ground for the southbounder. If you make it through there, you can do the Sierra Nevada, no problem."

"No wonder. Jeesh!"

"Is Golden still here?" Monica said.

I took a step back from our circle to peek around the corner. "He's still here. Jamie is saying we only need to expect precipitation for part of one afternoon. Whether it's rain or snow will depend on our elevation at the time, I guess. If it's just for one afternoon, how bad can it be?"

"What do you think, Katie?" Monica said.

"I think Golden has seen a lot in his time, so I give weight to his warning." She held up one hand. "But on the other hand, there is safety in numbers … assuming I'm still a part of the family."

"Oh, please! I just hope you don't regret it." Monica touched her forearm. "Please, don't feel like you have to stay with us out of kindness."

"If it gets too bad," SoGood said, "there are a few alternates we could take to get out to the eastern side of the range."

When I reentered the camp store, neither shopkeeper seemed to notice me. Not even when I stepped up to the glass counter did they turn. The man would be wintering in Onion Valley, and the woman would be flying home to Oklahoma. It had been a good season, but neither planned to return in the fall.

I cleared my throat and lifted the can of isobutane and let it fall to the glass with a click. The woman half tilted her head toward me. "Back again?"

"Do you have any KT tape? I couldn't find any."

"I have athletic tape." She nodded toward the far end of the store.

"I was able to find the athletic tape, thank you. I'm asking about KT tape."

"If you didn't see it, we don't have it. We close tomorrow for the season, so what you see is what we've got."

"You might be the last customer of the season." He turned his head to view the clock high on the wall behind him. "We are open for another hour and a half." He nodded toward the front door. "The campground will be open 'til the weekend, and the restaurant will serve breakfast in the morning."

"My kids will be happy to hear about the restaurant."

"You have kids out here?"

"Yes, we are hiking through on the PCT."

"You know there is a storm coming?" They looked at each other, and the man shook his head.

"We've been told."

I stepped away from the counter and fished my phone from my pocket to re-read Jamie's text. "Flurries Tuesday afternoon at high elevation according to Mountain Forecast."

This time when I stepped through the front door, Golden was shifting out of reverse across the gravel parking lot. He caught my eye and held his hand palms up through the open passenger window. I shook my head, and he shot me a thumbs-up. His tires kicked up dust, and his taillights disappeared behind the high bank bordering the turn.

1760.5

"Oh my gosh!" Aiden jostled my shoulder. "Dad, wake up."

I felt a light drop on my forehead. I couldn't see anything in the dark. "Is it raining?"

"Hurry, Dad. We have to get the tents set up."

Save Monica and Georgie, we were all scattered on more or less flat benches formed by the sprawling roots of a large tree. SoGood had set up on one of the two tent spaces nearby.

Aiden flicked on her penlight and put it between her teeth, and began to pull the rainfly from the top of her open backpack. She reached a foot over to kick June, and mumbled, "June, I need the tent. Now!"

"Is it raining?" Monica said. "Are you getting wet?"

"Wake up, buddy." I tapped the sole of Henry's foot. "Somebody else get out a flashlight, we've got to set up quick."

SoGood turned on her flashlight, and a dome of yellow illuminated below us. "Oh, I'm so sorry, you guys. Can I help with anything?"

I held my hands toward the sky. "It's just sprinkling. We should be okay."

"Are you sure?"

"This tree is blocking most of it, we just need to find a couple of flat places. Do you know what time it is?"

"It's 4:30," Georgie said. "Can you guys hold it down out there? We're trying to get some sleep."

Before I climbed into the tent, I scanned the area one last time with my flashlight. "Aiden, you left your clothes bag out." I lifted her vestibule and tossed the bag underneath.

When at last inside the tent, I pulled my quilt over my head, shivered, blew warm air into my hands, and slid toward Henry. "Come on bud, let's get some of that body heat working."

After I warmed, I dropped my quilt down to my neck and stared above me. Even in the dark, I could see the tent. I lay there, and listened, and felt no discontent, or hurry, or worry. A faint glow crept over the tent, unconcentrated, as though the moon, peeking through somewhere, diffused its light through the trees. The rain had passed within a half hour. "Was that it?" I wondered aloud. I don't know how long I looked at the tent. I dozed off for what felt like a moment, and it was dawn.

The view of Purple Lake opened near the outflow. I stepped off the trail on the high side of a natural grass-covered dike to drop to the back. Aiden stepped up beside me. "You can see why they named it Purple Lake."

"I can't figure out why it is so purple. I don't see any vegetation up the hill on the far side. It looks like it's all granite from here."

"It's something to do with the water, I'm sure."

I put my arm around her and pulled her close. "Aido, thanks for your help last night."

"Sure, Dad. You think it will rain again?"

"Do I think that was all of the storm?"

"Yes."

"No, I don't think that was all."

By mid-morning, bluebird skies broke through the heavy haze. We took a long lunch by a stream.

"Are we going to be here for a long time?" Henry said. "'Cause if we are, I'm going to fish." On his first cast, he pulled a small trout from the water in a wide arch over his head.

"Henry, you don't have to set the hook so hard. You have all the leverage with that long rod."

"That fish is tiny, Dad," Aiden said. "Why are they all so small up here?"

"Nothing does well year-round up this high. There's far less oxygen at this elevation."

"It's water, what does that have to do with oxygen?" she said.

"I thought you went to IB, Aiden." Georgie said. "Aren't IB kids supposed to be smart?"

"Whatever, Georgie. Dad's probably not right about that anyway. I think it's 'cause the big ones come up here to lay eggs and then go back down. You know, like salmon."

"You just keep thinking, Aido," I said. "That's what you are good at. It also has to do with limited seasonal food sources."

"I know for a fact I wouldn't last up here," SoGood said. "I like food way too much. Calories are so good."

"Wait," Monica said. "Is that where your name comes from?"

"Yes, I thought you had my Instagram."

"Vince does all that. I don't touch social media. But I am a foodie."

"Oh, me too. You guys, there is a Chinese place in Bishop that I am dying for. That's all I could think about in my tent this morning."

"I could go for some Chinese food right about now," Aiden said.

"I motivate myself in every section by the restaurants in the next town. There is this bakery in Tehachapi too …" SoGood rubbed her belly. "When we get there, it's cinnamon rolls for everyone, on me."

Henry set the hook, this time with the appropriate weight, dipped his hand into the water, and lifted a small trout. He set down the pole and walked toward me. "Look at this, its belly is orange and yellow. Do you think this is a golden trout?"

"It's not as gold as the ones I've seen in pictures. Maybe it's a hybrid."

"Dad," Georgie flipped over my pack, "where is your fishing rod?"

I threw my sleeping quilt off of me. "We have to get moving, dad-gummit. I hate waking up in the rain." I wandered through the groaning and stirring. "Keep your dry stuff dry. I have a feeling it's going to be a lot colder tonight. We'll have to stay walking to stay warm."

"It's still dark," Monica said. "What time is it?"

"You can feel the temperature dropping already," Aiden said.

Monica called for an early lunch at the first cloudbreak. "This looks as good a spot as any. Everyone, get your cups out and your food ready. Does anyone have anything in their clean bottles?"

Henry held one of his bottles high. "Both of mine are empty."

"Henry, have you not been drinking enough water?" Monica said. "You'll get dehydrated."

"I'm not dehydrated. You can't get dehydrated in the rain."

Aiden popped him in the arm. "Henry, that's so stupid. Give me your dirty. I'll go fill it up. Where'd you get that idea? How else are you gonna explain your nosebleed?"

"That's not from dehydration."

"Henry," I said. "Drink more water. June, you too."

"Here, Georgie, give me your bottle too." Aiden hopped up from her groundsheet. "When I get back, I'll boil the water for you, Mom, so you can work on your feet."

"Spread out your tents," I said, "and get them as dry as you can."

Monica tilted her head sideways toward the sky. "You think we have enough time?"

Ten minutes later we were walking disheveled after a hurried repack. We drank our crunchy rice meals from camp cups on the walk. June said it was too disgusting to finish.

"You will," I said. "Every bite."

"My throat is closing up, I can't swallow."

"Did I ever tell you about the time that happened to me, and your mom poured out my milk to a stray cat? We were on our honeymoon, and we had hiked up to the Shilthorn from Gimmelwald."

"You've told me this before, and I don't want to hear it again."

"Gimmelwald is in the Swiss Alps. We were hiking up a trail, and I dunked my shirt in a cattle trough on the way up the mountain, because it was such a hot day. But by the time we got to the top it was freezing. I didn't know anything was wrong with me until we got back down to the little town and bought some snacks with the last of our cash. This cat walked up on us when we sat down to eat. I tried to drink my milk, but I couldn't swallow anything. Your mom grabbed my milk and said, 'I guess you aren't using this,' and dumped it all out for the cat."

"I'm not even listening to you."

"You need the calories, June. Try and finish it."

"Why?"

"June, stop for a minute." I walked to her and put my hand on her shoulder to turn her toward me. "Look at me kid. Right in the eyes. I know it's annoying to eat on the way, and I know it's a pain to eat it when it's crunchy. But listen to me. I want you to do it because I said so. I want you to trust me when I say that I know what is best for you in this." She turned away. "June, look at me." She looked back toward me again. "Will you do it? Will you trust me?"

She nodded.

SoGood walked in stride behind Georgie and Henry and Aiden. "Do you guys know the whole album?"

"Probably," said Aiden. "Dad always plays us Van Morrison. Come on Henry, let's sing that one about rain."

"Which one is that?"

She started singing:

Half a mile to the county fair
And the rain came pouring down.

Henry hopped up to a rock face beside the trail and caught up to walk beside her and sang,

Me and Billy standing there
With a silver half a crown.

SoGood turned back and smiled at Monica. She put her hand to her heart and mouthed, "I like your kids."

The trail was a trough collecting the rain. We sloshed through the rocks with soaked shoes through the puddles. It wasn't bone-cracking cold, but damp-through, whole-body-shivers cold. It was the hang-my-cold-clothes-away-from-my-skin type of cold.

The mountain was leaking through rainwater cataracts into the stream down below us. "Can we add layers, Dad?" I shook my head.

"Can we take a break, Dad?"

"Where? If we stop, we will freeze. There is a cabin ahead--it says on my map--we can try that."

I pulled SoGood and Monica to the side. "Should we go off-trail to Muir Trail Ranch? I know that they're closed, but maybe there is cover. A porch. Something. It may be worth a try."

"What about that cabin you mentioned?" Monica said.

"It's past the junction to Muir Trail Ranch, so if we go on, we are more or less committed."

"If you want my opinion," SoGood said. "I say we go on and hope the cabin checks out. Worst case, we can just keep walking this afternoon. If we get too tired without any breaks, we can just set up early tonight and get a good start in the morning. I wouldn't want to waste effort going out to Muir Trail Ranch only to have it disappoint us. It is not as if we can get an extraction from there this late in the season anyway."

Not long after the junction, I stood before the cabin with rain dripping off my hood in front of my face. "Why would you even put a cabin out here without a front porch? I walk around it. Not even eaves. Are you kidding? And the rain. The rain is straight down, so we can't even hide on the leeward side." I looked for a log round to use for my break-in. It took me until I was standing with one hand on the door latch and a softball-sized rock in the other, to come to my senses. I dropped the rock and turned back toward the trail.

"Well?" Monica said when I returned to the group. But she had known my answer before she'd asked the question.

Georgie cried, and Aiden pulled her in tight.

"Something will turn up," I said. "Have faith."

SoGood encouraged the kids back onto the trail.

We found a ranger cabin above a short bridge, unmarked on my map. And though it was boarded and locked, it had a wide wrap-around porch that protected us from the rain. We huddled there, inside our sleeping bags to eat warm food, less for the food than for the warm. But for all of our down insulation, we stayed on the cold side of warm, so we cut our break short to get our blood moving again. "Walk yourselves warm, everybody," I said, and read what looked like despair in their eyes. "I know. Believe me, I know."

My feet were heavy. Snow would have been better. At least it would have
been drier.

Listening to Golden would have been better.

Listening to those nosy northbounders that told us to flip down to Lone Pine
would have been better.

Anything would have been better.

"Dammit, Anne. You may have been right."

After another SoGood and Monica confabulation, I was swayed. "Yes, let's
stop at the next tentsite we see."

I followed them from the trail, dropped my pack in the pinestraw, and
prepared for a final effort to make camp before dark.

June cried when she pulled out her tent. "Dad, it's soaked."

"Sleep in the tent with the other two girls, unless SoGood needs a warm
body. Henry can sleep in here with your mom and me."

"I'd take you, June," SoGood said, "but you'd probably be warmer in
there."

"Did you ever think you'd see three people pile into a Big Agnes Flycreek
two-man tent?" I said.

"It's quite impressive."

"Aiden, let's set up the third tent," I said. "Just throw everything in there.
We will dry out tomorrow. SoGood, you are welcome to use it for your wet
gear too." I apologized to Monica. "I need to help June for a few minutes,
or she'll lose her mind."

I rejoined Monica with the last of our setup and picked up my pack. "Henry, slide over." I knelt inside the vestibule. I dropped my pack inside it and opened it up.

Monica could see that something was wrong. "Vince, what is it?"

"My jacket," I stuttered. "Both my jacket and my quilt are soaked through."

"What are we going to do?"

"It isn't that."

"What is it?"

"I don't want to say what it is."

"Tell me."

I looked at my stiff, half frozen hands. "If I were here alone …" I shook my head and began to pull out the rest of my gear. I dropped my clothes bag inside the tent and patted it a couple of times. "If I were here alone …" I wiped my eyes. "Henry, slide this way, and I'll sleep between you and Mom. Let's move quickly."

I lay down and jammed my feet into Henry's toe box, and Monica wrapped the top of her quilt over me.

I turned and kissed her on the ear. "I am so glad I am not alone."

"I'm scared. What are we doing here?"

"The worst is behind us, I'm sure."

She matched my stare with wide eyes. "What are we doing here?"

1801.0.1

They are sleeping, one on each side of me, Monica and Henry. They have been sleeping for a long time now. I can see my breath. Before she fell asleep, June had called out from the other tent to announce the temperature. "Hey Daddo, it's fifteen degrees." I roll to my side and pull the flaps of their quilts over me. Inside there, together, we have made a warm place. We share a warm space.

Had I been alone, I would still be walking through the night, wet and cold. My pen light battery would have worn down fast, so I would have been walking in the dark as well. What else could I have done?

Our range has widened. Our range of comfort. I am comfortable walking in my shorts now in thirty-five degrees, even less if the sun's out. But there are limits. Limits that I don't define or overcome by sheer willpower. At a certain temperature in the wrong conditions, a human cannot survive. I look up toward the top of the tent. This thin layer of ultralight waterproof fabric is the only thing that stands between any of us and a desperate life and death situation. A thin piece of fabric. That's all.

Monica had said, "What are we doing here?"

At this very campsite? It is as far as we made it.

What are we doing in the Sierra? That's easy. We decided to push into the storm.

We could have chosen an easier trail. We'd been far more familiar with the Appalachian Mountains. It would have made more sense for us to go there. It's so close to home. It's far less remote. It has infrastructures long fixed in place for the hikers passing through.

Could it be we were drawn to the unfamiliar, the spectacular, the unknown?

Yet here we are on the Pacific Crest Trail, winding our way from one border to another border. From a border of what? To a border of what? As a concept, the whole thing is a bit arbitrary. Two borders formed upon the cessation of several conflicts, where nations and tribes pressed back and forth, until lines of empires were defined in the sand on the one end. And on the other end, in the trees. However these agreements or capitulations were finally reached, they dropped boundary stones to mark the new line. Then, if the stories I read are correct, some Boy-Scout-come-oil man woke in the night with a dream to call together a conference of trailing enthusiasts and commission them to link disparate, pre-existing fragments of trails from one boundary stone to the other, south to north, and this thing—that wasn't a thing—became the Pacific Crest Trail.

But when the trail cutters cut their way through these forests, why did it run right through this particular pass? What misdirection or redirection had they encountered? Were they following the old paths? Ancient paths? Which of its wild movements and shifts were inspired by geological consideration? Are some wide sweeps nods to long-forgotten property rights? Surely, some of its twists and turns enshrine a trail architect's miscalculation.

When we began our hike in Washington, I'd often repeated "what was I thinking?" as a refrain of self-doubt. Then, the same phrase poured from me as much in wonderment, almost a pat on my own back. But tonight, when I whisper it into the dark of the tent, the former intent has returned, and with fangs. "What was I thinking, dragging us here?"

I roll to my side, drape my arm over Monica, and fall asleep.

I know that I dreamt, but I cannot remember the dream when I wake.

1801.0.2

I woke up with my back pressed to Monica's. I rolled over to my opposite side and rested my chin on her shoulder.

She cracked an eye open. "What time is it?"

"I know what we are doing here."

"What are you talking about?"

"Last night, you asked what we were doing here. I woke up this morning, and I knew. At least, I think I know."

She stared at me.

"We wake every day and force a first step onto the trail, and then we force another, and another 'til the end of the day. And each day we are taking another bite out of this thing. And, yeah, some days are worse than others. Some days we would rather be anywhere else. Especially in this horrible weather. But it's the thing that is in front of us to do, so we do it. I had no idea how big or how hard it would be when we began. I'm not sure I'd have begun it, had I known. But all it took to get here was one step in front of the other. And all it takes from here is one step in front of the other. Yesterday we were stretched to our limit, but we made it through."

"That's what you woke me to say?"

"Yeah, I guess I could have waited to say it 'til you were awake."

"Or said it with fewer words."

"Alright, it's just following the trail. That's all it is. Just following the trail." I lay on my back and smiled. "Whatever it is."

I sat up to maneuver my way over Henry. I slid him toward Monica and tucked the flaps of their quilts back around them and zipped my wet down jacket over my rain shell. I swung my feet out the mesh door and reached for my shoe. Ice flaked off when I first stretched it open. It took several minutes to pry it pliant enough to create room for my foot. I blew on my hands long enough to feel them again and reached for my other shoe.

Once out of the tent, I stretched my arms toward the sky and turned to look around the glade. Another tent, dark green, stood less than forty feet from us. Beyond it, a thin wisp of smoke rose from a fire pit beyond it. I rubbed my eyes. Through the trees I saw a man walking with care and scanning the ground. He looked toward me, and I waved.

I sat down on a rock beside the fire, and he continued to wander through the nearby trees. I extended my hands toward the flame until I couldn't bear the heat. I moved forward and squatted over the fire ring. After a while, steam began to rise from my shirt.

I turned when I heard a stick crack behind me. "You scared me." I held my hand to my chest. "I didn't hear you coming." I turned back to the fire. "You were stealthy last night. I didn't even know anyone else had come in."

He nodded toward his tent. "We didn't get here until after dark." And sat down on a rock to my right before tossing a small chunk of wood onto the flame.

"I'm surprised you were able to find any dry wood out here."

"When it started raining yesterday," he said, "I looked under logs and rocks as we went along." He held up his hand. "Wood chips and kindling like this. Full of pitch." He tossed a piece to me. "You can smell it."

"How did you know to do that?"

"My grandfather taught me."

"I thought I was dreaming when I saw the smoke. Are you sure you aren't an angel?"

"Far from it," he laughed. "But I am a missionary kid, so you might say I have connections, however far I may have wandered." He bent for a long stick beside him and piled coals against one of the logs. "One thing I do believe is that this is the highest achievement in fire building in my lifetime."

He smiled and stared in silence into the fire for a long time. "I'm less sure about the rest of that stuff, now."

"I'll believe enough for the both of us. You are a gift from God this morning. Just wait 'til my kids see this fire. You'll be a hero." I nodded toward the far side of the glade. "Looks like the sun is about to hit there. I'm going to grab a rope so I can dry some stuff out. You are welcome to use it."

"We're gonna head out as soon as we pack up."

"I think I'll let mine sleep in." I looked up at the sky. "My friend sent a message that it's supposed to be clear 'til at least eleven o'clock. Most of our stuff is soaked. My down quilt too. Maybe it'll give us a chance to dry out."

"A down quilt?"

I nodded.

"How did you stay warm?"

"Three of us slept in that two-man tent over there." I pressed my hands to my knees and stood up. "Do you mind if I invite them all over to the fire?"

"Not at all. I was about to round up some more wood."

I strung a line across a sun patch and returned with damp gear. The sun patch had already changed places, so I restrung the line. Every so often I left to adjust the line. By 9:30 everything was dry, save my quilt. I pulled it from the line, draped it over my arm, and walked toward the fire. All of their feet were resting on a rock in the fire ring. And their laughter rang through the trees. I stopped to watch them for a moment that I might delay what I would have to say.

"Alright everyone, I guess we've enjoyed the fire about as long as we can."

SoGood looked through the canopy toward the sky above. "We should get going before it moves in."

At ten thousand feet elevation, the snow began to fall. We huddled together, and SoGood pulled out her phone. "There is an emergency shelter at the top of Muir Pass. I think this might qualify as an emergency."

Aiden bounced up and down on the balls of her feet. "You think?" she said.

"It's good that we made it up high when we did," SoGood said.

"But it's snowing," Aiden said. "Why is that good?"

"Because it isn't raining," I said. "And rain is much worse. At least we can stay dry in the snow. It shouldn't get too bad, it looks pretty light."

In three miles, we started up across an incline, blanketed by four inches of snow. Tucked into some boulders down to the left stood a green tent.

A figure stood by the door with his arms held up high. "Woohoo! You got this."

"Look, Dad, that's him. That's our angel," June said.

We plowed on, and snow fell heavier around us. It piled up under our feet until at last, within a few miles, we were sloughing through powder eight inches deep. June pushed on ahead of me, steady and strong. Even so, we fell further behind, until the last of the others faded from sight, as some apparition into a cloud of white.

A good way into the last climb, I checked my phone for the distance. I said, "You are doing great, kid. Almost there."

"I don't mind the snow at all." She turned back and shrugged. When she looked forward again, she pointed through the blur and said, "Dad, I can see the top of the hut now. Can you?"

"Very soon, kid, we will be cozy and dry."

***

When I stepped past the heavy, wooden dutch door, into the dank hut, I could see that it was crowded. The clothesline that crisscrossed the room dipped low, draped heavy as it was with damp clothes. In the middle of the room stood a tent. A hiker crawled out of it and stood in front of me. We had not seen him before. "I can move it over to make room for you guys," he said and bent to grab the front corner of the tent. He ducked under the clothesline and slid it to the far end away from the door.

I stepped toward SoGood and whispered, "Why does he have his tent set up?"

She shrugged.

"Henry," Monica said, "you need to get into your dry clothes."

 He sat rigid on the stone bench as if frozen in place.

Monica dropped her quilt onto her Tyvek and walked to him. "Henry, let's go," she said, "get in your sleeping bag."

He stared straight ahead. "I can't move, Mom."

She put a hand on his shoulder and turned to me. "Is he okay?"

"I don't know." I hopped over Aiden and joined them. "Buddy, look at me." I squatted down and lifted his chin. His eyes seemed to me almost vacant. When I rested my hands on his, they felt cold. I turned them over, palms up. They were red.

"Did you have your gloves on?"

He shook his head slowly.

"Come on buddy, let's get you out of these wet clothes and into your quilt." I threw a look toward Monica. "Will you help him get changed? He can sleep between me and the furnace. We'll get him warm."

Within minutes, we were lined up like seven sardines. Henry was stuffed in tight, warming between June and me. I rolled to my side facing him and threw my arm over him onto June's shoulder. "You are going to be okay, buddy."

We were all silent for a few minutes. "Can you believe we are inside, guys?" Aiden said, "Isn't this great, Mom?"

"Better in here, than out there."

After a while, SoGood broke the silence. "I'm glad I'm a Strawbridge today."

"We are so glad you're with us," Monica said.

"Good night, everyone," I said.

We were all quiet for a few minutes more when Aiden said, "Dangit! Did anyone else feel that?"

"What is it?" Monica said.

"I just got a drop in my eye."

"Me too," June said. "But not in my eye. On my forehead."

"Oh no, it could be condensation." I dug for my flashlight and found the two damp rainflies in order to cover our quilts. "This won't really keep us from getting wet, but it may help for a while."

When I lay down again, Monica whispered in my ear, "I think we would have been better off outside."

I found her hand and squeezed it. "I think you are right."

Before first light, I slipped out from under the sticky tent fly and tiptoed over bodies toward the door. I pushed open the top of the half door and cracked the small row of icicles that had formed on the eave in the night. I looked into the gray mist of the predawn, shut the door, and made my way in the dark back to Monica.

"What does it look like out there?"

"It's bad," I said. "We may want to consider going out at Bishop Pass if it doesn't clear up."

I dozed off again for a while and woke up flooded in light from the wide-open door. Though she was only a dark silhouette against the bright light behind her, I could tell it was Aiden. She turned and said, "Dad, check this out. All the clouds are gone. It's a beautiful day."

1822.6

The hiker bounded into the opening. For all its dinginess, his golden shirt glowed. He clapped his hands together, flashed a toothy grin, and said, "People! At last. My people." He held his hands wide to the sky. "Thank God!" He took a stride toward us. "Now, you must be the Strawbridges."

"We are," SoGood said. "And you must be Airborne." She turned to Monica. "This is the other yoyo I was telling you about."

"What's yoyo mean again?" Georgie said.

"It means I am a glutton for punishment," Airborne said.

"What it means, Georgie, is that he started in Mexico, walked to Canada, and is now walking back to Mexico," I said.

Airborne pulled his groundsheet from his pack and unfurled it. "I've been walking with Starter, and he has been talking about your family." He sat down and pulled his pack toward him. "He loves you guys."

"The Starter of the Garden Club trail family?" I said. "We last saw him at Crater Lake lodge. He had skipped down two hundred miles when we saw him there. He must be making good time."

"He was up high for the worst of the storm, up on Silver Pass. He told me he was about ready to lay down and die, so he was making all sorts of deals with God. He said he made a promise to change if God would save him. About just as he said it, he looked up and saw a little protected area up under a boulder with a pile of dry wood. So he was able to get a fire going."

"We spent the night up in the Muir Shelter last night," June said.

"Oh, that's good timing."

"You'd think so," I said. "But it dripped on us all night. We've argued all morning about whether or not to push on. If we can't get dried out, we are thinking of heading out from here over Bishop Pass. That's why we stopped at the junction."

"I was thinking the same thing." Airborne looked up at the sky. "It's been nice until now, but these two lines of clouds seem to be moving toward each other from opposite sides of the sky."

"Monica," I said. "I don't want to have to walk fourteen miles out and then all the way back in, so if we can push on to Kearsarge, I'd feel better."

She shook her head and turned to Airborne. "What about you? What are you going to do?"

"I feel a lot better about it now that I've seen you guys. I nearly went hypothermic while I was setting up my tent last night. I couldn't move my thumbs by the time I got inside. I had to hold my food bar like this"—he tapped the heels of his hands together—"and tear it open with my teeth. I could tell it was getting bad, because I was starting to get delirious."

I waved my hand in Henry's direction. "Henry was out of it last night, bad. We think he was hypothermic, but the furnace and I got him warmed up. Didn't we, Bug?"

"Hypothermia is no joke," Airborne said, reached into his pack and pulled out a large food bag and shook it. "This thing was full when I left Red's Meadows." He worked his hand around the inside of the bag and came out with a full sized squeeze bottle of Mayonnaise. When he popped open the top, he squeezed a long stream into his mouth. "Ahh. The best hiker food."

"I can't believe I'm saying this," Monica said. "But that actually looks good."

I lay down onto my back and tilted my hat over my eyes to block the sun. When I woke from my nap, I rose and hobbled over to touch my quilt. Monica looked at me as if to inquire.

"It's dry," I said.

"I'm game to go on," SoGood said. "If the rest of our family is."

Not long after we left the junction behind us, Henry dropped back to ask me a question. "Dad, do you care if I walk faster with SoGood and Airborne?"

"As long as you take Aiden with you, I don't mind."

"Can I go with them too?" Georgie said.

1838.4

Airborne caught me on a climb and settled in to keep pace behind me. I offered to let him pass, but he declined. "We saw your tent this morning on this side of Mather," I said. "Was that Green with you?"

"He should be coming up any minute."

"June pitched a fit on the other side of the pass late last night, just after we made it up this side of the Golden Staircase. I wanted to make it over the top to get down to lower elevation, but she wouldn't move. We couldn't have stood around much longer. Usually, if they pitch a fit, it's more of a parenting issue. But last night, it was dangerous. SoGood walks a layer light, and we were getting cold fast." I looked back toward the pass. "It must have been in the low teens."

"Well, you owe her a thank you. It was so cold on this side of the pass without any trees to block the wind. I couldn't even get out of my tent till nine-thirty this morning."

"I do wish we had been able to see the Golden Staircase in the daylight."

"I already told this to your wife when I saw her. When I got to the top of Mather last night, I was warm from the climb, so I took a break to look back. Your flashlights, when you were climbing, were moving in and out of the rocks, back and forth on the switchbacks. I was mesmerized. I must have watched for thirty minutes. It was the most beautiful sight I've seen since I started this trail. It's gotta be cool to do all this with your kids."

"I had plans to take it slow through the Sierra, to force myself to take it all in, but this storm has us wrecked. Now, I just want to get out of here as fast as we possibly can."

"Are you stopping in Bishop?"

"Yes, we are going out at Kearsarge. How about you?"

"I have a friend packing in my resupply over Kearsarge, so I don't have to go out."

"I don't like the idea of hiking four miles out and back in, but I think my crew is ready for a break." I looked at the sky. "Especially with a possibility of a second wave of this storm."

"Are you stopping for lunch?"

I pointed my trekking pole toward a pond in the meadow below. "I think we will set up there. SoGood has a leak in her groundpad that she couldn't find."

"I meant to tell you, too, your boy, Henry, can walk. I mean, really walk. I couldn't shake him coming up that pass the other day. Starter was waiting for me near the top, and he didn't see that Henry was behind me. He just saw me breathing heavy, and he was confused because he's not used to seeing me that way. I was like, 'It's this kid, man.' I was pushing like hell to keep ahead of him, trying to see if I could go hard enough that he'd ask me to slow down, and every time I would look back, there's this little thirteen-year-old right on my heels. And, for all I can tell, he's not even phased by it."

"Oh, man, sorry about that. When he asked if he could walk with you, I thought you had invited him."

"I invited him. Starter and I have laughed about it a few times. It's more that I couldn't believe how hard he could hike. He was born for it."

I took a few steps more and turned. "Airborne. This might seem a little dramatic, but running into you when we did yesterday, it couldn't have come at a better time."

"The trail provides," he said. "It always does."

In the late afternoon, the trail wound its way up a cut and between two gray granite walls that encroached it, ever tighter. I paused to study them more closely. The rock itself was dotted with black and orange flecks. Lines and cracks cutting through at strange angles. If I had ropes, I might have been able to climb the rock face to the left. After another long look, I wondered if I might even be able to free climb it.

As I finished the last of the rise, I came to two large boulders that crowded the trail. When I threaded through them to the other side, I spotted Aiden ahead, sitting beside the trail on her pack looking away from me up a long, u-shaped valley. It wasn't until I was within a few steps of her, that she turned. "What's up, kid?" I said.

"I just felt like walking in the back with you. And, I mean, what better place to go slow than in these aspens?" She swept her arm up-trail toward the dense stand of trees. "It's nice to be walking through here when they are changing colors."

"Cold and all?"

"It's worth it. In my opinion."

"I do like the way the leaves flutter and you see all different colors. We are almost to Rae Lakes, the place that inspired this hike."

"What do you mean?"

"You remember that trip that Mom and I took with Chris and Savannah? We are almost to it. When we get to the suspension bridge in three miles, we will be walking a part of the same loop that we took. From there, I think it's only a few miles to Rae Lakes. Even before we talked about a thru-hike, I told your mom I wanted to bring you guys back here. These lakes are amazing. There are giant trout swimming around in them. I swear they are two feet long. That's the whole reason I carried this Tenkara rod with me.”

“Georgie isn’t going to like crossing a suspension bridge.”

“I think she’s better with heights now than she was.”

“She was telling me earlier that she was nervous about it.”

“That’s funny. She didn’t say anything to me.”

Beyond the bridge about ten minutes later, I sat on a pine log in a large tentsite. I reached a hand down to pat Georgie’s head. “That wasn’t so bad.”

“It wasn’t as bad as I thought it would be.”

“You want to know something funny?”

“What?”

“You know that place I was so excited to show you?”

“The one you came to with Uncle Chris and Aunt Savannah that time?”

“I was just talking to Mom and to SoGood. They’re ready to get out of here. Out of the mountains and down into town. We are making such good time today that we could be on the other side of Kearsarge pretty early in the morning.”

“And?”

“It means that we might walk into Rae Lakes after dark and be gone before it gets light in the morning.”

“So we won’t even get to see it?” She laughed. “What about the fishing?”

“I guess we’ll have to come back another time.”

1865.5

"This whole valley was farmed at one time, Aiden. Were you not listening to our driver at all?" I stretched backward over my backpack to look up at her.

"I wasn't paying attention." She stepped up on the curb and back down to the pavement.

"So, Mulholland came up from L.A. and bought up all the ranches and farmland throughout Onion Valley. Then when he carved out the water rights, he sold it back to them."

"What does that mean?" Georgie said.

"It means that all the water underneath, and everything that comes from the sky belongs to Los Angeles, and these farmers have to buy their own water if they want to use it."

"That's stupid," Aiden said. "It's their land, it should be their water."

"Supposedly, there was a huge lake in the valley that is all dried up now."

"Look, Dad," Georgie pointed. "It's Ms. McGuyver walking up here from the main road."

After we made our greetings, I said. "You're headed back out there? Did you hear there might be a second wave of the storm?"

"I don't mind it at all, I like the cold weather."

"Even in that cold rain and snow?" Aiden said.

"I'm from Finland, so I winter-camp all the time. Where is the rest of the family?"

"We had to get separate hitches down from the trailhead. We are waiting down here for them before we go to the road together and find a hitch the rest of the way to the hotel. Our driver went back up to get the others. Maybe he will take a third trip. Who knows?"

"Is it hard to get hitches with six people?"

"We've had to split up most of the time," I said. "Monica was not excited about that the first time we had to do that back in Washington. Steven's Pass, wasn't it, Aiden? The lady that finally picked us up scolded us for hitchhiking with our kids."

"Hey, it got us a ride, didn't it?" Aiden said.

"After that first time, Monica got a lot more comfortable."

"It is illegal in most places in Finland, and I never thought I would feel comfortable catching rides with strangers." Ms. McGuyver resituated her pack and looked down toward the highway. "If nobody stops soon, maybe I will ask the person who is driving your family."

Within a few minutes, a couple pulled over in a well-used SUV and rolled down their passenger window. The man spoke from the driver's seat, "We can take you if you mind riding in the back with the dog?"

The woman in the passenger seat turned toward the driver and said something that I could not hear, then opened her door and stepped out. "Let's put your pack in the back, and you take the front seat. He's a sweet dog, but he'll be curious about a stranger. I'll sit in the back with him."

Before the car's brake lights came on at the first bend, Monica, Henry, and June's ride passed them on its way toward us. I pulled out their packs and thanked the driver, who made a quick U-turn and headed back up the hill toward the trailhead. "That was nice of him, wasn't it?" I shielded my eyes and scanned the mountain above us to see if I could spot his car on one of the turns.

Monica touched my elbow and said, "Let's go to the main road and catch a ride to the hotel. I'm tired of feeling so filthy."

Georgie's raised arm was enough to hail the first passing van. The driver slid open the side door and leaned in to resituate a child's car seat, and said, "Where can I drop you?"

I gave her the name of the hotel, but Monica interrupted. "Let's go to the grocery store first, I need to pick up a few things."

Two hours later I was sitting on the edge of the bed in the hotel room waiting for my turn in the shower. I looked across to where Monica sat on the far bed when I heard a knock at the door.

"I forgot to tell you." She stood up and moved around the far side of the bed. "I ran into Bear Hair at the grocery store and invited her to come by."

"Is she staying with us?"

"I was going to invite her." She stopped in front of me and touched my shoulder. "I thought you could sleep on the floor with Henry, and she can share the bed with me."

When Monica swung the door open, Bear Hair stumbled forward into her open arms. Bear Hair wept. They stood in their embrace for a long time. "Oh, Bear Hair, you should stay with us. Please, just stay with us." Monica walked her to the far bed where they sat down together. She took Bear Hair's hands into her own. "Tell me, what happened out there?"

"The first night was so cold, I couldn't keep my pad from deflating. Whenever I woke up, I blew it up again and did push-ups. At least I was dry that night. I tried to find the hole all the next day. Then I thought maybe just to walk through the night, because that day, I was soaked through completely. And it was so much colder even than the night before. I couldn't walk through the dark. It was too dark, and I knew I didn't have enough battery left in my headlamp or my phone, and I couldn't let the phone die, because if I got lost … anyway …"

Henry tapped my knee and whispered from the side of his mouth, "At least she has a headlamp now."

"I kept trying to walk in the dark, but I got so tired. I fell asleep walking, so I had to set up my tent, and everything was wet. I finally gave up blowing up my groundpad, so I had to set my alarm on my watch to wake me up every fifteen minutes to eat an Oreo cookie. I gave up in the middle of the night and started walking. When I came to the trailhead, no one was there, so I had to camp there until someone gave me a ride out this morning."

"Good we didn't come out there, Dad," June said. "We might not have found a ride."

"Where did you all finally come out?"

"Kearsarge," I said.

"Will you stay with us, Bear Hair?" Monica hugged her again.

Aiden touched my shoulder and whispered, "What about dinner? Aren't we meeting SoGood for Chinese food?"

"I'll message her after I shower."

1887.0.1

"Why are we even doing this?" Henry slunk backward against the tree in the dark. "This is so stupid. It's not even on the trail."

"Dude, Mount Whitney is the tallest mountain in the lower forty-eight United States, come on. Normally, you have to apply for a permit through a lottery, but our PCT permit lets us do it for free."

"Why would you think I would care about that?"

I reached into my pocket to pull out my phone. "It's 2am, everybody, let's get going."

"How long is this going to take?" Aiden said.

"It's eight wasted miles off-trail," Henry said.

"It's pretty dark out tonight, Dad," Aiden said. "Do I have time to find my flashlight?"

For forty-five minutes, we shuffled step for step through the darkness. When the trail began its first climb up from the valley, June threw her poles down and refused to take another step farther.

Monica and I stepped to the side so that the kids couldn't hear us. "What are you going to do?" she said. "She can't act like this."

"I'll run her back to the tent and catch up to you guys. If we don't keep moving, everyone is going to miss the sunrise."

"You are going to leave her by herself all day?"

"I'll tell her she isn't allowed to leave the tent. Seriously, you guys go ahead. Don't worry about me."

I joined June and walked in step behind her for forty-five minutes back to the tent without saying a word. I held my tongue and told myself over and over to let this anger pass, to sort it out on the other side of this feeling. She would soon be in her tent. When she was, I zipped it up without a word and turned to try and catch the others.

June, I can't believe you would do this. Now you got me climbing fast in the dark to catch up, and I keep finding myself way off track. If I crack my shin again, I swear. It's weird, it's almost easier without the flashlight. At least then I can intuit the trail and get closer to used-to-the-dark. Holy hell, their lights are so far up that climb. That's some serious switchbacking. My head hurts. June, I am so annoyed. We came to do this thing together. There is going to be some kind of punishment for this. Something. My head hurts, and I feel like I might throw up.

It was light outside before I caught them. Georgie did not see me coming up from behind her. "Hey, kid. Wait for me. Don't step on that ice. If you slip here, you might fall forever."

Aiden heard me and waved me over to where she stood. "Come check this out, Dad. The sun is coming right through this hole in the rocks. It's so warm."

The gap opened a wide window to Onion Valley below. "It's crazy to be able to see ten thousand feet down like this." I turned my face to the side and felt the sun warm my cheek. "I guess we missed the sunrise." I turned my back to the sun and muttered June's name under my breath.

Monica patted my upper arm with her palm. "You are going to have to let that go."

"Dad," Georgie reached out her hand from behind me. "Dad, you forgot me. Can you come help me down these steps? I'm afraid I might slip on the ice."

When I stepped up the two steps to stand beside her, I clasped her hand and pointed along the ridge toward a wide slope. "Once we get there, it won't take us more than a few minutes to get to the top."

We crossed above thirteen thousand five hundred feet at the base of a talus field. I got lightheaded, so I sat on a rock and dropped my head between my knees. Georgie put her hand on my shoulder. "You okay dad?" she said.

"I don't know, I should be. I have some of that pre-throw up feeling. How about you? Are you any better?"

"It feels like I'm on a ship's deck where everything is moving."

"We can go down, Georgie. We don't need to go to the top."

"You think I'm going to quit now? I came this far, didn't I?"

The highest rock at the summit was crowded with day hikers who'd come up from the opposite side. In the background a ghostly mist wafted up from Onion Valley below. We stood on the flat rock overlook only long enough to trouble a stranger to take our picture. I turned to Henry on the way off the rock and said, "It would be far more impressive coming up this side, don't you think?

At the first switchback above our descent, I called ahead to Monica. "I forgot to sign the logbook. I'll be right back."

When I flipped the book open, I discovered our five names already recorded in Aiden's handwriting. I traced my fingers across them and said aloud, "Only five names. Only five." I paused. "June, I'm so sorry. It isn't the same if you aren't here with us. It's like we may as well not even have come."

"You okay, man?" a hiker said.

I wiped my eyes.

Again, I touched our names in the book. "It's only five names, and it's supposed to be six. She couldn't make it."

"Who couldn't make it?"

"My second daughter. June is her name. The whole idea of this thing was to be together, you know? And it just doesn't feel right for her not to be here."

"How?" He put his head down and folded his hands in front of him. "How did you lose her?"

"Lose her?"

1887.0.2

Henry and I walked parallel through the high grass with our Tenkara rods held high. I looked toward where he walked 30 feet away. He looked back toward me and smiled. Beyond him, the backside of Mount Whitney, from which we'd descended just hours before, stood as a desolate backdrop. Behind our backs, in the trees, the girls were ensconced in their tents, well into their afternoon naps. June had reported that she had slept herself all morning throughout our absence, but it had not stopped her from sleeping again.

We crested the rise before us and rolled along a gentle shoulder toward a narrow creek with a stained brown rocky bottom that gurgled softly through small and various pools.

"This should be good, bud," I said. "I bet nobody ever fishes up here." I pointed upstream and nodded, and Henry veered off to follow my direction. I dropped my pole beside me to the ground and fished in my pocket for my small tin can of flies. With the lid flipped open, I touched a few of the flies with my fingertips. "I don't suppose it matters," I said aloud. "These fish would probably eat anything."

On my first cast a small golden trout flashed at the fly. I overreacted and missed him. "Hey, Henry," I called out. "Dollar, dollar, dollar."

He lifted his hands as if in a question.

"One dollar for the first, one for the biggest, and one for the most. Let's go." I taunted Henry.

"I'm gonna win," he said.

I caught the first fish, but I overdid it on my hookset again and flung the 4-inch fish over my head in a wide arc. As I separated the grass to find the flopping fish, I called, "Whoop, woop, Henry, take that! That's a dollar to me."

Henry also pulled too hard on his first hookset, and loosed from the hook, the fish flew thirty feet through the air before landing on the high bank behind him. He dipped his hands in the stream and raced to it. When he found his fish, he made his way to me along the high crest of the bank. "Dad, did you bring your phone? I want a picture."

"I think we have the advantage of these little guys with these long rods," I said. "We need to go easy on our hooksets."

He smiled down at me and extended the fish in both hands. "Mine is the biggest. That's a dollar to me."

"So far, you have the biggest," I said. "But that dollar is not very secure, 'cause I'm coming for you."

"They are so yellow. Why are they like that?"

"These fish are unique to the Sierra and only live in these high elevations. As far as I know, you can't catch them anywhere else, unless they've introduced them somewhere. But I'm sure this is the only place in the world where they are native."

We snapped picture after picture of fish after fish and made our way upstream at a slow pace, pool by pool. After two hours or so, a long shadow crept over the stream from the high cliff above us. I walked up to the shelf to sit in the sun.

I watched Henry fish by himself for the better part of an hour. I called down to him when he caught what looked like it might be his biggest one yet. "Want a picture of that one?"

"Don't you think we have enough pictures?" he called back.

I lay back, clasping my hands behind my head and scanned the high cliff wall beyond Henry and followed the ridge line toward the cut where we'd climbed Mount Whitney. There is a fine balance between pushing kids toward their potential and enjoying them right where they are. June has run in the red the whole time, always at her limit. I'm not sure I could have asked anything more from her. If I had, I'm not sure she could have given it. Henry has had to push past impatience, because he's been capable of so much more. He's had to overcome boredom and envy born of wanting to be elsewhere. And of knowing he could already been done. On some days, I had doubted the good of the entire endeavor, but not that day. Not in the meadow in the shadow of Whitney lying down in the warm grass.

"Wow!" Henry called and pulled hard on his rod. The fish stayed in the water and fought back. Water splashed high when Henry stepped into the pool to his knees and followed the fish to give it slack.

"My gosh, he is going to catch that thing." I raced to him with my phone in my hand. Before I made it to him, he had the fish in his two hands and stood on the bank with the widest of grins.

He laughed and a tear dropped from his eye. "I got the biggest by far now. There's no way you're going to catch me, Dad."

1900

After the cold burned off in the morning, during the hour when we would free our hands from our pockets, we came upon Skybird. She was resting on a sunny patch of sand that was covered by a thin layer of pinestraw. She invited us to join her, so we tossed out our Tyveks and lay down. After the kids peppered her with a first wave of stories, she pointed toward the far side of the trail. "Are you taking a picture here too?"

Across the trail, a collection of rocks had been arranged in the shape of a number. "Is this mile nineteen hundred?" I said. "We have taken a picture of our feet at every hundred-mile marker." I opened my phone, scrolled to the first one of the kind that I found, and handed it to her.

"The one made of pinecones. You made that? We took a picture there too, so we must have been right behind you." She tossed my phone back. "How was Whitney for you guys? Did you summit at sunrise?"

"I didn't even go up Whitney," June said. "I slept all morning long in my tent."

Skybird looked at me.

"She stayed in her tent while the rest of us summited."

"And Dad gave me a trail name because of it," June said.

"What is the trail name?"

"He called me Frankie, because Frankie refuses all the jumps. And I refused to go up Whitney, so my dad thought that it would be fitting."

"Frankie is the horse that she rides," Monica said. "And he's not always cooperative with June when she tries to take him over the jumps."

"Oh, June." Skybird held her hand to her mouth. "That's …" She hesitated. "Funny?"

"He gave me a choice of a punishment, because he was frustrated." She looked toward me as if to ask permission. When I smiled back at her, she continued, "He said I either had to come back with him someday to do Whitney or accept a trail name."

Skybird looked toward me.

"I thought for sure she would take the Whitney offer," I said.

"I don't know why you even suggested that. She was never going to choose it," Monica said.

"She's the only one with a trail name," Aiden said. "And that stinks."

"Skybird," Henry waved his arm up and down until she acknowledged him. "That creek in the meadow has tons of fish in it. We caught maybe …" He looked at me. "Thirty or forty golden trout, while the girls all slept in their tents."

"Wow. That's amazing. Did you eat them?"

"We didn't know if we were allowed," Monica said.

"How big were they?"

"About"—Henry held up his hands five inches apart—"this big."

"So, not very big," Monica said.

We all turned at that moment when a backpack-less hiker burst into the clearing with her hands over her face.

Skybird jumped to her feet and ran toward her. "Are you okay, Grizz?"

"My phone," she said and buried her head into Skybird's chest. "I lost my phone. It's the second time. My mom just bought me a new one too."

Monica joined them and patted Grizz's back with a soft hand. "Can we help you find it?"

"I think I know right where I dropped it." She stepped back from Skybird and laced the fingers of both hands behind her head. "It must be at the water source three miles back."

"Can one of us go with you?" I said.

Grizz shook her head and crossed her arms over her thin t-shirt and shivered. Monica reached out to place a hand on one of Grizz's arms and rubbed her arm as if she would warm her.

"It's fine, thank you." She reached a hand to her waist and touched her jacket. "I have my rain shell."

With our mood dampened, I called an end to the break. I turned back as we left the clearing and said, "She's going to get cold when it gets dark."

A half a mile down-trail, Monica said, "Oh no. Look at this." She bent and came up with a phone and turned to me wide-eyed. "Poor Grizz."

"It's going to be dark soon." I reached for the phone, turned it over several times in my hands, and looked toward the sky. "Do you think I can catch her?"

For the first mile, whenever I came to an opening in the trees, I stood stock-still until my breathing slowed and my pulse stopped pounding in my ears, then I called out through the quiet in the hope of a response. No response came, not even an echo. The silence itself seemed oppressive. After the first mile, I slowed to a fast walk. After another half mile, I quit calling out. "When it gets dark, she is going to freeze." I squeezed my hand tight around my rain shell. "We are going to freeze," I said, and then another thought hit me, "Surely, she'll turn around if she reaches the water and can't find her phone." I broke into a run again, and soon again, stopped. "What's the rush?

You aren't going to overtake her. She'll stop at the water. She has to stop sometime."

When I arrived, Grizz was sitting on the far side of the small stream, halfway up a small slope with her head between her knees. She did not look up.

"Grizz, Monica found your phone."

She placed her hand over her mouth and shook with sobbing. I hopped over the creek and held out her phone. She reached for it without saying a word and sat down again on the bank. I sat apart. After what felt like a long time, she said, "I fell apart. Over a phone. It's just a phone, and I am usually so strong. I just fell apart."

"I don't know."

"It's more than a phone." She pressed the power button and the screen came on. "It's my journal. And all my pictures. Most of my trip. Everything. I already lost the first part when I lost the first one."

I nodded.

Her lips tightened and she half-smiled, but her eyes seemed as if fixed on something distant. We sat like that for a long time.

"Falling apart is a daily occurrence with our crew," I said. "We call it cry-thirty when it comes."
She looked up and half-smiled.

"My June Bug is always a hair's breadth from losing it. Although, to be fair, it's a bit like that back home too. But out here, shoot, we get everything in its most concentrated form. Three times now we have been this close,"—I pinched my fingers closely together and squinted through them toward her —"to packing it up and heading home. I'm not talking about the, it's-a-bad-day-I-wish-we-weren't-out-here kind of go home, I'm talking about the where-is-the-nearest-airport kind of go home."

Grizz smiled and shook her head. "Why didn't you?"

"The worst one, I guess, was after she and Monica had a serious fight. She threw herself down on the trail and wouldn't budge. Whenever she'd lost it before that, I'd been able to talk her back into pushing on. Mostly using techniques from this book I read before we started the trail"

"What was it?"

"It isn't about hiking or anything. It's called *Never Split the Difference*. It's kind of an 'art of the deal' book by a former FBI hostage negotiator. But don't kid yourself, trying to coax these people down the trail is like negotiating with a bunch of terrorists. Basically, you start with mirroring, so I would say, 'you are staying right here?' Then you summarize. 'It seems like you are asking me to leave you here.' I guess, ultimately, you want to invite them to help you solve your problem. 'How' questions are good for that. Something like, 'June, you are my fourteen-year-old daughter, and I love you. How can I leave you here?' or 'June, they will be worried about us. How can we leave the rest of our family out there scared and wondering what's happened to us?'

"Isn't that a little manipulative."

"It could be, for sure. Especially if the thing you were inviting them into wasn't good for them, but I was pretty convinced that dying on the trail wasn't in her best interest. The other thing he says, that I think is really cool, is that you have to approach everyone with unconditional positive regard. That, I think, is what gives you the best chance of moving all of his techniques away from being manipulative and moving them to a higher level of listening and understanding. Because, I think, at its core, what it does is it helps you to get people talking. And when people talk you can find out what they really want. Either way, I can tell you, it wasn't working that night. That kid was a brick wall."

I held up my finger. "Sorry for going off on that tangent. The point is that all this stuff that had worked so well before, wasn't working. I couldn't make her budge.

"All of a sudden,"—I waved my hands out in front of me as though I would conjure a spell—"SoGood, I think you know her, appeared out of nowhere and said, 'How are you doing?' Of course, I lied … at first. I'd lied to the three hikers before her, so I'm not sure why I corrected myself that time and decided to tell her the truth. I told her, 'June's having a rough day.'

"Well, it couldn't have been better timing for June, because it turned out that SoGood's favorite milk goat was named June. Which, you would appreciate a whole lot more if I were any kind of storyteller. My June Bug is my animal whisperer. She practically lives for her two goats at home. So there is nothing in the world SoGood could have said that would have been better for us at that moment."

"That's really cool timing." Grizz smiled. "Did she start walking again after that?"

"What was so cool for me," I said. "Was that it had nothing to do with me or with my ability to persuade her." I paused. "It felt like a miracle."

Grizz leaned forward and picked up a few pieces of pinestraw. "I have been sitting here thinking that something about Monica finding my phone was miraculous. I haven't thought about the possibility of that kind of thing in a long time, so it sounds weird even to say it."

"I think that it's happening all the time. God is not some distant, way-out-there, absentee landlord." I laughed.

"Why are you laughing?"

"A line from a song just popped in my head. Have you ever listened to Josh Ritter?"

She shook her head.

"He's got this one song where he's mostly just raging at a distant God. The line goes, 'he made the earth in seven days, and ever since just been a' walkin' away.' It's funny to me that he talks about God walking, and somehow walking out here has made me more aware of a present and active God, not less."

"The trail provides."

"Exactly, that serendipity,"—I raised my hands to make air quotes,—"that everyone celebrates when they say, 'the trail provides,' I think it's the providence of a God who is right here with us."

"I haven't thought about this stuff in a long time," she said.

I drew a circle in the dirt with my finger, and we sat in silence for a long time. I rolled sideways to push myself to my feet. "You must be getting cold." I offered a hand to help her up. "You want to head back?"

We jogged for a few minutes after we left the water. When we slowed to a walk, I said, "I don't know what I'd do if I lost my phone. I would have freaked out too, if I were you."

It was dark before we parted at the junction. Grizz made her way through the trees toward a dim light in Skybird's tent. While I waited to hear the confirmation of their reunion, I pulled my puffy jacket from my pack and put it on. At last, their voices rang out clear through cold night, and I turned to walk into the dark alone.

1902

Above me, the dark sky, like some jet black, inked ocean, is pockmarked with incandescent stars. At my feet, flickers of light dance on the pinestraw, off-cast from a pre-risen moon beyond the ridge to my left. I bend to study the ridgeline through sparse trees. I have seen moonrises out here that crest horizons, only to slide low and crabwise across the sky for a while and then drop from sight again. I could, if I wanted, scramble up the shallow incline through the trees for fifty yards to stand on the cliff's edge and look down, five thousand feet above the wide, desert floor. The two of us together, the moon and I, would keep watch like sentinels as Onion Valley sleeps. But my thoughts break apart, it is only seven o'clock. Everyone down there in houses will have flipped their lights on and cranked up the heat, and I am isolated in this wild and quiet place. When I breathe out, clouds of vapor form and linger longer than is normal, and I stuff my fingers in the pocket of my puffy jacket. I'll save the visit to the cliff for another time. I don't want any detours.

Before long the trees grow tighter together and crowd the trail. It is harder to see. I pull my pen light from my pocket and click it on. The branches around me reflect as brilliant white, almost blinding. New sounds wake in my ears, the cracking of sticks and the rustle of leaves. I laugh in the knowledge that in the truest place in my mind, I know it is only the rising wind that has caused it, but this new, unsettled feeling will not dissipate. Intuiting my way in near darkness would be preferable to this half-pretense of sight, so I turn off my flashlight, and wait. Pressing my thumbs to my eyes, I raise bright circles and wait longer. One heavy wind gust shakes the trees above me, and then all is still. Still blind, I fish my beanie from my back pouch and pull it down tight over my ears.

They will be there in the camp, knowing that I'm coming. Surely, they'll camp just off-trail.

If I could study the contours on the map, I might be able to guess their destination. I squeeze my phone through my hip belt pouch and reach for the zipper, but I stop. If I look at the screen, I'll lose all the progress I've made, adjusting to the dark, so I pull my hand away.

They'll have already eaten and crawled into their tents. I laugh. But I have one of the tents. I throw my hand up to my mouth and laugh again at the oversight. Henry will have jumped in with one of them, but it will be a tight squeeze. The trail is brighter now, or maybe my eyes have adjusted. I can move toward my family at a good pace.

They are my target and my destination. I whisper their names on the breeze.

What is it, this thing that we are doing? And why does it light up my soul? When we opened ourselves to this possibility, we opened the door to adventure. And since we began, every step has been a decision at the margins of the possible.

"There's nothing like a human for walking," Ben Bishop had said, and he was right. Sure, at the beginning, it was all grind and discomfort. But after three weeks, when the rust broke loose, we stepped into the swing of it. And then, even on the hardest days of grinding, there was always an afternoon window when everything felt right, even the light. Every day, beyond a certain mile marker–an arbitrary objective–something in my brain would ring out, "Did you have any idea that a human could do this?"

I can imagine Georgie in her tent, as if I am there with her now, dropping her curly hair to her clothes bag. I can hear Aiden harrumphing, "Get your hair out of my face."

We fight now as if we are home, because we are now home here, wherever we sleep. In Lakeland, our thermostat is set at seventy-eight degrees all year round. Tonight, here, it will be cold, below twenty degrees, and tomorrow the sun will beat us down. But we've pushed these margins out wide now. I look down to my shorts as if in proof. Other than my puffy jacket, I will wear the same thing in either extreme.

This is a comfort gained on the far side of discomfort. A million tiny sacrifices, tiny deaths on the way to a sort of a union. I can feel my quads on this hill, but they don't burn anymore, not ever. They are tuned to it, in tune with the task. This harmonization between tool and task has a magic about it. It is an act of creative participation in the way we were made, in a place that was made for us.

It's just walking, I know, but it's walking at the outer parts of our limits. I didn't know humans could walk 30 miles a day on repeat. Especially eleven-year-old humans.

It has been here, in this place, beyond the certain, that I have found myself flooded with this feeling of wonder.

I stumble on a root and stop my fall with my hands. I push myself up and brush my hands together and laugh.

I laugh out loud at myself for having wandered so far into reverie. I thank the root out loud for the reminder. "Thank you, root."

But I do not want to repeat the mistake, so I watch my feet. I can see a hint of blue from my new, roomy, size sixteen Altras. A northbound Sierra section hiker had called them clown shoes, and he wasn't wrong. I spread my toes apart from each other as if to explore the space. "Well, no wonder I tripped on that root. These things really are clown shoes." Since I put them on just before Red's Meadows, I've had feeling in all of my toes. If anyone ever asks me gear questions, I'll tell them, "Start with the shoes, and be sure they are the right ones for you."

With each stride, I'd hear a ticking but I can't figure out what it is. I catch a flash of my shoestring in the moonlight and then it makes sense. After I retie the shoe and double-knot it, I stand to stretch my arms wide toward the trees. A settled feeling of belonging comes over me and I skip like a child for a few yards. Before I slow down into my walking pace. I hear a stick crack off-trail, followed by the sound of a voice, "Dad, we are over here."

I found Henry sitting on his bear canister with his sleeping quilt wrapped around him. "I guess it's you and me tonight, eh buddy? Why aren't you waiting in one of the tents?

"'Cause you have our tent."

"Will you start setting it up? I need to say something to June. Give me a minute." I crawled under the vestibule of June's tent. "June Bug?" I unzipped the mesh and reached for her hand. "June Bug, can I tell you something?"

"What is it, Daddo?"

"Remember how we talked about the idea that your suffering might help you to help others someday?"

"Yeah."

"Well, your story meant a lot to Grizz. She said it reminded her that she wasn't alone."

"What story?"

"I told her about the time when Aunt Katie told us about her milk goat, and how perfect the timing was when she came along."

June smiled and pulled me to her for an upside down, makeshift hug. "I'm glad, Daddo. I can't believe her favorite milk goat was named June, just like me."

"It's a great story, June." Monica said. "It is always better when you're not alone."

"Your mom has some bionic hearing, doesn't she?" I whispered.

"No," Monica said. "You are incapable of whispering."

1950.8

We lay tucked inside the shade line beneath the sandy wall on the outer bend of a gully. Below us, the dry stream faded into the brush and into the brown and into the dust. Georgie shifted herself on her dust-covered Tyvek and lay back down again. She rolled her head toward me and her wild hair spread about, all ringlet and tangle. Her very movement a sigh.

Monica rested her chin on my shoulder to look at Georgie. "She looks so much older now. I think her hair color has changed."

"We've been out here a long time."

"It's faded a lot." She reached her hand to Georgie's forehead and said, "Your face is so dirty." She traced her fingers underneath the curls. "Look how red it is under there. How long has it been since you've showered?"

"Mom, it's fine. I'm taking a shower later today."

"I've decided," Henry said. "I'm not even going to take one single shower in all of California."

Monica pulled her hand from Georgie's hair, wiped it on the side of her pants, and rolled back onto her back. "You guys are gross."

"How long 'til we get there, Dad?" Georgie said.

"That's up to you. How fast are you planning to walk? Now that we are past the Sierra, it's all downhill to Mexico."

"I mean between here and town."

"Not far. We follow this water course down to the road, so it must be all down. You can look it up if you want."

"Fine, give me your phone," Georgie said and turned her head up toward the bank. "We are going to lose the shade soon."

"Hey, Mom," Aiden said. "Press your ear to the ground. You can actually hear the water moving underneath us. It's so crazy."

At the top of the wash behind us, a brown fiberglass trail marker bore a tattered sticker with a fading outline of the emblem of the Pacific Crest Trail. I closed my eyes. For a moment it was as though I could see past all the trail markers, high mountain passes, tears, laughter, arguments, anger, joy, and pain. "Almost there, guys."

"How far is it to Kennedy Meadows South, Georgie?" Henry said. "Did you look it up yet?"

"3.2 miles, and it's all gentle down."

"Can I see?" June said.

"Come over here and look. I don't feel like getting up."

"Just throw it to me."

"Can I throw it to her?" Georgie looked at me.

I nodded.

"Are we staying in town tonight?" Aiden said.

"I don't know how much of a town it is, kiddo," I said. "I don't even think there is anywhere to stay. We were planning to just do a quick resupply and maybe grab a burger," I said. "Are you okay with that, Monica?"

"As long as we can take showers."

"If there is nowhere to stay," Aiden said. "How can we shower; that makes no sense?"

"There are showers at the burger place," Monica said. "I know, isn't that ridiculous?"

Georgie peeked over my arm. "Are there milkshakes at this restaurant that has showers?"

I rolled toward Monica and touched my beard to her ear. "Can you believe that we've made it?"

"I don't know why you keep saying that. We still have a long way to go."

"Because, when you've made it to Kennedy Meadows South, you've made it. That's what they say. At least we're past the hardest part." I half-turned my head. "Georgie, did you check the mile marker here?"

"I have the phone, Dad," June said. "We are at mile 1950.8."

"1950.8, so that's ..." Aiden said.

"Aiden, let June try to figure it out," I said. "Go ahead, Bug. You can do this."

Aiden stuck her tongue out at me. "It's seven hundred."

"He told you not to help me!"

"It's not seven hundred, June. Take your time." We lay in silence for a while. I rose and stepped out of the shadow and turned my face toward the sun. "Let's get moving, guys."

June said, "Is it seven hundred and sixteen miles?"

"You got it," I said. "Good job, kid."

Aiden huffed. "That's the same thing I said, practically."

While still sitting down, Monica folded her groundsheet and stuffed it into the mesh pouch on the back of her pack. She stood up with a groan.

I watched her first halting steps.

"You think she's okay, Dad?" Georgie whispered.

"I don't know. I hope so. Probably. You can go on ahead with the others, I have to pee."

"You think we will make it to the border before my birthday?"

Wedged between two scrubby creosote bushes, I looked up along the mouth of the long canyon. "We are going to make it," I said aloud. I snapped my waistband back into place and swung into my pack in one smooth motion and climbed onto the trail. "Wait up, Georgie. I'm coming."

1955

"I heard that if we make it to Mexico, we might be the largest family to have ever thru-hiked the trail southbound," I said, leaning on the counter in Triple Crown Outfitters.

Yogi smiled. "I'm pretty sure you'll be the largest family ever to have thru-hiked this trail either direction."

Yogi dispensed knowledge of the trail as effortlessly as she did the packages we had mailed ahead for her to hold.

"Who is she, anyway?" Aiden nodded toward the entrance to the store as we sat down to do our resupply.

"She's hiked the Triple Crown twice."

"What is that?"

"This trail, the Appalachian Trail, and the Continental Divide Trail; the three together are called the Triple Crown. She did all three of them, twice. And this one she did in the nineties, before it was so well maintained. She did it without any GPS apps. All of her navigation was by map and compass."

Aiden made an airy whistling sound and shook her head.

"You know what else she told me? They used to have to carry seven liters of water at all times, just in case."

"That's an extra fifteen pounds, Dad? That would make it so much harder."

"She's the first woman to ever have done it. Others have done it since, but not many. Brazil Nut has."

"And she just set up this store in this tiny little town?"

"She did. It's a great spot for it too, because this place marks the end of the Sierra. From here it's all easier than what we've done. Well, the water carries are longer in the desert, but there shouldn't be anything to stop us now, as long as we all stay healthy and no one gets injured."

"What about Mom's feet?"

I shrugged. "She's about got that figured out." I grabbed her knee and squeezed. "Ready for some Grumpy Bear's? I could eat a horse."

At Grumpy Bear's diner, the man behind the counter loudly declared that the town's population had been grossly exaggerated to compel the telephone company to provide service to the residents.

"But the sign says, 'Population 64,'" I said.

"Sure, if you count llamas and horses," the man said.

Aiden raised herself onto her tiptoes to whisper in my ear.

I laughed. "Are you sure, kid?"

"Oh yeah." She smiled.

I gave her a nod, and she ordered a double bacon cheeseburger all the way with hashbrowns, eggs, and avocado.

Spatz, Skybird, and Grizz caught our attention from across the restaurant and motioned for us to join them at their table. When we sat down Skybird said, "Are you Strawbridges heading out today?"

"We're just passing through," I said. "Have you looked at the water report for the next section? My map is still downloading."

"It looked like some long carries," she said. "But nothing you can't handle. Salty is almost to the border, and he says it's not that bad. Do you have a target date to finish?"

"No, we don't. Do you?"

"Some of us have flights to catch and have to go a little faster, but we don't want to split up, so we may all push. Salty said it can be done in thirty days."

"We are a little touch and go with Monica's feet," I said. "So this may be a last goodbye for us."

***

We walked out of town down the empty highway, all six of us side by side. Not a car passed from either direction. When they all dropped onto the dusty path at the junction without breaking stride, I paused to take a last glance north. Not far beyond the road, the trail bent beyond a bush and disappeared. Beside the bush, a brown fiberglass marker shuddered in the breeze. Before turning around, I called out to Monica, "Wait up, I'm coming."

1958

"There are bones everywhere out here," Monica said. "It's not an easy place for things to live."

I slid the cow skull with my toe and looked down the dry trail. In many ways this was not the desert I expected. There was no tumbleweed piled against fences, no sand dunes, and no cacti across the wide valley. Small, scraggly piñon grew above unfriendly creosote bushes all sloping away toward the wash. The creek we had followed for a few miles had disappeared now as if swallowed into the rough sand.

"The horns are almost completely intact," Monica said. "How old do you think that is?"

"Probably not too old. This one still has some hide attached. But you get the feeling things can be one hundred or one thousand years old out here, and still be well preserved."

"I've been feeling that way all day. Like we are walking through an ancient place. It's almost like we aren't supposed to be here."

1964

"I can't believe you have reception," I said. "Who was that?"

"Michele."

"Oh, how is Dax? Did his feet ever recover?"

"She said he misses the trail. He's been boiling water every morning and eating oatmeal straight out of the pouch. 'In solidarity with the Strawbridges,' he says."

"That's nice of him to suffer with us."

"That's what I said, but she said he loves it, so not to give him too much credit."

SoGood was standing under a pinion pine just off-trail when we saw her. She swept her foot and kicked a pinecone away. "I can't decide if I want to set up my tent or not."

"I am definitely not going to set up a tent," Aiden said.

"If you are asking me," Monica said, "I'd set it up."

SoGood opted to sleep in the open.

We all sat on our groundsheets for a while into the dark. "That was hard," I said. "There was more elevation change than I would have expected, but it could be my new heavy pack. I think I carried too much water."

"You know what they say," SoGood said. "You pack your fears. If water is your thing, you are going to carry it even if it's overkill. As far as the elevation goes, this is still the Sierra, so the mountains are just about the same in terms of contour. They are just a little bit lower in overall elevation."

"If you add in these long water carries," Aiden said. "It might be worse."

By next mid-morning, Georgie and I had dropped well to the back. She cried as she walked.

"I don't think it helps to talk about it, Dad. Just let me cry, I'll be fine."

We hiked for an hour before she stopped in front of me and leaned over her trekking poles with a sigh. She turned her head to look up at me.

"I wasn't going to say anything, kid. Take your time."

"It isn't that. It's just that I thought I was over all the cry-thirties. I thought after the Sierra it would be easy."

"I did too. If it helps, SoGood said this is the last hardest thing." I paused. "There have been too many last hardest things."

She stood up straight again and looked out across the valley below. "Dad, how do you deal with the despair coming on? I mean, when you see it starting to get a hold of you."

I leaned over my trekking poles and didn't speak.

"I don't know why I thought everything would be different when we left the road. I guess it's because we kept saying that once we finished the Sierra, we would be home free. So now that we are here and it's not flat and cruisy, it feels so much harder. I thought we'd be making hay all day every day."

"What is the Lord up to, Georgie?"

She smirked at me. "I guess that is supposed to make everything better."

2010

"If you are looking for your people, I believe they went that way." He pointed downhill and slumped backward into his external frame pack. When he did, his cookpot clinked against the exposed aluminum metal frame. He gave a half turn to the faded bandana that was tied around his neck, pinched it near the middle, and wiped the underside of his chin. He turned his sun-raw, leathery face to me as if to demand a response.

"I'm waiting for a couple more of my kids. They are still behind me," I said. "How is your hike going?"

"It's going."

"What's your name?"

"My name is Limbo."

"Like the game with the stick?"

"Not that Limbo."

"Are you a southbounder? We haven't seen you before."

"For now, yes, I am southbound."

"What do you think of the desert so far?"

"The desert is to be endured. A final test."

"It's been a test so far. Yogi told us we'd be the largest family ever to have completed this trail."

"The largest family? Do you really believe that?"

"I don't see why not. She seems to be well connected in the PCT networks."

"These trails were here long before the Pacific Crest Trail Association appointed itself curator. You are not the largest by a long way. Look below you to the valleys. Have you considered the names? Santa Cruz, San Jose, San Francisco, San Rafael. And where are you going, if not San Luis Obispo, Santa Maria, Santa Barbara? The distances between them are not an accident. They are all of them missions. One day's walk apart. Oases all, against the wolves. Against the night. This is the land of the pilgrim and the sojourner. You are not the first, nor the largest, nor the last. How many carcasses did you see before you arrived in the desert? How many skeletons?"

"Not very many."

"How many have you seen since?"

"More than a few."

"This is a place of dust and dry bone, and the bone remains. Life here leaves no trace. It is only death that is remembered."

"This all seems a bit melodramatic. Isn't it just walking, after all?"

He pushed himself to his feet, hoisted his heavy pack, and walked on.

I dropped my pack at the spring and pulled out my two water bottles along with an extra water bladder. "It's a long way to the next water, everybody. If you don't want to walk a long way off-trail, you'd better camel up."

"I'll be fine," Henry said. "I don't need much water."

"I'm going to drink a couple liters," I said. "So get comfortable."

"Henry keeps adjusting the straw he made, and it's muddying the water," Aiden said. "Leave it alone, Henry, it's fine."

I sat beside Monica to wait my turn. "Did you meet that guy at the junction?"

"What guy?"

"He was some kind of wannabe sage. You are sure you didn't see him? He told me he saw you guys."

"I didn't see anybody."

I touched my shoulder. "External frame backpack with an aluminum frame."

She shook her head again.

"How far did you say to the next water?" Aiden said.

2011

It is as if the Sierra was slid into a dehumidifier. In the waterless waste, all the greens dissolved into a washed-out blue-gray. Dusty piñon pine, prickly sage, and Joshua tree. Water is scarce here, but what water there is, cannot cloak itself well in this place. Bright greens and yellows pop in cottonwood cuts to betray even a trickle. In the cuts in the mornings, even where the water flows well below ground, it is colder, and greener. Water is everything here. Fox Mill Spring, Joshua Tree Spring, Walker Pass Spring, McIver's Spring, Landers Meadow Spring, Water Hole Mine Spring, Robin Bird Spring. And in between springs are cisterns and deep wells, and volunteer-placed water caches. And water is life.

2042

"Dad," Aiden turned her head as if in slow motion and held her pose as if to gather effort to swallow before she spoke. "I … Do you think I could use your trekking poles?" I handed both of mine to her.

Monica stepped past me and reached a hand to Aiden's forehead, "Oh, Aiden, you're so clammy," and turned to me with wide eyes.

"She says she is nauseous," I said, "I don't know what it is, but I'll stay with her in the back if you want to go on and catch up to the others?"

Monica nodded. As she passed, she whispered, "Keep a close eye on her."

Aiden stood for a long while staring up the trail as if to gather strength. As if, through force of will, she would pull the top of the hill down to herself. "I wish I could throw up, Dad. I think I would feel better."

After a while, she labored forward with even steps. I gave her space, until she stepped off trail to lean over the bushes. She called for me and held her hand toward me without looking back. When I grabbed her hand, she said, "No, Dad, I wanted you to hand me my water," and gave a half-hearted chuckle. I gathered her hair from the side of her face and held it. She remained in that position for a while.

"I don't think anything more is going to come," I said.

She shook her head and stood up straight. "I wish I could throw up again and make it all feel better. What do you think it is, Dad?"

"It could just be the flu. You don't think you got into some bad water, do you?"

She made a slight motion with her finger down the hill. "I guess it could have been that water cache from yesterday. That one was full of dead flies."

"You didn't drink from that bottle, did you?"

"No, but it makes me think the others may not have been so clean." She let out a long exhale, and said, "Sorry if I'm slowing everyone down."

"You are doing great. This is about the pace June and I walk. At least, when we're on a climb."

"I don't know how you stand going this slow." She pointed towards the ground. "Could you pick up those trekking poles? I don't feel like bending down."

After two hours of unbroken steps, she called my name.

"What is it, Aido?"

"I think I found it."

"Found what?"

"The perfect pace, where I am nauseous, but I stay just on this side of throwing up."

 When we came upon the others resting in the shade at the top of the next long climb, I pointed toward them. Monica stood up and walked toward me. "I'll take a turn in the back with her till the next water, if you want to walk in the front."

"'Til Robin Bird Spring? Sure, I can do that. I'll sit with you and Aiden for a while and then catch up to them."

I caught June quickly and fell into her pace. After a while, she said, "Go catch Georgie and Henry, Dad. I know you want to. I can tell."

They were standing in the middle of a switchback laughing when I caught them, breathless. "What's wrong, Dad?" Georgie said.

"I had to work to catch you two," I said. "Why were you two laughing?"

"We've been working on a song we wrote about food cravings. Do you want to hear it? It's kind of silly."

"That's okay, sing it."

On the 12th day of Christmas
My true love gave to me
12 strips of bacon
11 Chick-fil-A's
10 bowls of ice cream
9 Snickers Bars
8 strawberries
7 plates of fries
6 boiled eggs
5 egg pancakes
4 caramel milkshakes
3 Burger Kings
2 apple fritters
And a basket of chicken wings

"Oh man, you guys. That makes me hungry, but you don't have to worry. We are going to have a feast when we get to Tehachapi."

The stupor of the afternoon descended, and we passed through unremarkable terrain, treeless, brown, and cactus laden. Rows of windmills dotted the landscape in varied states of disrepair. After a last water stop, a cattle trough, we spread out along the ridge. "It's just a turnout by the interstate. Mom will call an Uber. Wait for us there."

***

Henry sat atop his backpack and cast a lazy look across the gravel toward me. He tipped his water bottle and drained the last of it into his mouth. Aiden toed the sole of his shoe. "How much flavoring do you put in that stuff, Henry? Your teeth are all red."

440

I dropped my pack beside them and sat down.

"How's Aiden?" Henry said.

"She's walking with your mom."

After a half hour of waiting, we saw Monica's hat appear. When I stood up to greet them, I noticed that something about the place seemed familiar. I pulled out my phone, kicked the sole of Henry's foot, and pointed. "You don't recognize this place?" I turned my phone toward him. "I didn't either at first."

"The Browns last picture challenge?"

"It's the third and last one, you guys," I said and turned my head up toward the slope. "One in Oregon near Shelter Cove, the one in Toualome Meadows in the middle of the Sierra, and now this one. It feels pretty awesome. You can almost picture their van peeling out from this gravel parking lot."

"Yeah," Henry said. "And Mr. Jamie was probably barking orders about keeping to the schedule or something."

Before June or Monica or Aiden sat down, we assembled ourselves just as the Browns had in front of the same wooden fence post. "They were right here, guys, in this exact place, in this exact pose."

"That's it," Monica said. "I can't believe we did the last of the Brown's picture challenges."

"If that's the last one," Henry said. "Can we finally go home?"

"Hey, Vince." Monica touched my elbow and motioned me to her with her finger.

"What is it?"

"I think I'm coming down with whatever Aiden has." She put a hand to her stomach. "It's bad."

A black car turned off in front of us a few minutes later.

"Are you kidding?" Monica said. "A Prius? How are we going to fit in that?"

2088.0.1

I woke long before dawn in the dark hotel room in the desert town of Tehachapi. I stared at the ceiling for a long time. When I lifted the covers and swung around to sit up, it took several searching taps with my feet to find enough space on the floor to stand. There was camping gear piled on every open space, table, and chair.

When we arrived the night before, I'd said, "Let's do it now. If we don't air all our stuff out, we'll leave it till the last thing on the way out of town, and then it will be too late." Monica had disagreed. She likes order.

I tiptoed my way to the lone body in the midst of the rubble and shook him gently. "The breakfast buffet is opening soon," I whispered. "Do you want to go downstairs with me?"

He rubbed his eyes and sat up. "Is anyone else coming with us?"

"Everyone is sick except Georgie, and she'll want to sleep in."

When we reached the lobby, we discovered that the breakfast buffet was already open. The attendant nodded toward two tables with men in reflective vests. "It was a special request."

After we returned to our table from the buffet a second time, a man at the adjoining table said, "Back for more, eh? Your boy sure can put it away." He stuffed his reflector vest into his hard hat and placed it on the table beside him.

"We burn through the calories while we are out there on-trail, so we are making up for lost time." I pulled my plate toward me and lifted my fork. "This isn't too bad for a hotel buffet. What project are you guys working on here?"

"A few pumps and water mains up at the dam."

"L.A. water, I'm guessing? Where are they pumping the water?"

"Up to the reservoir?"

"Up?"

"Yeah. They pump it up at night to drop it in the daytime."

"I guess I don't quite understand that. It's got to be a net energy loss, right?"

"Electricity is cheaper at night, because there's so much less demand. They make a few pennies on the difference selling it back into the grid in the daytime." He pointed toward Henry, "I think Young Fella's trying to get your attention."

"What is it, bud?"

"Dad, let's go back to the hot tub."

"To take a break before round three?"

As we stood, the man said, "When you make your way back, try the waffles."

When we went upstairs later that morning to check on the girls, I asked Henry to tell Monica what he ate. "All four rounds, Henry. Go ahead, list it off."

"The first round I had sausage, eggs, and a banana. Then we went to the hot tub. Second round was two waffles, more eggs, and more sausage." He held up a finger. "Then it was," he paused as if for effect, "hot tub. The third round was cereal, Cinnamon toast crunch, two bowls, plus, a waffle and two muffins. Hot tub. For the fourth round, I just did everything all over again."

"Why are you telling me this?" she said. "I haven't been able to hold anything down for two days."

"Aiden," I said. "You and Georgie need to get down there, so you don't miss the buffet." I sat down beside Monica and put my hand on her forehead. "Can I get you anything?"

"Do I still have a fever? Feel my head."

"It doesn't feel hot to me."

"Do you mind shutting the blinds? I think I just need sleep."

I walked toward the window, "Henry, what do you think? Round five."

"I'm stuffed. I don't know."

"Can you guys just cut it out?" June said, "and stop talking about food? You are making me want to throw up."

After lunch, Henry and Georgie and I walked under the porte cochere and through the automatic glass doors. They carried on through the lobby, and I went upstairs. I cracked the door open into the dark room.

"Shut the door," Aiden said, "We are all sleeping in here."

"I brought you lunch from the Vietnamese place. Where do you want it?"

"I want it in my belly. I am so hungry."

I nodded toward the other bed. "They haven't moved at all since we left?" I slipped my hand into Monica's and sat down beside her.

"Oh hey," she said. "When did you get back? Where are Henry and Georgie?"

"Hot tub."

"By themselves?"

"It's that nice day clerk on the desk now. They'll be fine. We ate at a Vietnamese place and sat next to a couple from Georgia. They were really fun. Of course, I made an idiot of myself."

"How did you do that?"

"Well, you know how I told you about the guy Henry and I met this morning? The one working on the dam project? Well, I started complaining to that guy from Georgia about it being a net energy loss."

"And?"

"Well, he looked at me like I was an idiot and said,—in this thick southern accent—'Well, sir, you can't store power.' I felt so dumb."

"Why is that dumb?" Aiden said.

"I was getting all hot and bothered about them wasting energy to pump water up at night, only to run it downhill in the morning, but you need the energy in the daytime to support the grid. They buy it cheap at night to move the water up and sell for a profit in the day when it is in high demand, so it's not as dumb an idea as I thought."

"Dad, are you just trying to convince us to night hike?" Aiden said.

2088.0.2

I held up a finger and mouthed, "Just a minute," and answered the phone. "Hey Grammy, yes, I'm here with Henry as we speak, having a milkshake. Georgie too, she wants me to say…Grammy says 'Hi' guys…Yes, we are having a great time, well, not Monica. She and June are back at the hotel… still in bed." I held my hand over the phone. "Give me a second, guys," and I walked outside.

When I shut the door behind me I found a nearby park bench in the shade. I nodded to the stranger sitting there and pointed to the empty side of the bench. She inched over to make a little more room for me. I cupped my hand over the phone so as to not disturb her. "No, Grammy, they have absolutely no idea…I didn't give it away, don't worry…Tomorrow morning, nine a.m., right? I'll meet you in the lobby."

I turned to the woman. Thick white hair peeked out in curls beneath her crocheted beanie. When I smiled at her, she smiled back. The creases on her sun-worn face deepened. "You seem like you belong in the desert," I said.

Her whole body shook with laughter, and she uncrossed her arms to touch my wrist. "Now that is an odd way to begin a conversation with a stranger."

"Some people just don't feel like strangers," I said. "I don't mean offense." I looked out across the road toward the train depot and beyond it. The beige floor of the desert stretching flat to the foothills, seemed almost a living thing. Dancing waves of light distorted as the morning heat burned off.

"Is this your first time in town?"

"Yes ma'am. Tehachapi is an interesting place."

She nodded toward the depot. "It's a rail town in its most modern iteration."

"And before that?"

"Ranchers, farmers." She pointed toward the mountains. "Miners, but they were only passing through." Her tarnished silver bracelets jangled when she lifted her hand up toward her chest. "Kawaiisu before that." She smiled. "Depending on the time of year."

She nodded toward my phone. "Planning a little surprise, eh?"

I held my finger to my lips and said, "Shh."

She leaned forward and turned toward the restaurant. She nodded toward the table where Henry sat. I turned as well. When he had my attention, he shook his empty milkshake glass. Beside me on the bench, the woman chuckled. "Looks like he wants another."

When I sat down at the table, Georgie said. "What was that all about, anyway?"

"That was just Grammy, calling to wish Aiden a happy birthday. Remind me to call her back when we get back to the hotel."

She tapped the window of the restaurant. "I meant that lady you were talking to. Although, now that you mention it, you were acting suspicious."

I shrugged my shoulders and raised my eyebrows. "Do you guys want to see if we can arrange to have lunch with SoGood tomorrow?"

"I thought she'd be gone by now."

"She has family visiting. I think it's her brother."

"I wish we had some family here too," she said. "That would be nice."

"At least we have milkshakes," Henry said. "Lots of milkshakes, and in my mind that makes up for it."

"You aren't getting tired of milkshakes?" I said. "We've been to all three ice cream places in town, twice each."

"What do you think?" He took a loud slurp through his straw. "Do you think I'm tired of milkshakes?"

***

The next morning, I woke when my phone buzzed beside me, lifted my covers, and tiptoed across the dark room toward the door. Henry saw me and dropped the flap of his quilt from his torso and started to stand up.

I put a hand on his head, pointed to my phone, and whispered, "It's Grammy, I'm just going to talk to her in the hallway."

"She's here, isn't she?" he said. "That's why you've been acting funny."

I shook my head.

447

Grammy skipped toward me across the parking lot to give me a hug. "How are my babies?"

"Pardon all these crazy things." Grampy leaned in for his own hug. "Grammy went a little bit nuts with all these balloons."

Grammy said, "How bad are they?"

"I brought Monica breakfast this morning, so I think she's almost over it. June was eating a bagel when I came downstairs. We should be recovered enough to walk out late this afternoon. I hope you can walk with us. But not before we have a giant cinnamon roll for lunch. We have a date with a German bakery down the street, and you are invited."

"Are you going to forget about me?" Monica's sister said, and she hugged me.

"Shannon, I never could."

"How long have you guys been stuck here in Tehachapi?" she said.

"Four days. Today is our fourth day." I bent to the side to look past her. "Shannon, did you bring a backpack?"

"Oh yeah, I'll be hitting the trail with you. At least for one night. Then I'll hike back out."

We stood in the hall outside the room, the four of us. I hugged them each again in turn. "This is perfect timing, you guys, truly. What a great surprise this will be for them."

"How do you want us to do it?" they whispered.

"Knock like its housekeeping. Just give me a minute to get in there and get the camera set up."

"Just get me in there," Grammy said. "I need to love on them."

When the knock came, Monica looked at me.

"Henry," I said, "go answer the door."

I watched Monica.

She looked at me. "What is this? Are you up to something?" She leaned sideways to look at the door. At the first sound of her mother's voice, her whole body shook with sobbing. She threw her arms wide, and cried, "Momma!"

2097

I hugged Grammy goodbye beneath the towering windmill a few steps from their rental car. "We will see you tomorrow night at the water cache. She stepped back from me and turned to Shannon to give her a hug. "So Shannon, we will be back here in the morning just after sunrise, right? And you'll know how to find your way back without them?"

Shannon pumped her fist, "Oh yeah, I'll be a professional after tonight." She spun a quick half-turn to show off her backpack "I mean, check this thing out. You can tell I know what I'm doing."

Shannon stood with us and waved goodbye to Grammy and Grampy as their car kicked up dust on the way back to the main road. She turned toward the trail and said, "I'm all about it. Give me the whole experience."

"Aunt Shannon, this is awesome," Aiden said as we left the road to follow the wash along the dry creek in the dark. "Mom, are you finally going to cowboy camp with us? Aunt Shannon said she is going to."

"I've done it before," Monica said. "Once at least, before the Sierra. I guess I could do it again tonight."

"Woohoo!" Henry said. "Mom's cowboy camping!"

"How did you even hear about cowboy camping?" Monica said.

"I'm not even sure what it is, really." Shannon said. "Jamie and Creigh told me to tell you I wanted to do it. It sounds fun."

"You sleep outside on the ground without any tents," Aiden said.

"Oh yeah, I am so doing that," Shannon said. "Monica, why don't you like to do that?"

"It just kind of freaks me out. You don't know what's out there."

"'Cause a tent is gonna protect you, right, Mom?" June said.

We walked for a while in silence along the wide wash and into the shadow of a grove of cottonwood trees. The trail cut back toward the highway to avoid a steep cutbank.

Shannon stumbled. "How can you guys find your way in the dark?"

"If we get lost, we have a map on our phones," Aiden said.

"How do your phones work without reception?"

"It comes from up there." Georgie pointed into the night sky. "GPS."

"What about when you get separated? Don't you walk by yourselves a lot?"

"They're all pretty good now at finding their way," Monica said.

The trail turned again to parallel the wash and emerged from the cottonwoods. I stopped to look up. There were no clouds in the sky. The voices of the others drifted away as I looked up. A satellite and a plane moved toward each other across the night sky as if on a path to collision, despite their disparate orbits. When I arrived beneath the large oak tree where they had stopped, Monica looked up and said, "We thought we shouldn't get too far from the road, so Shannon doesn't have too long a walk in the morning."

"It's a great spot," I said.

Shannon dropped her pack to the dirt and clapped her hands. "Okay, let's get our cowboy camping on."

We spread our groundsheets side by side between the tree and a row of bushes nearby. Henry lay down and pulled his quilt over him.

"Wait, you sleep right on the ground? Where are your ground pads?" Shannon said.

"I'm on my groundsheet," Henry said and slid to his left and lifted a corner of his flattened square of bubble wrap. "And this is my ground pad."

"I think they are crazy," Monica said. "They tried to talk me into sending my groundpad home."

"You mean your royal mattress, Mom?" Aiden said.

Shannon laughed. "Royal mattress?"

"They make fun of me for not sleeping on the hard ground."

"In my defense," I said. "I was getting sick of having to repair them all the time. Especially Henry's."

"You mean June's," Henry said.

June sniggered.

After we were all lying down, Shannon said, "What kind of tree is this?"

"I'm sure it's some kind of oak," Aiden said. "The stars are just so-so tonight. It's probably how close we are to the city."

"I bet you guys have seen some stars."

"Oh, there was this one time, Aunt Shannon," Henry said. "When we came back over Kearsarge Pass in the dark. There was this crazy explosion up in the sky. We had no idea what it was. It went like, 'Spoosh' and all these fire trails went out from it. There was lots of smoke. Aiden thought it was Jesus coming back."

"I did not think that, Henry. I was just joking."

For a long time into the dark, Shannon and Monica spoke in hushed tones and giggled.

I heard something scurry in the bushes and laughed.

"What was that?" Monica said. "Oh my gosh, you guys, I knew I shouldn't have cowboy camped."

"Henry probably just threw a stick," Aiden said.

"Nope. I didn't," he said, "and neither did Dad."

"Relax, Monica," Shannon said. "It's probably just acorns."

For an hour at random, or in response to any sound, someone would call out, "Acorns," until Monica said, "That's enough, everybody. Go to sleep."

We waved goodbye to Shannon in the morning. "It's just right down there. Follow your Guthooks. You have that water cache waypoint marked for later tonight," I said. "In about twenty-two miles—I'll see you then."

2113

I dropped my pack against the base of the sharp bank on the high side of the wash beside Aiden and asked, "How long have you guys been here?"

"Not long, Dad."

Up the dry cut, there were hints of a seasonal stream's passage. Ruts running through low veins, bordered by scattered tufts of dry grass. "There's a nice cold pocket here, have you found the water?"

Aiden turned her head toward me. "I was thinking that this is where you said we'd find water."

"You didn't see any?"

"You have eyes, don't you?"

"You didn't look over there?" I pointed across the trail toward the downslope. "We don't have any other water till later tonight, so this could be bad."

I pushed myself to my feet and crossed over to look down. "I don't see any green," I said and walked toward them. "It's cold enough here that you know there's water running beneath the ground from the top."

Aiden slapped the side of her leg. "Henry, that's it, we never looked up. Come on, let's go look up-wash. We'll come back down and get you if we find it."

Monica kicked my toes, and I shielded my eyes to look up at her. She pulled her hat from her head and fanned her face with it. "Can you pull my water bottle out for me?"

I sat up and stretched toward her. "If you can bend down."

"Wasn't there supposed to be water here? I'm almost out."

"Henry and Aiden have gone up there to look for it." I patted the ground beside me. "Have a seat."

Monica dropped her pack with a thunk and sat down beside me. She bent from the waist and reached for her toes. "I'm so tight." When she straightened again, she reached high, linked her hands and stretched back. "Oh, that feels good."

When I patted the ground again, she slid over and leaned against me. She rolled her head to rest on my chest and sighed. "I could fall asleep."

And I fell asleep.

It was Aiden's call from up-wash that woke me. "We found it! Just bring your bottles, it's a pretty long walk."

I pushed myself to my feet and reached my hand toward Monica. As we followed Aiden from twenty yards back, Monica leaned in to say, "They are pretty good at this now."

2147.8

"Wait up, Dad." Henry pointed into the valley below. "Look back down there." Between mobile homes and ramshackle houses, a metal pipe, 12 feet across, disappeared across the sands of the Mojave Desert.

"It's the LA Aqueduct. The water in that pipe runs from here to Los Angeles. Probably thirty miles as the crow flies. Dadgum water thieves." I laughed. "Still, it's fun to see these iconic PCT places in real life."

He pointed toward the valley again. "That's not what I mean. Look where the pipe comes toward the mountain down there. We came up all the way this way, but it's the exact wrong way." He raised his arm to point south. Mexico is that way."

"Airborne says they might be changing up the route and might not even cross the Mojave here anymore." I pointed across the horizon to a range along the far side. "I think someday, the trail will go that way. Apparently, some private owner is putting the land into a natural preservation land trust."

"They should just make the trail go the way we are wanting to go."

"You think you could be a better trail designer?"

"I know I could. This stupid trail hardly takes you to any water anymore."

"Oh, dude, that reminds me. I meant to download the latest comments on Guthooks before we left the valley. I need to take my phone out of airplane mode. I hope we get coverage up here somewhere."

"How far is water?"

"A few of the sources coming up were drying out. I just want to make sure we can still count on them."

My phone rang near the top of the ridge. It seemed an alien thing here, that ring. "Old what's-his-name," I said into the phone, "I'll never forget old what's-his-name. Mr. Blatter! How are you?"

"Oh, I can't complain. If I did, who would listen?"

"Speaking of … How is your wife?"

"Oh, you must not have heard. She fell off the back steps at the farm and broke her femur. And you know our son's house is way back on the other side of the property. That back door locks automatically, so she tried to call out for somebody for a while, I guess. Finally, she just decided to drag herself all the way around to the front. I was down in the city for my treatments at the time."

"They don't make them like her anymore."

"You got that right."

I could picture him. Mr. Blatter, almost half hunched over, would be scratching his scalp as if puzzling out some equation. He'd spent his life in the mechanical trades, mostly big boilers. When they'd come down from Michigan to that first winter in Florida dragging that rickety fifth wheel behind, we had no idea they'd return every winter. I asked my dad if he knew they would be parking it in our yard for so many years. He would only say, "That Mr. Blatter, he's one of a kind."

Once, in the middle of a rain barrel project on the back side of a house, I had asked Mr. Blatter for his advice. I'd tapped one of my three elevated fifty-gallon drums. "Yeah? Just tie them in as a series," he'd said while scratching his scalp.

"But the pipe's underneath them?"

He had squinted his eyes and looked at me sideways. "So? What's the problem? Just tie them together?"

"Do I run a gutter over the top to each of them? And how will it fill them up evenly?

Then he twisted his face up and growled like a pirate. "Water seeks its own level, Vince. You know that. Come on!"

When I rounded the turn, I was still on the phone. Georgie was waiting, and she turned her head sideways to indicate my phone.

"Mr. Blatter," I mouthed.

"I got Georgie here, Mr. Blatter, you want to talk to her?"

Georgie walked ahead of me with the phone against her ear. She occasionally responded with an "mhm" or a "yessir" until she turned and handed me the phone again.

"Mr. Blatter?" Silence. "Mr. Blatter? I guess I lost him." I set the phone to airplane mode again. "That was fun, eh, Georgie?"

"Mr. Blatter is nice, isn't he?"

"He sure is. He knows a lot about the world, and how it works."

"Is it weird that you are friends with someone that old?" she said. "Is he over eighty or something?"

"You think that's weird?"

"Well, that means when you were born, he was almost the age you are now. It just seems like it might be weird."

"Someday you and I will be more like friends or peers than a dad and a daughter."

"How did you get to be friends with Mr. Blatter?"

"He was your great-grandfather's friend first. When they first started coming down from Michigan, I would have lunch with them sometimes. I spent a good bit of time with my grandpa toward the end."

"Did you know Great-Grandpa was dying?"

"Only in the way that you know everyone is going to die. I didn't know he was going to drive into the back of a flatbed truck."

"Why was he driving in the middle of the night anyway?"

"Do you not know this? Grandma, your great-grandma, was starting to lose connection to her memories. Sometimes she would wake up in the middle of the night convinced they were in someone else's home. She would say she needed to get back to her childhood home in Wauwatosa. That's in Wisconsin. Grandpa would just play right along and tell her to pack a suitcase. He would drive around for a couple hours and bring her back to the house. Who thinks of that? I wish you could have known him."

"I don't really remember him at all."

"He was up for anything. You know when he fought in the Pacific, in World War II, he took some of his men to steal a big bulldozer from the army in the middle of the night?"

"Why did they do that?"

"Because the Army had a nice basketball court, and the Marines never had any money for that kind of thing, so he 'borrowed' the bulldozer and built one."

"How old was he?"

"He was around twenty-one. Pretty young, right? He was in college in Beloit and had just married Grandma, and because he was a college man, they made him an officer. When he first got to the Pacific, almost all of the men that were under him had already fought at Iwo Jima and Peleliu, so they would have been resentful of an officer who'd never been in battle. Uncle Ted says he just went around to all the lead guys and said, 'I don't know why they made me an officer, so what do you think we ought to do?'"

"And that worked?"

"He was Scout and Recon on Okinawa, and he made it back alive. It must have."

"What's Scout and Recon?"

"Their job was to go find where the enemy were hiding. Okinawa was a different kind of warfare than they'd seen before. Before that, the Japanese had always engaged with force on the beachhead. On Okinawa, they pulled back into the hills and set up ambushes."

At the crest of the climb, the trail turned to cut through dry grass across a long flat through a forest of towering ponderosa pines. Through the trees, a half mile off in the distance, a low and round ridge wrapped nearly all around us and back toward the drop. I wondered if it had been a caldera. To the right of us two large and lone twin boulders stood in the trees. "Look at those things Georgie."

"They look like frozen giants from The Hobbit," she said.

"Can you imagine hiking into these trees knowing there was someone waiting to kill you? Grandpa said the first Japanese soldier he ever saw was trying to sneak across a road using cut branches to make himself look like a bush."

"I guess that didn't work too well."

"He didn't tell me what happened after that," I said. "At one of those Marine Corps reunions Uncle Ted thanked one of Grandpa's marine buddies for bringing his dad back alive. Ted said the guy got a little mad at him and said, 'Make no mistake, not a man in this platoon would have come back alive if it hadn't been for your father.' Ted got to meet a man who Grandpa had saved."

"He saved someone's life?"

"I guess the guy had gotten too far advanced and was pinned down on a hill out front, and Grandpa went out there to get him all by himself. It's amazing he lived to have grandkids."

"Was Grandpa alive then, when Great Grandpa went to war?"

"No."

"Then we wouldn't be alive either."

We walked for a while. "He almost never talked about it. He would say, 'We lived those horrors so people back home would never have to see it.' Of course, toward the end, he talked more about it."

"Like what?"

"One time, he was invited to speak to a middle school class. One kid asked him why the knife had the serrated edge on the back side?'"

"I don't get it."

"He told them that if you cut your way into a body, the pressure builds up around the knife and locks it in, so you need the serration to help cut your way back out."

"Yikes." She stopped. "How would you be normal after all that?"

"Many aren't. Your great grandpa handled it better than most. He seemed almost to be bigger than life. Little things didn't seem to get to him. As if he felt lucky to be alive. Everything, I mean everything, was an adventure."

"Maybe that's where you get it?"

"I don't have an ounce of what he had, Georgie. But he sure got excited about seeing it in his grandkids. You know, one summer, I came home from college and got a wild idea to go buy silver in Mexico and bring it back to sell it in the sorority houses in the fall. I told him about it, and five minutes later he gave me enough money to buy,"—I held out my hands,—"About this much silver."

"How much?"

"This much."

"Dad, that's almost as big as a basketball."

"Oh yeah, in three days, I was on a plane to Mexico with your Aunt Luchrysta. I brought her because I thought she knew Spanish."

"You said that like she didn't." She looked back at me over her shoulder.

I laughed. "I didn't know that until we got there. We walked around Taxco, where all the silver mining is, until we found one that had a storefront. I pushed Aunt Luchrysta up to the counter, and she froze. Not a word of Spanish. She tried to tell me later she'd lost it when she lived in Brazil for the summer."

"What did you do?"

"I came home with a whole lot of silver, or something that looked a lot like silver. Some of the stuff that I sold started to turn green."

"Dad!"

"After that, every time I would go over to Grandpa's house, he'd rub his hands together and say, 'What are we getting into next?'"

"Was he rich or something?"

"Not in money, but he sure loved adventure."

"Dad, do you think he would have liked us doing this?"

2188

It was a hard day. A hot day. If we spoke, it was sparingly. It was a day to be endured.

But in the hottest part of the afternoon, Aiden and I rounded a tight bend into a soft breeze. I let out a shout and pointed down the hill to where a thick stand of entangled cottonwoods lined the drainage that bordered the highway. "Ahh, shade, sweet, blessed shade."

The moment I dropped into the shade line, my skin cooled against my sweaty shirt. I freed one of my shoulders, turned back to Aiden, and smiled, "We are going to be here awhile."

She pointed past me into the alcove and shook her head. "Somebody trashed this place."

Plastic jugs, jars, and bottles were piled up everywhere. Paper trash and plastic bags lay in scattered piles as well, half-buried in dirt. On the high side of the opening, someone had arranged three broken folding chairs side by side. I kicked a one-gallon jug from my path and sat on the torn folding chairs. After I adjusted myself to fit inside the exposed aluminum frame, I waved a hand toward the empty chair to my right, and, intoning a kingly voice, said, "Sittest thou beside me, dear daughter."

Aiden declined and leaned on a lone oak tree. She did not take off her pack. "Can we not go somewhere else? I seriously think I might gag."

"There's no shade anywhere else. Are you sure of those jugs have any water in them?"

She covered her nose and bent again to inspect them and gave me a thumbs down.

Henry announced his presence by shaking a one-gallon jug. "This one only has dead flies in it." He put his ear to it and shook it again. "Oh cool." He tapped it against his hand as if it were an instrument and started to dance. "This kind of sounds like a maraca."

"Do you not smell it, Henry?" Aiden said.

"Smell what? It isn't that bad."

The three other girls stopped just outside the alcove. Monica scrunched up her face.

"Is there no water here, Dad?" June said. "Do you think all this trash is because of the water cache?"

I reached for a crusty pair of jeans with my trekking pole and held them up. "Not these anyway."

"Or this bra." Henry dropped his gallon jug and reached into some bushes.

"Gross, Henry," Monica said. "Not with your hands." She turned toward me as if to recruit my assistance.

"Bouquet Canyon Road."

"Yeah, It's a bouquet of something, alright."

A cheerful voice called down from the trail above us. "Strawbridges! What's up, guys?" I knew it was Airborne before I could see him. He and Dahn stepped into the glade and stopped side by side in front of the chairs. "We were trying to catch you before you made it to the cache," he said. "In case you drank up all the water."

"There's nothing here," Henry said. "Unless you are looking for trash." And as if to prove his point, kicked his one-gallon jug into the trees,

"It smells disgusting." Aiden said.

Airborne lifted his chin and took a sniff. "At least there is shade." He reached an arm back to pluck an empty one-liter bottle from his side pouch, shook it, and said, "I'm gonna run up there and yogi some. Dahn, you want some water?"

Dahn dropped his pack, grabbed his two bottles, and together, they jogged up the steep bank toward the road.

"What is a yogi?" Monica said. "I know what a yogi is in yoga, but what did he mean?"

It was not long before we heard tires grind to a stop on gravel. A few short minutes later, they came bounding into the clearing with cold bottled waters in their arms. Airborne, however, had one of his arms behind his back. "And,"—he announced and waited for our full attention,—"Who wants a beer?"

I jumped to my feet.

"Dude, it's the desert, every laborer out here carries a cooler full of water in the back of their truck. He lifted his beer high in the air, "And the best ones have beer." He nodded up toward the road. "You take Henry and Georgie up there, you can get all the water you want."

"Let's go try it, Georgie." I lifted my beer high as if returning a toast and brought it down again to press against my cheek. "After I'm done with this beer."

With our toes on the lip of the pavement, we threw our hands roadward toward the first truck we saw. The driver flashed his lights and pulled onto the gravel after he passed us. By the time we jogged to him, he had hopped over his tailgate and popped open the top of a styrofoam cooler. "Gatorade?" He smiled and tossed two bottles to me.

He honked his horn as he eased onto the highway. "This is amazing isn't it, Georgie?"

Standing above the tight offshoot above the down trail, Georgie touched her bottle of blue Gatorade to the back of her neck and turned one last time toward the empty road. She said, "thank you," in a half-whisper and turned her face up toward me. "People are nice, Dad."

Airborne stopped himself mid-story when we returned. I urged him to continue.

"Well, anyway, I was with Snacks that day, and we were flying. We'd been hitting 40's for days, so we were tired and looking for a restaurant to stop in when we hit town. We were down on the road trying to catch a hitch, when Brazil Nut pops out of the trees." He pushed himself to his feet with his trekking poles in his hands, threw his chin foreward, and assumed the stance of a downhill skier. "She looks left and right, and then boom, takes off, straight up the other side—Dahn, tell them—you walked with her."

"I walked with her one day." Dahn smiled. "She and I walked fifty miles together, but the funny thing was that the next day she woke me up, and said,"—Dahn attempted a Brazilian accent—"'Oh, Dahn, that was great, but today you want to do a long one?'"

"What?" Aiden said. "Fifty miles isn't enough?"

"I told you she's crazy," Airborne said.

"Says the man yoyoing the trail," Monica said.

"There's crazy," Airborne said. "And then there's crazy. But hers is the good kind of crazy. You know what, though? After all that, she ended up missing the fastest known time for the PCT by just two days."

He leaned forward and twisted a few strands of grass between his fingers, and spoke in a quieter tone, "You guys will get so much from being out here."

"And you've gotten it two times over, doing a yoyo," I said. "Think of what you've learned."

"You know, it's funny. People ask me that all the time. They ask me what profound things I have learned out here. But it's so much. Well, you know what I mean, 'cause you've lived it. It's like, even if I could wrap my head around all of it, I couldn't put it into words." He paused. "I've stopped trying to answer them. Now, I just tell them I've learned I am pretty good at walking."

"That's great," I laughed. "I'm gonna have to use that."

"Will you all be staying at Hiker Heaven too?" Dahn said.

Monica and I looked at each other. I shrugged.

Before we reached town, Henry claimed to see a roadrunner race past. He could only convince Aiden of the truth in his claim. June stopped on the side of the road on the outskirts of town above a practice pen to watch two men take turns releasing calves to practice their tie-down roping. She'd have stood there for hours, had I not dragged her away. It was near dark when we were led to our seats in the Mexican restaurant in Agua Dulce. The waitress had returned with our drinks before Airborne's dingy, yellow shirt caught my eye through the front door.

"We thought you'd get here before us," I said.

"Oh man, did you see that guy parked across the street from the cache?"

"Yeah, we talked to him for a few minutes," I said and elbowed Georgie. "Someone yogied some water from him."

"Ken Lancaster," he said. "Now, that is one awesome guy. We told him the cache there was empty, so he said, 'Hop in boys.' We ended up helping him refill about ten five-gallon jugs. Not only that, but he also wanted to load out the trash, and that took a lot longer than we expected. There were three truckloads of that stuff." Airborne paused and bent to hug the woman at the table beside us, "Sorry I'm late, Mom."

She smiled and shook her head. "Oh, Jon, I knew exactly what to expect." She stood and said, "Now you give your mom a proper hug."

"Mom," he said, "I want you to meet the mom of the Family I was telling you about. Monica, meet my mom."

I was out in the front holding Monica's hand on the walk across town back to Hiker Heaven when Henry ran from the back to grab my opposite hand. "Guess what, Dad? This is so cool. Airborne is a soccer coach in the L.A. Galaxy Youth Academy."

2200

Dahn stood over the frying pan in the small kitchen of the single wide trailer. He held an open tin can up to the light to re-read the label. He shrugged, dumped it in, and then looked at me over his shoulder. "It's in the bean family anyway," he said. "But it beats trail food. Are you guys taking off today?"

I turned to look through the window across the wide yard at Hiker Haven. "Sometime after lunch." I pointed toward the side of the house between us and the gate. "She keeps the hiker boxes in the garage?"

"Yes, just lift up on the garage door," Dahn said. "She has racks and racks of boxes, and they are all labeled. You'll find whatever you need."

The chair squeaked when I pushed back from the small kitchen table. "I'll wait for Monica. I can't remember what it was that she wanted me to look for." I looked over the half wall toward the living room. Aiden lay on her stomach on the mattress of the fold out couch. She lay facing the television with her chin in her hands as if she were watching something. I moved crabwise and leaned over to get a view of the television. "The TV is off, Aiden. What are you doing?"

"You said we could watch something."

"Did you look through them to see if there was anything worth watching?"

She huffed and pushed herself up from the bed. "I'm looking now."

Monica stepped through a door at the end of the narrow, faux-wood-paneled hallway with a towel draped over one arm. She smiled at me and turned left to enter the bathroom. After a failed first effort, she shouldered the door again to gain access. When it opened, she smiled and waved.

I turned back to Dahn. "Donna seems like a pretty neat lady," I said. "Airborne said this might be their last season."

"Do you know her story at all?" He raised his eyes. "She is as good as they come. I can give you the gist, but you should look her up. Donna Saufley."

"When we get to town," Georgie framed her words in air quotes with her fingers, "eh, Dad?"

"What does she mean by that?" Dahn smiled.

"Georgie is keeping a running list of things I'm supposed to have looked up. Aren't you, you little turd?" I stuck my tongue out at her, and then turned back to Dahn. "I guess about everyone has stayed here. We saw the wall covered with signatures back there."

He pointed down the hallway. "In that first bedroom?"

I nodded. "We watched a video on YouTube of an eleven-year-old who hiked the trail some years back."

"Scrambler," Georgie said. "I found her name on the wall back there, Dad."

"Did you sign it too, Georgie?" Dahn said.

"I would if I had a marker."

"I'll find you one. Donna would want you to sign it." He turned down the burner and held one hand over the pot as if to test the heat coming off of it. "Let that sit a minute." He returned a few minutes later with a marker.

"Dad," Aiden said. "They have *Butch Cassidy and the Sundance Kid*."

"I know what we'll be watching, then," Henry said.

After the movie was over, the kids lay down for a late morning nap. Monica and I sat on the porch folding laundry. The shade from the porch kept the sun from our eyes, but everything below our necks was warmed by the sun.

I placed my hand on a folded stack of clothes. "Want me to run this stuff in there to them?"

"No, let's just sit." She picked up her chair, moved it toward the railing, and turned her face up toward the sun. "It's peaceful here. It feels nice."

"It's great, isn't it?" I nodded toward the yard.

"It is, but I think it would be hard for me to be this hospitable, especially when it gets crazy. I wonder why she does this?"

"Dahn said her story is similar to the Dinsmores'. She kept seeing these dirty hikers walk through. One day, down at the restaurant, she saw a hiker washing herself in the restroom, and thought, 'That's it, no more of that,' and invited the hiker home so she could have a warm shower."

"This is a lot more than a warm shower."

"'Over forty thousand warm showers through the years' is what he told me."

Monica smiled. "Amazing."

Past the corner of the garage at the far end of the property, I saw a full-sized white truck stop in front of the gate. Donna hopped from the truck and opened the gate to pull into the driveway. I heard the truck door close, and the garage door open.

From the still open gate, I scanned my way back along the fence that ran the length of the yard. A deep ivy enveloped it all the way down. In the far corner, a different type of flower bearing vine covered a portico. Beneath it, there were two wooden benches encircling a small fire pit. "There are pictures of this place covered with tents, every square inch of this yard. She's created quite the oasis here in the desert."

Monica pointed toward the portico, "Is that Dahn over there? I thought he was still inside."

"All I can see are legs. That vine on the frame is blocking my view. Do you think it's honeysuckle?"

She tapped my leg. "You should go say hi."

A few moments later I tapped on the wood frame through the honeysuckle. "Hey, Dahn. Mind if I join you?"

"Be my guest." He tapped the empty space on the swing to his right.

I sat down. "What are you doing?"

"Taking in the view."

"Of the backyard? I guess it's not an ordinary backyard, is it?"

"It is far more than that," he said. "It's an oasis."

I heard the truck door slam, and the ignition crank. I leaned forward. Donna dropped the gear shift into reverse and looked over. She waved. "Shoot," I said. "I meant to go over and say hello to her."

Dahn picked up a book from between us.

"I didn't know you were reading," I said. "I'm sorry to interrupt."

"I've finished it."

"What is it?"

"It's a story of questing," he said, "funny enough."

"If you had it to sum up in a sentence, what would you say?"

"Home is the place from which you adventure, and the place to which you can always return."

"Oh, man. I'll be home soon."

"What is home to you?" he said.

"Home is my uncle's back porch deck. When I get there, I will tell him these stories, even the worst ones, and he will say, 'Cheer up, you are worse than you think you are, but more loved than you ever dared dream.'"

"That doesn't sound like a bad home to return to."

I stood up from the swing.

"Oh, I almost forgot," he said. "Donna asked me to get a picture of you while you are here. I can take it for you before you leave."

2215

Henry stood high to the side of the trail near the rounded top of a sandy dune. I picked my way through the scraggly, desert brush to climb up beside him. He pointed below us to where a reflective umbrella bobbed through the scrub.

"You think that's Lafours?" I said.

He tilted his head toward me and scrunched up his face.

"The one everyone called Poopfinger."

He shook his head. "But they don't say poop, do they, Dad? Anyway, he's long gone. All those people left us in the dust."

"I don't really get the whole umbrella thing. It never rains."

"They don't carry it only for the rain," he said. "It's for the sun too."

"Would you want to carry it? I don't think I could justify the extra weight."

"No."

"By the way, Donna, from Hiker Heaven, is mailing your raincoat downtrail for us. She wouldn't take any money for postage, so you are going to have to send her a thank you note."

"Why would anyone care if they got a letter?"

"You wouldn't want someone to send you a thank you note if you went out of your way for them?"

"No."

"You are going to write her a letter, Henry."

"Why?"

"How about, because I said so?" I reached my arm around his shoulder and pulled him to me. "This is one of those times when you get to work on that obedience muscle."

Henry shielded his eyes and looked above us toward the bright, blue sky. "I don't think I'm gonna need a raincoat again."

"L.A. probably drinks up all the rainwater around here before it hits the ground anyway. Do you want to start looking for a place to eat lunch?"

"How far have we gone?"

"Eleven miles … twelve maybe."

"I told you."

"Told me what?"

"We'd be done already if they didn't take so long.

"Henry, what about your mom's feet?

He shrugged.

"You go ahead and stop at the first place you find shade. I'll wait for the girls."

After I ate, I scraped the bottom of my cup with my spork to free the last bit of rice, and squeezed a few drops of water into the cup. I tipped it up after swishing it around a few times, and I heard Aiden groan.

"Why do you do that? It's gross."

"What's gross, Aiden?"

"Drinking the water you clean your cup with."

"It's all going to the same place, and I don't waste water."

"I just think it's gross."

"I think this lunch spot is gross," I said. "Couldn't you guys have found a spot where we didn't have to sit with our feet hanging over the trail?" I shifted on my Tyvek to pull out the slack, and the dry leaves crunched beneath it. "It's like everything in the desert was designed for discomfort. These leaves keep poking me in the back."

"It kind of stinks too," she said, "like a dead smell, but not a wet and musty kind of dead, more like an old kind of dead. At least there's nobody out here but us. Maybe Airborne and Dahn, and they are way ahead of us by now."

"Henry and I saw a guy earlier who had one of those umbrellas like Lafours."

"Like who?"

"You remember Poopfinger, Aiden?"

"Yeah, but they don't call him Poopfinger, do they, Dad? Still, one person is more than we've seen in a while."

"Airborne said they might see us again because they were getting off-trail one more time," Henry said.

I lay back and covered my eyes with my forearm, "I don't mind this spot as long as I don't get woken up from my nap."

"You are napping?" Aiden said. "I thought we wanted to make twenty-six miles today."

"We'll see. Mom's feet are hurting."

"You are going to take a nap right on the trail?"

"Hey, you are the one that chose this spot." I reached in my pocket and pulled out my phone. There was just enough connection to upload an Instagram post. After it loaded, I scrolled through my feed.

"What are you doing over there?" Monica said.

"I'm catching up on people's posts."

"I thought you were posting pictures."

"I did already. Do you all remember that guy we met up at the very beginning of the trail? The one who made his own Pemmican as his only food?"

"Nobody even met him, Dad. Except you." Aiden said. "You were the only one that stopped to talk to him."

"He quit at Kennedy Meadows South. But listen to his reason for why he quit. He says in his post, 'I did what I came to do.'"

"What's wrong with that?" Monica said.

Aiden laughed and adopted a deep voice. "It's about the journey, not the destination."

"Come on, Aiden," Monica said. "Why can't it be true that he got out of it all that he needed?"

"I guess so," Aiden said and looked at me.

"We're not saying he didn't, Monica. But there is no way that guy was at his house stuffing his pack for the last time on the night before he came to trail, thinking, 'I know I said I am going to hike the PCT, but what I truly want to do is make it down through the Sierra Nevada, and then stop with only the desert to go.'"

"I don't get why someone would do that?" Aiden said. "The desert is the easiest part. After Tehachapi anyway."

"I would quit if you'd let me," Henry said.

"You are lying," Aiden said.

"I don't think he is," Monica said. "Are you, Henry?"

"Nope."

***

When I woke, I heard Monica say, "I don't have any water, can one of you clean my cup?"

"Not me," Henry said.

"Not you, huh?" I said. "I'm surprised you didn't jump up to serve someone else."

Monica huffed, and we sat for a while. The only sound was of her calf massage ball rolling against her groundsheet as she worked on her calf.

After a few minutes of quiet, Henry broke the silence and said, "You know, I hadn't thought much about it, but I don't see myself as the service type."

2235

Henry and I hopped on the painted crosswalk hashes to cross over the scenic Angeles Forest Highway well ahead of schedule. When we reached the far side of the road, we sat down on our packs to wait for the others.

"Who are all of our cousins that are coming?" he said.

"Almost all of the ones that live in Long Beach. It's not that far. Uncle Kevin and Aunt Susan are bringing Samuel and Uncle Will is bringing two of his kids."

He turned to look up the hill behind us. "Are we all just sleeping in the parking lot?"

"The map says there is a privy in the parking lot, so there may be some tent sites. If not, we can just sleep on the pavement. I leaned forward and looked down the roadway to the paved driveway. "I don't see the fire station, though, there is supposed to be a fire station or something nearby, but maybe it is just up there.""

Monica and Georgie crossed the road together. She stopped in front of me and reached into her side pouch for her water bottle and unscrewed the top. "Are you sure they are coming?" She shook her bottle and held it out in front of her. "I hope they bring some water, I'm almost out. Do they know we are here?"

"They'll be here. I got a message from Kevin a while ago. He said I confused them with my directions. He'll meet us here at the fire station."

Georgie tapped me on the shoulder. "Mom said you have the shovel."

"You don't need a shovel, because there is a privy right up here in the parking lot, Georgie. I could see the top of it from across the road."

"A privy, Dad? That's gross."

"You'd rather dig a hole?" I slung my arm out of my shoulder strap and dug in my back pouch for the shovel kit.

When Georgie disappeared up the driveway, I said, "We may as well go up and check this place out. I'll shoot Kevin another text and let him know where to find us."

When the first carload of cousins pulled in, the kids rushed it. "They're here! They're here!"

"Uncle Will, can we help you set the tent up?"

"Thanks, Aiden, but it just pops up on the truck, so there isn't really much to set up."

"Are you kidding me? That's so convenient. Come on, William." She reached her hands out and swung her young cousin up into her arms for a hug and carried him across the parking lot. She held him on her hip and watched as Will climbed on his open tailgate and pulled a lever. The army green tent popped open in one movement, and Will flipped another lever to lock it in place. Aiden turned her head to catch my eye, her mouth agape.

The second truck came with the hotplate. Uncle Kevin dropped it on the tailgate and hooked up the propane. He bought meat for the meal from a special market he knew. My offer for help was rejected with an almost imperceptible shake of his head. "I've got a system."

His wife Susan patted my shoulder and laughed. "Oh yes, he's got a system."

Kevin laughed too. "I'm a little particular, I guess, but we've gotten into car camping a bit lately. Let me show you what I've done with the truck." I watched over his shoulder as he flipped a hinged 2x4 support system up from the floor, leaned both seats forward, and fitted a slab of plywood into place. He hit it with the heel of his hand. "Sam and I are a comfortable fit, but we aren't giants like your people."

While Keven stood over the sizzling meat, Henry stood guard with his paper plate in his hand.

I tousled his hair. "What do you think, boy?"

"I'll tell you what I think." He rubbed his belly. "I think I'm glad Uncle Kevin came."

Susan laughed.

After dark, the adults sat at the picnic table with wine. I sat beside Will on the tailgate, and his son William slipped in as if from nowhere and reached up to place a hand on his dad's knee. His attempt to shield his whisper with his hand was unsuccessful. "Dad, can we spend the night out with the big cousins?"

Will leaned in close. "Grab your sleeping bag out of the truck." William turned and gave Aiden a thumbs up.

Aiden cheered when William gave her a thumbs up. She said, "When you come back, squeeze in between June and me … unless you need me to help you."

They scanned the sky calling out shooting stars for a while. During one lull, Aiden and June pointed out constellations. William seemed somewhat confused. "Aiden, could I ask you a question? What are all those lights up there?"

"What lights are you talking about, William?"

"The lights we are seeing," he pointed. "Up in the sky."

"Do you mean stars?" Aiden said, as if uncertain.

"Oh, I didn't know that's what stars looked like. And Aiden?" he said.

"What is it, William?"

"The big one? What's that big star?"

I listened in, unbelieving.

"The big star, William? You mean that one?"

He nodded.

"William," Aiden said. "That's called the moon."

Will laughed and held up his wine glass to toast me. "We don't get out much. But to be fair, the smog is bad in L.A."

I turned again to look toward the kids. Aiden placed her palm across William's forehead and moved her mouth close to his ear. She spoke with animation, "Sometimes, that moon is so bright that it lights our path when we walk through the night."

"Dad, look, it's Airborne!" Henry said.

Airborne popped out of the dark sedan before it stopped moving and landed in a sort of surfer stance, a lanky silhouette against the low hanging sun. In one motion, he swung open the back door and into his pack. He then spun around, slammed the door shut, tapped the top of the car, and offered the driver a theatrical wave. He strode across the parking lot with a big grin and opened his arms wide. "Strawbridges!"

"What are you doing here?" Monica said. "We thought you were way ahead of us."

"I got off-trail for another wedding. I'm meeting Dahn down the hill. He's got a trail angel lined up for us in Wrightwood."

"What about that guy that dropped you off?" I said. "He couldn't take you to town?"

"This is as far as he could take me. I'll restart a few miles back that way in the morning."

"We'd planned to make a couple more miles toward Cajon Pass tonight, but we need to go into town to top off our food for tomorrow."

"Plus," Aiden said, "It's freezing up here."

"Come down the hill into Wrightwood. It's a great town. I guarantee you'll find a trail angel. If you don't find someone at the grocery store, there's a list of trail angels posted at the library."

"We've tried to catch a ride for about an hour. We haven't seen anything but sports cars, so we gave up." I turned toward Monica. "Is the Uber coming?"

"I think the driver confirmed." She held her phone above her head and looked at the screen. "But then I lost coverage. They should have been here a while ago if they were coming."

"Where did you start today?" he said.

"Right in the middle of the trail," Henry said. "Like, two hundred feet from a perfect spot."

"The best spot is always just a few feet ahead." Airborne's pack ground against the pavement as he slid it toward Henry and sat down. He fished around in the top pocket, pulled out a Snickers bar, broke it, and offered up a piece. After Henry accepted, he said, "Isn't that always the way, Henry?"

"We walked in the dark pretty late last night," I said. "We couldn't find anything flat, it was all a ledge traverse for miles."

When Airborne said, "you didn't step on any yellow frogs did you?" Monica shot a wide-eyed look in my direction. He held his hand out as if to comfort her and laughed. "Don't worry, I'm a vault. Tell me about it, Henry."

"Dad didn't want to take the long way around the yellow frog closure, even though you aren't supposed to walk through there."

"Henry," I said. "You are going to have to be more careful when you tell that part of the story. The truth is, Airborne, I didn't want to walk a winding two-lane mountain road with four kids in the dark."

"Anyway, he pretended he didn't see the junction out of there to come up to the re-route. By then, it was so dark we got out the flashlights, but not all of them, you know. We usually walk with one in the front and one in the back. But then Aiden fell, and her water bottle popped out of her pocket and bounced." He motioned with his hand. "Bump, bump, bump." He gave a long whistle and dropped his hand to the ground. "Boom!" He nodded at Airborne. "It was a long way down. That was kinda scary, so we got all our flashlights out, and then walked forever and ever, because there was no flat place."

"Yeah, and you told us," June said. "Dad told us we were going to stop right after that."

"What was it?" Henry looked at Monica. "Two hours?"

"At least."

"We slept right on the trail, 'cause it was the first place we found that was flat enough. Dad said we were the only ones stupid enough to walk the Yellow Frog in the dark, so no one would be coming by. But it wasn't all that flat anyway."

"At least there were trees below us to stop us if we rolled," I said.

"I was so mad at him, Airborne," Monica said. "I probably cried for the last hour because my feet hurt so bad."

"I was going to ask about your feet. Did you ever figure out what was wrong with them?"

"It's plantar fasciitis." Monica lifted her cork ball. "This thing has helped if I take time to rub out my calves at lunch every day, but lately it's been getting a lot worse."

"You don't want to be near us when the pain kicks in," I said. "I imagine you'll be way past us after tomorrow."

"You never know," he said. "I keep thinking I've seen the last of you guys, and you pop up again."

"Tell him about what we did today at Baden Powell," June said.

Monica tapped June's knee. "He doesn't want to hear all our stories."

"I want to hear, June," Airborne said. "Why don't you tell me?"

June tried to begin her story several times but laughed herself out of speaking.

"Oh, Junie. I'll tell him," Aiden said. "Dad and June were the last to the top. You know where the trail comes right near the summit, there's that junction by the big tree with all the roots. Everyone was already lying down for lunch. He tried to get everybody to go up to the summit because it's only like four hundred and thirty-two feet away from the junction to get to the top, but nobody would go."

"Except me," Georgie said.

"Well, except Georgie." Aiden waved a hand toward Georgie as if to dismiss her. "She went with him."

"What did Henry say?"

"Henry said, 'I've seen better,'" June said.

"That's just what I thought he would say. You didn't miss much, Henry. The view wasn't that great today because of the smoke from the Paradise Fire. Usually, you can see the ocean from up there."

"And then," June said. "And then he said he already went to the top of Whitney, so he's not going to summit anything else."

"Red line only," Henry said. "Unless it's a shortcut, I'll take an alternate route if it's a shortcut."

"No, you won't," Aiden said. "We didn't come this far not to do the whole thing."

"We already missed thirty miles for that fire closure, so I don't get what's the big deal," he said. "You guys get all hung up on the stupid records."

"You did what you came to do, huh?" I said.

"That's right."

"I'll tell you what I'd like to do right now," Aiden said. "I'd like to get a ride."

Airborne hopped to his feet. "I'll get you one."

Just then a white Prius rounded the bend. Airborne jumped out into the lane and held out both of his hands. The car slowed. After it swerved around him in the far lane, it veered off the road and came to a stop a few hundred feet away. Its red brake lights gave way to white reverse lights. When the driver pulled back even with us, he leaned over and pushed open the passenger door. "Come on in, I'll take as many as you can fit."

Standing behind his car, he rattled off the specifications of the subwoofer that filled his car's rear compartment.

Airborne laughed and looked us over. "I guess your backpacks will have to go in your laps."

I bumped Georgie with my elbow. "Let's go. The biggest and smallest in front."

After all of us, save June, had squeezed into our places, Airborne picked up her pack and passed it across the back seat. June and Airborne looked at each other and laughed. "Alright June, here we go."

When she sat down, one half of her hung out the door, he leaned against her shoulder and gained her a few inches on the slide. He backed away, held both hands up as though he were nervous she might totter. "Hold it there June. Don't move an inch. I'll shut the door."

By the time I rolled down the window to shout back a thank you, Airborne was already out in the street throwing his hands out to halt the driver of an oncoming pickup truck.

As we rolled away, I turned to the driver. "This has to be the most people you've had in your car."

"Maybe the most people," he said, "but it's not the most weight. I have a couple of friends that are big boys. I had this thing dragging the ground when I had all of them in here."

2282.3.2

"We don't have anywhere to stay yet. We may just catch a ride back up to the pass if we can't find anything."

"Airborne and I are staying with a trail angel here," Dahn said. "Where are the kids?"

"Somewhere in there,"—I waved beyond the registers into the grocery store,—"grabbing food for the next section. I'm done making these decisions for them. They can live on cheese puffs and peanut butter for all I care. I gave up somewhere around the time SoGood shared a big cinnamon roll with them."

"Are you going to do the McDonald's challenge coming out of Cajon?"

I turned my head.

"Some people load up on Mcdonald's and carry through to the next resupply eating only Mcdonald's."

"That sounds disgusting."

"I figured Monica wouldn't let you get away with that." Dahn nodded past me toward the nearest register. "She's a good parent."

Henry waved his arms for my attention and lifted a squeeze bottle of mayonnaise. He held it up as if to squirt it into his mouth. Dahn smiled. "Where did they get that idea, I wonder?"

Before I turned around again, a man had sidled in beside Dahn. As though perceiving my interest in the words on his T-shirt, the man pinched it to lift it from his chest for me to read. "It's true, too," he said.

"So you used to have superpowers?" I said.

"Until my psychiatrist took them away." He reached out his hand for me to shake it. "Are you hiking with Dahn and Airborne?"

"Oh, I can't keep up with them."

"Well, if you don't have a place to stay tonight, you could come stay at ours. It's not luxurious, but we could squeeze you in. There are only a few rules: don't let The Dude out; that's the name of my cat, take a shower, and most importantly, you have to let my wife work on your feet."

"They are a family, Mike," Dahn said. "A dad, a mom, and four kids."

"How old are the kids?"

"Sixteen down to eleven," I said. "Wait. No, my oldest just turned seventeen."

"I think we could make that work. What do you think, Dahn? We could just push that couch out of the way and they could sleep where the coffee table is. You've seen it."

"That's a kind offer," I said.

"I'll just grab another bag of hamburger buns. You guys like hamburgers, right? I mixed up a batch of homemade mayonnaise today. What do you think, Dahn?"

"It's your house, Mike," Dahn said. Mike squeezed past Henry at the register and shuffled down the condiment aisle.

"Vince, you don't have to feel obligated to come. There is a list of trail angels over on the door of the library. I'm sure you could find something."

"Do you not want us to come? I don't want to impose."

"It isn't that, believe me. I'd love to hang out with you all. I just hope it isn't an uncomfortable experience for you."

Monica walked toward me with a fresh towel draped over her arm. She leaned in and spoke from the side of her mouth in a soft voice. "Are you going to eat any of the mayonnaise?"

"Don't you think it would be rude not to?"

"I'm going to take a shower. Maybe it will be gone when I get back."

Henry turned and looked up at us out of the corner of his eye. He reached up to grab the corner of a blue porcelain bowl. The heavy glob of mayonnaise inside jiggled. He looked back and shrugged.

I leaned down and whispered in his ear. "I think it just looks green because of the bowl."

Aiden took a step back from the front of the line. "What's green?" she said.

Dahn sniggered.

I held a finger to my mouth to shush her.

As if he'd been waiting for his cue, Mike parted the plastic beaded ropes that hung from the door frame to the room at the back of his house. He reached his leg back and swept the large cat into the room. "Get out of the honeymoon suite, you nosey cat. Don't mind The Dude, and he won't mind you. If he wants to rub up against you, don't pet him. He's very particular and has been known to scratch, but only small children." He winked at Georgie. "I won't be long with the next round of burgers, gotta pop out to the grill. Who's up next in the shower? Is anyone in there?" He walked down the hall and pressed his ear to the bathroom door. "I don't hear the water running. Why don't you hop in there, Airborne? We don't need to have the Strawbridges hog all the hot water."

"You know what? I'm good, thanks. I'd rather wait, anyway."

"Alright, but you know the rules. If you stay here, you have to shower. If you don't shower, you won't get to have my wife work on your feet. And you'd be missing a treat. She used to work in a chiropractor's office, and she learned how to massage feet. The first hiker we had for dinner five years ago … the girl's feet were so bad. Her blisters were all infected. She ended up staying here for three weeks to heal. We told her she could stay the rest of the season if she wanted, and she was planning to stay two weeks, if I remember right, but she ended up having a family emergency ... Was it? Anyway, she had to get out of here in a hurry. My wife rubbed her feet every night. Airborne, you sure you don't want to hop in that shower. You don't want to miss this foot rub, I can tell you."

"You know what? I'm good. I think these kids probably need it more than I do."

"I think it's a pretty big deal what you are about to do though, isn't it?" Mike said. "I don't think I've ever met a Yoyoer. How many people did you tell me have ever done that, Dahn?"

"Five." Dahn turned back from the counter and pointed the peanut butter knife in Airborne's direction. "Including this guy."

"You know, Mike, the Strawbridges are the largest family to ever thru-hike the PCT," Airborne said. "I think their feat is probably more important, so maybe we should focus on their feet."

"And Mom's feet are hurting, Dad," June said. "Good we came here to stay."

The bathroom door creaked open, and Monica came out with a towel wrapped around her hair. She tiptoed across the deep green deep shag carpet and stood beside me. "What's going on?"

"Mike says his wife is going to fix your feet right up," Airborne said.

"If she can help, that would be great." Monica touched a hand to the towel twisted around her hair.

After dinner, Henry and I carried the coffee table and placed it against a wall of dusty cardboard boxes that lined the stair rail to the lower level. I sat down and leaned my back against the couch. Aiden sat beside me and put her hands palms down to the carpet and rubbed a wide circle. "This carpet is comfortable."

"It's a deep shag, Aiden. Have you ever seen shag carpet?"

"No, but I think we will sleep well tonight. It's really thick and comfy."

June sat down and leaned her head on Aiden's shoulder. I tapped each of them on the leg and nodded across the room. Georgie and Henry were on their knees, one on either side of Dahn, and leaning toward a computer screen. Dahn held his pointer finger over the mouse. "Are you ready?"

"What are they doing, Dad?" Aiden said.

"I think it's some kind of geography quiz game."

"Dahn is about to get a surprise." June attempted to whisper and then made a sound somewhere between a snort and a giggle.

Dahn turned. "What was that, June?"

"Nothing." Aiden shot a hand to June's mouth.

June yanked Aiden's hand away. "You'll see."

A few minutes later, Dahn shook his head. "You two know more than most of my geography students ever learn." He turned to Monica. "Good homeschooling, Mom."

Leslie squeezed Monica's ankle and said, "Honey don't move. I'm working on your cuticles. You don't want me to cut you."

Airborne groaned from where he sat on the hearth. I looked across to him. He caught my eye and shook his head.

When Leslie declared Monica finished, she confirmed Mike's claim that their romance had begun at the curling lanes. And in what seemed an attempt to prove it, she fumbled around between two of the cardboard boxes to lift a red and white curling stone by its large handle. "This thing is forty pounds. Mike couldn't believe how easily I could lift it when we met." She tiptoed over our legs toward the fireplace where Airborne sat. "Check this thing out, Airborne. See if you can hold this up." She leaned with it over his feet to hand him the stone.

He swung himself sideways to pull his feet up beside him on the hearth. "You know what, I'm good. I think I am going to take a shower after all." He snatched up a small pouch from beside him and darted across the room toward the bathroom.

Mike stuck his head through the plastic beads in the doorway. "Are you sure you all don't want to stay for a few days? This is fun."

2307

I held my phone high in the air and looked down the trail toward the dirt road from where I had returned in my search for cell phone coverage. Angie picked up on the third ring, and I put the phone to my ear. "Angie, I don't even know if you can get to this location."

"I can't believe you are so close. Where are you, exactly?"

"We're about five miles out of Cajon Pass."

"Cajon Pass?"

"Interstate 15. We tried to make it all the way there, but Monica's feet gave out, so we stopped at a road crossing about five or six miles from the interstate. I don't think we can make it that far tonight."

"Oh, her poor feet."

"I'll drop you a pin that should get you to the dirt road where we are now. It might not be exact, but it will be close. I had to climb back up to get enough coverage, so text the SAT number if you can't get here."

"I'm on the way, as soon as I find my keys. Kaia is going to be so excited to see your kids."

When I made it down to the road, they were huddled together beside the dirt road at the bottom of the dry swale. I put my hand on Aiden's head. "Hey kiddo, get your quilt out. We will be here for a while."

"You think she can make it down this road?"

"I hope so," I spread my groundsheet beside her and stamped smooth a couple of hard clumps of dirt. I stood behind Monica and reached down and rubbed her shoulders.

"Oh, that's so nice," she said.

"Did you guys see Dahn pass?"

"You can still see him," Henry pointed. "He just started climbing that cut. Did you know he doesn't carry a flashlight or a tent? One time he had to sleep in a privy when it rained."

"I wonder what privy it was," Aiden said. "He's lucky he found one."

I tapped Monica's shoulder. "Are you feeling better?"

"I'm so sorry for all that back there. My feet hurt so bad."

"Yeah, Mom," Aiden said. "You went crazy back there."

"I just didn't want to be pushed."

"But nobody was even pushing you," Aiden said. "At lunch you were the one that wanted to push for Cajon Pass. It's not even our fault."

"Aiden," I said and held my finger to my lips.

"No, it's okay, she's right. I don't know what got into me."

"When we get back on-trail, we need to limit our miles to twenty," I said. "That seems to be about the time your head starts spinning around in circles."

"If we …" Monica said. "I don't know if I am going to be able to do this. I think it might be too much." She turned her face toward me. "What if you guys were to finish without me? I could come back when I'm better to finish it up."

"No way," I said. "It's all of us or none at all."

"I'll go home," said Henry. "For Mom."

Aiden punched him in the shoulder.

"I'm serious," Henry said. "If she can't do it, we can't do it."

I searched his face. "I think he was actually serious, Aiden." I spread my Tyvek on the ground beside Monica and lay down. "Let's see if Angie knows someone who can look at it. She's a nurse."

Above us the light faded, and the first stars appeared against the dark sky.

Far out toward the horizon, headlights cut through dark lines of a cattle gate and lit up the dirt road between us. As the lights moved slowly toward us, the rumble on the dirt road increased. "Do you think it's her?" Monica said.

I stood to my feet and stepped over the shoulder to wait. The white pickup truck came to a slow stop with a piercing, metallic whine from the brakes. The driver leaned across the front bench seat and cranked down the window by hand. "You okay out here?"

"Is this road accessible by a two-wheel drive car?"

"Yes, it shouldn't be a problem so long as they can find their way in."

"We have someone coming for us. I dropped them a pin to this location."

He touched a hand to the brim of his cowboy hat and eased his truck forward. "Ya'll stay safe out here."

I sat down beside Monica again. She leaned into me. "I feel far less safe here, nearer the cities than I do in the more remote areas. Does anyone else feel that way?"

We hailed two more cars over the next hour. The third car was Angie's. We encircled her in the road for a few moments, hugging happy greetings before we squeezed into the back of her warm van. Back at their house, after we all took our showers, Kaia leaned over the couch and held a picture in front of June and Aiden, and her lips tightened into a sly smile.

"What is that, Kaia?" Kaia held up the picture so her mother could see. Angie clapped her hands. "Let's replicate that pose tonight!" Then she winced. "Do you remember that night, Georgie?"

Georgie held her hand to the scar on her forehead. "I remember."

Angie put her hand over her mouth. "I felt so terrible."

"Oh please," Monica touched Angie's knee. "If it didn't happen at your house, it would have happened somewhere else."

"But she had to get stitches," Angie said.

"We've never once blamed you for it. Besides, this way we always have something to remind us of you."

After the kids went to bed, I came back downstairs to join Monica and Angie in the kitchen. "Where do I put this?" I held up my empty glass.

"Did you want anything else? A beer or something?"

I declined and looked at Monica. "Did you figure anything out about the feet?"

"I have an appointment for her tomorrow with my doctor," Angie said. "We are going to get x-rays and go from there."

"This is so amazing," Monica said. "Thank you, Angie."

"It's so great to have you guys here in California. Has it been four years already?"

"When did I coach Kaia last, Monica? I think it was when she and Aiden were eleven years old. So, yeah, something like that."

By mid-morning of the next day, we were pulling the van into the parking lot at Angie's clinic. Kaia leaned forward from the second-row seat and pointed me toward the back side of the building. "That's it there. You can just park anywhere you find an empty spot."

Angie was waiting by the back door. I stepped from the van and walked toward her. "Well? What is the verdict?"

"Nothing is broken, but my doctor was trying to tell Monica to rest. I pulled the doctor into the other room and I said"—Angie held up her pointer finger —"I told her, I said, 'Listen here, they are on a mission, so don't you try and stop them.' She asked me how many miles you had left, and you should have seen her face when I told her you still had three hundred miles to go. I could tell she was hesitant, but she said, 'okay.' She doesn't think there is danger of causing a fracture or permanent damage. Any more so than there already is. I think she's just worried about the pain level. She offered to give Monica an injection, but Monica didn't want to do that."

"Monica was okay with everything else?"

"I think she wants to stay two more nights to rest, but yes, she seemed good with it."

"Are you sure you can put up with us that long?"

"Are you kidding? Kaia will be ecstatic. You don't want to be out on the trail on Halloween night. There is some crazy stuff that goes on out there in the desert."

On the first night after we left Angie's, we crossed fifty feet beyond a high junction of a gravel mountain road. The wind ruffled our groundsheets as we flipped them open to lay down side by side on the rounded knoll. The wide sky above us was alive with bright stars. All around us, down in the valleys, clusters of orange lights, some steady, some blinking, marked out the street grids of various cities. Monica propped herself on her elbows. "I'm glad I finally started cowboy camping. Just look at those stars."

"We were telling you that all the time, Mom," June said.

Georgie rolled to her side. "When did you even start?"

"Ever since Shannon. Remember the night of the acorns?"

"Speaking of acorns," Aiden said, "I think I might have heard one of those acorns moving around in the bushes earlier, Mom, and the sound was coming from over near you."

"Mom, she's only teasing, don't believe her," June said and rolled on her side toward me. "When is your brother coming out again, Dad?"

"Stephen? He will be here for the last forty miles."

"That doesn't tell me anything,"

"That tells you everything, June," Aiden said. "We walk more than nineteen every day, and not more than twenty-two. It's the rule. So it's …"

"Don't say it Aiden," June said. "Can you let me try to figure it out?"

"How many days do I add for resupply, Dad?"

"Give it two, just to be safe."

"Is it eighteen days?"

"You got it, Bug."

"That feels like a long time, Dad," Georgie said.

"It won't feel like a long time."

"Why not?"

"Because people are coming. Lots of people."

"Are some of them surprises? Or do we already know?"

"Yes, some are surprises."

"Are you going to tell us who, at least?"

"Some you already know about. Some you don't, and the ones you don't know about, you won't know about."

"I know it's Mr. Brickhouse tomorrow," said Henry. "I hope he brings us some Chick-fil-A."

"Mr. Brickhouse isn't coming tomorrow, buddy." I said. "He comes the day after tomorrow."

"Quit talking, everybody," Monica said. "Go to sleep." Then she whispered to me, "Do I know about everyone that is coming?"

"I don't think so," I whispered.

"What don't you think so, Dad?" Aiden said.

2327.0.2

It is the end of another long day. We are arranged, shoulder to shoulder in a sardine line tonight, and I am on one of the ends. Monica is beside me. Our overlapped groundsheets fit inside two rows of bushes that seem as though they've been cut out for us. I lie awake long after they sleep. The gentle ridgeline on the opposite shore of the lake is sharply defined by the pale light from a bright moon that still lingers somewhere beneath the horizon. It is quiet and calm, but for the gentle and rhythmic lapping of waves on the lake's shore. I can hear myself breathe. I can feel the beat of my heart. The wind whispers in the bushes. I look across all of their faces beside me, and they are asleep. The sky is crowded tonight with bright stars. Another shooting star splits the sky. "Did you see that?" I whisper.

"I did," Georgie whispers back.

"I thought I was the only one awake."

"Why did you ask if someone saw it then?"

"Just in case."

"That one looked like it had sparks coming off its tail, Dad."

"I thought it would never fade."

"Goodnight, Dad, I'm getting sleepy."

"Goodnight."

Some time later, a soothing voice woke me. I did not hear the words that he spoke when he woke me. He spoke again with an unhurried cadence, "I didn't want to startle you."

"You are night hiking, huh? Do you like night hiking?"

"I do," he said. "Do you mind if I rest here with you for a minute?"

"Please do." I heard him sit down on the far side of the trail. "I like night hiking too, but these others don't, so we don't."

"Are you all hiking together?"

"Yes. We are a family."

"A family, family?"

"My wife and four kids, yes."

"Do you have trail names?"

"Some call us 'The Family,' but we just go by our surname."

"Which is?"

"Strawbridge."

"Well, Dad Strawbridge, I am Walking Home."

"I like that. Where is your home?"

"It's a name I picked up several years ago on another trail. How far are you going?"

"All the way."

"And you are thru-hikers?"

"In a few hundred miles we are, yes."

"How have you enjoyed hiking in a southbound direction?"

"I like it, but I don't have anything else to compare it to."

"I am headed south also, but I have hiked the whole thing a few times before in both directions."

"I talked with a man in the desert, just outside of Kennedy Meadows South. It kind of messed me up. I've been questioning our choice to go southbound ever since."

"Why is that?"

"He spoke of the desert as though it were a test. 'A test for enduring,' he said."

"I could see that, I guess."

"Sure, but my problem is that I think of deserts as places of preparation, especially if it involves a test. I see it as almost a cleansing for what is to come."

"What's wrong with that?"

"Well, if the desert is preparing for what is to come, for the quest, for the mission, or however you want to think about it, then northbound would make a whole lot more sense because you'd go through the desert at the beginning."

"Ahh, I see what you mean," he said. "But you are thinking of the end of the trail as an ending. I don't see it the same way."

"It's my first trail."

"Think of it this way. Maybe everything from the border was preparing you for the desert, and the desert is the final preparation before you truly begin."

"I like that better. Much better."

"Life is a trail, man. This thru-hiking stuff is all a little bit make-believe."

"At the moment, it feels pretty real to me."

"Don't get me wrong, it will leave an impression on you. Especially on the kids, but I'm not sure they will ever appreciate how much they've been shaped by it. This is now a part of their childhood. It will probably just seem like normal life to them."

"I was thinking about that earlier today. I was imagining standing on the sideline at Georgie's soccer games in the fall and watching her run around on the field with all of her teammates after she's been through all this. I wonder if she will be different."

"I have no doubt, but it's surprising how quickly we forget. Maybe you could do something to help her remember. Did you take a lot of pictures or keep a journal? You know, something to remind her about all that she lived through and learned out here."

"I have a lot of that stuff, especially pictures and videos." We were both silent for a while. "The trouble with video is that we won't have any footage of the most intense moments. That's when you shut the camera and miss all the stuff you'd most like to have captured."

"You could write it all down. Did you journal?"

"That's something to think about."

He shifted his position and fell into silence for a long while. "I'm getting a little cold," he said. "I'd better get moving, but it was nice to meet you."

"Enjoy," I said. "Walking Home."

After a while, Georgie whispered, "Dad?"

"I didn't know you were awake."

"I am," she said. "I liked him."

"Did you?"

"Yeah, he seemed nice," she said. "Could you even see his face?"

"I never did. Did you see it?"

"No."

2327.0.3

I am still awake. I do not wake as often in the night now, but, earlier in the day, at lunch, I had slept for an hour, so tonight I am not tired. The stars dim a little. A bright, white moon peeks over the horizon. I prop myself to my elbows and look across the water to follow its elongated reflection to the far shore. It is almost blinding against the dark water. I flip open the flap of my quilt and walk barefoot across the cool ground.

I stand at the water's edge. A fluorescent lamp has now come into view across the lake to the left. Its light is interrupted by the railing, and the wire, and the coils of the hydropower station standing as some sentinel atop the far dam.

I take a deep breath, as much air as I can take in. I press my lips closed and imagine I am moving the breath all around my body. Toward my right foot first, then I pull it back to guide it down to my left. Toward each of my hands, and then toward my head. I imagine the air flowing as if through a valve into the occipital lobe and then like some child on the greatest of flume rides, through the various tubes of each lobe. When I grow lightheaded, I gasp and breathe in again. I repeat all of this three more times. Afterward, I take even steps into the water, maintaining a slow, steady movement until I am submerged to my neck. "I do not feel the cold, I only feel its power."

I dog-paddle in the direction of the moon for a while and stop to tread water. After one lung-filling inhale, I sweep my hands up to swim down. Above the disrupted surface of the lake, stars shake and shimmer. I let out more air, and I am held suspended. With arms extended I sweep myself in a circle. Something is happening here. Some becoming thing. Something of becoming. I stop spinning and remain suspended again. This silence is pregnant. A ripe and pregnant pause full of longing. I wish I could stay longer, but I need air.

I step onto shore, turn to face the moon again and scrape water from my skin. A wave of warmth envelopes me. I stand still for a long time until I am dry. I turn and walk toward the others across the cold ground, and I lie down.

When Monica shakes me awake in the morning, the sun is above the horizon.

2330.7

We settle into our twenty-mile-a-day rhythm, and it's easy to plan. And people come. So many people.

A white van slows beside the dirt road, and the door slides wide while it is still moving. Scott Brickhouse, with his beautiful bald head, jumps to the ground, and I run toward him. "Hombre de Pollo." I look past him. "Who have you got with you?"

"It's Patrick and Dequan.

After a few minutes, I say, "This talking stuff is great, but we'd better get moving. We've got miles to make."

"What's the hurry?" Henry says. "We will make it there, easy."

I whisper to Scott, "I have a cousin joining us, but it's still a secret."

"How far are we planning to go today anyway, Henry?"

"Always twenty miles," Henry says. "It's the same every day."

We climb back up to the trail and Scott says, "Group-o photo," and we smile.

"Let's all reassemble at the parking lot eight miles up, everybody," I say. "If we get separated."

2340.9

"I knew you were up to something," Georgie says as she peeks up at me from inside her Uncle Chris's embrace.

"Savannah and I will camp out with you tonight," he said. "We'll come back out this way to the car in the morning."

A few miles on we cross above Deep Creek Hot Springs and I shield Georgie's eyes beneath my hands. "There's a naked dude right there, kid, don't look down."

"What is with all the toilet paper everywhere?" Savannah says. "It would be such a beautiful canyon without all this trash and graffiti."

"We promise, the whole trail is not this way. There are more and more day hikers that come out from L.A. now."

"And when is your brother coming to join you?"

"Tis nigh on a fortnight," Henry says.

Savannah bursts out laughing. "A fortnight? What on earth?"

"Henry," Aiden says. "Like you even know what that means."

"It's in that one stupid book you made me listen to."

"Well, you didn't have to listen to it if you didn't want to."

2347

"Come on, Uncle Scott, are you going to force me to answer?" Aiden says.

"Yes, everyone has to give a high and a low. You're the last one."

"Of the whole trail?"

"Of the entire trail."

"I'm going to go with … tonight. I never dreamed we would cowboy camp with so many. I mean, eleven people at once?"

"What about your low?" Scott said.

"I don't have one."

"Come on Aiden, you have to."

"If I had to say a low, it would be that you didn't bring us Chick-fil-A. We were sure you would."

Everyone laughs.

"Hey, come on, Aiden. I'm ultralight now, I can't carry extra. I learned the hard way the last time I hiked with your dad."

2357

Dequan "Dequans" it the next day. At least, that's what it has come to be known as. He walks into lunch and falls face down flat on the dirt. He sleeps for two hours without moving.

I carry his pack near the end of the day until the pickup van is in sight. I offer it back to save his good reputation. He carries it again only until June offers to help. "Please," he says. "Take it. I have no more pride."

At dinner Aiden says, "I don't see why we couldn't call it The Grandy."

"Oh no," Dequan says. "I don't mind. You can call it The Dequan. I earned it."

2381

I coax Henry, soliciting his commiseration. "Aren't you annoyed at how slow we are going? We could be there by now if we could just go."

"This has been good for Mom's feet, Dad. We will get there when we get there."

I search his face for a hint of sarcasm and find none.

2436.7

"In the spring," Aiden says. "I bet you can't even cross here."

"That water line is pretty high," I say. "Where is your mom?"

Aiden nods downstream. "Soaking her feet."

I text Rob to let him know we will see him at 7:35 in the morning, and balance across the large, tumbled-smooth river rocks in search of a good place to sleep.

Rob greets us in the morning with Starbucks, big smiles and big hugs. He is a boisterous and bouncy step counter. "Sixty thousand," he calls out that night after dark.

"Tomorrow," I say, "over San Jacinto around 5:30 p.m., we will meet my cousin and take the spur into town."

"Did Aunt Luchrysta come all the way out to California just to see us?" June says.

"No, she just happened to be out here. She has a conference not too far away."

"I thought you said we had dinner with Angie and Kaia," Aiden says.

"Yes, they'll be there too, when we get down the hill."

"Isn't that spur a long way off-trail," Monica says.

"There's an eleven-mile fire closure right after, and no safe way around it. Angie will drop us back to trail the day after tomorrow on the far side."

"After church?"

"Yes, we can finally go."

In the morning, Rob woke, again bouncy. He called down from another off-trail overlook, "Come on Henry, there is so much to see."

"Nah, Mr. Rob, I'm good here. My energy serves one single purpose, and that's to get me down trail."

2470

A day's hike beyond San Jacinto we camp in a saddle up high. Below, another city sparkles but dims the stars in the sky. "What is that city, Daddo?"

"I don't know the name, but it's pretty."

"You know it's gotta be called San Something-or-other," Aiden said.

"I feel less safe this close to people," Monica says. "Does anyone else feel that way now?"

2503

Chad Johnston's van is parked in the turnout at the top of the hill when we arrive. The side door slides open and six kids spill out. All of them named something starting with the letter J. It takes us until the last slice of pizza is gone to learn all of their names, but we practice until we get it right. Chad's wife has brought Monica a salad, and they sit to the side and they talk.

"The thing that kind of trips me out, though," Chad says, "is time. We've been following along from the beginning, and the whole summer we've been up and down the West Coast. It's not that you aren't walking fast, but you are walking … It's almost like your family has stepped into a whole different realm of time."

Another car swings in and slides to a stop beside the Johnstons' van, and everyone looks over. Columbus pops out with his arms open wide. "Hey, guys!" He runs straight to the kids.

Blue Bear climbs out of the passenger side and waves to Monica.

Monica shakes her head and looks at me. "You knew about this?"

When the sun sets, it gets too cold to be stationary, so we hug Chad, his wife, and all the little J Johnstons goodbye.

When they are gone, I say, "Thanks so much for coming, Columbus and Blue Bear."

He says, "No way, you don't get rid of us that easily, we are camping out with you tonight."

The kids cheer.

We walk a quarter of a mile from the highway and spread out on the ground.

"You really picked up the pace," Columbus says.

"We caught The King in Belden," June says. "We were blasting Disney songs on our speakers when we caught him."

"Funny thing about that," Columbus says. "They don't sell Advil P.M. where The King is from in New Zealand. He had been taking it for four hundred miles before Shivers helped him figure it out."

"He sleepwalked for four hundred miles?" Aiden says. "Henry, that sounds like something you would do."

When the quiet settles around us, Columbus sits up as if slapped. "Adrienne, look at that tree." He stands up and walks to it. He touches his hand to a small branch. "Remember? Right here is where Salty hung his food bag. We were here guys, right here. Not that long ago."

The following morning, we hug them goodbye and begin another twenty-mile day. Georgie says, "Adrienne? I don't think I ever would have guessed her name would be Adrienne."

2537

I set a target for lunch. When we arrive, I set a new target.

"Why are we moving again, Dad?" Aiden says. "This place is fine."

"There's a better spot a mile away." I reach for my phone and send a text through the Garmin. "We have to change it up, Neil. Abort on this road. It won't work. It's not even a road anymore. Let's shoot for the next one down trail. I'll send details."

"Who are you messaging?" Monica says.

"I'm just making some final arrangements with Stephen about where he and Silas will meet us."

I see Monica's brother descending the switchbacks beyond the ravine, long before anyone else does. He is hugging the kids near the bottom by the time Monica spots him. She turns to me. "Is that Neil?" She punches my shoulder. "That's who you were texting?" And she runs.

"I parked about a mile up the road, and I had to run," he says. "I was afraid I would miss you." He looks down at Monica again and pulls her to him once more. "Oh, it's so good to see you guys."

She hugs him tight and holds on. "What are you doing here?"

"I extended a layover through L.A., and I rented a car, which, by the way, was not made to drive on that road. I was hoping the timing would work out so that I could be with you at the border, but this will have to do."

"Momma came. Daddy came. Shannon came, and you came too," Monica says. "I can't believe that you all came."

2554

"Henry," I call, and he waits on the far side of the road. "When I tell you to wait, boy, you wait. You don't have a map. How do you think you won't lose the trail?"

He lifts his arm and points with two fingers as if weaving around the near cut toward the distant, high saddle.

"Well, you happen to be right this time, but don't do it again."

2578

L.A. day hikers stop us to talk, and they marvel. Though one couple scolds us for "that little girl out in front, all alone."

Another friend named Chad, Chad Gray, joins us for pie and ice cream in Julian, and we pick up our last resupply.

Under a bridge on the way out of town, we sit down in the shade.

"What's this?" Aiden picks up a plastic bag from under a rock. It has a note inside. "It's for us, guys, from Bear Hair, SoGood, and Smiles. Look, Sprites and Skittles for everyone here."

We wait there for the cool of the evening. We don't have many miles to go to reach twenty.

"How far until Stephen and Silas?" Henry says.

"Why don't you guess?" I say.

"I'll guess the day after tomorrow, around 1:30?" Georgie says.

"I'll guess 1:45," Aiden says. "Just to be safe."

"And then, Aiden?" I say. "How many days after that?"

"Just two days left."

"I guess you could see it that way," I say, "but I wouldn't discount tomorrow. I'd call it the morning of the third day."

2615.2

"Wow, you guys are so stinky." Stephen opened his arms wide. "Forty miles of desert and you're done."

"Maple!" Georgie said and scooped up the poodle. "Silas, I can't believe you brought Maple."

"She said we weren't allowed to come back without her."

"How are you guys doing?" Stephen said. "How are Monica's feet?"

"We've had this thing licked since we dialed in a limit at twenty miles a day," I said. "I think we finally found our groove."

"Tell him about the milkshakes you promised, Dad," Georgie said.

"Yeah, how far until we get to have milkshakes, Vince?"

"Twenty miles."

"So one day, exactly. What are we waiting on, kids? Let's get this train moving."

"When you think about it," Aiden dropped her chin to the grid-patterned patio table the next day, "Strawbridge doesn't make a whole lot of sense. "Aunt Lucia would say"—she imitated her great aunt's voice—"'The best part about being a Strawbridge is that you get to be one, so you don't have to marry one.'" She tossed her straw wrapper at Silas. "Silas Strawberry, how are you liking your strawberry milkshake?"

"Silas Strawberry? At school, they call me that. It's annoying."

"That's dumb," Aiden said. "How hard is Strawbridge to remember?"

"You've already said why it's hard," I said. "It doesn't make sense."

"Yeah. I mean, what is a Strawbridge anyway?"

"Aunt Lucia says the name comes from England," I said. "And that we were the ones that put straw on the bridges when it rained, so it didn't get too muddy and slick. You know, so the carts could pass over the bridges."

"Wouldn't that make us the Bridgestrawers?" Aiden said.

"We could call my dad," I said. "I can use the store's wifi to call out."

"Put it on speaker," she said.

My dad recounted a wide range of Strawbridge stories, including one connecting the family to a man named Seth Kinman. "He made gifts of elk and deer antler chairs to a few presidents, including Abraham Lincoln."

"How were we connected to him, again?"

"He was the nephew of the Strawbridge widow," my dad said, "but the one you should talk to about this is my cousin, your Uncle Rob Urish."

"Okay, what's his number? I'll call him right now."

After I hung up, Aiden said, "Are you really going to call Uncle Rob, Dad?"

"Why not? You have something going on? It could be fun to find out some of these things. Histories tend to get fuzzy as you trace them backward in time. It might be good if we go ahead and lock it in while we are at it."

Uncle Rob answered on the third ring. "What is it you are hoping to find out?"

"I'm here with the kids, and we are trying to discover exactly what a Strawbridge is. I am realizing that I don't actually know."

"What is it that you understand it to be from the oral tradition?"

"Yes, let's call it the oral tradition." I laughed. "Other than Great-Grandma marrying her student who also happened to be her father's hired hand, I don't know much. I guess, as far as Illinois Strawbridges go, the way I have always told it is that there were three Strawbridge brothers that fled west after robbing a bank. Two of the brothers changed their names to Trowbridge. One kept the name, Benjamin Strawbridge. He became a sheriff and drowned while chasing a criminal into the Susquehanna River. I make that Benjamin the grandfather of my great-grandfather."

"That's almost right. The Benjamin that drowned was a ferryman, Benjamin T. It was his son Benjamin, a shoemaker by trade, who became the sheriff in Williamsport, PA, and eventually moved west. You are right that the son Benjamin is your great-grandfather's grandfather. The claim on our side as to the motivation for the name change is that the sheriff's step-father got on the wrong side of the law and high-tailed it to central Illinois where he restored his step-son's surnames to Trowbridge in order to avoid apprehension."

"Restored?"

"The first of the family to immigrate to this country was of Irish descent. He was a fellow named Shuebel Trowbridge from Belfast. According to family lore, he was self-conscious about his unusual name, so he would never spell it out. We have several letters and official documents from the early 1800s where he signed 'S Trowbridge.' The surname was 'corrupted' over time and Shuebel's descendants became Strawbridges."

After I said goodbye to Uncle Rob, Aiden said, "You are telling me after all of this time, we aren't even Strawbridges. Our name is actually supposed to be Trowbridge?"

"You are a Strawbridge, kid, however you came to be one."

"That makes more sense," June said. "Strawbridge is a weird name."

"You think Trowbridge makes more sense?" Aiden said.

"Don't worry, girls," I said. "At least, you get to change your name when you get married. Henry is stuck with it."

"That's true." Aiden laughed. "I guess Aunt Lucia was right."

"When you take a new name," I said. "Your job will be to make another name great." I picked up my milkshake. "Does anyone else have to go to the bathroom before we leave?"

After I flushed the toilet, I shimmied past the sink and reached for the door handle, but the door swung open and hit me.

"Sorry, Dad," Henry said.

I stepped through the front door of the market and heard the bus brakes squeak. When the door opened, Troubadour burst out with arms open and ran to us. "Strawbridges!" He gave high fives all around.

"Looks like your driver is leaving you," I said. "You don't want to miss your bus."

Troubadour backed into the road blowing kisses. "Get to that border, and come visit me in Asheville this summer, so I can play for you. Come see a show."

"How will we find you?"

He jumped onto the bottom step of the bus and turned. "My name out there is Pat Zim. Look me up."

"Could we go?" Aiden said as soon as the bus pulled away. "Oh, I almost forgot to fill up my water. Georgie, don't forget to fill up your water."

"I have plenty." Georgie touched my forearm. "Dad, have you seen that moss trick that Mr. Chad Grey showed us? There's this brown moss on the rocks all over the place. It looks dead. But if you drip water on it, it starts moving and turns green in probably less than thirty seconds."

"Yeah, Uncle Vince," Silas said. "We can show you."

A few miles later, June sat not far above the base of a hill, leaning back over her pack with dirt streaks running down her face. "Daddo, I can't do it."

I sat down beside her.

"I know, and I know I can do it 'cause my legs are strong enough now. I just can't make myself go."

I put my arm around her.

"I just stopped to tie my shoe, and they wouldn't wait for me. It's harder for me when I feel behind and alone. Why do I always do this?" We sat in silence for a while. "It's like I forget to remember that I'm stronger now."

"This is the very last hill, Bug," I said. "One more and you can be done forever!"

"Good, 'cause I'm retired. she heaved herself to her feet and extended her hand. "Come on, Dad, let's go. Do you think these miles are just gonna walk themselves?"

We took a few steps together. "How far is it to the top?"

"You sure you want to know?"

She nodded.

"Almost two miles."

"I can do that," she said.

2643.8

Stephen threw off his quilt and stepped to the edge of the flat and belted out a song.

Oh for a thousand tongues to sing
My great Redeemer's praise,
The glories of my God and King,
The triumphs of his grace!

"Ugh, Silas," Aiden said. "Your dad's worse than mine."

Stephen turned back with his arms widespread to the heavens, a dark silhouette backlit by the morning sun. "Today is the day! What an amazing day. You guys. Aren't you excited?"

Monica stretched her hands high and yawned. "Do we even need to get snacks out?"

"It's nine miles," I said. "I doubt we are going to stop anywhere, but you might pull out a few bars."

"How long did it take you guys to get across the desert?" Stephen said.

"It was supposed to take thirty days," I said. "According to Skybird."

"Cut it out, Dad," Aiden said. "Can't you just enjoy it for once?"

"Hang on, Stephen." I pulled out my phone. "I'll pull up a picture and check. Here's one from that spot with SoGood outside of Kennedy Meadows South. It will have been forty days, so not bad."

"Are you kidding me? Forty days? Could that be more perfect?"

2645

Georgie stood beneath the several buzzing wires strung between two transmission towers on the remnant of an old roadbed. She tilted her head up to read a square yellow sign. I stopped beside her and told June that we would catch up.

"What does it mean, Dad?"

"It's a warning."

"What about?"

"You can guess from the pictures."

"I see the sun and mountains. A snake, and a few cacti." She touched the sign. "This looks like some guy drowning. And that circle thing around the words. What does 'No hay agua potable,' mean?"

"That there is no water here that you can drink."

"But why is it in Spanish?"

"We are near the border. This is a warning to people who have snuck into the country that the desert is a dangerous place."

"I didn't know the desert was dangerous."

"It is if you aren't prepared for it."

"What does the whole warning say?"

"It says, 'Be careful, don't expose your life to the elements. It has value,' or something like that."

"I'd like to know Spanish."

"Me too."

2649.9.1

"Dad, what is that?" Georgie slipped her hand into mine.

I looked into her eyes. We both looked up again together. Behind the chain link fence people milled about the yard. Some leaned against the cinder block wall. Some sat or half-sat on one of two picnic tables. A boy, about Georgie's height, gripped the fence with his hands.

"He's looking right at you, Georgie."

"There's razor wire on the top of the fence, Dad."

"It's a detainment center."

She looked up at me again and squeezed my hand. She waved at the boy.

The boy waved back.

2649.9.2

I sat in the gravel not far from the pavement at the final road crossing before the border. My Garmin beeped, and I reached for it. "It's Jamie."

J: You okay? You've been stationary for an hour, and the border is close.

V: Some of them walked down to the store in Campo. We are waiting for some SoCal friends who are coming to walk the last little bit with us.

J: Today is the day. You better text me the minute you touch.

V: Thank you. I will. Thank you ... For everything.

2649.9.3

"Dad, what are you even talking about?" Henry and I sat with our legs splayed out before us onto the gravel turnout on the last highway crossing of the trail.

I re-situated myself on my Tyvek and pulled a small rock from beneath it, threw it at Henry's shoe and leaned back again against my backpack.

"You missed," he said.

"Basically, all I am trying to say is that when I die, I am not sure there will have been anything I've ever done that I will be prouder of." I tapped the side of his leg. "This was a pretty big deal, you know?"

"Did you say that both of your Chad friends are coming? How are we supposed to tell them apart?"

"You've met them both. One is Chad Grey, and one is Chad Johnston."

"What am I supposed to call them?"

"You call one Mr. Johnston and one Mr. Grey. What do you think? You've been in California too long, kid. You have no respect for your elders."

"Mr. Johnston is the one with all the kids?"

"Yes, do you remember their names?"

"I remember that all of their names started with the letter J."

"What about you, Aiden? June? Do either of you know?"

"Six of them, right?" Aiden held up her hand to count. "James and Joshua were the boys. Jessa, Johnna, Josephine … I can't remember the last one."

"You are kidding me, right?" June said.

I laughed. "Tell her, June."

"It's June."

"Oh my gosh, June. How could I forget?"

"It's Juniper," I said. "But they call her June."

"What about the other Chad's son's name?"

"That's easy," Henry said. "His name is Sam."

"And they are all going to be here to walk with us to the finish?" Aiden said.

"All of them. Plus, Brian and Jana and their two boys, Jack and Rhett."

"It's a lot of people."

"It's a lot of people. They should be here any minute."

Chad Grey hit the brakes and cut the wheel to slide to a stop on the gravel shoulder beside the road.

We coughed and waved away the dust. I slapped Henry on the knee and squeezed. "What do you think, bud? Are you ready?"

He did not push my hand away.

Chad popped out of the car and rubbed his hands together. "Let's do this!"

I groaned and stood to my feet.

Henry looked up at me and smirked. "Dad, I don't think I'll be touching the border today. I did what I came to do."

"You little turd. Oh no you don't!" Aiden punched him. "You are going down there to the monument if I have to drag you myself."

"You know what?" Henry smirked. "I think I will go with you." And he reached up his hand.

The other Chad parked his van just beyond us, and all six of his kids filed out.

"I think Brian and Jana can catch up," I said. "They say they're only a few minutes out."

The path from the pavement was wide and soft. Laughter of friends and partial conversations flitted and floated about me.

"Wait up, Silas," Georgie said. "It's kind of cool, isn't it? You and your dad were here in the beginning, and you'll be here through to the end."

"That's true, Georgie. I'm gonna call it my border-border hike. Maybe people will think I walked the whole thing."

"Does it feel strange to be at the finish?" Chad said.

"I wouldn't know how to describe the way it feels," I said.

"Just soak it up, man. You don't have to talk."

"I'm gonna run to catch Silas," Henry said. "He's going to try to touch the monument before I do."

"Go get him, buddy!" Chad shouted after him.

June dropped Juniper's hand and skipped back toward me. "I have to go to the bathroom, Dad. Will you wait? I don't want to be last."

"She's just like my Juniper," Chad said.

We crested the rise, and I saw the monument. "Look at this first, my June," I said. "There it is."

"Yep, there it is," Chad said. "Is it the same as the one at the north end of the trail?"

"It's the same shape anyway. The same size, and same configuration. This one is made of stone. Even so, something else is very different about it."

"Or maybe you are different?"

"One would hope."

"It's okay, Dad," June said. "You can wait down there near the monument, but don't touch it without me."

"Go on ahead, Chad. I'll catch up. I'm going to walk alone for the last bit."

At the monument Jana pulled plastic flutes from a picnic basket and poured sparkling grape juice around.

"There's champagne too," she whispered. "For you two."

I filled Monica's flute. "I know you've been hurting for a long time. Thank you for enduring the pain."

Monica wiped her eyes. "I'm so proud of us."

Aiden brushed past me and spilled my champagne. "Hey, Georgie," she said, "let me lift you up."

"Oh hey, Georgie," Silas said. "I'll hand Maple up there to you so she can be in the picture."

I refilled my glass. "It was a good idea that you had, Monica."

Monica put her head on my chest and said, "I don't like Georgie sitting so high on that top post."

Georgie palmed the flat of the top post and teetered. She twisted herself around to a seated position and reached her hands down toward Silas. When she sat upright again, she tucked Maple under her arm.

"Way to go, Georgie!" I said.

She turned toward me and lifted her hand to her lips and kissed her fingers, then blew the kiss in my direction. I made a motion as if to catch it then pulled Monica to me again.

"Listen to this one, guys …" Aiden picked up the logbook and read.

"Who was that last one?" Monica said.

"That was The King. But, Mom, listen to this, Tig, Hanz and Franz, Relish, Airborne, Spatz, Potter, SoGood, Smiles, Swarm and Vamp." She looked up. "Vamp made it. That is awesome! Poopfinger, Bear Hair … and look, Chip, Skybird, and Grizz must have finished together like they planned, they all signed on the same day … Ms. McGuyver, Troubadour, The Lightning Brothers, and Newsfeed, we don't know who Newsfeed is, do we? Peach … well, DMV, Green, The Kid, Snacks, Twig, Jen, Salty … All of them. They all signed it and wrote their stories down too."

"Did you see Trouble's name?" Georgie said.

"She's behind us," Henry said. "By about two weeks, I'd say."

"Trouble made it through the Sierra?" Monica said. "I'm so glad she is going to make it."

"Mom," Aiden said. "The Columbus and Bluebear one, you gotta hear this … It's so funny, where was that? I'm going to read it again, so you can hear."

"Let me look, Aiden," Monica said. She touched my hand and nodded to the monument. "Have you touched it yet?"

"Not yet, I'm waiting for June."

"Ta-da!" June jumped sideways in front of me. "The caboose has arrived."

I reached a hand behind her back, and we took the final few steps of the trail together. "You go first, June."

"No, Dad. Let's go together."

We interlaced our fingers.

"Your story is here too, June, and it's a good one."

"On three," she said. "Ready, Daddo?"

We held our hands pressed against the monument for a long while. "This thing," I said. "This thing holds many stories." I pulled June to me and said, "I'm proud of you, Bug."

Henry bumped into June, plopped his pack against the base of the monument, and unclipped the top. He pulled out his sleeping quilt and tossed it to the ground. Then he reached in again.

"What are you doing, Henry?" June said.

"Trying to find something, June. Hang on." He pulled out the tent fly he carried, his clothes and food bags, and reached in again. Then he smiled. With his hand still in his bag, he called, "Mom, do you have your phone? I need a picture." His Coke can clinked when he placed it on the monument. "Now," he said, "Now, I did what I came to do."

We took pictures. So many pictures, and I poured out the last of the champagne.

2652.2

Aiden walked toward me through the crowd and put her hand on my shoulder. "Hey, Dad, you want to go check out the border wall with me?"

"Yeah, let's go look."

When we arrived at the base of the wall, we banged the heels of our hands against the solid, metal panel and looked up toward its top. I fitted my eye to a rusted-out hole "Look through there, Aido. There is a whole lot of desert."

She nodded.

"What do you think? Want to keep going?"

"I mean, I would, but …" She smiled.

We stood there in the shade beneath the border wall for a long time. I turned to lean with my back against it. To the north, beyond our happy crowd at the monument, the trail wound up to the top of the rise. A hiker came into view and looked down. He stood for a long time, as if deciding.

"Do we know who that is?" Aiden pointed. She jumped up and down waving her arms as if to invite him in. "Why would he not come to the finish?"

When the hiker turned away, the sun flashed against the metal bar of his external frame backpack. "Maybe he didn't see it, Aiden."

"But it's so obvious."

"That's what I like about you, kid. You've got vision and the rest of the world wears bifocals." I paused. "I would love to know what you learned out there on the trail. Do you think you could put it into words?"

She kicked the ground a few times. "I guess," she paused for a while and then smiled up at me. "I guess I learned I'm pretty good at walking."

Our large company of revelers began filing away from the monument and out toward the road. Monica raised her hand and waved, as if to invite us in.

"Can you believe this, Aiden?"

"We did it, Dad." She brushed a strand of hair from her face. "We did it. Now, let's go home."

RATHER THAN AN EPILOGUE...

A Day on Trail
By Aiden Strawbridge

The 5:00 a.m. wake-up call is Dad's too-cheerful voice. I roll over and try to push through the fog of a headache and smack June to get her moving. The same thing is happening in the other two tents. Henry, my dad, and I are universally hated in the mornings.

Breakfast is a cup of cereal mixed with cold chocolate water; if you're lucky, you might have an extra Pop-Tart too. We eat in our sleeping bags, trying to stay cozy for as long as possible. If there are other hikers nearby, we do our best to argue without waking them up. Needless to say, morning is not considered the favorite time of day.

By the time we hit the trail, it's usually past the scheduled departure time, and the next hour consists of Dad's continued griping. By 9:00, we're warmed up enough to start smiling again. Henry and I sing silly songs or tell jokes, while Georgie and June laugh at chipmunks. The next hour increases in speed and cheerfulness, and we take a few breaks to admire the views or eat a snack.

At around 10:00, we start to feel the aches and pains of yesterday. My mom's feet continue to hurt, Georgie trips over every single root in her path, and June and my dad stop to massage and stretch their legs. Henry and I often ask for a lunch spot to stop, locate it on the map, and take off for it. We are not likely to see the rest of the family until the designated lunch spot.

We're all extremely grateful when we do reach lunch at around 12:30. By that time we have usually covered ten to thirteen miles and are ready for a break. We sit down by a lake or stream to filter water, take off our shoes, and pull out our foodbags to see what we have. I have been officially fired from boiling the water, so Mom or Georgie do the cooking. While we wait the seven minutes for our rice to cook, we stretch and rub our feet. We add as many calories to our rice as we can, and snack continually (I do, anyway). Our lunches last anywhere from an hour to two hours depending on how far we plan to go that day. We use that time to wash our clothes and ourselves as well as eat.

After another slow start and more griping, we head out for the afternoon haul. The afternoon is by far the most fun part of the day for me. I love the thought that we have already done so many miles and are closing in on bedtime. I am more alert and cheerful in the afternoon, and for some reason the scenery is more beautiful to me. Everybody else seems to hate it. Georgie and June have a daily "cry-thirty" in the afternoon, and everyone is tired and irritable. Amusing yourself is more difficult, so you turn to music and books for distraction. We kids enjoy listening to music from movies and trying to reenact the whole thing in our heads. The afternoon is almost a "quiet time" whose silence is occasionally broken by questions like, "How many more miles?"

As it gets closer to seven, we seem to slow down. It's very trying for those who want to go fast enough to beat the sunset. The sun turns orange as it gets lower in the sky, and the light shining on the trees looks like orange spray paint. We hurt and we cry, but we always make it up that last hill.

When we finally do make it to camp at around eight, we collapse in our tents from exhaustion, eat a peanut butter wrap, and go to sleep.

The days are long and hard, but there are amazing moments: lunch by a perfect swimming lake, ridge hikes through volcanic rock at sunset, and watching the emotional and spiritual battles inside everyone around me as they fight their way through the day to a well-earned rest. It is an experience that I wouldn't pass up for anything.

ACKNOWLEDGMENTS

We have come to the naming of names. The long list of the "this hike was made possible by" names. Every time I come to one of these lists, I close the book. It's okay to close it. Go ahead. We are not offended. This list is for us and for *our* remembering.

Now that it is just the two of us, please know that you are among those who have pressed your fingerprint onto our lives in ways that only we know. You have made this grand adventure possible with a word, a whisper, or a hand. You have doubted and believed along with us. You have joined us on trail. You have lifted our spirits. You have been co-adventurers with us in the journey of the trail and of this book. This is your story as much as it is ours.

Watch, if you will, a short film by Elina Osborne about her hike on the Pacific Crest Trail. It is called *It is the People.* You are our people.

THANK YOU:

Rick, Dellynne, Stephen, Silas, Lee, Michael, Joy, Tim-o, Tina, Christin, Ben, Erica, Ted, and Samuel Strawbridge, Paul, Marie, and Neil Amato, Steve and Shannon Sloan, Jamie and Creigh Brown, Doug Horch, Christopher Boll, Billy Ivey, Martha Linder, Anthony Shamoun, Scott Brickhouse, Dane Parker, Allen Conner, Lee Harrelson, George and Rebecca Womble, Henry Harrell, Rob Hunt, Luchrysta Caswell, Dequan Green, Patrick Njubi, Dax Gibson, Dustin Prickett, Grandy Streets, Chris and Savannah Eaves-Kohlbrenner, Chad, Melanie, and Sam Gray, Brian, Jana, Rett, and Jack Owen, Jeremy, Mei, and Gideon Owen, Chad, Erika, Jessa, Juniper, Johnna, and Joshua Johnston, Dahn Pratt, Jon "Airborne" Schwarze, Katie "SoGood" Radosevic, Nick and Adrienne "Columbus and Blue Bear" Taylor, Malou "Bear Hair" Mauren, Kevin, Susan, and Sam Sheby, Will, Milliy, and William Campbell, Angie and Kaya Hashioka, John Smith, Rick and Donna Samuelson, Tim and Marcia Lloyd, Donald Higgenbothem, Jerrod Parker, Barry Ginn, Susan Morris, Rachel Caswell, Joel and Debbie Chandler, Mark and Linda Kirby, Chrystl Eaves, Brian and Kari Seeley, Brad Williams, Jackie Burridge, Kelley Wilson, Craig Mozhdehi, Andy Baker, Jon Brock, Deanna Bayless, Tom and Kathy Oates, Tim and Allison McNabb, Joaquin Martinez and Sandra Saldana

VINCE STRAWBRIDGE:

Vince wouldn't have ventured into the outdoors if the housing market hadn't taken a nosedive, making hiking suddenly look like the only affordable vacation option. He didn't even like walking—but his wife did, and that was enough to pique his interest. Like everything else he gets into, though, he took it one step too far. Or in this case, 8,000 miles worth of steps too far, dragging Monica and the kids down three of the longest trails in the United States. In 2021 they became the largest family to have completed the hiker's Triple Crown.

At the moment, he and his youngest (who, for some inexplicable reason, still talks to him) are off on the gap year of a lifetime. By now they will have walked the Great Divide Trail through the Canadian Rockies, and soon they will trek a brand-new 3,000-kilometer trail through the French Alps and down through the Pyrenees. And when he's not lost somewhere in the mountains? You'll catch him building docks and seawalls in central Florida, probably daydreaming about his next adventure.